Sustainable Partnership and Investment Strategies for Startups and SMEs

Biswajit Paul
University of Gour Banga, India

Sandeep Poddar
Lincoln University College, Malaysia

A volume in the Advances in Logistics,
Operations, and Management Science (ALOMS)
Book Series

Published in the United States of America by
IGI Global
Business Science Reference (an imprint of IGI Global)
701 E. Chocolate Avenue
Hershey PA, USA 17033
Tel: 717-533-8845
Fax: 717-533-8661
E-mail: cust@igi-global.com
Web site: http://www.igi-global.com

Library of Congress Cataloging-in-Publication Data

Names: Paul, Biswajit (Editor), 1984- editor. | Poddar, Sandeep, editor.
Title: Sustainable partnership and investment strategies for startups and
  SMEs / edited by Biswajit Paul, Sandeep Poddar.
Description: Hershey, PA : Business Science Reference, [2024] | Includes
  bibliographical references and index. | Summary: "In a broader sense,
  businesses and societies can find strategies that will move towards all
  three goals-environmental protection, social wellbeing, and economic
  development-at the same time. The proposed book will assemble research
  contributions from different authors that will definitely help the
  researchers by highlighting and recognizing different new aspects of
  strategies of society, business organizations, entrepreneurships,
  startups, and SMEs in the light of sustainable development"-- Provided
  by publisher.
Identifiers: LCCN 2024007194 (print) | LCCN 2024007195 (ebook) | ISBN
  9798369321973 (hardcover) | ISBN 9798369321980 (ebook)
Subjects: LCSH: Partnership. | Strategic planning. | Sustainable
  development.
Classification: LCC HD69.S8 .S87 2024 (print) | LCC HD69.S8 (ebook) | DDC
  338.7--dc23/eng/20240318
LC record available at https://lccn.loc.gov/2024007194
LC ebook record available at https://lccn.loc.gov/2024007195

This book is published in the IGI Global book series Advances in Logistics, Operations, and Management Science (ALOMS) (ISSN: 2327-350X; eISSN: 2327-3518)

British Cataloguing in Publication Data
A Cataloguing in Publication record for this book is available from the British Library.

For electronic access to this publication, please contact: eresources@igi-global.com.

Foreword

In today's entrepreneurial environment, sustainable development is crucial, especially for startups and SMEs. For startups and SMEs, the book Sustainable Partnership and Investment plans for Startups and SMEs offers comprehensive guidance on developing plans that align with the Sustainable Development Goals (SDGs). For the sake of both corporate success and societal well-being, it emphasizes how crucial it is to concentrate on a few number of SDGs. The book also argues for a paradigm shift in how environmental issues are understood and addressed, highlighting the necessity of true development that is socially and environmentally sustainable.

I am delighted to present this indispensable manual, "Sustainable Partnership and Investment Strategies for Startups and SMEs," with much enthusiasm. Startups and small to medium-sized firms (SMEs) are vital to innovation, economic growth, and significant global community transformation in today's dynamic and always changing business environment.

This book is more than just a theoretical discussion; it's a useful guide with plenty of doable recommendations, actual case studies, and professional insights. In order to help readers succeed in the cutthroat business world of today and make a real difference, I provide them with the knowledge, frameworks, and tools necessary to navigate the complexity of partnership agreements and comprehend the subtleties of impact investing.

I applaud their commitment to advancing sustainable entrepreneurship and enabling companies to add value in ways that benefit society and the environment in addition to their bottom line. I hope this book will help and inspire you as you make your way through the thrilling and difficult world of contemporary business.

Writing the Foreword for this International Edited Volume of IGI Global, "Sustainable Partnership and Investment Strategies for Start-ups and SMEs," makes me feel completely content. Start-ups and small—to medium-sized firms (SMEs) are vital to innovation, economic growth, and employment creation in today's ever-changing business environment. For company leaders and entrepreneurs alike, deciphering the nuances of sustainable partnerships and investment plans may be challenging. The value of sustainability in collaborations and investments is one of the major topics this book delves into.

In this insightful and comprehensive book, I delve deep into the intricacies of sustainable partnership development and investment strategies tailored specifically for startups and SMEs. Using my years of experience and industry knowledge, I offer firms insightful analysis, useful guidance, and doable tactics to help them succeed in a market that is becoming increasingly competitive.

The ground-breaking book Sustainable Partnership and Investment Strategies for Start-ups and SMEs offers priceless insights into promoting long-term success in the fast-paced business world. Written by renowned authorities in the area, it is essential reading for anybody interested in sustainable business growth, as well as investors, small—and medium-sized business (SME) owners, and prospective entre-preneurs.

However, IGI Global's entire publication team deserves recognition for their work in releasing this edited volume. The editors of this edited volume, Professor (Dr.) Sandeep Poddar, Deputy Vice-Chancellor (Research & Innovation), Lincoln University College, Malaysia, and Dr. Biswajit Paul, of the PG and Research Department of Commerce, University of Gour Banga, India, deserve a hearty round of applause for their tireless work and persuasive academic ideas. In conclusion, I hope readers will find this book a priceless tool in their quest to create enduring and prosperous companies.

Entrepreneurship is widely recognized for its positive impact on society, creating employment, eco-nomic expansion, and consumer well-being. This collection of research provides a nuanced understand-ing of key concepts of Asian entrepreneurship, highlighting the cultural and historical factors that have shaped the field and the importance of government policy and cultural values.

Léo-Paul Dana
LUT, Lappeenranta, Finland & Dalhousie University Halifax, Canada

Suhaiza Hanim Binti Dato Mohamad Zailani
Department of Decision Science, Faculty of Business and Economics, University Malaya, Malaysia

Preface

At present, 'making sustainable business strategies' is a bigger issue than it has ever been before. The relationship between present needs and future imperatives defines our contemporary challenges, especially within the realms of societal aspirations, business enterprises, Startups, and SMEs. The dynamic nature of today's entrepreneurial landscape, characterized by ceaseless challenges and constant change, underscores the urgency to align strategies with the imperatives of sustainable development. At the core of its spirit are the abovementioned importance, the book *Sustainable Partnership and Investment Strategies for Startups and SMEs* examines this issue and the intersection between sustainable development and the practical nuances of navigating the modern entrepreneurial landscape. It explores key themes and strategies for fostering sustainability in the business landscape. The book emphasizes balancing economic viability, environmental protection, and social equity, and highlights the importance of innovative approaches, technological advancements, and stakeholder partnerships. The critical role of SMEs and Startups in driving sustainable economic growth, job creation, and innovation is examined. The book provides insights into investment strategies aligned with Sustainable Development Goal 8 to promote inclusive and sustainable economic growth. This book will be helpful for making sustainable and responsible entrepreneurship.

However, Startups and Small and Medium-sized businesses, or SMEs, are the cornerstone of any flourishing economy and serve as a potent engine for national growth (Hu, 2010, Imeokparia & Ediagbonya, 2014, Madanchian *et al.* 2015). Despite being smaller in size than large organisations, these dynamic businesses are essential for promoting social advancement, economic growth, and innovation. The power of Startups and SMEs to create employment is one of their greatest contributions. Their adaptable framework and wide variety of activities make an ideal environment for job prospects. This is especially important in emerging nations where a lot of people are looking for job. Startups and SMEs serve as a safety net, taking in surplus labour and promoting inclusive growth by giving a larger segment of society access to sources of income. According to ILO data, individuals as workers and micro- and small businesses make up an astounding 70% of all employment globally. More than 50% of GDP is contributed by SMEs in the majority of OECD nations. While the contribution varies by sector, it is most significant in the service sector, where SMEs make up at least 60% of GDP in almost all OECD nations (https://www.ilo.org/infostories/en-GB/Stories/Employment/SMEs).

Furthermore, Startups and SMEs are essential to the advancement of regional development. Small and startup businesses typically spread out geographically, in contrast to major organisations that have a tendency to settle in urban areas. They make use of nearby resources, satisfy specific demands in the region, and support the local economy. This minimises the gap between urban and rural areas and promotes balanced growth. Startups and SMEs have an impact that goes beyond the financial domain. They guarantee that customers have access to a greater variety of goods and services at reasonable costs and prevent monopolies from emerging by fostering a diversified and competitive economic environment. This promotes a sound business environment and enhances financial stability in as a whole.

However, the contribution of Startups and SMEs should not be constrained by the limits of economic stability; rather, it should equally contribute to ensuring the world's sustainable development. The earth and its inhabitants have suffered as a result of the recent trajectory of global economic growth, which has been fuelled by business and entrepreneurial activity (Rahman *et al.* 2021). At present, it has become a chestnut that environmental problems are substantial. The studies such as Hayzoun *et al.* (2014); Ratha (2019); Jermsittiparsert (2021); Siddique (2021); Sharma & Verma (2023); Mosikari (2024) found the adverse impacts of business activities on environment. So, to maintain or ensure the environmental sustainability, role of business organisations including Startups and SMEs is predominant.

Against the backdrop of a constantly evolving world, the objective of the book comes to the forefront. Today's business and entrepreneurial practices grapple with an ever-changing environment, demanding contemporary and flexible business and investment strategies. Focusing on investment strategies for Startups and SMEs, it is not just a strategic imperative but a requirement for societal well-being and enduring today's business success.

This book's target audience includes a wide range of stakeholders who have an interest in the sustainability and success of Startups and SMEs. These pages contain valuable insight for business owners and entrepreneurs looking to expand their operations while upholding sustainability principles. The several viable frameworks for sustainable investment are also covered in this book. Investors will be guided by this and made aware of sustainable investment opportunities, enabling them to allocate their capital to worthwhile projects and maximise returns while adhering to environmental, social, and governance (ESG) criteria.

This book must have a significant socio-economic value in business research. It will bring together high-level public and private sector decision makers as well as entrepreneurs, investors and researchers. It aims at building a bridge and linking startups and SMEs to investors, financiers and established corporates in the region to create business partnerships and joint ventures. Additionally, the insights and recommendations offered in this book will be helpful to the policymakers who are interested in creating an environment that supports sustainable Startups and SMEs.

However, this book contains **fifteen** research chapters to address their respective research objectives. Several research chapters have been collected from academicians and researchers having common research interests to share their insights relating to this area.

Chapter 1 underlines the usage of cloud computing in modern business. This chapter specifically put emphasis on the critical role of one of the revolutionized the concept of information networking and infrastructure i.e., 'Super Cloud' to ensure sustainable business practices. The chapter is having a significant exploration into the super cloud, a new phase of cloud computing, offers scalability, performance, and accessibility, but its impact on sustainability initiatives is crucial. This chaper also explores the interconnectedness and potential synergies between super cloud adoption and sustainable business practices, emphasizing the importance of ethical and social responsibility. **Pertinency: This chapter will help the businesses including the Startups and SMEs to make their strategies in information networking and soft infrastructure related issues.**

Chapter 2 titled 'Framework for Corporate Governance and Disclosure Requirements for Small and Medium-Sized Enterprises (SMEs)' aims to establish comprehensive guidelines for regulating all aspects to ensure the effectiveness of its implementation. The interviewees will offer novel and practi-

systems. This is because they require a strategy to manage their companies to realize their ambitions (Ndagu & Obuobi, 2010).

Large corporations value effective management and governance structures more because they recognize their critical role in ensuring their continued profitability (Grandori, 2022; Kotabe & Helsen, 2022). Unsurprisingly, they can investigate opportunities in one part of the world while managing operations in another. SMEs should have the same mentality toward conducting business.

Small and medium-sized businesses in Malaysia have a perfect chance of propelling the country's economy forward (Ghouri, 2023; Teoh et al., 2023; Mendoza & Tadeo,2023; Murdiati et al., 2023). The guidelines for SME corporate governance may require a different approach, one that considers the advisory role that boards of directors play in addition to controlling and monitoring the company (Teixeira & Carvalho, 2024; Xue et al., 2024; Nasrallah & El Khoury, 2022).

SMEs in Malaysia encounter various obstacles in the current business landscape. Key obstacles encompass restricted financial accessibility, a dearth of proficient labor, exorbitant operational expenses, and fierce rivalry from larger enterprises. In addition, small and medium-sized enterprises (SMEs) frequently face limitations regarding resources and marketing knowledge, hindering their ability to advertise their products and services efficiently (Corvello et al., 2023; Thekkoote, 2024; Macca et al., 2024; Ji et al., 2024). These obstacles can impede the growth and competitiveness of small and medium-sized enterprises (SMEs) in the market. Nevertheless, by implementing effective strategies and receiving adequate support, small and medium-sized enterprises (SMEs) can successfully overcome these obstacles and flourish within the business environment of Malaysia (Abdulaziz et al., 2023; Talib et al., 2023; Islam et al., 2023; Hisham, 2023; Rahman et al., 2016; Muhammad et al., 2010; Ramli et al., 2022).

According to Hamad and Karoui (2011), much research has yet to be done on how corporate governance and SMEs are connected. Research has yet to be conducted on small and medium-sized enterprises' corporate governance framework and disclosure requirements. As a result, this study aims to investigate the attitudes held by small and medium-sized enterprises (SMEs) regarding corporate governance framework and disclosure requirements for small and medium-sized enterprises.

The second section briefly overviews corporate governance, while the third discusses the research methodology. The fourth section examines the findings, and the last section concludes the chapter.

CORPORATE GOVERNANCE

One of the phenomena that emerged in the last twenty years is corporate governance (Li & Singal, 2022; Lu & Yan, 2022; Kjaer, 2023). The global economy experienced a period of significant expansion in the second half of the 20th century. Because of such a significant increase in population, the economic institutions also developed significantly. A significant number of adjustments were made to the structures of the financial institutions as well as their operating systems.

Unhappily, that economic growth did not come without a price tag. However, as a result of its actions, humanity was forced to experience a significant number of catastrophes. The most prominent feature of the era was undoubtedly the series of economic crises that followed each other. Examples of those tragedies are the financial crises in the United States in 1930, 1975, and 1997, and South East Asia. Following each previous crisis, modifications were made to the regulatory and supervisory frameworks that were in place.

During the past two decades, corporate governance has received significant focus from state governments' economic entities and regulatory authorities (Tong et al., 2022; Stiglitz, 2022; Cini & Borragán, 2022). It is because, following a series of reoccurring financial crises, governments and economic analysts realized they were caused by a lack of good governance and an appropriate corporate framework. It is the reason why this is the case. As a result, nations worldwide endeavored to synchronize the regulations and guidelines governing corporate governance. In other words, the first step guarantees the viability of the essential economic institutions, and the second step guarantees the nation's economic stability. Countries and local authorities attempted to regulate corporations by passing laws that required them to fulfill specific requirements and codes. These requirements and codes included the structure of the board of directors, stakeholders' rights, reports' disclosure, and other requirements.

Various state stock exchanges, corporations, and institutional investors have collaborated to develop corporate governance principles and codes with the assistance of local authorities and international organizations (Panait et al., 2022; Eltweri et al., 2022).

As a result, every nation has its own distinct set of codes and frameworks for corporate governance tailored to the needs of the companies and firms in that nation. However, before the OECD's code was accepted in 1999, there had never been an internationally recognized standard for good corporate governance. The IFSB guidelines and principles for institutions offering Islamic financial services (2006) serve as the corporate governance standard for Islamic corporations.

What exactly does "corporate governance" entail?

The Malaysian Security Commission provided the following definition of corporate governance: "The process and structure used to direct and manage the business and affairs of the company towards enhancing business prosperity and corporate accountability with the ultimate objective of increasing long-term shareholder value while taking into consideration the interests of other stakeholders" (MCCG. 2012).

The Organization for Economic Co-operative Development defined corporate governance as a "set of relationships between a company's management, its board, its shareholders, and other stakeholders" (OECD, 2004).

According to the World Bank's definition, governance is "the exercise of political authority and the use of institutional resources to manage society's problems and affairs."

After reading these two definitions of corporate governance, the reader will better understand what corporate governance entails. To put it more simply, corporate governance is the collection of practices, rules, policies, laws, and codes that influence how a firm (or company) is directed, regulated, or controlled. Corporate governance can be defined as the process and structure used to direct and manage an institution's business and affairs to enhance business prosperity and corporate accountability with the ultimate goal of realizing long-term shareholder value while simultaneously taking into account the interests of other stakeholders. This definition emphasizes the importance of balancing the needs of shareholders with those of other stakeholders. In addition, corporate governance encompasses the relationships between the numerous stakeholders involved in the company and the goals the corporation is governed to achieve.

Modern corporations' primary outside stakeholder groups are shareholders, debt holders, creditors, suppliers, customers, and societies impacted by the company. Other stakeholders include customers and suppliers. The corporation's internal stakeholders are the board of directors, executive managers, and other corporate employees. Corporate governance refers to the processes by which boards oversee the

Table 6. Stakeholder relations

S.no	Stakeholder Relations	Mean	Standard Deviation
1	The SME should establish precise function priorities for the stakeholders	3.67	1.528
2	The SME should establish a clear SOP in handling and managing customer relationship	4.00	1.000
3	The SME should formalize ethical standards through a code of conduct and ensure its compliance	4.00	1.000
4	The SME should manage and govern the organization's account properly for the stakeholders	4.00	1.000
5	The SME should have procedures to protect resources and allocate them to make planned progress toward the organization's defined purpose	4.33	0.577
6	The SME should ensure that stakeholders, where appropriate, can and do hold management to account	3.67	0.577
7	The SME should ensure that it has priority for the most important customers, partners, and regulators	3.67	1.528

Source: Researchers' own calculation

The company will expand with the stakeholders because its success and future expansion opportunities depend on them. The success of any organization, including SMEs, depends on several factors, and one of the most critical factors is stakeholder engagement. For instance, the network of suppliers and partners that are essential to the operation of the business; if there is a lack of transparency and accountability, this will have a significant impact on both the key suppliers and other organizations, in addition to the regulatory body. Gaining the general public's confidence and receiving recognition from various stakeholders can be accomplished by accurately disclosing the SME's accounting practices.

Small and medium-sized enterprises (SMEs) have a variety of motivations for forming partnerships with their stakeholders. These partnerships are increasingly becoming essential to many SMEs' strategies for surviving, maintaining, and ensuring growth. Alliances are created by small and medium-sized enterprises (SMEs) to improve their businesses, lower their risks, or increase their access to resources. We can differentiate between four distinct kinds of partnerships: strategic alliances between non-competitors, competition, strategic partnerships between competitors, joint ventures to develop new businesses, and buyer-supplier relationships to ensure reliable supplies. Moreover, for any of them to have faith in an SME, they required accounting disclosure.

The interviewees' thoughts on stakeholder relations and the board of directors are examined through seven questions. Each question was based on a Likert scale with five different options. There is a range of options from one to five, with one representing "not at all important," two representing "slightly important," three representing "important," four representing "fairly important," and five representing "very important." According to ten SMEs, corporate governance policies and procedures are critical; however, the mean values and standard deviations vary. According to the findings, the lowest possible mean value for those five questions is 3.67. Furthermore, these seven subcomponents are significant, and SMEs should evaluate them consistently.

CONCLUSION AND AREA FOR FURTHER RESEARCH

This paper offered an analysis of the governance principles applicable to SMEs. Moreover, it examined how it played out in the real world. It reaffirms the significance of accountability and transparency and protects SMEs from potential crises. In addition to the discussion that was presented earlier, raise awareness about the significance of engaging in governance practices in a highly competitive world like the one we live in a situation in which there is poor governance can lead to instability, which in turn can affect the whole society because the economy and society are intertwined. The current economic crisis has brought to our attention the significance of adequately governing organizations in such a way as to assist in the defense of the legal interests of the stakeholders associated with it. The findings indicated that the government initiative undertaken by the Malaysian government had produced positive results, which will result in a positive impact in the long run. The industry will benefit Malaysia's small and medium-sized enterprises in the long run.

Further investigation is needed to explore the framework of corporate governance and disclosure requirements for small and medium-sized enterprises (SMEs), as it is a crucial research area. Although there has been some advancement in this field, there are still numerous deficiencies in our comprehension of the most optimal methods for creating efficient governance and disclosure frameworks for small and medium-sized enterprises (SMEs).

An area that could be explored in future research is the evaluation of the efficacy of current governance and disclosure frameworks for small and medium-sized enterprises (SMEs) in various countries and regions. Through the process of comparing and contrasting the methods employed by various jurisdictions, researchers can discern the most effective strategies and pinpoint areas that require enhancement in the development and execution of these frameworks.

Another crucial field of study focuses on the influence of governance and disclosure regulations on the performance and competitiveness of small and medium-sized enterprises (SMEs). While certain studies have indicated that these prerequisites can enhance the fiscal performance and standing of small and medium-sized enterprises (SMEs), others have expressed apprehensions that excessive regulation could impede innovation and expansion in these companies. Future research should investigate the trade-offs between regulatory compliance and innovation in small and medium-sized enterprises (SMEs). Additionally, it should aim to identify strategies that can effectively balance these competing demands.

Additional research is necessary to investigate the attitudes and behaviors of small and medium-sized enterprises (SMEs) regarding governance and disclosure requirements. While certain companies may perceive these requirements as onerous and expensive, others may regard them as a chance to enhance their operations and reputation. Policymakers and regulators could enhance the effectiveness of governance and disclosure frameworks for SMEs by comprehending the factors that impact their attitudes towards these aspects. This understanding would facilitate the design of frameworks more likely to be adopted and embraced by these firms.

To summarize, investigating the framework governing corporate governance and disclosure obligations for small and medium-sized enterprises (SMEs) is a crucial research topic requiring additional examination. Researchers can enhance the design and implementation of frameworks for small and medium-sized enterprises (SMEs) by evaluating their effectiveness, studying the influence of governance and disclosure requirements on SME performance, and analyzing the attitudes and behaviors of SMEs towards these requirements. This research can contribute to the global growth and prosperity of SMEs.

Ogbechie, C., & Arije, A. (2023). Corporate Governance in Africa: Key Challenges and Running Effective Boards. In *Sustainable and Responsible Business in Africa: Studies in Ethical Leadership* (pp. 265–290). Springer Nature Switzerland.

Organization for Economic Co-operation and Development. (2004). *OECD Principles of Corporate Governance*. OECD Publications Service.

Panait, M., Ionescu, R., Radulescu, I. G., & Rjoub, H. (2022). The Corporate Social Responsibility on Capital Market: Myth or Reality? In Research Anthology on Developing Socially Responsible Businesses (pp. 1721-1754). IGI Global.

Rahman, N. A., Yaacob, Z., & Radzi, R. M. (2016). The challenges among Malaysian SME: A theoretical perspective. *WORLD (Oakland, Calif.)*, *6*(3), 124–132.

Ramli, A. M., Asby, P. N. K., Noor, H. M., & Afrizal, T. (2022). Challenges Encountered by SMEs in Tourism Industry: A review from 2017 to 2021. *Journal of ASIAN Behavioural Studies*, *7*(21), 1–13. doi:10.21834/jabs.v7i21.405

Rashid, A., Akmal, M., & Shah, S. M. A. R. (2024). Corporate governance and risk management in Islamic and convectional financial institutions: Explaining the role of institutional quality. *Journal of Islamic Accounting and Business Research*, *15*(3), 466–498. doi:10.1108/JIABR-12-2021-0317

Razak, D. A., Abdullah, M. A., & Ersoy, A. (2018). Small, medium enterprises (SMEs) in Turkey and Malaysia a comparative discussion on issues and challenges. *International Journal of Business, Economics, and Law*, *10*(49), 2–591.

Roche, J. (2005). *Corporate governance in Asia*. Routledge. doi:10.4324/9780203461723

Rost, B. (2010). Basel committee on banking supervision. In *Handbook of transnational economic governance regimes* (pp. 319–328). Brill Nijhoff. doi:10.1163/ej.9789004163300.i-1081.238

Sarah, R. M. (2017). The benefits of good corporate governance to small and medium enterprises (SMEs) in South Africa: A view on top 20 and bottom 20 JSE listed companies. *Problems and Perspectives in Management*, (15, Iss. 4), 271–27. doi:10.21511/ppm.15(4-1).2017.11

Schlierer, H. J., Werner, A., Signori, S., Garriga, E., von Weltzien Hoivik, H., Van Rossem, A., & Fassin, Y. (2012). How do European SME owner-managers make sense of 'stakeholder management?': Insights from a cross-national study. *Journal of Business Ethics*, *109*(1), 39–51. doi:10.1007/s10551-012-1378-3

Sekeran, U., & Bougie, R. (2010). *Research method for business: skin building Approach* (5th ed.). John Wiley and Sons Ltd.

Shah, W. U. H., Hao, G., Yan, H., Yasmeen, R., Padda, I. U. H., & Ullah, A. (2022). The impact of trade, financial development and government integrity on energy efficiency: An analysis from G7-Countries. *Energy*, *255*, 124507. doi:10.1016/j.energy.2022.124507

Shiau, W. L., Hsu, P. Y., & Wang, J. Z. (2009). Development of measures to assess the ERP adoption of small and medium enterprises. *Journal of Enterprise Information Management*, *22*(1/2), 99–118. doi:10.1108/17410390910922859

Stiglitz, J. E. (2022). More instruments and broader goals: Moving toward the Post-Washington consensus. *Revista de Economia Política*, *19*(1), 101–128. doi:10.1590/0101-31571999-1084

Stoelhorst, J. W., & Vishwanathan, P. (2024). Beyond primacy: A stakeholder theory of corporate governance. *Academy of Management Review*, *49*(1), 107–134. doi:10.5465/amr.2020.0268

Sumaiyah, A. A., & Rosli, M. (2011). The relationship between business model and performance of manufacturing small and medium enterprises in Malaysia. *African Journal of Business Management*, *5*(22), 8918–8932. doi:10.5897/AJBM11.474

Tahir, H. M., Razak, N. A., & Rentah, F. (2018, March). The contributions of small and medium enterprises (SMEs) On Malaysian economic growth: A sectoral analysis. In *International Conference on Kansei Engineering & Emotion Research* (pp. 704 711). Springer, Singapore.

Talib, N. A. C., Abd Razak, N., & Mahmud, N. (2023). Enhancing Small and Medium Enterprise Performance through Supply Chain Integration: A Case Study of Malaysia. *Information Management and Business Review*, *15*(3 (I)), 405–417. doi:10.22610/imbr.v15i3(I).3551

Teixeira, J. F., & Carvalho, A. O. (2024). Corporate governance in SMEs: A systematic literature review and future research. *Corporate Governance (Bradford)*, *24*(2), 303–326. doi:10.1108/CG-04-2023-0135

Teoh, M. F., Ahmad, N. H., Abdul-Halim, H., & Kan, W. H. (2023). Digital business model innovation among small and medium-sized enterprises (SMEs). *Global Business and Organizational Excellence*, *42*(6), 5–18. doi:10.1002/joe.22200

Thekkoote, R. (2024). Factors influencing small and medium-sized enterprise (SME) resilience during the COVID-19 outbreak. *The TQM Journal*, *36*(2), 523–545. doi:10.1108/TQM-08-2022-0266

Tong, T., Chen, X., Singh, T., & Li, B. (2022). *Corporate governance and the outward foreign direct investment: Firm-level evidence from China*. Economic Analysis and Policy.

Tongco, M.D.C. (2007). *Purposive sampling as a tool for informant selection.*

Ulupui, I. G. K. A., Zairin, G. M., Musyaffi, A. M., & Sutanti, F. D. (2024). Navigating uncertainties: A tri-factorial evaluation of risk management adoption in MSMEs. *Cogent Business & Management*, *11*(1), 2311161. doi:10.1080/23311975.2024.2311161

Williams, C. (2011). Research methods. [JBER]. *Journal of Business & Economics Research*, *5*(3). doi:10.19030/jber.v5i3.2532 PMID:21543382

Xue, S., Genmao, Z., Boxin, H., Jiahui, H., & Salman, S. A. (2024). The Perception of SMEs towards the Corporate Governance in Malaysia. *The Journal of Research Administration*, *6*(1).

Yousef, H. A., ElSabry, E. A., & Adris, A. E. (2024). Impact of technology management in improving sustainability performance for Egyptian petroleum refineries and petrochemical companies. *International Journal of Energy Sector Management*, *18*(3), 517–538. doi:10.1108/IJESM-02-2023-0002

Zafar, A., & Mustafa, S. (2017). SMEs and its role in economic and socio-economic development of Pakistan. *International Journal of Academic Research in Accounting, Finance and Management Sciences, 6*(4).

Zhang, L., Zhang, X., An, J., Zhang, W., & Yao, J. (2022). Examining the Role of Stakeholder Oriented Corporate Governance in Achieving Sustainable Development: Evidence from the SME CSR in the Context of China. *Sustainability (Basel)*, *14*(13), 8181. doi:10.3390/su14138181

Zhang, Z., Zhu, H., Zhou, Z., & Zou, K. (2022). How does innovation matter for sustainable performance? Evidence from small and medium-sized enterprises. *Journal of Business Research*, *153*, 251–265. doi:10.1016/j.jbusres.2022.08.034

Zheng, Y., Rashid, M. H. U., Siddik, A. B., Wei, W., & Hossain, S. Z. (2022). Corporate social responsibility disclosure and firm's productivity: Evidence from the banking industry in Bangladesh. *Sustainability (Basel)*, *14*(10), 6237. doi:10.3390/su14106237

Chapter 3

How Does Green Finance Reduce the Adverse Effect of Global Climate Change Issues:
An Investigation

Sandip Basak
Dwijendralal College, India

Ashish Kumar Sana
University of Calcutta, India

ABSTRACT

In the context of global emergence of green bond market to tackle the global issue of climate change, this study takes an initiative to highlight the world-wide present status of green bond as a support to tackle this kind of challenge and to achieve UN-specified sustainable development goals. This study is exploratory in nature. This study identified that China remained the largest emerging market issuer. China has issued more than $30 billion in green bonds each year since 2016. Considering the outcome of (COP – 27) held in Egypt in November 2022, it is of prime importance for every nation to focus on emergence of green bond market and thereby issuance of green bonds. Still green bond market is in nascent stage and potentially less liquid. It is the responsibility of the government of any nation to emphasize such a market for getting a sustainable green future.

INTRODUCTION

Green Bond is a vital instrument in the area of sustainable finance which is a long-term approach to finance and investing, giving emphasize on long-term thinking, decision-making and value creation and has also been described as the interrelationships that exists between ESG issues on the one hand, and financing, lending and investment decisions on the other and long-term oriented financial decision-making that integrates ESG considerations. One of the most important instruments of sustainable finance is "Green

DOI: 10.4018/979-8-3693-2197-3.ch003

Bond". Green Bonds are issued to raise funds for climate and environmental programs, and are generally issued by Governments, Corporations and financial institutions. Multilateral Development Banks including the European Investment Bank and World Bank originally bought them to market in 2007 but issuance has really picked up in recent years with new issues topping US$ 258 billion worldwide 2019. The green bond market is maturing with outstanding issuance of green bonds passing US$ 1 trillion total issuance since inception in September 2020, more than 10 times the size of the market in 2015. The majority of the green bonds issued are green "use of proceeds" or asset-linked bonds. Basically, funds raised from these bonds are reserved for green projects but supported by the issuer's entire balance sheet. Again, the decision relating to 'Zero-tolerance' against the 'Greenwashing' (Greenwashing happens when a company makes an environmental claim about something the organization is doing that is intended to promote a sense of environmental impact that doesn't exist.) taken by the representatives of COP – 27 (The 2022 United Nations Climate Change Conference or Conference of the Parties of the UNFCCC, more commonly referred to as COP27, was the 27th United Nations Climate Change conference, held from November 6 until November 20, 2022 in Sharm El Sheikh, Egypt.) attending countries highly supports the issue of Green Bonds. Considering the need of Green Bond at the moment of preparing climate action plan, this study takes an initiative to highlight the relationship between Green Bond Market and Sustainability Development Goals.

And this study consists of six sections: Section – I provides the background of the study; Section – II highlights the review of literatures; Section – III mentions the objectives of the study; Section – IV describes the research methodology used in this study; Section – V explains analysis and findings of the study and Section – VI concludes the study with some recommendations.

Emergence of Sustainable Finance

Sustainable finance is the set of financial regulations, standards, principles, norms and products that helps achieving a particular environmental objective of a business concern. It allows the financial system to connect with the economy and its populations by financing its agents while maintaining a growth objective related to environmental development. Basically, capital for sustainable finance is available from investors who want to take part in financing enterprises involved in projects with high environmental or social value including projects that will have an impact that the investors may experience directly. Businesses have a key role to play in the evolution and growth of sustainable finance by embracing ESG-focused financing instruments and related practices such as more robust disclosures of their ESG performance (Agarwal et. al., 2020, pp. 3300-3301). For example, Apple has issued green bonds to finance energy efficiency projects and Starbucks used a sustainable bond to raise $500 million to underwrite ethical coffee production. Between September 2016 and June 2020, Mitsubishi UFG Financial Group issued seven Green Bonds, one Social Bond and one Sustainability Bond for a total amount of $3.2 billion equivalent.

ESG and Fixed Income Instruments

For many years, ESG investing was not considered relevant for fixed income, as bond holders do not have voting rights and therefore has less influence on a company than equity investors. Contrary to stocks, bond investors' primary focus is on alleviating the risk of default rather than gaining upside potential (which is naturally capped) and returning the principle invested (Getting money back) at a future date. However, because of ESG's increasing influence over credit ratings and investors' increasing engagement with debt issuers, the fixed income sector is starting to play catch-up. Particularly given the distinct range of debt instruments, issuers and maturities, fixed income investors are integrating ESG considerations into their analysis as ESG investing expands to all areas of the market and ESG metrics help spot new risk factors.

For many companies, there is a preference to raise funds through bond issuance as this can be more efficient and less expensive than giving up equity, particularly when benchmark interest rates are low. Therefore, the bond market is considerably bigger than the equity market, and many companies are realizing the increasing relevance of good ESG processes to attract bond investors.

GREEN BOND – Conceptual Analysis

Green Bond is that type of bond instrument where the proceeds can be exclusively applied to financing the green projects. In other words, it can be stated that Green Bonds raise funds for conducting any climate-change related programs or environmental programs that are related to upgradation of environment within which a firm continues its operations, and are generally issued by Governments of different countries, Corporations in different cities and several Financial Institutions who are ready to finance any kind of feasible green projects. Globally the issuance of Green Bonds has been growing exponentially since 2013 (Cortellini & Panetta, 2021, pp. 1-2). The growth of Green Bonds market in the last few years can partly be attributed to an overarching trend towards including Environmental, Social and 8 Governance (ESG) issues in the decision process for investments by institutional investors (Deschryver & Mariz, 2020, pp. 3-5). Currently, over USD 45 trillion of global asset under management (AUM) incorporate ESG issues into investment decisions and are signatory to Principles of Responsible Investments (PRI). In addition, since more than half (55 percent) of the asset base of institutional investors is exposed to climate risks (including heavier regulation of dirty industries), participation in green bonds also provides an option for investors to diversify their portfolios.

Focused Area

- Projects in renewable energy and electric transportation generally receive the highest rating, as they are focused on the long-term objective of a zero-carbon economy.
- Bonds covering questionable energy efficiency in green building projects would have a lower rating.
- Improvements to fossil fuel infrastructure including technologies intended to reduce the environmental impact of coal burning would be considered ineligible; while such projects could generate environmental benefits, prolonging the useful life of fossil fuel assets is not consistent with an eligible green project.
- Nuclear energy projects, despite their zero-carbon benefits, are also excluded due to the prospective environmental impacts of radioactive waste.

Difference between Green Bond and Blue Bond

Blue bonds are sustainability bonds to finance projects that protect the ocean and related ecosystems. This can include projects to support sustainable fisheries, protection of coral reefs and other fragile ecosystems, or reducing pollution and acidification. All blue bonds are green bonds, but not all green bonds are blue bonds.

Difference between Traditional Bond and Green Bond

The Green Bonds can be differentiated from Traditional Bonds based on the basis of four different angles which are described below.

- **Subscription** - Green Bonds are oversubscribed compared to standard bonds. The trend is consistent across all Green Bond markets. This occurs primarily because of the huge demand-supply outmatch for Green Bonds, the volume of Green Bond issuances fail to match high demand, leading to increased issuance or oversubscription.
- **Liquidity** - Market research indicates that green bonds are less liquid assets than standard bonds. Several factors impact liquidity. In green bonds market, this is particularly because of the small size, indicating scarcity of funds for buyers.
- **Risk** - Comparison of credit risk of green bonds and conventional bonds reveals identical characteristics, implying that green and conventional bonds from the same issuer face similar credit risks. However, green bonds are exposed to additional risks due to climate-change phenomenon and natural calamities, called environmental risks. This also involves the risk of greenwashing, which means that the funds may be used for activities that are not as green as the investor would desire.
- **Returns** - Comparative return analysis reveals mixed results for yields of green bonds in comparison to standard bonds. The returns have been observed to vary across bonds of different currency denominations and across different time periods, making it difficult to assess the comparative monetary advantage of green bond investing.

Classification

The Green Bond Principles (GBP) begin by defining Green Bonds as "any type of bond instrument where the proceeds will be exclusively applied to finance or refinance, in part or in full, new and/or existing eligible Green Projects and which are aligned with the four core components of the GBP." The GBP recognized four types of Green Bonds, noting that additional types may emerge as the market develops:

Standard Green Use of Proceeds Bond: A standard recourse-to-the-issuer debt obligation aligned with the GBP for which the proceeds are held in a sub-portfolio or otherwise tracked by the issuer and attested to by a formal internal process that is linked to the issuer's lending and investment operations for projects.

Green Revenue Bond: A non-recourse-to-the-issuer debt obligation aligned with the GBP in which the credit exposure in the bond is to the pledged cash flows of the revenue streams, fees, taxes etc., and whose use of proceeds goes to related or unrelated green project(s).

Green Project Bond: A project bond for a single or multiple Green Project(s) for which the investor has direct exposure to the risk of the project(s) with or without potential recourse to the issuer, and that is aligned with the GBP. This type of bond is limited in scope to a particular underlying green project, meaning that investors have recourse only to assets related to the project.

Green Securitized Bond: A bond collateralized by one or more specific Green Project(s), including but not limited to covered bonds, ABS, MBS, and other structures; and aligned with the GBP. The first source of repayment is generally the cash flows of the assets. Basically, these debt instruments involve a group of projects gathered together into a single debt portfolio with bondholders having recourse to the assets underlying the full set of projects.

Green Bond Principles

The Green Bond Principles (GBP) are a set of voluntary guidelines that aim to promote transparency and integrity in the market. The four constituents of the GBP establish the minimum requirements for a green bond label:

- Announcing the qualified project classifications up front
- Working to determine environmental sustainability objectives
- Reporting at least annually on the quantified use of proceeds
- Ensuring funds are ring-fenced for the projects declared

REVIEW OF LITERATURE

There are several studies that discussed the present scenario of sustainable investing across different nations. Few studies are available regarding how the corporates of different countries are getting inclined day by day towards adoption of ESG investing as well as ESG reporting. Agarwal et. al. (2020) stated that Green Finance is still an early stage in Asian Countries and thereby facing several challenges. Kumar and Kundalia (2023) in their paper examined the role and scope of green bonds in India's financial and fiscal landscape. It discussed the various types of green bonds available in India, the regulatory framework governing their issuance and the potential benefits of investing in green bonds. The paper also highlighted the challenges associated with green bonds in India and suggests measures to promote their growth. Wang and Wang (2022) examined the relationship between the performance of ESG dimensions and green bond issuance from the perspective of listed firms in the emerging market. The results indicated that decent ESG practices not only increase the propensity in green bond issuance by listed firms but also help them issue more green bonds. However, the authors identified the negative effect of financial performance in issuing green bonds when combining the effect of ESG performance. Verma and Agarwal (2020) in their study signified Socially Responsible Investing (SRI) through investing in Energy Efficiency, Green Infrastructure, Renewable Energy and Water Improvement. The study also analyzed green bonds from a comprehensive viewpoint. The authors in their study also asked for a need to have an intensified push by the government to the private sector to issue and invest in bonds. So, a policy of tax benefits to the issuers as well as investors could help overcome the existing need of funds for environmental projects. Cheong and Choi (2020) made a survey of recent academic developments in the literature on green bonds, which have become an important financial instrument in socially responsible investment. This study provided a review of papers that studied the market pricing of green bonds, the economic and environmental effects of green bond financing, as well as legal and institutional issues in the green bond market. Clapp et. al. (2015) in their study stated that green bonds were a promising financial instrument for robust investment decisions in consideration of climate and environmental risks and potential impacts. They also argued that green bonds are a simple financial instrument that, when coupled with climate science, can make a positive investment in a low-carbon climate resilient future. A company or institution that issues a green bond also needs to coordinate across its internal financial and environmental departments, sending a signal to investors that it is better prepared to proactively manage climate risk. Arora and Raj (2020) in their study argued that the green bond market is characterized by a diverse investor base, high demand and huge potential for growth, a dilemma often faced by the investors is whether green bonds offer higher returns on investment than traditional bonds? They concluded that the financial performance of green bonds is comparable to that of standard bonds, except liquidity. The market size and growth are largely restricted due to ignorance of market players towards green assets and investing know-how. Lack of standardization of market procedures increases the risk of greenwashing making green bonds potentially less attractive to investors. Till date, the market has thrived largely without government support. Ahmed et. al. (2022), using the Capital Asset Pricing Model, Fama–French Three Factor, Carhart Four Factor and Fama–French Five Factor pricing models, in their study provided empirical evidence that the announcement of green bonds issuance led to positively abnormal return on stocks. They divided their dataset into two parts. The first part of the dataset was from 01/01/2013 to 30/06/2018 and later part analysed the period from 01/07/2018 to 30/06/2022. The consistent results highlighted the firms' and investors' efforts towards climate action (SDG13) and strongly suggested that green bonds played an important role as a bridge to the SDGs. Antoniuk and Leirvik (2021) investigated in their study the impact of unexpected political events on the risk and returns of green bonds and their correlation with other assets. They applied a traditional and regression-based event study and found that events related to climate change policy impact green bonds indices. Green bonds indices anticipated the 2015 Paris Agreement on climate change as a favorable event, whereas the 2016 US Presidential Election had a significant negative impact. The negative impact of the US withdrawal from the Paris agreement was more prominent for municipal but not corporate green bonds. All three events also had a similar effect on green bonds performance in the long term. The results implied that, despite the benefits of issuing green bonds, there were substantial risks that were difficult to hedge. Maltais and Nykvist (2020) in their study addressed the broader questions of what attracted investors and issuers to the green bond market, the role of green bonds in shifting capital to more sustainable economic activity, and how green bonds impacted the way organisations work with sustainability. Using Sweden as a case study, they provided insights into the rapid growth of the green bond market and how green bonds affect market participants' engagement with sustainability that were easily missed if one focused only on how green bonds were marketed. Another interesting result for this study was the extent to which both investors and issuers called for more leadership, long-term planning, and stronger climate policy from the state as the most important factors in increasing the availability of bankable green investments.

Based on the available literatures, it is clear that most of the literatures are dealt with the pricing and liquidity mechanism of Green Bond Market and essentialities of Green Bond Market but there is a dearth of literatures stating the relationship among Green Bond and UN Sustainability Development Goals. Even very few literatures are dealt with the present scenario of Green Bond market across the world and how the emergence of Green Bond Market helps to tackle the climate change issues. Thus, this study aims to bridge the gap.

OBJECTIVES OF THE STUDY

This study has two specific objectives which are –

- To study the world-wide present status of Green Bond.

- To establish Green Bond as a vital instrument to achieve UN specified Sustainable Development Goals for solving climate change issues.

DATABASE & METHODOLOGY

This section comprises of three sections which are (a) Area of study, (b) Sample period and (c) Parameters of the analysis. The study is based on exploratory analysis. No statistical tool is applied here. To analyse the relationship between issuance of Green Bond and UN specified Sustainable Development Goals, the world is categorized in six regions. These are – (a) Africa, (b) Asia-Pacific, (c) Europe, (d) North America, (e) Latin America and (f) Supranational. Sample Period is ranging from 2014 – 2022. And six Sustainable Development Goals are taken into consideration which are – (a) SDG – 6, (b) SDG – 7, (c) SDG – 9, (d) SDG – 11, (e) SDG – 13, (f) SDG – 15.

ANALYSIS & FINDINGS

World-wide Listing of Green Bonds

Stock Exchanges continue to be major promoters of ESG disclosure. Uniquely positioned as a channel between issuers and investors, these bodies have the opportunity to promote more efficient capital markets that generate long-term value. There is consensus that those promoting high-quality ESG information enable investors to better evaluate fundamental drivers of value creation and help companies navigate, comply with or stay ahead of regulations that require disclosure of financially material ESG information. This methodology is also applicable in case of Green Bonds too. In Table – 1, country-wise and date-wise issue of Green Bonds and in which Stock Exchanges those have been listed are disclosed.

Table 1. Listing of green bonds in stock exchanges

Name of Stock Exchange	Operating Countries	Types of Dedicated Segment	Launch Date
Oslo Stock Exchange	Norway	Green Bonds	Jan-15
Stockholm Stock Exchange	Sweden	Sustainable Bonds	Jun-15
London Stock Exchange	United Kingdom	Green, Social & Sustainable Bonds	Jul-15
Shanghai Stock Exchange	China	Green Bonds	Mar-16
Mexico Stock Exchange	Mexico	Green Bonds	Aug-16
Luxembourg Stock Exchange	Luxembourg	Green, Social & Sustainable Bonds	Sep-16
Italian Stock Exchange	Italian	Green &Social Bonds	Mar-17
Taipei Stock Exchange	Taiwan	Green Bonds	May-17
Johannesburg Stock Exchange	South Africa	Green Bonds	Oct-17
Japan Stock Exchange	Tokyo	Green & Social Bonds	Jan-18
Vienna Stock Exchange	Austria	Green & Social Bonds	Mar-18
NASDAQ Nordics & Baltics Exchange	Europe	Sustainable Bonds	May-18
The International Stock Exchange	St. Peter Port, Guernsey	Green Bonds	Nov-18
Frankfurt Stock Exchange	Germany	Green Bonds	Nov-18
Moscow Stock Exchange	Russia	Green & Social Bonds	Aug-19
Euronext	Netherland	Green Bonds	Nov-19
NASDAQ Sustainable Bond Network	NASDAQ	Green, Social & Sustainable Bonds	Dec-19

Source: Compiled by the Researchers

From Table – 1, it is identified that there are different types of sustainability bonds listed in 19 Stock Exchanges across the world from the year 2015 to 2019. Only two Stock Exchanges (Stockholm Stock Exchange and NASDAQ Nordics & Baltics Exchange) showed that their listed bonds are Sustainable Bonds, though sometimes sustainable and green bonds are used interchangeably. Remaining Seventeen stock Exchanges reported clear focus on listing of Green Bonds.

IFC: Creating a Market for Green Bonds

International Finance Corporation (IFC) is the largest global development institution focused on the private sector in developing countries. IFC, a member of the World Bank Group, advances economic development and improves the lives of people by encouraging the growth of the private sector in developing countries. Besides, Amundi is a French Asset Management Company. It is largest Asset manager in Europe and one of the 10 biggest investment managers in the world. In 2018, IFC and Amundi launched the Amundi Planet Emerging Green One Fund (AP EGO) to stimulate demand for green bonds in emerging markets. As of August 2022, AP EGO had $1.4 billion under management, of which 77.8 percent are green bonds, well above the interim target of 50 percent by February 2023. Most interesting fact is that they were continuously increasing investment in the Green Bond as far as the fund is concerned. In 2018, IFC launched the Green Bond Technical Assistance Program (GB-TAP) to create a market for green bonds in developing countries. The GB-TAP offers a range of activities and initiatives to foster the supply of emerging market green bonds, both in terms of volume and quality, by training banks in emerging markets, setting standards, and disseminating best practices across the industry.

IFC: Green Bond eligible Project Commitment (Regional Analysis)

As of June 30, 2022, IFC Green Bond proceeds supported 257 green bond eligible projects. The total committed amount for these projects is $10.4 billion, of which $9 billion has been disbursed.

Table 2. Regional analysis of commitment through green bonds (USD millions)

Latin America and the Caribbean									
	FY14	**FY15**	**FY16**	**FY17**	**FY18**	**FY19**	**FY20**	**FY21**	**FY22**
Commitments	618	422	90	534	406	252	330	101	249
Disbursements	156	551	210	449	357	208	171	146	301
Europe and Central Asia									
	FY14	**FY15**	**FY16**	**FY17**	**FY18**	**FY19**	**FY20**	**FY21**	**FY22**
Commitments	178	370	284	320	834	121	119	109	197
Disbursements	66	228	265	312	833	183	255	49	220
Middle East and North Africa									
	FY14	**FY15**	**FY16**	**FY17**	**FY18**	**FY19**	**FY20**	**FY21**	**FY22**
Commitments	55	59	119	137	265	45	108	100	69
Disbursements	9	34	86	184	75	148	62	79	213
South Asia									
	FY14	**FY15**	**FY16**	**FY17**	**FY18**	**FY19**	**FY20**	**FY21**	**FY22**
Commitments	62	239	200	299	297	122	84	14	60
Disbursements	11	125	154	194	200	248	75	10	39
East Asia and the Pacific									
	FY14	**FY15**	**FY16**	**FY17**	**FY18**	**FY19**	**FY20**	**FY21**	**FY22**
Commitments			229	204	340	325	38	366	313
Disbursements			18	179	427	306	47	198	323
Sub-Saharan Africa									
	FY14	**FY15**	**FY16**	**FY17**	**FY18**	**FY19**	**FY20**	**FY21**	**FY22**
Commitments	23	43	39	36	63	20	17	350	120
Disbursements		19	21	22	14	42	32	183	199

Source: IFC, 2022, Green and Social Bond Impact Report

Table – 2 reflects that the world is benefited due to the commitments made by the IFC with a purpose to make a green environment and thereby providing a sustainable future to the future generations. It is the commitment of the IFC to make the world "Green for all".

World Bank: Commitment Through Green Bonds (Sectoral Analysis)

The mission of the World Bank is to end extreme poverty and boost shared prosperity in a sustainable manner. Tackling climate change plays a critical role in achieving these goals. Through World Bank Green Bonds, investors make an impact by supporting the financing of a wide range of projects across many sectors that address climate change. As of June 30, 2019, Renewable Energy & Energy Efficiency and Clean Transportation made up the largest portion in the Green Bond eligible projects portfolio. They comprise approximately 66% of all Green Bond commitments.

Table 3. Commitment of World Bank through green bonds

Amounts in Eq. US$ billion	Committed			Allocated & Outstanding
	Mitigation	Adaptation	Total	
Renewable Energy & Energy Efficiency	6.1	0.1	6.2	4.4
Clean Transportation	5	0.2	5.1	3.1
Water & Wastewater	0.1	1.3	1.3	0.8
Solid Waste Management	0.1	0	0.1	0.1
Agriculture, Land Use, Forests & Ecological Resources	0.5	2.4	2.9	1.3
Resilient Infrastructure, Built Environment & Other	1	0.4	1.4	0.8
Total	12.8	4.3	17.2	10.5
Percentage	75%	25%	100%	

Source: World Bank, 2019, Green Bond Impact Report

Table – 3 reflects that World bank has given emphasize on renewable energy and energy efficiency along with clean transportation to a great extent but the said bank did not give that much emphasize on solid-waste management and preservation of water and recycling of waste water. A mediocre focus is given on use of agricultural land and forest maintenance.

In the past 11 years, the World Bank has issued 158 Green Bonds in 21 currencies for a total of over US$13 billion in funding to support the transition to low-carbon and climate resilient growth. During FY19 (July 1, 2018 to June 30, 2019), the World Bank issued US$2.7 billion equivalent in 24 transactions in 10 currencies. In FY19, 16 new projects were added to the Green Bond eligible project portfolio bringing the number of eligible projects to 106 and the total commitments to US$17.2 billion. Of these commitments, US$11.9 billion in Green Bond proceeds were allocated and disbursed to support projects in 31 countries. As of June 30, 2019, the East Asia & Pacific region made up the greatest portion of the Green Bond eligible projects and comprises approximately 34% of all Green Bond commitments. The region includes China, Indonesia, Philippines, Timor-Leste, and Vietnam.

Geography of the Green Bond Market

Green Bonds have been issued in 23 jurisdictions including 14 markets of the G20 and in 23 currencies. These are shown below:

- **GBD** – The countries where Green Bonds are issued for domestic and foreign investors: Australia, Austria, Canada, China, EU, France, Germany, Hong Kong, China, India, Italy, Japan, Mexico, Netherlands, Norway, Peru, South Africa, Spain, Sweden, the UK and the USA.
- **GBF** – The countries where Green Bonds are issued for foreign investors only: Brazil, Switzerland and Chinese Taipei.
- **GBC** – The currencies which are associated with issuance of Green Bonds: AUD, BRL, CAD, CHF, COP, EUR, GBP, HUF, IDR, INR, JPY, MXN, MYR, NOK, NZD, PEN, PLN, RMB, RUB, SEK, TRY, USD, ZAR.
- **GBM** – The G20 markets where Green Bonds are traded: Australia, Brazil, Canada, China, EU, France, Germany, India, Italy, Japan, Mexico, South Africa, UK, USA.

Emerging Market Green Bond Issuance, 2019

Bond market conditions were supportive of debt issuance in 2019, with total issues by all sectors from emerging markets amounting to $1.7 trillion, up from $1.4 trillion in 2018. Whereas bond issues by China rose by 21 percent, issuance in emerging markets other than China increased only 11 percent. Stronger growth in green bond issues outside China was attributable to increasing awareness and know-how about green bonds among both issuers and investors as well as to demand for ESG products. Indeed, the incorporation of these instruments into investor strategies gained considerable momentum in 2019. Globally, ESG-dedicated funds hold about $850 billion in assets under management. The entry of emerging market issuers into this space has been quite recent but encouraging, enabling them to tap into strong demand for green bonds to secure capital from both domestic and international investors.

Table 4. Emerging market green bond issuance, 2019

Country	Volume($million)	Country	Volume($million)
China	34338.2	Peru	652.3
India	3195.6	Malaysia	475.2
Chile	2924.9	Ukraine	357.9
Poland	2478.2	Panama	200
Philippines	1498	Ecuador	150
UAE	1270	Mexico	129
Brazil	1258.8	Nigeria	106.3
Czech Republic	832.7	Turkey	100
Indonesia	750	Kenya	41.5
Thailand	734.4	Costa Rica	3.5
South Africa	724.2	Barbados	1.5

Source: IFC, 2019, Emerging Market Green Bond Report

China remained the largest emerging market issuer. Although China has issued more than $30 billion in green bonds each year since 2016, its issuance in 2019 declined by 7 percent from a year before. Other emerging markets drove the overall growth in 2019 with $18 billion of issues, nearly triple that in 2018. The largest volumes were registered by India, followed by Chile, Poland, the Philippines, the United Arab Emirates, and Brazil. New entrants to the green bond market included Barbados, the Czech Republic, Ecuador, Panama, and Ukraine, demonstrating the increasing geographical diversification of the green bond market across all regions.

Outside China, the region moved to the forefront of green bond market development. Southeast Asian countries have been stepping up issuance, with another sovereign green bond from Indonesia ($750 million), a green sukuk from Malaysia, and a mix of corporations and financial institutions issuing in the Philippines and Thailand. In South Asia, benchmark-sized issuances from nonfinancial corporates in India included those from Adani, Greenko and Renew, with the use of proceeds going to renewable energy. After a slow year in 2018, issuance in Latin America and the Caribbean grew rapidly in 2019, buoyed by two sovereign issues from Chile and new entrants including Barbados, Ecuador, and Panama. With 40 issuers from 11 countries, the region has the largest number of countries with nascent green bond markets. Poland again led Europe and Central Asia with a sovereign bond issuance of €2 billion, as well as several by financial institutions. Both the Czech Republic and Ukraine saw debut issues from nonfinancial corporates, and private placements from financial institutions in Turkey added to the region's totals. The Middle East and North Africa saw $1.2 billion in green sukuk issuance from the United Arab Emirates company Majid Al Futtaim. Green bond market activity in Sub-Saharan Africa included a repeat sovereign issue by Nigeria, financial and corporate offerings in South Africa, and a debut green bond from a corporate in Kenya.

Green Bond Market in India

The Green Bond Market in India has already gained its importance with the help of two types of Green Bonds – One was issued by Indore Municipal Corporation (IMC) in 2017 and another one is Sovereign Green Bond issued for first time in 25th January 2023 by Reserve Bank of India.

Types of Green Bonds in Indian Green Bond Market –

- Green Bond as issued by IMC in 2017
- Sovereign Green Bond as issued by RBI in 2023

The National Stock Exchange (NSE) has listed the first green bonds on its platform from Indore Municipal Corporation. Green bonds are debt securities designated to finance environment-friendly projects. India's municipal bond market is growing rapidly, with fund raising growing three-fold since 2017. Indore Municipal Corporation had filed for another round of ₹250 crore fund raising. It has raised ₹6,252 crore through this route, compared to ₹2,342 crore in 2017. This shows that the government fixed-income market is back on investors' radar. Yield on the benchmark 10-year government securities has risen to 7.4 per cent from a low 5.8 per cent in June 2020. Municipal bonds provide an alternative means of financing for urban local bodies, reducing dependence on central and state grants. Most urban infra bonds may be categorised as green bonds given that proceeds are predominantly targeted towards energy, transport, water management, sewage treatment, energy saving and so on.

The Government of India joined the Sovereign Green Bonds Club on 25 January 2023 when the Ministry of Finance priced an INR 80 billion (USD 1 billion two tranche deal split equally between five- and ten-years tenors. The deal attracted oversubscription of more than four times, enabling primary market spread compression of two basis points on the 10-year, and three basis points on the 5-year tranche. The five-year bond was allocated to 32 investors and the 10-year to 57 investors according to Reserve Bank of India. On 09ᵗʰ February each tranche was reopened for INR 40 billion (USD 500 million) increasing India's total green liabilities to INR 160 billion (USD 2 billion).

The full auction results as declared by RBI on January 25, 2023 is given in the Table – 5.

Table 5. Sovereign green bonds: Full auction results

	Auction Results	NEW GOI SGrB 2028	NEW GOI SGrB 2023
I.	Notified Amount	INR 4000 Crore	INR 4000 Crore
II.	Underwriting Notified amount	INR 4000 Crore	INR 4000 Crore
III.	Competitive Bids Received		
	Number	96	170
	amount	INR 13525 Crore	INR 19367 Crore
IV.	Cut-off price /yield	7.10%	7.29%
V.	Competitive bids accepted		
	Number	32	57
	Amount	INR 3993.124 Crore	INR 3948.646 Crore
VI.	Partial Allotment percentage of Competitive Bids	81.62%	22.15%
		(11 Bids)	(23 Bids)
VII.	Weighted Average Price/yield	100	100
		(WAY: 7.1000%)	(WAY: 7.2900%)
VIII.	Non-Competitive Bids Received		
	Number	2	4
	amount	INR 6.876 Crore	INR 51.354 Crore
IX.	Non-Competitive Bids Accepted		
	Number	2	4
	amount	INR 6.876 Crore	INR 51.354 Crore
X.	Amount of Underwriting accepted from primary dealers	INR 4000 Crore	INR 4000 Crore
XI.	Devolvement of Primary Dealers	NIL	NIL

Source: Reserve Bank of India, 2023, Sovereign Green Bonds – Full Auction Results

Most significant fact is that the proceeds from the Sovereign Green Bonds in India will go towards projects that meet the decarbonisation targets, which include achieving net-zero emissions by 2070, reducing emission intensity of GDP by 45 per cent by 2030 over the 2005 levels, and increasing the share of non-fossil fuel energy resources to 40 per cent by 2030.

The country's sovereign green bond framework, published in October 2022, identifies how the proceeds from green bonds will be allocated to projects like renewable energy, energy efficiency, clean transportation, sustainable water and waste management, and green buildings. In India, there are some issues (https://www.cbd.int/financial/doc/india-greenbonds2015.pdf) associated with the development of Green Bond Market which are –

● Interest arbitrage against normal bonds does not exist.
● Green Bonds Investments are not social funds.
● The bond tenures are still low against requirement.

Relationship Between Green Bond and Sustainability Development Goals

The United Nations Sustainable Development Goals (SDGs) made an urgent call for action by all the countries across the globe with an aim to end poverty, improve health and education, reduce inequality, and spur economic growth – all of these are intended to be achieved while tackling climate change and working to protect environment and preserve earth. However, these goals cannot be achieved unless money is mobilized to finance climate change mitigation and adaptation efforts across the world. Different ways of financing are there but the most favourable way of financing the efforts to achieve SDGs is Green Bonds.

Green Bond Investment supports six SDGs out of seventeen SDGs as specified by United nations. These are –

● **Clean Water and Sanitation (SDG – 6):** Clean water and sanitation (SDG - 6) accounts for 11% of green bond issuance to date. A recent example of Green Bond investment in this is Cape Town's Certified Green bond, which financed clean water and sanitation assets (SDG – 7) that are both low carbon and climate resilient.
● **Clean Energy (SDG – 7):** Clean energy (SDG7) remains the largest share of the green bond market (40%), though the share has fallen as the market has diversified over the last few years. Nigeria's sovereign green bond for example allocated the majority of proceeds to renewable energy expansion (SDG - 7).
● **Sustainable Industry, Innovation and Infrastructure (SDG - 9):** Low carbon buildings are the second largest segment of the Green Bond market to date (24%), followed by low carbon transport (15%). India Railways Finance Corporation offers up a best-practice example of a Green Bond from the transport sector with proceeds allocated to electrified rail, a low emission transport solution. Lithuania's sovereign green bond financed energy efficient multifamily housing.
● **Sustainable Cities and Communities (SDG - 11):** Many of the assets financed by Green Bonds are located in cities and they address the Goal of sustainable cities and communities (SDG - 11). Cape Town's Green Bond for water supports sustainable cities (SDG - 11) as well as climate action (SDG - 13) - illustrating how a single asset contributes to several SDGs at once.
● **Climate Action (SDG – 13):** The rapidly growing Green Finance sphere is already providing capital for assets that simultaneously contribute to climate action (SDG - 13) and many other SDGs. In the Green Bond Market, the vast majority of proceeds to date is allocated to climate mitigation and adaptation & resilience, with only a small share allocated to other green assets.
● **Life on land (SDG – 15):** A smaller share of Green Bonds (3%) is also financing sustainable forestry and agriculture, contributing to life on land (SDG - 15). Almost half the Green Bonds issued in Brazil (a global agriculture exporter) have a sustainable forestry or land use component. Poland's Sovereign Green Bond included sustainable agriculture, afforestation, conservation and restoration of natural habitat.

Region-Wise Green Bond Issuance

To finance SDGs, every region of the globe has already issued Green Bonds. Here in Table – 6, how much amount has already been raised by the different regions through issuing Green Bonds over last 9 years ranging from 2014 – 2022 is summarized.

Table 6. Green bond issuance (US$ billion)

Region	2014	2015	2016	2017	2018	2019	2020	2021	2022
Africa	0.1	NF	0.2	0.3	0.2	0.9	1.2	0.4	0.3
Asia-Pacific	1.6	3.6	26.5	35.5	48.5	66.9	52.7	143.3	133.4
Europe	17.9	19.6	25.8	60.6	67.1	120.3	162.9	294.3	228.6
Latin America	0.2	1.1	1.6	4	2.4	5.2	10.9	9.1	3.1
North America	7.4	12.8	20.8	48.7	38.9	62.7	61.5	103.9	76.6
Supranational	9.4	8.4	10.2	9.5	12.1	13.1	13.8	31.4	45.1

Source: https://www.climatebonds.net/market/data/

From Table – 6, it is observed that, Europe stands as the pioneer among all the regions as far as Green Bond Issue is concerned. Europe has raised US$ 294.3 billion which is highest among other regions followed by Asia-Pacific and North America respectively. Africa and Latin America are still far behind than other regions. So, this study concludes that unlike other regions, Europe and Asia – Pacific are absolutely aware of the SDG financing through issue of Green Bonds.

Financing SDGs Through Green Bonds

Whenever there is an issue of Green Bond, the purpose is to finance the SDGs. In Table – 7, it is shown how proceeds from issue of Green Bond is utilized for the purpose of successful achievement of SDGs.

Table 7. Use of proceeds from green bond

Particulars	2014	2015	2016	2017	2018	2019	2020	2021	2022
Energy (SDG – 7)	18.3	23.7	33.2	53	53.7	85	104.8	200.9	158.3
Buildings (SDG – 9)	7.5	8.3	17.9	46.3	46.9	81.4	82.6	164.8	122.3
Transport (SDG – 9)	4.2	5.9	12.7	23.9	30.7	52.5	68.2	96.9	91.6
Water (SDG – 6)	2.7	4	10.7	19.8	18.1	24.9	18.1	36.7	33.2
Waste (SDG – 6)	1.1	1.5	4.4	6.1	7.6	9.7	7.8	24.6	24
Land Use (SDG – 15)	1.5	0.6	1.7	5.3	7.3	8.9	15.5	30.9	26.5
Industry (SDG – 9)	NF	0.7	0.1	0.2	0.8	1.7	0.9	7.7	4.1

Source: https://www.climatebonds.net/market/data/

Table – 7 exhibits that throughout the globe, from 2014 onwards, proceeds from Green Bond is basically used to finance energy conservation (SDG – 7), development of infrastructure (SDG – 9), treatment of water and providing clean environment (SDG – 6) and proper utilization of land (SDG – 15). Looking at 2021, it can be stated that conservation of energy i.e., SDG – 7 is in top priority list to most of the countries at the time of spending proceeds of Green Bonds. After that countries are worried about development of infrastructures. Most significant fact is that there is a sharp and steady rise in the spendings for SDGs from 2014 to 2021 as the proceeds are coming more and more through the issue of Green Bonds. In a nutshell, it is a positive initiative taken by the people of different countries to achieve a Green Environment and thereby achieving a sustainable future in the long-term.

Financing Climate Action (SDG – 13) Through Green Bonds

Most of the countries began turning to green after the Paris Agreement on climate change were adopted in 2015. Some facts are given here to show how Green Bond financed the SDG – 13.

Fiji: In 2016, Fiji became the first emerging market to issue a Green Bond raising $50 million for climate resilience.

Egypt: In 2020, Egypt's $750 million sovereign green bond was the first in the Middle East and North Africa. It also raised funds for investments in clean transportation and sustainable water management. The Green Bond also financed investments in sustainable water and waste-water management projects benefiting 16.9 million people.

Indonesia: In 2021, a sustainability bond in Indonesia **is** supporting the Sidrap Wind Farm in South Sulawesi – one of the largest islands in the Indonesian Archipelago. The project, which runs through 2028, will install 30 wind turbines and send enough renewable energy to the South Sulawesi national grid to power over 70,000 homes. The bond was issued by a non-bank financial institution, PT Indonesia Infrastructure Finance, established by the Government of Indonesia, the World Bank Group, Asian Development Bank and other multilateral institutions. The project is part of a plan to increase the amount of renewable energy in Indonesia's power grid while reducing coal and diesel.

Colombia: Colombia, recognized for its efforts to green its economy, issued Latin America's first green bond in a local currency (Colombian pesos) in 2021. he $511.4 million-equivalent bond being named sovereign green bond were issued to support 27 investment projects in sustainable water management, ecosystem services and biodiversity protection, renewable energy and clean and sustainable transport, including funding for the first line of the Bogotá metro.

Malaysia: Green bonds are also helping to finance green projects in the Islamic world. A $481.9 construction project in Kuala Lumpur, Malaysia, is funded in part by a green sukuk, an interest-free bond that generates returns to investors without infringing the principles of Shari'ah (Islamic law). The project backs energy-efficient construction of 83 floors of office space and is the first in Malaysia to qualify for triple platinum green building accreditation.

Thus, the different countries already started to issue Green Bonds for the purpose of taking steps to achieve a green planet.

Criticisms of Green Bond Market

Keeping in mind the effectiveness of Green Bond Market towards achieving a sustainable environment and the significance of Green Bonds in the arena of Sustainable Investing, it is the responsibility of the researchers to highlight the limitations of such green instrument which are –

- Green Bond Market is small and nascent in nature and potentially less liquid.
- The Bond Size is too small.
- Lack of unified standards can raise confusion and possibility for reputational risk if green integrity of bond questioned.
- Limited scope for legal enforcement of green integrity.
- Lack of standardisation can lead to complexities in research and a need for extra due diligence that may not always be fulfilled.

"Transition Bond" – A Threat or Alternative to Green Bond?

AXA Investment Managers (AXA IM) were the first to advance the idea of "Transition Bonds", focusing on new instruments for carbon-intensive companies that are actively decarbonizing (for example, fossil fuel companies) but unable to issue green bonds. Such companies lack suitable green assets to issue a green bond. Therefore, Transition Bonds provide an alternative source of funding explicitly aimed at helping them become greener. The idea is that they could depend on the use-of-proceeds approach, which supports green bonds. The funds need to be exclusively used to fully or partly finance or refinance specified projects and the issuer needs to justify their significance from the standpoint of commercial transformation and climate transition.

CONCLUSION AND RECOMMENDATIONS

The evolving green bond market faces a range of specific challenges and barriers to its further evolution and growth. Policy makers have a suite of options available to overcome these barriers and help to grow a sustainable green bond market with integrity. Considering the outcome of United Nations Climate Change Conference (COP – 27) held in Egypt on November 2022 and the global requirement of achieving Sustainable Development Goals 2030, it is of prime importance for every nation to focus on emergence of Green Bond Market and thereby issuance of Green Bonds. Even World Bank and International Finance Corporation helped some nations to go for emerging Green Bond Market. Still Green Bond Market is small and nascent in nature and potentially less liquid. But at the end of the day, keeping in mind the effectiveness of Green Bond to tackle the climate change issues, it is the responsibility of the Government of any nation to emphasize on such a market for getting a sustainable green future. This study also recommends for some globally accepted unified Standards for the purpose of regulation of such market. Otherwise, the purpose of issuance of Green Bond will simply go into vain.

REFERENCES

Agarwal, V., Thakkar, K., Jain, R., & Keerthan, D. (2020). Sustainable Financing: A Study on effect and development of green bonds in Asia. [IJCRT]. *International Journal of Creative Research Thoughts*, *8*(10), 3299–3314.

Ahmed R., Yusuf F. & Ishaque M. (2022). Green bonds as a bridge to the UN sustainable development goals on environment: A climate change empirical investigation. *International Journal of Financial Economics*. . doi:10.1002/ijfe.2787

Antoniuk Y. & Leirvik T. (2021). Climate Transition Risk and the Impact on Green Bonds. *Journal of Risk and Financial Management*. . doi:10.3390/jrfm14120597

Arora, R., & Raj, M. (2020). A Comparative Study on the performance of Green and Traditional Bonds. *International Journal of Business and Management Invention.*, *9*(7), 40–46. doi:10.35629/8028-0907034046

Cheong, C., & Choi, J. (2020). Green Bonds: A Survey. *Journal of Derivatives and Quantitative Studies.*, *28*(4), 175–189. doi:10.1108/JDQS-09-2020-0024

Clapp, C., Alfsen, K., Torvanger, A., & Lund, H. (2015). Commentary: Influence of Climate Science on Financial Decisions. *Nature Climate Change*, *5*(2), 83–85. doi:10.1038/nclimate2495

Cortellini, G., & Panetta, I. (2021). Green Bond: A Systematic Literature Review for Future Research Agendas. *Journal of Risk and Financial Management*, *14*(589), 1–29. doi:10.3390/jrfm14120589

Deschryver, P., & Mariz, F. (2020). What Future for the Green Bond Market? How Can Policymakers, Companies, and Investors Unlock the Potential of the Green Bond Market? *Journal of Risk and Financial Management*, *13*(61), 1–26. https://www.climatebonds.net/market/data/. doi:10.3390/jrfm13030061

International Finance Corporation. (2019), *Emerging Market Green Bonds Report*. IFC. https://www.ifc.org/content/dam/ifc/doc/mgrt/amundi-ifc-research-paper-2018.pdf

International Finance Corporation. (2022), *Green and Social Bond Impact Report*. IFC. https://www.ifc.org/content/dam/ifc/doc/2023/IFC-GreenSocialBondReport-Final.pdf

Kumar S. and Kundalia L. (2023). Green Bonds – Role and Scope in India's Financial and Fiscal Landscape. *The Journal of Indian Institute of Banking & Finance*.

Maltais A. & Nykvist B. (2020). Understanding the role of green bonds in advancing sustainability. *Journal of Sustainable Finance & Investment*. . doi:10.1080/20430795.2020.1724864

Reserve Bank of India. (2023), *Sovereign Green Bonds – Full Auction Results*. Reserve Bank of India. https://www.rbi.org.in/scripts/BS_PressReleaseDisplay.aspx?prid=55190

Verma, A., & Agarwal, R. (2020). A Study of Green Bond market in India: A Critical Review. *International Symposium on Fusion of Science and Technology (ISFT 2020)*. ACM. 10.1088/1757-899X/804/1/012052

Wang, S., & Wang, D. (2022). Exploring the relationship between ESG performance and Green Bond Issuance. *Frontiers in Public Health*, *10*, 1–13. doi:10.3389/fpubh.2022.897577 PMID:35692317

World Bank. (2019), *Green Bond Impact Report*. World Bank. https://documents1.worldbank.org/curated/en/961221573041494528/pdf/Financial-Year-2019.pdf

World Bank. (2022), *Sustainable Development Bonds & Green Bonds Impact Report*. World Bank. https://thedocs.worldbank.org/en/doc/33420eed17c2a23660b46dc208b01815-0340022023/original/World-Bank-IBRD-Impact-Report-FY22.pdf

Chapter 4
How to Enhance the Cooperation Between Science and Economy Towards a Sustainable Future:
Evidence From Serbia

Marija Mosurović Ružičić

Institute of Economic Sciences, Belgrade, Serbia

Marija Lazarević Moravčević

Institute of Economic Sciences, Belgrade, Serbia

Mihailo Paunovic

Institute of Economic Sciences, Belgrade, Serbia

ABSTRACT

Sustainability has emerged as a significant and pressing issue, garnering attention from researchers, institutions, global corporations, and economies, aiming to enhance human well-being comprehensively. Within this Sustainable Development Agenda 2030, Research and Development Institutions (RDI) play an important role as catalysts for societal transformation and researching diverse societal challenges. This chapter analyses the two indicators related to achieving the sustainable development goals: research and development expenditure as a proportion of Gross Domestic Product (GDP) and researchers (in full-time equivalent) per million inhabitants. The research aims to highlight the importance of the scientific research sector as a partner for collaboration with the business community in achieving sustainable development. This chapter will also analyse some data related to Serbia. In the context of developing countries, the concept of sustainability holds great potential for improving their position within the regional context.

DOI: 10.4018/979-8-3693-2197-3.ch004

INTRODUCTION

Nowadays, the influences from the environment compel organisations to generate strategies in the context of sustainable development. Organisations that follow sustainability initiatives can establish a link between technological innovations, organisational elements, and market demand more easily (Schaltegger et al., 2016).

As the economic theory in the field of innovation has developed, the focus has first shifted from research and development, as a key factor of innovative behaviour, to the market that ensures innovation placement. Moreover, the development of information and communication technologies and the knowledge about the creation of new ideas have improved the business paradigm; therefore, information technologies and human capital have become more prominent, i.e. knowledge exchange and cooperation in the area of research and development (Sengupta, 2014). The imperative is now to network all the actors of the innovation system and to enable their mutual interaction not only towards obtaining economic benefits, but also towards the anticipation of social challenges, and responding to them as well (OECD, 2011).

Sustainable development goals, which are presented in the document The Agenda for Sustainable Development, define the priorities of societies' development and represent a framework for improving human prosperity in all spheres (Griggs et al., 2014; Ružičić et al., 2021; United Nations, 2015). The Agenda specifies that the fields of science, technology and innovation present the accelerators of SDGs implementation. In this way, these areas have become part of a strong institutional mechanism providing a better flow of knowledge between countries (Guo et al., 2022).

The role of Research and Development Institutions (RDIs) in the context of achieving sustainable development goals can be viewed in several ways. Research and Development Institutions are the agents of social changes since they research various social challenges that a society faces, and in this regard these institutions develop their strategies in accordance with the SDGs (Pakkan et al., 2022). The strategies of research and development institutions are a reflection of the events in the modern environment. As for developing countries, the context of sustainability enables the improvement of the position of these countries in the regional context where research and development institutions play a significant role (Filho et al., 2021). Nowadays, research and development institutions are facing the challenges of restructuring as a result of new demands and influences from an unpredictable environment. In the economies facing the process of privatisation, liberalisation and lack of public funding for financing research and development, the organisations engaged in research and development are forced to reconsider the state and type of the activities they are engaged in; in particular, to what extent they should develop their cooperation with customers and suppliers, what kind of personnel is needed, assessment of the resources of management, the importance and potential of the market, and the like. All these activities require careful strategic management. One of the mistakes that developing countries make is that they simply copy the model of developed countries. Research and development should be in accordance with the needs identified within the national innovation system (Arnold et al., 2010).

The concept of sustainability has gained significance recently and has become a primary area of focus for researchers, institutions, global companies and economies. Along with advancements in science and research methods, there is a lot of resources and research that can contribute to the development of modern systems, economy, industry, education, etc. Research not only helps overcome obstacles, but also supports innovation and directs decision-makers' attention to sustainability problems within organisations and society. Thus, everyone strives to benefit from scientific development and achieve sustainability, which brings plenty rewards to those who are successful (Jouda & Abu Dan, 2022).

The intention of this paper is to address the research question: what is the role and significance of research, development, and innovation in contributing to the achievement of all Sustainable Development Goals (SDGs). However, special attention will be paid to the analysis of the indicators specified within Target *9.5. Enhance scientific research, upgrade the technological capabilities of industrial sectors in all countries, in particular developing countries, including, by 2030, encouraging innovation and substantially increasing the number of research and development workers per 1 million people and public and private research and development spending* (United Nations, 2015).

A desk-research method was utilised in the paper and secondary sources of data were the papers and publications from scientific journals and other professional literature. The main indicators of achieving the target will be analysed, that is, *Research and Development Expenditure as a Proportion of GDP* and *Researchers* (in full-time equivalent) per million inhabitants. The aim of the research is to underline the importance of the scientific research sector as a partner for the cooperation with the economy for the sake of sustainable development. The chapter will also analyse some data related to Serbia, with the intention to show the degree of the connection between science and economy.

Research and Development Institutions (RDIs)

The environment in which research and development institutions operate is turbulent, full of uncertainty and risk. Investing in research and development activities is capital-intensive and the results can only be seen in a future period or quite often there are no results, and/or it is necessary to abandon certain scientific research project during the implementation process itself. Taking everything into account, the strategic approach to the management of research and development institutions is gaining more and more importance. There is a mismatch between the research that takes place within research and development institutions and the needs of a society, in particular, the needs of the industry. The research should be viewed in a complex technological and social context that places the emphasis on intra-disciplinary collaboration (Jain et al., 2010). In addition, the cooperation should be seen in a wider context as an interaction between all actors of the national innovation system. Research and development institutions increasingly tend to function as business enterprises that plan, organise and deliver their *business products and services*. This does not only imply entrepreneurial behaviour such as taking risks, but also displays a strategic approach to the commercialisation of scientific research results. The literature in the field of research, development and innovation indicates that companies do not cooperate sufficiently with institutes and faculties on the development of innovation. For example, a research study conducted by Paunović et al., 2022 indicate that small firms (family and non-family firms) introduce many business process innovations, but the firms themselves introduce those innovations. Actually, companies ought to have successful implementation mechanisms to realise innovation in the market. This approach involves a methodical approach to problem-solving and is most effective when accompanied by a well-defined strategy and decision-making system. A significant increase in research and development activities, as well as the costs incurred on that basis, highlight the need to establish an efficient strategic management system in research and development institutions which is important not only for improving the performance of the scientific research sector, but also for improving the performance of the national economy as a whole (Ružičić Mosurović & Obradović, 2020). The so-called *scientific revolution* has affected almost every area of life, so that there is almost no nation - at least in Europe - whose economic development is not seen through the influence of scientific research work on the lives of citizens, as well as the ability to put scientific research work into the function of making a profit (Libik, 1969).

On the other hand, a large number of institutes is financed largely from national budgets, so the processes that take place should be in accordance with the policies at the national level, especially with the policies in the field of research, development, and innovation.

The importance of scientific research institutions is primarily seen through a process of creating knowledge. Universities produce highly educated staff and engineers who will be in a position to create new knowledge. Institutes and research centres, just like universities, perform the function of creating knowledge and driving technological progress (Chaves & Monzón, 2012; Nelson, 1993). Scientific research in research and development institutions aims to improve the existing knowledge base, while research and development activities strive to direct research and development towards market requirements. In research and development institutions, alongside the activities related to research and development, also the activities related to research dissemination and technology transfer are often performed. Recently, various infrastructural solutions that can enhance the performance of these activities are becoming more prominent.

According to the Official Journal of the European Union 2006/C 323/1 (European Union, 2006), research and development institutions, institutes and higher education institutions categorise scientific research into fundamental research, industrial research and experimental development in line with the UNESCO and OECD classification. Based on its definition, it is obvious that a research and development institution represents a common determinant both for scientific research institutes and higher education institutions. In institutes, the predominant activity is research and development; while at universities, it is education provision. However, institutes and faculties should not be viewed as competitors, but as a complementary system. Universities are traditionally recognised as the main centres of research and development. In cases when research and development needed to be promoted at the national level in a certain field, universities were often considered to be a suitable place for the formation of new organisational units and institutions. Most of them are mainly state-funded and some are financed from private and non-profit sectors and, more recently, from the business sector (OECD, 2015). A large part of the literature recognises and places emphasis on higher education institutions, institutes and research centres for achieving technological progress and, ultimately, economic growth.

Regardless of the fact that research institutes are significant sources of expenditure when it comes to research and development activities, almost half of the research and development expenditure from public funds go to these organisations, yet they were insufficiently statistically mapped for a long time. Actually, they were rather neglected, especially when it comes to the operation of national European policies, and, consequently, in that context their contribution to the development of the European Research Area was also limited. However, the actual situation in practice indicates that institutes have a significant role within the European Innovation System, regardless of the financing method, which mostly limits them to the national level (Arnold et al., 2010). The same authors (Arnold et al., 2010) classified research and development institutions into: scientific research institutes, government laboratories, and research and technology organisations (RTOs). The definition of the institutional units participating in the performance of R&D activities is of fundamental importance for the collection of the data related to R&D. Important methodological recommendations for the collection, processing and the analysis of the data from the field of research and development are presented in *the Frascati Manual*. The first two versions of the manual included only natural sciences and engineering, while social sciences and humanities were incorporated in the third edition of the manual. The latest, sixth edition (OECD, 2015) represents the most significant revision of the original. It analyses thoroughly research and development process in the contemporary complex business environment. Within this edition of the manual, the classification by sector of the organisations performing research and development is proposed: business enterprise, government, higher education, private non-profit sector, and the rest of the world.

The definition of research and development has evolved over time under the influence of the environment and the development of the scientific research system itself. Godin (2003) noted that all definitions are based on *continuous and systematic searching for new facts*. The evolution of the term *systematically* started from the initial emphasis on the term *scientific method* leading to the later emphasis on *institutional research*. The word *research* is derived from a Latin word *quaestio, -ionis*, and, etymologically speaking, the root originates from the Proto-Italic **<kwai-s-e/o*, which when translated means: to acquire knowledge or skill; to learn based on experience; and to acquire something thanks to hard work and effort. The verb *quaero*, in Latin, has a wide range of meanings: to search, investigate, desire, consider, plan, strive for a goal, yearn to learn and master something, examine, conduct a judicial investigation, and scrutinise. All the abovementioned meanings are condensed in the noun *quaestio*, directly deriving from this verb, and it best illustrates what the term *research* implies today (Ružičić Mosurović & Obradović, 2020).

Research and experimental development (R&D) comprises creative and systematic work undertaken in order to increase the stock of knowledge – including knowledge of humankind, culture and society – and to devise new applications of available knowledge (OECD, 2015, p. 44). The definition includes fundamental research, applied research and experimental development, i.e. the research aimed at increasing the general knowledge base without a specific goal, which can also be purpose-driven research in accordance with predefined development goals and/or tasks commissioned by various clients, mostly for the needs of the industry. Based on the characteristics of research and development activities within the Frascati Manual, five basic categories are identified (OECD, 2015):

- *Research and development activities aim to make new discoveries.* The goal of research and development activities at the operational level is the acquisition of new knowledge, yet this should be adapted to different contexts dictated by the fact which sector is taken into account.
- *Research and development activities are based on original but not obvious concepts and hypotheses.* Basically, research and development activities generate new knowledge; in addition to improving the knowledge already existing as part of products and processes, the knowledge that supports the development of new concepts and ideas is also generated.
- *Research and development activities are accompanied by uncertainty regarding the final outcome.* Due to uncertainty, the costs of research and development, the type of results and the time period cannot be precisely estimated, therefore, there are some deviations in these categories. When it comes to basic research, whose main goal is to expand the boundaries of formal knowledge, there is even the possibility of not achieving a certain result at all.
- *Research and development activities should be planned and budgeted*, through a developed management and budgeting system conditioned by the type of the project's research and development activities.
- *Research and development activities should lead to the possibility of transferring new knowledge.* In business environment, results are protected by secrecy or other intellectual property protection; nevertheless, processes and results are expected to be useful to other researchers in a company.

Based on the above, the OECD classification indicates that research and development refers to fundamental research, applied research and experimental development, which is generally in line with the UNESCO classification and Eurostat classification. The authors (Elken & Wollscheid, 2016) pointed out the broad coverage of the term *research* itself since it is used not only as a denominator for basic research, applied and experimental development, but also for the other activities undertaken by academics, such as scientific thinking, curriculum development, consulting, etc. They also believe that the very concept of research differs between countries, cultural and linguistic areas.

Management patterns in RDIs are created according to the features of the scientific research work performed in them. Research and development activities are risky by their nature; therefore, it is rather difficult to measure and evaluate theses results. The strategic management of these organisations should be flexible; the autonomy of researchers should not be limited, as this could adversely affect their creativity. Furthermore, research and development institutions have to serve both public and private (e.g. the industry) interests, which further impedes the process of strategic management (Güldenberg & Leitner, 2008). Basic research activities always strive to make new discoveries, based on original concepts (or their interpretations) or hypotheses. Frequently, one never knows precisely what the end result will be (as well as the amount of time and resources needed to achieve the goal). Applied research and development are generally planned activities, having an appropriate budget and the aim to achieve the results that can be either transferable or that can be implemented in the market (OECD, 2015). When it comes to applied research, it should suit more the needs of the industry. It is necessary to pay special attention to the strategic level of the research and to improve the possibility of transferring knowledge and technology in the industry. Moreover, it is important for research and development institutions to have a developed institutional capacity that will enable market-oriented research and development activities through the establishment of the cooperation between scientific research institutions (regardless of the type of financing) and the economy. It has been proved in practice that research and development institutions are often less successful and achieve poorer performance due to an academic way of thinking and not thinking in a businesslike way, especially when it comes to the organisations financed from public funds (Thuriaux et al., 2000). The authors, Mazzoleni & Nelson (2007) believe that research institutes that are financed from public funds, often within universities, but this is not the rule, are marked as important structural elements of economic development.

Changes in the economic international environment and increasing scientifically based new technologies influence the increase in the importance of these organisations in the future. Universities and publicly funded laboratories have contributed to the development of the various forms that define the technological capabilities of countries and economic sectors. Economists' interest in the analysis of economic growth lies in the fact that even very small changes in the long-term rate of economic growth bring about significant differences in the achieved level of living standards between countries in the long term (Ružičić Mosurović & Obradović, 2020).

There is a consensus in the literature on the positive correlation of the investment in research and development and the rate of economic growth. The author Khan (2015) systematised theoretical and empirical research to explore the place and impact of research and development on economic growth. His research indicated that developing countries should follow this model to achieve sustainable economic growth. Economic growth rates differ between countries in the long run. A country that is a technological follower, but also has a large share of human capital in the total capital, can catch up and even take the lead in a limited period of time. Whereas, a country that is a technological leader will remain in that position as long as it manages to maintain the advantage in human capital accumulation rate. Taking everything in account, it can be concluded that countries with a better education system are more inclined to bridge the technological gap compared to the other countries (Mervar, 1999, 2003).

R&D Science Towards Sustainable Science

There is a mismatch between the research taking place within research and development institutions, the needs of society, and the needs perceived by industry (Jain et al., 2010; Smit & Hessels, 2021). The research undertaken should be viewed in a complex technological and social context that emphasises interdisciplinary collaboration (Jain et al., 2010).

In the second half of the last century, RDIs experienced rapid but fundamental changes, leading to the creation of new organisational forms of knowledge creation. In the early nineties, the authors Etzkowitz & Leydesdorff (1995) developed the Triple Helix model that represents a framework for understanding the complex relationship and interaction between three key actors in the innovation process: academia (research institutes and universities), industry, and government. The model proved that the interactions between the main actors in the model boost economic growth. Research and development institutions strive more and more to function as business enterprises that plan, organise and deliver their business products and services, which does not only imply undertaking entrepreneurial behaviour in terms of taking risks, but also a strategic approach to the commercialisation of scientific research results.

At the beginning of this century, as a consequence of the need to reconceptualise the origin and creation of knowledge as well as its usage in the modern business context, the authors Carayannis & Campbell (2009) developed the Quadruple Helix Model (Cai & Lattu, 2022; Carayannis & Campbell, 2014, 2009). The Quadruple Helix Model includes a fourth helix: civil society, which represents the involvement of citizens; non-governmental organisations; and other societal actors in the innovation process. By involving civil society in the innovation process, the Quadruple Helix model seeks to promote more democratic and inclusive innovation and ensure that the benefits of innovation are more widely shared. This model has been used to guide policy-making and research in a variety of fields toward sustainable development. Bearing in mind the socio-ecological transition, which emerged at the beginning of this century, the same authors proposed the Quintuple Helix model which also encompasses the environmental dimension (Cai & Lattu, 2022; Carayannis et al., 2021). It is the necessity of the cooperation and the close link between environment, government, industry, social society and academia that the Quintuple Helix model underlines when it comes to sustainable development. Consequently, the innovation designed in this way will be more inclusive and responsible as it can simultaneously satisfy the needs of both society and the environment.

As a consequence of the current events, it is essential to apply sustainable development as a new paradigm of development accepted by a large number of governmental and non-governmental organizations. Over the past few years, the term *sustainable development* (SD) has emerged as the latest determinant of development. Sustainable development concept represents the integration of three concepts: the concept of development referring to social and economic growth while respecting environmental limitations, the concept of resources (i.e. equal distribution of resources to ensure the quality of life for all), and the concept of future generations which implies the even use of resources to provide a certain quality of life for future generations (Klarin, 2018). Sustainable development is based on three interconnected pillars, the first one is social (people), the second one represents the environment (the planet), and the last one is the economy, i.e. prosperity (Neves, 2018).

Bearing in mind the abovementioned things and as a logical reflection of the events from the past period, a large number of organisations started including the concept of sustainability in their strategic management strategies, although they still did not fully understand it in a holistic way, i.e. not being merely focused on profit (Jouda & Abu Dan, 2022). The sustainability of the firm can be understud as achiement of development goals, overcoming financial limits in oder to promote long-term sustainability (Đuričin et al., 2022). The new changes in today's scientific research system have influenced the need to establish a new concept of science - sustainable science. Sustainable science is of profound importance for achieving sustainable development; what is more, it brings scientific and research work closer to people. Knowledge and the use of knowledge to achieve sustainability need to be clearly defined; there ought to be a clear connection between users and producers of knowledge, which implies significant changes in the organisation itself and the implementation of science (Jouda & Abu Dan, 2022; Spangenberg, 2011). The author Song (2021) have reviewed the literature on "sustainability science" indicating that academic or scientific research is related to something that has already been done in the past or there is intention to be done in the present and/or future in a way to generate new knowledge. In addition, it is important to objectify it in such a way that it can contribute to a specific research field or a community.

Sustainability science is a multidisciplinary and interdisciplinary field of research that focuses on understanding interactions between social, economic and environmental systems and identifies the solutions for tackling global sustainability challenges. This approach underlines the importance of addressing social and economic equity, and the need to consider the long-term impacts of our actions on the environment and future generations. The very concept of sustainable science was created as a result of the need to improve research at the global level in order to solve social challenges, which implies multidisciplinary and interdisciplinary scientific cooperation. As a result of these initiatives, the International Science Council was formed in 2018, created through the integration of the International Science Union and the International Social Science Council, which highlighted the importance of unique coordination of natural as well as social sciences and humanities at the global level (Shrivastava et al., 2020). "Sustainability Science is research and education that results in new knowledge, technology, innovation and holistic understanding which will allow societies to better address global and local sustainability challenges" (UNESCO, 2017, p.1).

Sustainability Science brings together the knowledge of researchers from different areas and promotes the common concept of the work of researchers from all scientific research institutions (faculties and institutes). The concept Sustainability Science integrates the knowledge of researchers from research and development institutions (faculties and institutes) including also interested stakeholders outside academia with the aim to overcome specific social challenges. In this way, Sustainable Science could be a tool for promoting and implementing Sustainable Development Goals (Shrivastava et al., 2020; UNESCO, 2017). Namely, the concept is based on multidisciplinarity that connects natural sciences with social sciences and humanities, integrates basic and applied research, respecting the three pillars of sustainability: the environment-economy-society (Cai & Zhou, 2014).

The authors (Kauffman, 2009; Spangenberg, 2011) after analysing a wide range of definitions of Sustainability Science differentiated three common features:

(1) Sustainability Science needs to be action-oriented, regardless of the fact whether it is based on applied or basic research. Methodological pluralism is one of the basic features of Sustainability Science.
(2) Sustainability Science integrates the process of analysis and evaluation, that is, connects knowledge and policy action to solve complex scientific issues. Therefore, through multidisciplinary interaction, it is possible to create added value and put forward recommendations for decision makers.
(3) Sustainability Science should be based on interdisciplinarity, implemented in a way that includes an interdisciplinary concept, i.e connecting disciplines while having a specific goal.

To achieve this aim, it is necessary to make radical changes in the organisations that conduct scientific research work. The authors (Shrivastava et al., 2020) examined incremental changes in research and development institutions and defined certain recommendations on how science could initiate the transformation of the entire society by changing the approach of solving the environmental problems not based solely on considering only a scientific-technological dimension, but also including a wider social context. They highlighted the importance of reviewing the context of change itself. Sustainability Science should be oriented towards SDGs and should encourage the transformation process through the challenging roles that the transformation process itself imposes, through transformation and acceptance of strategies and policies, both at the organisational and national levels.

Research and Development in a Function of Achieving SDGs

Sustainable development goals, which are presented in the document the Agenda for Sustainable Development, define the priorities of societal development and represent a framework for collective action with the aim of achieving a better future for all, solving social, economic and environmental issues that hinder the global progress (Ružičić et al., 2021; United Nations, 2015; Yamaguchi et al., 2023). The Agenda was adopted in 2015 and identifies 17 interconnected sustainable development goals with 169 related targets. Never before have world leaders agreed to create such a unique common policy. All countries worldwide face specific challenges in terms of achieving sustainable development, especially developing countries, underdeveloped countries, and the countries in conflict (United Nations, 2015). The European Union supported this document within *Europe's strategy for international cooperation in a changing world*, emphasising the importance of international cooperation regarding the development of innovation partnerships within the framework with sustainable development goals in order to ensure better life and future generation. It is anticipated that the improvement of the cooperation will take place in several groups of countries: industrialised non-EU countries and emerging economies, EFTA countries, the Western Balkans, Turkey, European Neighbourhood Policy countries, and the United Kingdom. Moreover, it is planned to deepen the cooperation with Africa in the field of research and innovation with the purpose of accelerating and improving sustainable and inclusive development towards knowledge-based economies (European Commission, 2021).

Within the aforementioned agenda, Sustainable Development Goal 9 is particularly dedicated to research, development and innovation - *Build resilient infrastructure, promote inclusive and sustainable industrialisation and foster innovation* - which will be discussed in more detail in this paper. The established target for this goal is*: Enhance scientific research, upgrade the technological capabilities of industrial sectors in all countries, in particular developing countries, including, by 2030, encouraging innovation and substantially increasing the number of research and development workers per 1 million people and public and private research and development spending* (United Nations, 2015, p. 25). Later, in 2017, the global indicator framework was adopted in the form of an annex referring to the 2030 Agenda for Sustainable Development. According to the resolution, the indicator framework would be revised on annual basis, and its comprehensive reviewing would be performed at the sessions at the Statistical Commission in 2020 and 2025, when they were planned to be held. It was envisaged that the member countries would additionally, at the national level, supplement these general indicators with complementary ones (UN General Assembly, 2017). In this document, the following are the indicators related to Target 9.5, which will be further discussed in this chapter (UN General Assembly, 2017, p. 13):

- *"Research and development expenditure as a proportion of GDP and Researchers (in full-time equivalent) per million inhabitants;*
- *Researchers (in full-time equivalent) per million inhabitants*

As already mentioned earlier in the paper, the OECD developed and created the Frascati Manual, aiming to define methodological guidelines for systematic, uniform and analytical data collection in the field of research and development, which enabled the creation of the base in the field of research and development at the national and international level (OECD, 2015; Ružičić Mosurović & Obradović, 2020). These guidelines, as well as various statistical bases at the European and global level, enable monitoring of these indicators and, based on that, move towards the previously defined goal of sustainable development - Goal 9 intended to build strong infrastructure that promotes sustainable industrialisation and encourages innovation.

The monitoring of these indicators, especially in the context of the achievement of sustainable development goals, is clearly depicted in the UNESCO Institute for Statistics database (Table 1).

Table 1. Research and development expenditure as a proportion of GDP (GERD)

Time	2015	2016	2017	2018	2019	2020
World	1.69	1.70	1.72	1.75	1.81	1.93
Landlocked Developing Countries	0.23	0.22	0.21	0.19	0.19	0.20
Least Developed Countries	0.27	0.27	0.26	0.26	0.27	0.27
Small Island Developing States	1.06	1.01	0.97	0.96	0.99	1.00
Sub-Saharan Africa	0.35	0.36	0.36	0.34	0.32	0.32
Northern Africa and Western Asia	0.75	0.76	0.78	0.81	0.85	0.90
Northern Africa	0.60	0.60	0.61	0.63	0.69	0.76
Western Asia	0.79	0.81	0.84	0.87	0.90	0.94
Central and Southern Asia	0.60	0.59	0.59	0.58	0.58	0.58
Central Asia	0.16	0.15	0.13	0.12	0.11	0.13
Southern Asia	0.63	0.62	0.62	0.61	0.61	0.61
Eastern and South-Eastern Asia	2.05	2.06	2.09	2.12	2.19	2.31
Eastern Asia	2.40	2.39	2.43	2.46	2.53	2.67
South-Eastern Asia	0.88	0.94	0.95	0.95	0.99	1.02
Latin America and the Caribbean	0.72	0.67	0.60	0.61	0.62	0.63
Oceania	1.78	1.77	1.76	1.74	1.73	1.73
Australia and New Zealand	1.83	1.82	1.81	1.79	1.77	1.77
Europe and Northern America	2.24	2.26	2.30	2.35	2.44	2.62
Europe	1.83	1.83	1.86	1.88	1.91	2.00
Northern America	2.69	2.75	2.79	2.88	3.03	3.30

Source: UNESCO Institute for Statistics (UIS) (UNESCO, 2022)

Research and development expenditure as a proportion of GDP (GERD) is the main statistical indicator that describes R&D activity of a country. Based on the data shown in Table 1, government budget allocations for R&D increased during the analysed period 2015-2020. There is a big difference between the allocations by region defined for monitoring SDGs.

GERD represents the expenditure for R&D activities of the national economy, which can be classified by sector into four categories:

- Business enterprises sector expenditure on R&D (BERD): represents the gross domestic expenditure on R&D component that is generated by business enterprises.
- Government expenditure on R&D (GOVERD): represents the expenditure from the government sector for research and development in the analysed period;
- Higher education expenditure on R&D (HERD): represents part of R&D that higher institutions allocate for research and development;
  -Private non-profit expenditure on R&D (PNPERD): also represents the gross domestic expenditure on R&D (GERD) component created by the units belonging to the private non-profit sector.

The figure 1 shows the allocations for R&D at the level of the European Union during the period 2011-2021. The allocated funds have upward trend; nevertheless, the growth line is most noticeable when it comes to the business sector (Figure 1). The researches related to the expenditure on R&D (BERD) have displayed that BERD is significant for technological progress that further encourages sustainable development and secures long-term growth, based on which, competitiveness is achieved as well (Williams et al., 2008).

Figure 1. Gross domestic expenditure on R&D by sector (% of GDP) during the period 2011- 2021
Source: Eurostat (online data code: rd_e_gerdtot) and OECD database, (Eurostat, 2022)

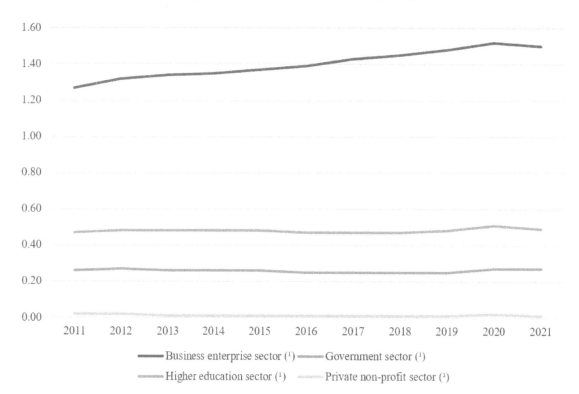

The information about how much money is spent on R&D is essential for national and global policy makers. Furthermore, that information gives us an insight into various aspects, such as who conducts and finances R&D, where it takes place, the purpose of conducting those activities, as well as the level of the interaction between institutions and sectors (OECD, 2015). The authors (Olaoye et al., 2021) examined the R&D investment and the government effectiveness in the selected African countries and showed that the innovation resulting from the investment in R&D and good governance at the highest level can encourage sustainable economic growth and development, meaning that African countries should strengthen and build their capacities for research and development.

Researches (in full-time equivalent) per million inhabitants: The statistical data about researchers are important indicators which illustrate the growth of the economy based on the knowledge and movement of highly qualified researchers.

Researches are professionals engaged in the conception or creation of new knowledge, products, processes, methods and systems, as well as in the management of the projects concerned (OECD/Eurostat, 2022).

Figure 2. Number of researchers during the period 2015-2020
Source: UNESCO Institute for Statistics (UIS) (UNESCO, 2022)

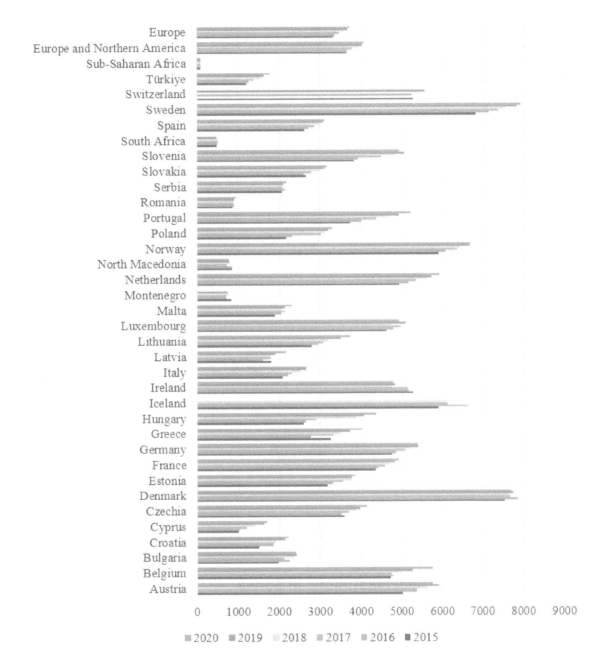

Figure 2 proves that in the period 2015-2020 there was an increase in the number of researchers, according to the data of the consolidation of OECD and Eurostat statistics (OECD/Eurostat, 2022). This number increased by over 50% at the level of the European Union, but a substantial growth rate was achieved in China - over 73%. If one were to analyse the structure of the growth of researchers, it is evident that the largest number of researchers comes from the business sector (Figure 2).

Figure 3. Researchers by sector, % of the total number of researchers in 2021
Sources: Eurostat (rd_p_persocc) and OECD database, (OECD/Eurostat, 2022)

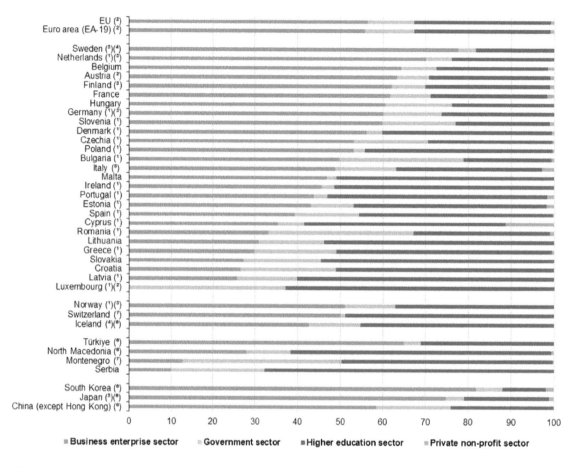

(¹) Provisional
(²) Estimates
(³) Definition differs
(⁴) Break in time series
(⁵) HES estimate
(⁶) 2020 data
(⁷) 2019 data

Research and Development Institutions in Serbia

The scientific research system in Serbia is in the process of transformation, aiming to use scientific research results as efficiently as possible. The scientific research institutions in Serbia are financed to the greatest extent from the funds provided by the Government of the Republic of Serbia. Other types of financing are recognised to a lesser extent, with the exception of research and development institutes that have direct contact with the economy.

Table 2. Gross domestic expenditure on R&D (%)

country/year	2015	2016	2017	2018	2019	2020
Serbia	0.81	0.84	0.87	0.92	0.89	0.91
Low income countries	0.26	0.25	0.24	0.24	0.23	0.23
Lower middle income countries	0.48	0.49	0.49	0.49	0.50	0.51
Middle income countries	1.10	1.13	1.13	1.15	1.21	1.30
Upper middle income countries	1.44	1.48	1.49	1.51	1.60	1.73
High income countries	2.37	2.38	2.43	2.50	2.57	2.74

Source: UNESCO Institute for Statistics (UIS)(UNESCO, 2022)

Serbia, as an upper middle income country, is below average regarding the allocation which should certainly be increased.

The existing strategy documents in Europe place a strong emphasis on enabling intelligent growth within the EU and setting the target for R&D investment to reach 3% of the European Union's (EU) GDP. Despite Serbia's notable economic reforms since 2000 and the acknowledgment of the importance of increased R&D, the country's R&D sector falls behind even in the group of upper middle income countries.

The Statistical Office of the Republic of Serbia has been applying Eurostat methodology since 2007, and accordingly, there is the statistics related to research and development expenditure as a proportion of GDP, by sector, during the period 2010–2021 which is shown in Figure 4.

Figure 4. Research and development expenditure as a proportion of GDP, by sector, 2010–2021 (%)
Source: Statistical Office of the Republic of Serbia, (Babović, 2023)

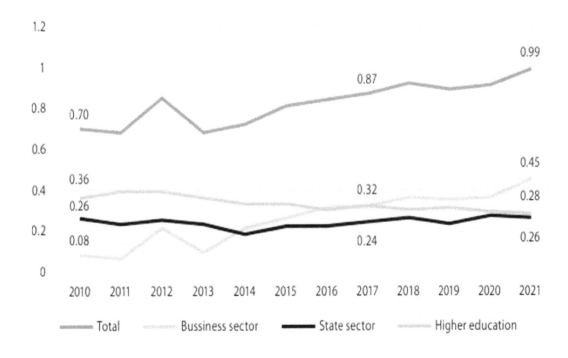

The data shown in Figure 4 match the data shown in Table 2, and the growing trend of the allocation from GDP for research and development is evident. However, that allocation is still insufficient to produce certain economic effects. However, the positive trend is the increase in the allocation rate from the business sector.

The increased number of researchers per one million inhabitants (Figure 2 and 3) indicates significant progress towards Target 9.5, although majority of researchers still come from the higher education sector.

The scientific research system of Serbia, as well as of most countries that are in the process of transition, encounters major challenges that can be systematised as follows (Racine et al., 2009; Ružičić Mosurović et al., 2021; Ružičić Mosurović & Obradović, 2020):

- The practical application of the conducted research has been constrained by limited experience. The research and development institutions primarily prioritise scientific achievements rather than the practical implementation of their findings. Although there is considerable interest in basic research, it frequently diverges from the requirements of the national economy, underscoring the importance of collaborating with international partners. However, a significant proportion of the national research and development institutions lack competitiveness at the global level.

- Deficiency in understanding the market demands is evident. The government has primarily extended its support to scientific research activities without adequately considering market justification. Consequently, this has resulted in a weak or almost non-existent connection between the scientific research sector and the industry.

- Ineffective management: Managers of RDI lack knowledge in strategic managing of RDIs. Some of them are not motivated to stimulate significant changes, they resist changes, with no intention to take any action. The governing boards of scientific research institutes often consist of members chosen for political reasons, who support organisational restructuring in a general sense. There is a significant lack of industry representatives who could make tangible contributions to the restructuring process.

- Migration of proactive research personnel: A significant number of scientists, driven by the desire for change, have left RDIs to join foreign company subsidiaries or foreign RDIs. They are attracted by better working conditions, both in terms of financial rewards and intellectual stimulation. There is a lack of interest in initiating substantial changes.

- RDIs in Serbia is facing transformation challenges and constant lack of financial resources, especially from the sources such as the market, foreign clients, European and other funds, etc. Besides that, there is still underdeveloped research infrastructure. Insufficent investment has been made in research capacity and equipment over a long period of time. The equipment is outdated, so it does not enable scientific research results to be research competitive.

The solution to these problems can be sought in the cooperation with other innovation stakeholders and the creation of appropriate infrastructural forms that can help improve the quality of scientific research results, diffusion, and knowledge and technology transfer. It is necessary to take advantage of the comparative advantage based on quality scientific research staff along with adequate management of knowledge and skills, and increase the participation of researchers in both domestic and foreign funds. Nowadays, the Government of the Republic of Serbia has initiated the transformation process of the scientific research system, which also includes RDI. The positive effects of this process are already visible, above all when it comes to establishing legislation standardisation that enables international competitiveness. However, if the specifics of scientific research work are taken into account, the essential effects will be seen only in a future period.

All the changes and macro-economic impacts of the transition environment have certainly had profound influence on the development of strategic management within research and development institutions. Not only is it important to invest in scientific research capacities and practice, but also to invest in improving the quality of management of the scientific research organisations, which have been neglected for a long time. It is vital to establish a connection between research and development policy and other policies.

CONCLUSION

The Agenda for Sustainable Development outlines the priorities for societal development and serves as a framework for enhancing human well-being in all spheres. Science, technology, and innovation are identified as important drivers for implementing the Sustainable Development Goals (SDGs). Research and development institutions play a vital role in the pursuit of sustainable development goals, manifesting its in multiple ways. They serve as agents of social change, such as by conducting research on various societal challenges and aligning their strategies with the SDGs. The concept of sustainable science emerges from today's dynamic environment. This approach highlights the importance of addressing social and economic equity while considering the long-term impacts of human actions on the environment and future generations. This entails significant changes in organisations and the implementation of scientific research. Research and Development activities generate new knowledge, but also contribute to a particular research field or a community.

This research gives insight into the importance of research, development and innovation from the perspective of their role and importance for the achievement of all SDGs. Special attention was paid to Target 9.5 and its indicators. The analysis of R&D expenditure as a percentage of GDP shows a growing trend, indicating a positive trajectory toward knowledge-based economic growth. The rise of business expenditure indicates enhanced collaboration between science and industry. Nevertheless, for more conclusive findings, it is necessary to conduct additional research and investigate the connection between R&D expenditure and research and development outcomes over the analysed period. This undertaking is extensive, making it a potential focus for future elaboration. Research, development, and innovation play a significant role in advancing the welfare of present and future generations by providing innovative solutions aligned with the objectives of the sustainable development goals.

The strategies of RDI reflect the dynamics of the modern environment. As for developing countries, the pursuit of sustainability enhances their position in the region with the research and development institutions playing a significant role in this regard. Research and Development (R&D) has the potential to foster sustainable entrepreneurial growth in developing nations by creating essential connections between education, business, and social needs. Consequently, these areas have become integral to a robust institutional mechanism that promotes knowledge transfer the exchange of knowledge between countries.

REFERENCES

Arnold, E., Barker, K., & Slipersæter, S. (2010). *Research Institutes in the ERA*. Europea. https://ec.europa.eu/research/era/index_en.htm

Assembly, G. (2030). *A/RES/71/313: Work of the Statistical Commission pertaining to the 2030 Agenda for Sustainable Development.*

Babović, M. (2023). *Progress report on the implementation od sustainable development goals by in the Republic of Serbia.* Statistical Office of the Republic of Serbia.

Cai, W., & Zhou, X. (2014). On the drivers of eco-innovation: Empirical evidence from China. *Journal of Cleaner Production, 79,* 239–248. doi:10.1016/j.jclepro.2014.05.035

Cai, Y., & Lattu, A. (2022). Triple Helix or Quadruple Helix: Which Model of Innovation to Choose for Empirical Studies? *Minerva, 60*(2), 257–280. doi:10.1007/s11024-021-09453-6

Carayannis, E. G., & Campbell, D. F. (2014). Developed democracies versus emerging autocracies: Arts, democracy, and innovation in Quadruple Helix innovation systems. *Journal of Innovation and Entrepreneurship, 3*(1), 12. doi:10.1186/s13731-014-0012-2

Carayannis, E. G., & Campbell, D. F. J. (2009). "Mode 3" and "Quadruple Helix": Toward a 21st century fractal innovation ecosystem. *International Journal of Technology Management, 46*(3/4), 201. doi:10.1504/IJTM.2009.023374

Carayannis, E. G., Grigoroudis, E., Stamati, D., & Valvi, T. (2021). Social Business Model Innovation: A Quadruple/Quintuple Helix-Based Social Innovation Ecosystem. *IEEE Transactions on Engineering Management, 68*(1), 235–248. doi:10.1109/TEM.2019.2914408

Chaves, R., & Monzón, J. L. (2012). Beyond the crisis: The social economy, prop of a new model of sustainable economic development. *Service Business, 6*(1), 5–26. doi:10.1007/s11628-011-0125-7

Đuričin, S., Beraha, I., Jovanović, O., Mosurović Ružičić, M., Lazarević-Moravčević, M., & Paunović, M. (2022). The Efficiency of National Innovation Policy Programs: The Case of Serbia. *Sustainability (Basel), 14*(14), 8483. doi:10.3390/su14148483

Elken, M., & Wollscheid, S. (2016). The relationship between research and education: typologies and indicators. In Research and Education.

EtzkowitzH.LeydesdorffL. (1995). The Triple Helix — University-Industry-Government Relations: A Laboratory for Knowledge Based Economic Development. *EASST Review, 14*(1), 14–19. https://ssrn.com/abstract=2480085

European Commission. (2021). *The EU's 2021-2027 long-term Budget and NextGenerationEU. Facts and figures.* (Issue September). Europea. https://op.europa.eu/en/publication-detail/-/publication/d3e77637-a963-11eb-9585-01aa75ed71a1/language-en

European Union. (2006). Community Framework for State Aid for Research and Development and. *Official Journal of the European Union,* 1–26. https://eur-lex.europa.eu/legal-content/EN/TXT/PDF/?uri=CELEX:52006XC1230(01)

Eurostat. (2022). *R&D Expenditure.* Eurostat. https://ec.europa.eu/eurostat/statistics-explained/index.php?title=R%26D_expenditure&oldid=551418#:~:text=In 2020%2C EU Research and,year when it recorded 2.23%25.&text=In 2020%2C the EU spent,compared with 1.97%25 in 2010.

Filho, W. L., Amaro, N., Avila, L. V., Brandli, L., Damke, L. I., Vasconcelos, C. R. P., Hernandez-Diaz, P. M., Frankenberger, F., Fritzen, B., Velazquez, L., & Salvia, A. (2021). Mapping sustainability initiatives in higher education institutions in Latin America. *Journal of Cleaner Production, 315*, 128093. doi:10.1016/j.jclepro.2021.128093

Godin, B. (2003). The emergence of S&T indicators: Why did governments supplement statistics with indicators? *Research Policy, 32*(4), 679–691. doi:10.1016/S0048-7333(02)00032-X

Griggs, D., Stafford Smith, M., Rockström, J., Öhman, M. C., Gaffney, O., Glaser, G., Kanie, N., Noble, I., Steffen, W., & Shyamsundar, P. (2014). An integrated framework for sustainable development goals. *Ecology and Society, 19*(4), art49. doi:10.5751/ES-07082-190449

Güldenberg, S., & Leitner, K.-H. (2008). *Strategy Processes in Research and Development Organisations: Why Knowledge Management is still more isolated than integrated.*

Guo, H., Huang, L., & Liang, D. (2022). Further promotion of sustainable development goals using science, technology, and innovation. *Innovation (Cambridge (Mass.)), 3*(6), 100325. doi:10.1016/j.xinn.2022.100325 PMID:36193207

Jain, R. K., Triandis, H. C., & Weick, C. W. (2010). Managing Research, Development, and Innovation: Managing the Unmanageable. In Managing Research, Development, and Innovation: Managing the Unmanageable. doi:10.1002/9780470917275

Jouda, H., & Abu Dan, M. (2022). The Role of Scientific Research on Sustainable Development Into Organizations. SSRN *Electronic Journal*. doi:10.2139/ssrn.4233050

Kauffman, J. (2009). Advancing sustainability science: Report on the International Conference on Sustainability Science (ICSS) 2009. *Sustainability Science, 4*(2), 233–242. doi:10.1007/s11625-009-0088-y

Khan, J. (2015). The Role of Research and Development in Economic Growth:a Review. *Journal of Economics Bibliography, 2*(3), 128–133. doi:10.1453/jeb.v2i3.480

Klarin, T. (2018). The Concept of Sustainable Development: From its Beginning to the Contemporary Issues. *Zagreb International Review of Economics and Business, 21*(1), 67–94. doi:10.2478/zireb-2018-0005

Libik, G. (1969). The Economic Assessment of Research and Development. *Management Science, 16*(1), 33–66. doi:10.1287/mnsc.16.1.33

Mazzoleni, R., & Nelson, R. R. (2007). Public research institutions and economic catch-up. *Research Policy, 36*(10), 1512–1528. Advance online publication. doi:10.1016/j.respol.2007.06.007

Mervar, A. (1999). PREGLED MODELA I METODA ISTRAŽIVANJA GOSPODARSKOG RASTA. *Privredna Kretanja i Ekonomska Politika.*

Mervar, A. (2003). Esej o novijim dorinosima teoriji ekonomskog rasta. *Ekonomski Pregled.*

NelsonR. R. (1993). National Innovation Systems: A Comparative. In *Analysis University of Illinois at Urbana-Champaign's Academy for Entrepreneurial Leadership Historical Research Reference in Entrepreneurship.* https://ssrn.com/abstract=1496195

Neves, P. (2018). *Literature Review on Sustainable Development - The spirit and critics of SD and SDGs*. How to Implement Partnerships Based on Sustainable Development (SD)to Achieve the Sustainable Development Goals (SDGs). https://doi.org/ OECD/Eurostat. (2022). *Researchers by sector 2021*. https://ec.europa.eu/eurostat/databrowser/view/rd_p_persocc/default/table?lang=en doi:10.13148/PN.2018.30.01.006

OECD. (2011). Fostering Innovation to Address Social Challenges. In *Innovation Strategy* (p. 99). https://www.oecd.org/sti/inno/47861327.pdf

OECD. (2015). The Measurement of Scientific, Technological and Innovation Activities. In *Frascati Manual 2015*. Guidelines for Collecting and Reporting Data on Research and Experimental Development.

Olaoye, I. J., Ayinde, O. E., Ajewole, O. O., & Adebisi, L. O. (2021). The role of research and development (R&D) expenditure and governance on economic growth in selected African countries. *African Journal of Science, Technology, Innovation and Development, 13*(6), 663–670. doi:10.1080/20421338 .2020.1799300

Pakkan, S., Sudhakar, C., Tripathi, S., & Rao, M. (2022). A correlation study of sustainable development goal (SDG) interactions. *Quality & Quantity*. doi:10.1007/s11135-022-01443-4 PMID:35729959

Paunović, M., Mosurović Ružičić, M., & Lazarević Moravčević, M. (2022). Business process innovations in family firms: evidence from Serbia. *Journal of Family Business Management*. doi:10.1108/JFBM-03-2022-0044

Racine, J. L., Goldberg, I., Goddard, J. G., Kuriakose, S., & Kapil, N. (2009). *Restructuring of Research and Development Institutes in Europe and Central Asia*.

Ružičić, M. M., Miletić, M., & Dobrota, M. (2021). Does a national innovation system encourage sustainability? Lessons from the construction industry in Serbia. *Sustainability (Basel), 13*(7), 3591. Advance online publication. doi:10.3390/su13073591

Ružičić Mosurović, M., & Obradović, V. (2020). *Strateško upravljanje projektima u naučnoistraživačkim organizacijama*. Udruženje za upravljanje projektima Srbije, IPMA Serbia.

Ružičić Mosurović, M., Obradović, V., & Iganjatović, M. (2021). Strategic Managinig Innovation in SROs in Serbia: Should it be resistible? *Responsible and Resistible Project Management*, 211–216. https://ipma.rs/wp-content/uploads/2022/10/Zbornik-2021.pdf

Schaltegger, S., Lüdeke-Freund, F., & Hansen, E. G. (2016). Business Models for Sustainability: A Co-Evolutionary Analysis of Sustainable Entrepreneurship, Innovation, and Transformation. *Organization & Environment, 29*(3), 264–289. doi:10.1177/1086026616633272

Sengupta, J. (2014). *Theory of Innovation*. Springer International Publishing. doi:10.1007/978-3-319-02183-6

Shrivastava, P., Stafford Smith, M., O'Brien, K., & Zsolnai, L. (2020). Transforming Sustainability Science to Generate Positive Social and Environmental Change Globally. *One Earth, 2*(4), 329–340. doi:10.1016/j.oneear.2020.04.010 PMID:33501419

Smit, J. P., & Hessels, L. K. (2021). The production of scientific and societal value in research evaluation: A review of societal impact assessment methods. *Research Evaluation, 30*(3), 323–335. doi:10.1093/reseval/rvab002

Song, D.-W. (2021). What is research? *WMU Journal of Maritime Affairs, 20*(4), 407–411. doi:10.1007/s13437-021-00256-w PMID:34895237

Spangenberg, J. H. (2011). Sustainability science: A review, an analysis and some empirical lessons. *Environmental Conservation, 38*(3), 275–287. doi:10.1017/S0376892911000270

Thuriaux, B., Arnold, E., & Couchot, C. (2000). Innovation and enterprise creation: Statistics and indicators. In Innovation (Issue 18).

UN General Assembly. (2017). *A/RES/71/313: Work of the Statistical Commission pertaining to the 2030 Agenda for Sustainable Development.*

UNESCO. (2017). *Guidelines on Sustainability Science in Research and Education.* UN. https://unesdoc.unesco.org/ark:/48223/pf0000260600

UNESCO. (2022). *Science, Technology and Innovation.* Institute for Statistics. http://data.uis.unesco.org/Index.aspx?DataSetCode=SCN_DS&lang=en# United

Williams, J., Debski, I., & White, R. T. (2008). *Business Expenditure on Research and Development in New Zealand - future potential and future industries.* Ministry of Research, Science, and Technology.

Yamaguchi, N. U., Bernardino, E. G., Ferreira, M. E. C., de Lima, B. P., Pascotini, M. R., & Yamaguchi, M. U. (2023). Sustainable development goals: A bibliometric analysis of literature reviews. *Environmental Science and Pollution Research International, 30*(3), 5502–5515. doi:10.1007/s11356-022-24379-6 PMID:36418837

Chapter 5
Influence of Industrialization and Energy Consumption on Environmental Sustainability:
Empirical Evidence From Asian Emerging Economies

Priyajit Kumar Ghosh
University of Gour Banga, India

Biswajit Paul
https://orcid.org/0000-0001-5935-5373
University of Gour Banga, India

ABSTRACT

This study assesses the influence of industrialization and energy consumption on the environmental sustainability for seven Asian emerging economies over the period 1990–2022 by using Panel ARDL estimation technique. Results show that industrialization adversely impacts environmental sustainability in the long run by discharging CO2, while energy consumption has a favourable environmental impact. In the short run, both factors have demonstrated overall as well as country specific adverse effects. Further, Dumitrescu Hurlin Panel causality results reported uni directional causal relationship moving from industrialization and energy consumption to carbon dioxide discharges. These results indicates that efforts of Asian emerging economies towards environmental sustainability are not sufficient. This study recommends policymakers consider different sustainability frameworks, increase awareness regarding adoption of environmental positive activities, and allocate more funding for environmental protection and technological innovation.

DOI: 10.4018/979-8-3693-2197-3.ch005

INTRODUCTION

The industry is often regarded as the lifeblood of any country, which ensures the socio-economic prosperity of that country and also helps that country to become self-reliant (Mgbemene, Nnaji & Nwozor, 2016; Singh & Kumar, 2023). The development of industrial activities often drives the level of manufacturing outputs. According to Kaldor's law, the growth in the manufacturing sector promotes economic development through several channels. Growth in the manufacturing sector enhances productivity and it absorbs a hung chunk of labour force from the labour market (Facevicova & Kynclova, 2020). Here, economies of scale, technical innovation, and higher labour productivity play a critical role in driving up productivity through lowering average production costs and increasing the level of manufacturing output (Millemaci & Ofria, 2014). This increase in manufacturing output eventually accelerates the economic development of a country (Mercan, Kızılkaya & Okde, 2015).

Over the past few decades, several economic studies have been done to check the applicability of Kaldor's law of manufacturing-based economic development in various countries. Mamgain (1999) investigated the applicability of Kaldor's law in different South Asian economies such as Singapore, Malaysia, South Korea, Mauritius, Thailand and Indonesia during the period from 1960 to 1988. This study found that growth in the manufacturing or industrial sector possessed a greater positive influence on productivity growth only in South Korea. Wells & Thirlwall (2003) empirically investigated the applicability of Kaldor's law of manufacturing based economic development hypothesis in various countries of the African region. This study documented that growth in the manufacturing or industrial sector possessed a greater positive influence on GDP growth than the agriculture or service sectors. Pata & Zengin (2020) checked the applicability of Kaldor's law in one of the upper middle-income countries i.e., Turkey. This study confirmed the validity of Kaldor's law of industry-based economic growth in Turkey. This study found an appreciable impact of industrial growth on both economic development and labor productivity in the industrial sector. Abdulgawad & El-Rasoul (2021) assessed the influential effect of the manufacturing sector on labour productivity and economic development in Saudi Arabia by using different long run and short run time series estimation techniques. This study found long run co-integrating relationship between the manufacturing sector, labour productivity and economic development in Saudi Arabia. This study also documented one-way causality moving from the manufacturing sector to labour productivity and economic development. Whereas, the study of Sallam (2021) identified both way causal relationship between the manufacturing sector and economic growth. The study of Ali et al. (2021) found the existence of Kaldor's law in developing countries. This study used a panel dataset of 105 developing countries and employed pooled OLS and GMM Models to assess the nexus between the productive efficiency of the manufacturing sector, technological advancement, and economic development. The results of this study captured the positive nexus between those three macro-economic factors. According to the results of this study technological advancement allows the manufacturing sector to take advantage of increasing returns to scale which helps them to achieve productive efficiency. This productive efficiency ultimately contributes to the economic development of nations. In contrast to this, the study of Edward & Ngasamiaku (2021) found the non-existence of Kaldor's law in Tanzania during the period from 1985 to 2017. This study identified the existence of one-way causality moving from economic development to manufacturing growth that defies Kaldor's law. The essential role of the manufacturing sector in fueling Jordan's economic growth from 1990 to 2019 was also highlighted in the study conducted by Alnegrish (2023). This study used the ARDL estimations technique to examine the effectiveness of Kaldor's law in Jordan. This study found that Kaldor's law was valid in Jordan during the study period as the results of the ARDL estimations technique documented growth in the manufacturing sector enhanced productivity. Ultimately, this increased productivity contributed to accelerating economic growth rates. Along with this, several other studies such as Ndiaya & Lv (2018), Chen & Xie (2019), Odeleye & Olunkwa (2019), Qaiser (2020), Udi, Bekun & Adedoyin, (2020), Sriyakul, Chienwattanasook & Chankoson, (2022), Appiah et al. (2023) have also been carried out to find the nexus between two major macro-economic factors i.e., industrialization and economic growth. All these studies reported the existence of a positive association between industrialization and economic growth. In addition to fostering economic development, industrial development addresses different social issues, including inequality, poverty, unemployment, etc. (Lavopa & Szirmai, 2012; Kumar, 2020; Erumban & De Vries, 2021).

Considering the vitality of the industrial sector, every country strives to accelerate its economic growth by fostering industrial development. The nineteenth and twentieth centuries witnessed how developed nations reap the benefits from the advancement of industries. However, in order to turn into industrialized nations, several emerging Asian economies, including China, India, Indonesia, Malaysia, Philippines, Thailand, and Vietnam have undertaken different initiatives and policy measures to drive industrial activity in recent decades. For instance, in India, during the year 1991, the adoption of the LPG policy greatly altered the country's economic structure and accelerated the country's industrial development (Kniivilä. 2007). The study of Nagaraj (2011) highlighted how these policy reforms help Indian manufacturing units to gain competitiveness and technological expertise from overseas. The study of Panagariya (2004) pointed out that in 1990's the robust industrial growth happened mainly due to a relaxation in industrial licensing and opening various industries for FDI. These results also corroborate with the study of Balasubramanyam & Mahambre (2001).

On the flip side, industrial development elevates the requirement for resources (such as energy) in tandem with socioeconomic development. The study of Shahbaz & Lean (2012) identified that industrialization raised the level of energy consumption. The study by Sadorsky (2014) found a positive relationship between those two variables. Simon (2016) reported the existence of both way causal relationship between industrialization and energy consumption in South Africa in long-term. Keho (2016) identified a positive relationship between industrial output and energy consumption in Sub-Saharan African countries from 1970 to 2011. These results also corroborate with the studies of Ma & Du (2012), Sadorsky (2013), Gungor & Simon (2017), Haider, Adil & Ganaie (2019), Sahoo & Sethi (2020).

Hence, based on above mentioned discussion it can be observed on the one hand higher level of industrial development enhances the demand for energy. On the other hand, it acts as a driver of economic growth through enhancing productivity. But several studies such as Opoku & Boachie (2020), Jermsittiparsert (2021) highlighted that despite of bringing economic prosperity in several countries, rapid industrialization often acted as one of the major contributors of environmental degradation since most of their activities put tremendous stress on natural ecosystems. In recent years, world is experiencing several unfavourable climate related issues such as a raise in GHG emissions, global temperature etc. Earlier reports of global organisations such as the International Energy Agency, showed that most of the industrialized economies such as USA, Japan, China emerged as the largest carbon dioxide emitters of the world (Mgbemene, Nnaji & Nwozor, 2016; Center for Climate and Energy Solutions, 2022).

In this regard, several researchers made an attempt to assess the effect of industrialization and energy use on the environment. However, the studies showed inconsistent findings across regions. The studies of Wang et al. (2011), Liu & Bae (2018), Majeed & Tauqir (2020), Rehman, Ma & Ozturk, (2021), and others reported a positive interaction between that industrialization, energy use, and environmental degradation. All these studies reported industrialization, and energy use led to CO_2 discharges, which in turn caused environmental damage. Conversely, the studies of Raheem & Ogebe (2017), Appia et al. (2019), Elfaki et al. (2022), and others revealed an inverse relationship between energy use, industrialization, and CO_2 discharges.

Considering the growing concern regarding climate-related issues, it is essential to determine and validate the relationship between industrialization, energy consumption, and environmental sustainability. Furthermore, considering the economic importance of Asia's emerging economies, research on the interaction between industrialization, energy use, and environmental sustainability in Asia's emerging economies is essential. In this regard, this study intends to examine the influence of industrialization and energy consumption on the environmental sustainability of seven Asian emerging economies over the period 1990–2022 by using the Panel ARDL estimation technique.

REVIEW OF LITERATURE

Several studies have been carried out to explore the interaction of industrialization, energy consumption, and environmental sustainability across various regions and time periods. A brief image of the select studies is portrayed below.

Wang et al. (2011) attempted to investigate the effects of China's heavy industrialization on carbon emissions during 1978 and 2008. The OLS estimation technique and error correction model were employed in this study to examine the short- and long-term relationships between the selected variables. According to the study's findings, China's carbon emissions were driven up by heavy industrialization in both the short and long terms. However, the long-term impact outweighed the short-term. In the short-term, a one-unit increase in the production of the heavy industry resulted in 0.146636 raise in carbon emissions, however, in the long run, it caused 0.278141 increase in carbon emissions. The study by Liu & Bae (2018) also confirmed the causal link among industrialization, energy intensity, economic development, and CO_2 discharge in China. This study found that industrialization and energy intensity exhibit a long-term effect on CO_2 discharge. The ARDL estimating technique's results showed that for every percent rise in industrialization and energy intensity, carbon emissions elevated by 0.3 and 1.1 percent, respectively. Using the ARDL model, Pata (2018)'s study demonstrated how various developmental activities put strain on the environment by releasing considerable amounts of carbon into the atmosphere in Turkey between 1974 and 2013. According to this study, the atmosphere has been contaminated with heat-trapping CO_2 as a result of urbanisation, industrial development, financial development, energy use, and economic growth. Majeed & Tauqir (2020) adopted the dynamic generalisation method of moments (GMM) approach and dynamic CCEMG estimation method to assess the overall and dynamic impact of industrialization and urbanisation on CO_2 discharge in 156 nations during 1990 to 2014. This study found a homogeneous as well as a positive relationship between urbanization, industrialization and CO_2 discharge. Furthermore, this study found that energy consumption i.e., one of the select control variables had a favourable impact on CO_2 discharge across all countries. In contrast, the effects of other control variables, i.e., economic growth and financial development varied amongst nations based on their corresponding stages of development. Rehman, Ma, & Ozturk (2021) applied a quantile regression analysis in their study to analyse the impact of industrialization and energy imports on CO_2 discharge in Pakistan during 1971 to 2019. They reported that CO_2 discharge reacted positively to industrialization and energy imports in Pakistan. The studies of Munir & Ameer (2020) in Pakistan; Ahmed et al. (2022)

in Asian Pasific region; Voumik & Ridwan (2023) in Argentina also highlighted how industrialization triggered environmental degradation in those selected region.

On the flipside, several studies documented an inverse relationship between industrialization, energy use, and CO2 emissions. Raheem & Ogebe (2017) concluded that industrialization directly exacerbates environmental degradation while indirectly it mitigating the environmental degradation in African nations. The study of Appia et al. (2019) used the ARDL estimating technique to assess the industrialization, energy intensity, economic advancement and CO2 discharge in Uganda. This study revealed that the combined effects of industrialization, energy intensity, and economic advancement led to a 2.46% reduction in emissions in Uganda. Nasir, Canh & Le (2021) found that industrialization had no significant effect on CO_2 emissions in Australia. The study of Elfaki et al. (2022) found that a negative interaction between industrialization and environmental deterioration in ASEAN + 3 nations. Whereas, the study of Idowu, Ohikhuare & Chowdhury (2023) stated that energy use and industrialization have no apparent short- or long-term effects on carbon emissions in OPEC countries. In the study, the interaction between the chosen variables was investigated by researchers using the Panel Autoregressive Distributed Lag Model.

After carefully studying earlier research, it appears that numerous studies have been conducted on the effects of industrialization and energy use on the environment in different countries and different time periods. But, most of these earlier studies presented mixed results regarding the effects of above mentioned two variables on the environment in different countries. In contrast, there is a paucity of comprehensive studies that focuses on the influence of industrialization and energy consumption on environmental sustainability in Asian emerging economies using the Panel ARDL model from 1990 to 2022. Considering this a significant research gap, the present study aims to investigate the influence of industrialization and energy consumption on the environmental sustainability in Asian emerging economies using the Panel ARDL model from 1990 to 2022. This Panel Autoregressive Distributed Lag (ARDL) Estimation or Pooled Mean Group (PMG) Test provides both long-run and short-run estimation results along with error correction terms. Further, this estimation technique also allows to capture the cross section wise existence of a short-run relationship between the select variables. In addition to this, this study employs the Dumitrescu Hurlin Panel Causality Test to examine the causal linkages between industrialization, energy consumption and environmental sustainability in Asian emerging economies.

RESEARCH METHODOLOGY

Data Source and Variable Selection

The present study considers seven major Asian emerging economies (i.e., China, Indonesia, India, Malaysia, Philippines, Thailand, and Vietnam) to investigate the influence of industrialization and energy consumption together on environmental sustainability. For this reason, this study collects data regarding the selected variables from two major databases i.e., World Bank and International Energy Agency from 1990 to 2022. The select variables are the level of Carbon Dioxide Discharge per capita (in metric tons), Industry Value Added (in constant 2015 US dollar), and Electricity Consumption (in terajoule). Table 1 demonstrates the description of selected variables and their related data sources.

Table 1. Summary of selected variables

Representation	Variables	Unit of measurement	Source
CO2	Carbon Dioxide Discharges (Zafar et al., 2020; Khan et al., 2022; Saqib et al., 2022; Tariq & Hassan, 2023; Liu et al. 2024)	Carbon Dioxide Emissions (measured in metric tons per capita) as proxy variable of environmental sustainability	World Bank (World Development Indicator)
IVA	Industry Value Added (Parveen, Khan & Farooq, 2019; Majeed & Tauqir, 2020; Sriyakul, Chienwattanasook & Chankoson, 2022; Ahmed et al., 2022)	Industry Value Added (constant 2015- measured in US dollar) as proxy variable of industrialization	World Bank (World Development Indicator)
EC	Energy Consumption (Ho & Siu, 2007; Zeng et al. 2018)	Electricity Consumption (measured in terajoule) as proxy variable of energy consumption	International Energy Agency (IEA)

Source: Researchers' own presentation

Present study proposes the following functional model to access the influence of industrialization and energy consumption on the environmental sustainability.

The proposed functional model is presented below:

Carbon Dioxide Discharges = f (Industrialization, Energy Consumption)

Based on the functional model mentioned above, the following econometric model is taken into consideration in this study.

$$L\_CO2_{it} = \beta_0 + \beta_1 L\_IVA_{it} + \beta_2 L\_EC_{it} + \varepsilon_{it} \tag{1}$$

Where,

$\beta_0, \beta_1, \beta_2, \beta_3 \ldots \beta_n$ = the model parameters
L_CO2_{it} = Carbon Dioxide Discharges of ith nation in t^{th} year (dependent variable).
L_IVA_{it} = Volume of Industry Value Added of ith nation in t^{th} year (independent variable)
L_EC_{it} = Amount of Energy Consumption of ith nation in t^{th} year (independent variable)
ε_{it} = Disturbance term occur in the model.

At first, this study performs a panel unit root test. Then panel cointegration tests are utilized which is used check the existence of cointegration relationship between the select variables. Then, the Panel ARDL or PMG estimation technique is used to estimate long-run as well as short-run relationships between variables. Then, the Wald Test is used to check whether or not the considered independent variables are adding some values to the model. Then Panel DOLS and FMOLS Models are used to confirm the results of the Panel ARDL estimation model. Finally, the Pairwise Dumitrescu Hurlin Panel Causality test is applied to analyse the existence as well as direction of causality between select variables.

Unit Root Test

To find out if there exists a unit root in the select series, the unit root test is required. For this study, several kinds of panel unit root tests are employed. This study considers the Levin, Lin and Chu, Im Pesaran and Shin W-statistic, ADF - Fiser Chi-square, and PP - Fiser Chi-square tests. All these tests consider the null hypothesis that indicates the presence of a unit root in the selected series. These techniques are widely considered in different earlier research studies also such as Adalı & Yüksel (2017), Alam et al. (2021), Magoti, Mabula & Ngong'ho (2020). Table 3 summarizes the results of these tests.

Panel Cointegration Test

In the case of panel data analysis, one of the important steps is – checking the existence of cointegrating relations among the select variables. If a cointegrating relationship exists among select variables then different panel estimation techniques can be performed according to their suitability. One of the most prominent tests that is used for panel cointegration is the Kao Test (Kao 1999). The null hypothesis of this test assumes that there is no cointegrating relationship among the selected variables. Several earlier studies such as Kalymbetova et al. (2021), Alam et al. (2021), Zafeiriou, Azam & Garefalakis (2022), and others used this Kao Test in their study to check the cointegrating relationship among the variables. The ADF test statistic of the Kao Test is demonstrated in Eq. (ii). Further, this study used traditional Johansen-Fisher panel cointegration test to assess the cointegrating relationship among select variables.

$$ADF = \frac{t\,ADF + \sqrt{6N\ \tilde{A}v\,\hat{}\,/2\,\tilde{A}u\,\hat{}}}{\sqrt{\tilde{A}v\,\hat{}\ o2\,/2\,\tilde{A}v\,\hat{}\,2 + 3\tilde{A}v\,\hat{}\,2\,/10\tilde{A}v\,\hat{}\ o2}} \tag{2}$$

where: N - cross-section data T - time series data

$\sigma_u\,\hat{}\,^2$ is the variance of 1st term i.e., u

$\sigma_v\,\hat{}\,^2$ is the variance of 2nd term i.e., v

$\sigma_u\,\hat{}$ is the standard deviation of 1st term i.e., u

$\sigma_v\,\hat{}$ is the standard deviation of 2nd term i.e., v

Panel ARDL Estimation or Pooled Mean Group (PMG) Test

Panel ARDL or PMG estimation approach (Pesaran, Shin & Smith, 1999) is considered as one of the most prominent approaches in panel data analyses specifically when select variables are integrated in a mixed order (i.e., I (0) and I (1)). It provides both long-run and short-run estimation results along with error correction term. Further, this Panel ARDL estimation allows to capture the cross-section wise existence of a short-run relationship between the select variables. Hence, this approach in one hand allows to check long-run and short-run relationship between the selected variables, and on the other hand, it allows to check country specific short-run estimation results.

The following is the long-run relationship model that is employed by the PMG estimate approach:

$$L\_CO2_{it} = \alpha_i + \sum_{j=2}^{p} \lambda_{ij}\, L\_CO2_{i,\,t-j} + \sum_{j=2}^{q} \delta_{1ij}\, L\_IVA_{i,\,t-j} + \sum_{j=2}^{r} \delta_{2ij}\, L\_EC_{i,\,t-j} + \varepsilon_{it} \tag{3}$$

Where, i represents countries (1, 2, 3... 20), t is the year (1990–2022), j is the optimum time lag, α_i is a group specific effect, λ_{ij} represents scalar term and ε_{it} indicates disturbance term.

The following is the short-run relationship model that is employed by the PMG estimate approach:

$$\Delta L\_CO2_{it} = \alpha_i + \phi_i (L\_CO2_{i, t-1} - \lambda_1 L\_IVA_{i, t-1} - \lambda_2 L\_EC_{i, t-1}) + \sum_{j=1}^{p} \lambda_{ij} \Delta L\_CO2_{i, t-j} + \sum_{j=1}^{q}$$

$$\delta_{1ij} L\_IVA_{i, t-j} + \sum_{j=0}^{r} \delta_{2ij} L\_EC_{i, t-j} + \varepsilon_{it} \tag{4}$$

where ϕ_i is the parameter that defines the error-correction term, which determines the pace at which changes in L_IVA, and L_EC cause CO2 to adapt to its long-term equilibrium. A negative and statistically significant value of this error-correction term suggests that select variables have a co-integrating relationship. λ_1 and λ_2 represents long run parameters of independent variables. Whereas, δ denotes the short-run parameters.

Wald Test

In order to reduce the chance of the problem of over fitted independent variables in the model and to check whether or not the considered independent variables are adding some values to the model, Wald Test is used in this study.

Panel DOLS and FMOLS Model

In order to verify the results of Panel ARDL estimation, this study further employ Panel DOLS and FMOLS Models. These models on one hand address the endogeneity problem and on other hand it eliminates serial correlation issue exists in the model Yahyaoui & Bouchoucha (2021). Several earlier studies such as Mehmood, Raza & Mureed (2014), Sharma, Kautish & Kumar (2021) and others also used to confirm the results of Panel ARDL estimation model.

Dumitrescu and Hurlin Panel Causality Test

At last, this study employs the Dumitrescu and Hurlin Panel Causality test (Dumitrescu and Hurlin, 2012) to determine the causal relationship between the select variables. This Dumitrescu and Hurlin Panel Causality test also provides reliable results even if there exists any cross-sectional dependency between selected countries.

Below is a representation of the Dumitrescu and Hurlin Panel Causality test:

$$Y_{i, t} = \alpha_i + \sum_{k=1}^{k} Y_i^{(k)} Y_{i, t-k} + \sum_{k=1}^{k} \beta_i^{(k)} X_{i, t-k} + \varepsilon_{i, t} \tag{5}$$

Here, the term x and y denote the select two variables for which causality analysis will be performed. The optimal lag interval is denoted by K. i stands for the selected countries (1, 2, ... 7), and t is the period of time (1990–2022).

RESULTS AND DISCUSSION

The descriptive statistics for the chosen variables in this study are first shown in this section (table 2). This descriptive statistic provides an overall description of the chosen variables.

Table 2. Summary of descriptive statistics of select variables

Variables	L_CO2	L_IVA	L_EC
Mean	0.6930	25.8297	5.1052
Median	0.6300	25.5493	4.8828
Maximum	2.0541	29.5029	9.0312
Minimum	-1.2418	23.1678	1.8718
Std. Dev.	0.8100	1.2991	1.5474
Skewness	0.0202	0.9427	0.6031
Kurtosis	2.1688	3.7406	3.0306
Observations	231	231	231

Source: Researchers' own estimation.

Table 2 demonstrates the description of the chosen variables in terms of their mean, median, maximum, minimum, standard deviation, skewness and kurtosis. It reveals that the mean value of the log of carbon dioxide discharges per capita is 0.6930, with 2.0541 and -1.2418 representing the highest and lowest values, respectively. The mean value of log of industry value added is 25.8297, with lowermost and highest values of 23.1678 and 29.5029. Whereas, the values of log of energy consumption varied between 9.0312 and 1.8718 with a mean value of 5.1052. The summary of descriptive statistics also shows the dispersion of data through standard deviation. The standard deviation value of the dependent variable i.e., carbon dioxide discharges per capita is 0.8100. While, the standard deviation values of two independent variables i.e., industry value added and energy consumption are 1.2991 and 1.5474 respectively. The positive skewness value makes it apparent that all of the variables have a right skew. Further, it can be inferred from the kurtosis value that data of select variables are normality distributed as kurtosis value ranges between -7 and $+7$ (Byrne, 2010; Hair et al., 2010).

Table 3. Results of different panel unit root tests

Variable	Statistic	Probability Value	Order of Integration
Levin, Lin and Chu Test			
L_CO2	-3.3547	0.0004	At level
L_IVA	-3.9806	0.0000	At level
L_EC	-5.4603	0.0000	At level
Im Pesaran and shin W-stat			
L_CO2	-4.7602	0.0000	At first difference
L_IVA	-5.4140	0.0000	At first difference
L_EC	-2.8543	0.0022	At level
ADF - Fiser Chi-square			
L_CO2	50.9107	0.0000	At first difference
L_IVA	57.2121	0.0000	At first difference
L_EC	33.8627	0.0022	At level
PP - Fiser Chi-square			
L_CO2	64.3127	0.0000	At level
L_IVA	28.7104	0.0114	At level
L_EC	58.3713	0.0000	At level

Source: Researchers' own calculation.

This study conducts panel unit root tests utilizing several techniques, including Levin, Lin and Chu (Levin, Lin & Chu, 2002), Im Pesaran and Shin W-stat (Im, Pesaran & Shin, 2003), ADF - Fiser Chi-square (Choi, 2001), and PP - Fiser Chi-square (Perron, 1988), after comprehending the description of chosen variables in the following stage. Several earlier studies (such as Olayungbo, 2021; Liu et al. 2023) performed these methods to check the stationarity of data. The Levin, Lin, and Chu test findings show that each select variable is stationary at level. A similar outcome is also noted when using the PP-Fiser Chi-square test. The PP-Fiser Chi-square test findings show that each of the select variables is stationary at level. While, the findings of Im Pesaran and Shin W-stat suggest only one variable is stationary at level i.e., L_EC and the other two variables i.e., L_CO2 and L_IVA are stationary at first difference. An analogous outcome to the Im Pesaran and Shin W-statistic is also noted in the ADF-Fiser Chi-square case. Here likewise, only one variable is stationary at level i.e., L_EC while the other two variables i.e., L_CO2 and L_IVA are stationary at first difference. Thus, the existence of a mixed order of integration is evident. Hence, the panel ARDL estimation technique can be applied as it can handle different orders of integration of variables (Mert, Bölük & Çağlar, 2019; Shaari, Abdul Karim & Zainol Abidin, 2020; Nguyen, 2021).

Table 4. Results of panel cointegration tests

Kao Test		
	T-stat.	Probability Value
Augmented Dickey Fuller (ADF)	-2.526038	0.0058
Residual Variance	0.002283	
HAC variance	0.002253	
Johansen Fisher Panel Cointegration Test		
	Fisher Stat. (from trace test)	**Probability Value**	**Fisher Stat. (from max-eigen test)**	**Probability Value**
None	57.39	0.0000	53.56	0.0000
At most 1	19.68	0.1407	16.12	0.3064
At most 2	23.99	0.0459	23.99	0.0459

Source: Researchers' own calculation.

Results of Panel Cointegration Tests are demonstrated in table 4. This test is performed to check the existence of cointegration relationship between the select variables. Results of Kao test show that select variables are cointegrated at 1% level of significance since the probability value of ADF statistic is less than 0.01. Similar to this, the Johansen Fisher panel cointegration test findings show that there is a cointegrating connection between the chosen variables since they disprove the null hypothesis of no cointegrating relationship.

Table 5. Long-run estimation results: Influence of industrialization and energy consumption on environmental sustainability (indicated by CO2)

Variable	Coefficient	Probability Value
L_IVA	0.6668	0.0023
L_EC	-0.4273	0.0762

Source: Researchers' own calculation

The results of Panel ARDL long-run estimation are reported in table 5. According to the results of Panel ARDL long-run estimation, the co-efficient value of L_VA is positive and significant at 1% level. This indicates that industrialization has a negative long-term impact on environmental sustainability because the increase in industrialization eventually results in higher carbon emissions.

The studies of Raheem & Ogebe (2017) and Dong et al. (2019) also underlined the adverse influence of industrialization on environmental degradation. While studies of Pata, (2018), Appiah et al. (2019) and Kwakwa, (2022) also found a similar unfavourable influence of industrialization on environmental degradation in Turkey, Uganda and Ghana respectively. The study of Ganda, (2019), and Wang et al. (2020) also reported the adverse influence of industrialization on environmental degradation in the context of BRICS and APEC countries respectively.

In opposite to this, the co-efficient value of L_EC is negative and significant at 10% level. This indicates that energy consumption has a favourable long-term impact on environmental sustainability because an increase in energy consumption eventually results in mitigating carbon emissions. This might be because now countries started to switch from non-renewable to renewable energy sources in order to meet their energy needs without endangering the environment.

Table 6. Short-run estimation results: Influence of industrialization and energy consumption on environmental sustainability (indicated by CO_2)

Variable	Coefficient	Probability Value
ECT	-0.0448	0.0326
D (L_IVA)	0.0761	0.5473
D (L_IVA (-1))	0.1511	0.0121
D (L_EC)	0.4517	0.0183
D (L_EC (-1))	0.1827	0.0397

Source: Researchers' own calculation

The results of Panel ARDL short-run estimation are reported in Table 6. The results of Panel ARDL short-run estimation are quite similar with the long-run results. According to the results of Panel ARDL short-run estimation, the co-efficient value of L_VA (lagging one year) is positive and significant at 5% level. This indicates that industrialization has a negative short-term impact on environmental sustainability because increase in industrialization eventually results in higher carbon emissions. Similar to this, the co-efficient value of L_EC is positive and significant at 5% level. This indicates that energy consumption has also adverse short-term impact on environmental sustainability because increase in energy consumption result in higher level of carbon emissions. This might be because most of the countries still heavily rely on the non-renewable conventional energy resources to meet their energy needs that actually endangering the environment. Further, table 5 highlights the coefficient value of the error correction term (ECT) which indicates whether or not select variables will converge to an equilibrium point. As the value of error correction term (ECT) is negative and significant at 5% level this implies select variables will converge to an equilibrium point.

Table 7. Results of country-specific panel ARDL short-run estimates

Variable	China	Indonesia	India	Malaysia	Philippines	Thailand	Vietnam
ECT	-0.0197*	-0.0351*	-0.0233*	-0.0607*	-0.1596*	-0.0271*	-0.0120*
D (L_IVA)	**-0.4692****	**0.2326****	0.0406	**0.4122***	**0.4954***	-0.1336	-0.0448
D (L_IVA (-1))	0.2868	0.0064	**0.1411***	-0.0059	0.0351	**0.1766***	**0.4174***
D (L_EC)	**1.0503****	0.2022	**0.7146***	-0.3489	**0.0474***	**0.8943***	**0.6019***
D (L_EC (-1))	**0.6089****	0.1483	0.0241	**0.2832***	**0.0133***	**0.2830***	-0.0818

Source: Researchers' own calculation.
*, **, *** indicates level of significance at 1%, 5% and 10%.

Results of Country-Specific Panel ARDL Short-run Estimates are presented in table 7. According to table 7, all the selected countries have negative and significant the coefficient values of error correction term (ECT). This implies that select variables of all the selected countries will converge to the equilibrium point in long run. In case of China, the co-efficient value of L_VA is negative and significant at 5% level. This indicates that industrialization has a favourable short-term impact on environmental sustainability. This result might be an effect of China's recent efforts to promote environmental sustainability, which have helped China to perform better than other nations in the course of action. As to the statistics released by Statista Research Department on July 6, 2023, China issued the largest amount of green bonds in 2022 (amounting to 85 billion in U.S. dollars), surpassing other developed countries such as the United States of America and Germany. For all the other selected countries, industrialization have an adverse short-term impact on environmental sustainability. For Indonesia, Malaysia and Philippines the co-efficient value of L_VA is positive and significant at 1% level. While for remaining countries i.e., India, Thailand and Vietnam the co-efficient value of L_VA is positive and significant at 1% level after one year lag. Similarly, energy consumption has demonstrated an adverse and statistically significant short-term impact on environmental sustainability for China, India, Malaysia, Philippines, Thailand and Vietnam.

Table 8. Results of the wald test

Test Stat.	Value	Probability Value
F-stat.	6.5343	0.0000
Chi-square	13.0686	0.0000

Source: Researchers' own calculation.

The empirical outcome of the Wald Test is demonstrated in table 8. Since the probability value of the F statistic is significant al 1% level, it implies that the select independent variables add values to the model and there is no need to exclude independent variables from the model.

Table 9. Results of panel DOLS and FMOLS models

Panel DOLS		
Variable	**Coefficient**	**Probability Value**
L_IVA	0.1986	0.0370
L_EC	0.4000	0.0000
Panel FMOLS		
Variable	**Coefficient**	**Probability Value**
L_IVA	0.2036	0.0000
L_EC	0.3957	0.0000

Source: Researchers' own calculation.

Table 9 summarises the findings of the FMOLS and DOLS models. In line with the Panel ARDL estimation results, the findings of the FMOLS and DOLS models confirm that the industrialization causes environmental degradation in Asian rising nations by exacerbating CO_2 discharge. Furthermore, the results of the FMOLS and DOLS models indicated that higher CO2 discharge was caused by higher energy consumption.

Table 10. Results of Dumitrescu Hurlin panel causality test

Null Hypothesis	W Stat.	Zbar - Stat.	Probability Value
L_IVA does not granger cause L_CO2	4.8431	3.0063	0.0026
L_CO2 does not granger cause L_IVA	3.7142	1.7384	0.0821
L_EC does not granger cause L_CO2	4.4886	2.6081	0.0091
L_CO2 does not granger cause L_EC	3.8273	1.8654	0.0621
L_EC does not granger cause L_IVA	3.8653	1.9080	0.0564
L_IVA does not granger cause L_EC	3.8174	1.8542	0.0063

Source: Researchers' own calculation.

The empirical results of the Dumitrescu Hurlin Panel Causality Test are demonstrated in table 10. The one-way causal relationship between industrialization and carbon dioxide discharges is observed by the statical significant value of the Panel Causality Test. Similarly, one way long-run causal relationship between energy consumption and carbon dioxide discharges is found since the probability value is significant at 1% level. Whereas, a uni-directional causal relationship from industrialization to energy consumption is reported at 5% level of significance. The studies of Sahoo & Sethi (2020), and Kahouli, Miled & Aloui (2022) also reported similar findings for India and Saudi Arabia respectively.

CONCLUSION

Various reports published by Global organizations *such as 'World Economic Outlook, April 2023: A Rocky Recovery' by IMF, and 'APAC Cross-Sector Outlook 2024', etc.* have underlined Asia's emerging economies' strong position in the context of economic growth, while all other advanced economies are grappling with a slowdown in growth. Here, the industrial sector plays a vital role in accelerating economic growth by enhancing industrial productivity. This industrial development unleashes several benefits in countries in numerous ways. It provides employment opportunities, enhances productivity, promotes exports, enhances cross-border activities, elevates poverty etc. On the other hand, this industrial sector requires a huge chunk of energy for the smooth conduction of industrial activity. According to the United Nations Industrial Development Organizations (UNIDO), the proportion of energy supply wanted for industry will increase to 50 percent in developing and transitioning countries. In this regard, the present study aims to investigate the influence of industrialization and energy consumption on environmental sustainability in Asian emerging economies by using the Panel ARDL estimation technique. The Panel ARDL long-run result shows that industrialization has a negative but statistically significant impact on environmental sustainability in select countries in the long run. While energy consumption has a favourable impact on environmental sustainability in the long run. In the short run, this study shows both industrialization and energy consumption have an adverse impact on environmental sustainability. This may be due to the fact that the approaches that industries of these countries follow are not sustainable in nature. Mostly all these countries are heavily relying on non-renewable conventional energy resources. Since all the select countries are in the growing phase, this result corroborates with the EKC hypothesis which states that at the initial stage of development, industrial and economic activity put pressure on the environment. But after a certain level, environmental degradation reduces as the countries started using advanced technologies to grab pollution and transiting towards renewable energy resources. The results of country-specific short run estimation results also indicate that industrialization and energy consumption demonstrated adverse impact on environmental sustainability for all the select countries. Further, Dumitrescu Hurlin Panel causality results identified uni directional causal relationship from industrialization to carbon dioxide discharges. Similarly, energy consumption causes carbon dioxide discharges. Further, industrialization causes energy consumption. So, it is clear that both industrialization and the energy that industries consume have a direct impact on environment. But the adverse impact of industrialization on environment shows that efforts of ASIAN emerging economies towards environmental sustainability are not sufficient. This study recommends policymakers to consider different sustainability framework at the time of framing policy regarding industrial development and energy consumption. Proper awareness should be made regarding how to adopt different environmental positive activities in industries. Further, the government should promote and industries should adopt various energy efficient practices and use different renewable energy and energy-saving equipment's in their operations. Apart from this both government and private institutions need to enhance their funding regarding environmental protection and technological innovation. Though this study delivers a novel insight regarding the connections between industrialization, energy consumption, and environmental sustainability, there remain a few areas that can be studied in future. This study considers seven countries from Asian emerging economies. More countries across the globe can be considered in future studies. Further, this study considers annual data of select variables from 1990 to 2022. This study period can be extended in future studies.

REFERENCES

Abdulgawad, R. E., & El-Rasoul, A. A. (2021). Kaldor's Hypotheses and The Role of Manufacturing Industries in Economic Growth in the Kingdom of Saudi Arabia. *Magallat al-Tanmiyat wa-al-Siyasat al-Iqtisadiyyat, 23*(1), 63-92. doi:10.34066/0271-023-001-003

Adali, Z., & Yüksel, S. (2017). Causality Relationship Between Foreign Direct Investments and Economic Improvement for Developing Economies. *Marmara Journal of Economics, 1*(2), 109–118. doi:10.24954/mjecon.2017.6

Ahmed, F., Ali, I., Kousar, S., & Ahmed, S. (2022). The environmental impact of industrialization and foreign direct investment: Empirical evidence from Asia-Pacific region. *Environmental Science and Pollution Research International, 29*(20), 1–15. doi:10.1007/s11356-021-17560-w PMID:34993824

Alam, M. S., Rabbani, M. R., Tausif, M. R., & Abey, J. (2021). Banks' performance and economic growth in India: A panel cointegration analysis. *Economies, 9*(1), 38. doi:10.3390/economies9010038

Ali, G., Shah, S. Z., Rafiq, S., & Khan, A. J. (2021). Inter-linkages between Manufacturing Sector Efficiency and Economic Growth of Developing Countries: Evidence from Kaldor's Growth Model. *Indian Journal of Economics and Business, 20*(1), 439–448.

Alnegrish, F. (2023). Manufacturing and Economic Growth in Jordan (A Test of Kaldor's Laws). *Central European Management Journal*, *31*(1), 46–59. doi:10.57030/23364890.cemj.31.1.5

Appiah, K., Du, J., Yeboah, M., & Appiah, R. (2019). Causal relationship between industrialization, energy intensity, economic growth and carbon dioxide emissions: Recent evidence from Uganda. *International Journal of Energy Economics and Policy*, *9*(2), 237. doi:10.32479/ijeep.7420

Appiah, M., Gyamfi, B. A., Adebayo, T. S., & Bekun, F. V. (2023). Do financial development, foreign direct investment, and economic growth enhance industrial development? Fresh evidence from Sub-Sahara African countries. *Portuguese Economic Journal*, *22*(2), 203–227. doi:10.1007/s10258-022-00207-0

Balasubramanyam, V. N., & Mahambre, V. (2001). *India's Economic Reforms and the Manufacturing Sector*. (Lancaster University Working Paper 2001/010).

Byrne, B. M. (2010). *Structural Equation Modeling with Amos Basic Concepts, Applications, and Programming* (2nd ed.). New York Taylor and Francis Group.

Center for Climate and Energy Solutions. (2022, December 1). *Global Emissions*. C2ES. https://www.c2es.org/content/international-emissions/

Chen, J., & Xie, L. (2019). Industrial policy, structural transformation and economic growth: Evidence from China. *Frontiers of Business Research in China*, *13*(1), 1–19. doi:10.1186/s11782-019-0065-y

Chen, J. H., & Huang, Y. F. (2013). The study of the relationship between carbon dioxide (CO2) emission and economic growth. *Journal of International and Global Economic Studies*, *6*(2), 45–61.

Choi, I. (2001). Unit root tests for panel data. *Journal of International Money and Finance*, *20*(2), 249–272. doi:10.1016/S0261-5606(00)00048-6

Dong, F., Wang, Y., Su, B., Hua, Y., & Zhang, Y. (2019). The process of peak CO2 emissions in developed economies: A perspective of industrialization and urbanization. *Resources, Conservation and Recycling*, *141*, 61–75. doi:10.1016/j.resconrec.2018.10.010

Edward, J. J., & Ngasamiaku, W. M. (2021). An Empirical Investigation of the Role of Manufacturing and Economic Growth: The Case Study of Tanzania. *ORSEA Journal, 11*(1).

Elfaki, K. E., Khan, Z., Kirikkaleli, D., & Khan, N. (2022). On the nexus between industrialization and carbon emissions: Evidence from ASEAN+3 economies. *Environmental Science and Pollution Research International*, *29*(21), 1–10. doi:10.1007/s11356-022-18560-0 PMID:35013968

Erumban, A. A., & De Vries, G. J. (2021). *Industrialization in developing countries: is it related to poverty reduction?* (UNU-WIDER Working Paper No. 2021/172). doi:10.35188/UNU-WIDER/2021/112-9

Facevicova, K., & Kynclova, P. (2020). How Industrial Development Matters To The Well-Being Of The Population, Some Statistical Evidence. United Nations Industrial Development Organization. Vienna: United Nations Industrial Development Organization.

Ganda, F. (2019). The impact of industrial practice on carbon emissions in the BRICS: A panel quantile regression analysis. *Progress in Industrial Ecology*. *Progress in Industrial Ecology*, *13*(1), 84–107. doi:10.1504/PIE.2019.098813

Gungor, H., & Simon, A. U. (2017). Energy consumption, finance and growth: The role of urbanization and industrialization in South Africa. *International Journal of Energy Economics and Policy*, *7*(3), 268–276.

Haider, S., Adil, M., & Ganaie, A. (2019). Does industrialisation and urbanisation affect energy consumption: A relative study of India and Iran? *Economic Bulletin*, *39*(1), 176–185.

Hair, J. F., Black, W. C., Babin, B. J., & Anderson, R. E. (2010). *Multivariate Data Analysis* (7th ed.). Pearson., https://books.google.co.in/books/about/Multivariate_Data_Analysis.html?id=SLRPLgAACAAJ&redir_esc=y

Ho, C. Y., & Siu, K. W. (2007). A dynamic equilibrium of electricity consumption and GDP in Hong Kong: An empirical investigation. *Energy Policy*, *35*(4), 2507–2513. doi:10.1016/j.enpol.2006.09.018

Idowu, A., Ohikhuare, O. M., & Chowdhury, M. A. (2023). Does industrialization trigger carbon emissions through energy consumption? Evidence from OPEC countries and high industrialised countries. *Quantitative Finance and Economics*, *7*(1), 165–186. doi:10.3934/QFE.2023009

Im, K. S., Pesaran, M. H., & Shin, Y. (2003). Testing for unit roots in heterogeneous panels. *Journal of Econometrics*, *115*(1), 53–74. doi:10.1016/S0304-4076(03)00092-7

Jermsittiparsert, K. (2021). Does urbanization, industrialization, and income unequal distribution lead to environmental degradation? Fresh evidence from ASEAN. *International Journal of Economics and Finance Studies*, *13*(2), 253–272. doi:10.34109/ijefs.20212012

Kahouli, B., Miled, K., & Aloui, Z. (2022). Do energy consumption, urbanization, and industrialization play a role in environmental degradation in the case of Saudi Arabia? *Energy Strategy Reviews*, *40*, 100814. doi:10.1016/j.esr.2022.100814

Kalymbetova, A., Zhetibayev, Z., Kambar, R., Ranov, Z., & Izatullayeva, B. (2021). The effect of oil prices on industrial production in oil-importing countries: Panel cointegration test. *International Journal of Energy Economics and Policy*, *11*(1), 186–192. doi:10.32479/ijeep.10439

Kao, C. (1999). Spurious regression and residual-based tests for cointegration in panel data. *Journal of Econometrics*, *90*(1), 1–44. doi:10.1016/S0304-4076(98)00023-2

Keho, Y. (2016). What drives energy consumption in developing countries? The experience of selected African countries. *Energy Policy*, *91*, 233–246. doi:10.1016/j.enpol.2016.01.010

Khan, S., Akbar, A., Nasim, I., Hedvičáková, M., & Bashir, F. (2022). Green finance development and environmental sustainability: A panel data analysis. *Frontiers in Environmental Science*, *10*, 2134. doi:10.3389/fenvs.2022.1039705

Kniivilä, M. (2007). Industrial development and economic growth: Implications for poverty reduction and income inequality. *Industrial development for the 21st century: Sustainable development perspectives, 1*(3), 295–333.

Kumar, N. (2020). *East Asia's Paths to Industrialization and Prosperity: Lessons for India and Other Late Comers in South Asia*. Economic and Social Commission for Asia and the Pacific (ESCAP). Available at https://www.unescap.org/sites/default/d8files/knowledge-products/SSWA%20Development_Paper_20-03_Asian%20transformation.pdf

Kwakwa, P. A. (2022). The effect of industrialization, militarization, and government expenditure on carbon dioxide emissions in Ghana. *Environmental Science and Pollution Research International*, *29*(56), 85229–85242. doi:10.1007/s11356-022-21187-w PMID:35794324

Lavopa, A., & Szirmai, A. (2012). *Industrialization, employment and poverty*. UNU-MERIT, Maastricht Economic and Social Research and Training Centre on Innovation and Technology. UNU-MERIT Working Papers No. 081. https://cris.maastrichtuniversity.nl/ws/portalfiles/portal/1218847/guid-98b8d5a0-0ae5-496a-bfbe-693becd28a20-ASSET1.0.pdf

Levin, A., Lin, C. F., & Chu, C. S. J. (2002). Unit root tests in panel data: Asymptotic and finite-sample properties. *Journal of Econometrics*, *108*(1), 1–24. doi:10.1016/S0304-4076(01)00098-7

Liu, H., Wong, W. K., Cong, P. T., Nassani, A. A., Haffar, M., & Abu-Rumman, A. (2023). Linkage among Urbanization, energy Consumption, economic growth and carbon Emissions. Panel data analysis for China using ARDL model. *Fuel*, *332*, 126122. doi:10.1016/j.fuel.2022.126122

Liu, K., Mahmoud, H. A., Liu, L., Halteh, K., Arnone, G., Shukurullaevich, N. K., & Alzoubi, H. M. (2024). Exploring the Nexus between Fintech, natural resources, urbanization, and environment sustainability in China: A QARDL study. *Resources Policy*, *89*, 104557. doi:10.1016/j.resourpol.2023.104557

Liu, X., & Bae, J. (2018). Urbanization and industrialization impact of CO2 emissions in China. *Journal of Cleaner Production*, *172*, 178–186. doi:10.1016/j.jclepro.2017.10.156

Ma, H., & Du, J. (2012). Influence of industrialization and urbanization on China's energy consumption. *Advanced Materials Research*, *524*, 3122–3128. . doi:10.4028/www.scientific.net/AMR.524-527.3122

Magoti, E., Mabula, S., & Ngong'ho, S. B. (2020). Triple Deficit Hypothesis: A Panel ARDL and Dumitrescu-Hurlin Panel Causality for East African Countries. *African Journal of Economic Review*, *8*(1), 144–161. doi:10.22004/ag.econ.301055

Majeed, M. T., & Tauqir, A. (2020). Effects of urbanization, industrialization, economic growth, energy consumption, financial development on carbon emissions: An extended STIRPAT model for heterogeneous income groups. [PJCSS]. *Pakistan Journal of Commerce and Social Sciences*, *14*(3), 652–681. https://hdl.handle.net/10419/224955

Mamgain, V. (1999). Are the Kaldor–Verdoorn Laws Applicable in the Newly Industrializing Countries? *Review of Development Economics*, *3*(3), 295–309. doi:10.1111/1467-9361.00069

Mehmood, B., Raza, S. H., & Mureed, S. (2014). Health expenditure, literacy and economic growth: PMG evidence from Asian countries. *Euro-Asian Journal of Economics and Finance*, *2*(4), 408–417.

Mercan, M., Kızılkaya, O., & Okde, B. (2015). Are The Kaldor's Laws Valid? Panel Data Analysis under Cross Section Dependency for NIC Countries. *Procedia Economics and Finance*, *23*, 140–145. doi:10.1016/S2212-5671(15)00399-8

Mert, M., Bölük, G., & Çağlar, A. E. (2019). Interrelationships among foreign direct investments, renewable energy, and CO 2 emissions for different European country groups: A panel ARDL approach. *Environmental Science and Pollution Research International*, *26*(21), 21495–21510. doi:10.1007/ s11356-019-05415-4 PMID:31127517

Mgbemene, C. A., Nnaji, C. C., & Nwozor, C. (2016). Industrialization and its backlash: Focus on climate change and its consequences. *Journal of Environmental Science and Technology, 9*(4), 301–316. doi:10.3923/jest.2016.301.316

Millemaci, E., & Ofria, F. (2014). Kaldor-Verdoorn's law and increasing returns to scale: A comparison across developed countries. *Journal of Economic Studies (Glasgow, Scotland), 41*(1), 140–162. doi:10.1108/JES-02-2012-0026

Munir, K., & Ameer, A. (2020). Nonlinear effect of FDI, economic growth, and industrialization on environmental quality: Evidence from Pakistan. *Management of Environmental Quality, 31*(1), 223–234. doi:10.1108/MEQ-10-2018-0186

Nagaraj, R. (2011). Industrial Performance, 1991-2008: A Review. In D. M. Nachane (Ed.), *India Development Report, Oxford University Press, 69-80.*

Nasir, M. A., Canh, N. P., & Le, T. N. L. (2021). Environmental degradation & role of financialisation, economic development, industrialisation and trade liberalisation. *Journal of Environmental Management, 277,* 111471. doi:10.1016/j.jenvman.2020.111471 PMID:33049616

Ndiaya, C., & Lv, K. (2018). Role of industrialization on economic growth: The experience of Senegal (1960-2017). *American Journal of Industrial and Business Management, 8*(10), 2072–2085. doi:10.4236/ajibm.2018.810137

Nguyen, Q. H. (2021). Impact of investment in tourism infrastructure development on attracting international visitors: A nonlinear panel ARDL approach using Vietnam's data. *Economies, 9*(3), 131. doi:10.3390/economies9030131

Odeleye, A. T., & Olunkwa, N. C. (2019). Industrialization: Panacea for economic growth. *Academic Journal of Economic Studies, 5*(2), 45-51. https://ir.unilag.edu.ng/handle/123456789/12302

Olayungbo, D. O. (2021). Global oil price and food prices in food importing and oil exporting developing countries: A panel ARDL analysis. *Heliyon, 7*(3), e06357. Advance online publication. doi:10.1016/j.heliyon.2021.e06357 PMID:33748459

Opoku, E. E. O., & Boachie, M. K. (2020). The environmental impact of industrialization and foreign direct investment. *Energy Policy, 137,* 111178. doi:10.1016/j.enpol.2019.111178

Panagariya, A., (2004), India in the 1980s and 1990s: A Triumph of Reforms. *International Monetary Fund. 4* (43). . doi:10.5089/9781451846355.001

Parveen, S., Khan, A. Q., & Farooq, S. (2019). The causal nexus of urbanization, industrialization, economic growth and environmental degradation: Evidence from Pakistan. *Review of Economics and Development Studies, 5*(4), 721–730. doi:10.26710/reads.v5i4.883

Pata, U. K. (2018). The effect of urbanization and industrialization on carbon emissions in Turkey: Evidence from ARDL bounds testing procedure. *Environmental Science and Pollution Research International, 25*(8), 7740–7747. doi:10.1007/s11356-017-1088-6 PMID:29288303

Pata, U. K., & Zengin, H. (2020). Testing Kaldor's growth laws for Turkey: New evidence from symmetric and asymmetric causality methods. *Çankırı Karatekin Üniversitesi İktisadi ve İdari Bilimler Fakültesi Dergisi, 10*(2), 713-729. doi:10.18074/ckuiibfd.625455

Perron, P. (1988). Trends and random walks in macroeconomic time series: Further evidence from a new approach. *Journal of Economic Dynamics & Control, 12*(2-3), 297–332. doi:10.1016/0165-1889(88)90043-7

Pesaran, M. H., Shin, Y., & Smith, R. P. (1999). Pooled mean group estimation of dynamic heterogeneous panels. *Journal of the American Statistical Association, 94*(446), 621–634. doi:10.1080/01621459.1999.10474156

Qaiser, S. (2020). Relationship Between Industrialization and Economic Growth: An Empirical Study of Pakistan. *International Journal of Management. Accounting & Economics, 7*(12). doi:10.5281/zenodo.4482746

Raheem, I. D., & Ogebe, J. O. (2017). CO2 emissions, urbanization and industrialization: Evidence from a direct and indirect heterogeneous panel analysis. *Management of Environmental Quality, 28*(6), 851–867. doi:10.1108/MEQ-09-2015-0177

Rehman, A., Ma, H., & Ozturk, I. (2021). Do industrialization, energy importations, and economic progress influence carbon emission in Pakistan. *Environmental Science and Pollution Research International, 28*(33), 45840–45852. doi:10.1007/s11356-021-13916-4 PMID:33881694

Sadorsky, P. (2013). Do urbanization and industrialization affect energy intensity in developing countries? *Energy Economics, 37*, 52–59. doi:10.1016/j.eneco.2013.01.009

Sadorsky, P. (2014). The effect of urbanization and industrialization on energy use in emerging economies: Implications for sustainable development. *American Journal of Economics and Sociology, 73*(2), 392–409. doi:10.1111/ajes.12072

Sahoo, M., & Sethi, N. (2020). Impact of industrialization, urbanization, and financial development on energy consumption: Empirical evidence from India. *Journal of Public Affairs, 20*(3), e2089. doi:10.1002/pa.2089

Sallam, M. (2021). The role of the manufacturing sector in promoting economic growth in the Saudi economy: A cointegration and VECM approach. *The Journal of Asian Finance. Economics and Business, 8*(7), 21–30. doi:10.13106/jafeb.2021.vol8.no7.0021

Saqib, N., Usman, M., Radulescu, M., Sinisi, C. I., Secara, C. G., & Tolea, C. (2022). Revisiting EKC hypothesis in context of renewable energy, human development and moderating role of technological innovations in E-7 countries? *Frontiers in Environmental Science, 10*, 2509. doi:10.3389/fenvs.2022.1077658

Shaari, M. S., Abdul Karim, Z., & Zainol Abidin, N. (2020). The effects of energy consumption and national output on CO2 emissions: New evidence from OIC countries using a panel ARDL analysis. *Sustainability (Basel), 12*(8), 3312. doi:10.3390/su12083312

Shahbaz, M., & Lean, H. H. (2012). Does financial development increase energy consumption? The role of industrialization and urbanization in Tunisia. *Energy Policy*, *40*, 473–479. doi:10.1016/j.enpol.2011.10.050

Sharma, R., Kautish, P., & Kumar, D. S. (2021). Assessing dynamism of crude oil demand in middle-income countries of South Asia: A panel data investigation. *Global Business Review*, *22*(1), 169–183. doi:10.1177/0972150918795367

Sharma, R. K. (2014). Industrial development of India in pre and post reform period. *IOSR Journal of Humanities and Social Science, 19*(10), 01-07.

Simon, A. U. (2016). *Financial Development and Energy Use (Consumption), Urbanization and Industrialization Role in South Africa* [Master's thesis, Eastern Mediterranean University (EMU)-Doğu Akdeniz Üniversitesi (DAÜ)]. http://i-rep.emu.edu.tr:8080/jspui/bitstream/11129/3600/1/simonangela.pdf

Singh, Y., & Kumar, Y. (2023). Economic Impact of Industrialization: A Social Study. *Research Journal of Philosophy & Social Sciences., XLIX*(1), 107–114. doi:10.31995/rjpsss.2023v49i01.15

Sriyakul, T., Chienwattanasook, K., & Chankoson, T. (2022). Does industrialization and renewable energy consumption determine economic growth? Empirical evidence from ASEAN countries. *International Journal of Economics and Finance Studies, 14*(03), 264-279. https://doi.org/. 20220073 doi:10.34109/ijefs

Statista. (2023). *Green bonds issued worldwide by country 2022.* Statista. https://www.statista.com/statistics/1289016/green-bonds-issued-worldwide-by-country/

Tariq, A., & Hassan, A. (2023). Role of green finance, environmental regulations, and economic development in the transition towards a sustainable environment. *Journal of Cleaner Production, 413*, 137425. doi:10.1016/j.jclepro.2023.137425

Udi, J., Bekun, F. V., & Adedoyin, F. F. (2020). Modeling the nexus between coal consumption, FDI inflow and economic expansion: Does industrialization matter in South Africa? *Environmental Science and Pollution Research International, 27*(10), 10553–10564. doi:10.1007/s11356-020-07691-x PMID:31939028

Voumik, L. C., & Ridwan, M. (2023). Impact of FDI, industrialization, and education on the environment in Argentina: ARDL approach. *Heliyon, 9*(1), e12872–e12872. doi:10.1016/j.heliyon.2023.e12872 PMID:36685391

Wang, Z., Rasool, Y., Zhang, B., Ahmed, Z., & Wang, B. (2020). Dynamic linkage among industrialisation, urbanisation, and CO2 emissions in APEC realms: Evidence based on DSUR estimation. *Structural Change and Economic Dynamics, 52*, 382–389. doi:10.1016/j.strueco.2019.12.001

Wang, Z., Shi, C., Li, Q., & Wang, G. (2011). Impact of heavy industrialization on the carbon emissions: An empirical study of China. *Energy Procedia, 5*, 2610–2616. doi:10.1016/j.egypro.2011.03.324

Wells, H., & Thirlwall, A. P. (2003). Testing Kaldor's growth laws across the countries of Africa. *African Development Review, 15*(2-3), 89–105. doi:10.1111/j.1467-8268.2003.00066.x

Yahyaoui, I., & Bouchoucha, N. (2021). The long-run relationship between ODA, growth and governance: An application of FMOLS and DOLS approaches. *African Development Review*, *33*(1), 38–54. doi:10.1111/1467-8268.12489

Zafar, A., Ullah, S., Majeed, M. T., & Yasmeen, R. (2020). Environmental pollution in Asian economies: Does the industrialisation matter? *OPEC Energy Review*, *44*(3), 227–248. doi:10.1111/opec.12181

Zafeiriou, E., Azam, M., & Garefalakis, A. (2022). Exploring environmental–economic performance linkages in EU agriculture: Evidence from a panel cointegration framework. *Management of Environmental Quality*, *34*(2), 469–491. doi:10.1108/MEQ-06-2022-0174

Zeng, B., Tan, Y., Xu, H., Quan, J., Wang, L., & Zhou, X. (2018). Forecasting the Electricity Consumption of Commercial Sector in Hong Kong Using a Novel Grey Dynamic Prediction Model. *Journal of Grey System*, *30*(1), 159.

KEY TERMS AND DEFINITIONS

Economic Development: This can be regarded as the process by which a nation enhances their capacity for production, generates wealth and improves the standard of life for its citizens.

Economies of Scale: It is a phenomenon in which an organization starts to obtain a cost advantage as a result of increasing the number of units it manufactures.

Environmental Sustainability: This concept advocates responsible human behaviour and economic advancement without endangering the environment.

Industrialization: It is the process by which a nation shapes its economy, shifting its dependence from agricultural to manufacturing.

Inequality: It represents the unequal distribution of resources among a nation's citizens.

Labour Productivity: It assesses how many goods or services that an employee is able to produce in a given time, typically in an hour.

Renewable Energy: It is regarded as energy that does not run out and is naturally regenerated.

Chapter 6
Innovation in Tourism and Startups in Eastern India

Sriparna Guha
https://orcid.org/0000-0003-3092-3722
Amity University, Kolkata, India

Anirban Mandal
ICFAI Business School, India

Fedric Kujur
Xavier Institute of Social Service, Ranchi, India

Sandeep Poddar
https://orcid.org/0000-0001-9771-877X
Lincoln University College, Malaysia

Samprit Chakrabarti
ICFAI Business School, India

ABSTRACT

Research conducted in the domain of smart city development reveals that the implementation of smart city initiatives has the propensity to draw individuals residing in the surrounding rural areas, as well as a growing influx of tourists. While numerous smart tourisms' approach primarily emphasise the advancement of technology, individuals, and institutional logic, the entrepreneurial ecosystem approach plays a crucial role in enhancing smart destinations. The objective of the current study is to examine novel initiatives pertaining to the advancement of startups in Eastern India. The study employed an exploratory and descriptive research design. Additionally, specific initiatives in the realm of tourist innovation, particularly those associated with startups, were also discovered. The findings of the study indicate that there exist guidelines associated with startups in the study area. The promotion of tourism can be facilitated through the implementation of several initiatives, which have been identified as contributing factors, including the provision of valuable experiences.

DOI: 10.4018/979-8-3693-2197-3.ch006

INTRODUCTION

Tourism is a rapidly rising industry and a sector that reflects the rise in personal income, leisure, and mobility. It is now considered one of the most significant components of human spatial behaviour. Travel and tourism contribute to employment creation for individuals with varying levels of qualifications, as supported by research conducted by Korinnyi and Tsyhanok (2020) and Pohuda and Rozmetova (2018). Unlike numerous other sectors, this particular industry has the capacity to expand without substantial investments, resulting in multiple advantages in terms of both generating cash and creating employment opportunities. Thus, tourism serves as a crucial sector in both the public and private domains for numerous countries (Abbate et al., 2019).

Tourism is a diverse field of inventive activity that encompasses various sectors of the economy, such as housing, transportation, communication, leisure, and food. Tourism not only generates novel offerings, but also leverages advancements adopted in other domains, such as cutting-edge practises in management, task execution, and the utilisation of recent scientific breakthroughs and technologies. These are employed by the tourism industry to enhance the quality of products and services sought by the market. The integration of cutting-edge information technology has the potential to significantly enhance the development of tourism products and services, as well as improve the efficiency of hotel management and ticket reservation processes (Abbate et al., 2019).

Different literatures demonstrate that the tourism business, including cultural tourism and art, is always evolving in response to advancements in technology and innovative solutions (Gusakov et al., 2016; Bertasini, 2020; Khan & Maria, 2022). This development is driven by the growing demands and behaviours of end customers, as well as the desire and requirement of firms to acquire competitive advantages or preserve their positions in relation to their competitors. Startups thrive in this niche as fertile ground, serving as idea incubators for larger and established organisations or potential future ventures. The tourism industry has witnessed a paradigm shift on both the supply and demand sides and this industry is undergoing significant structural changes, with technology playing a crucial role (Pavlatos, 2021). Tourist destinations are embracing innovative planning and management approaches to effectively address these changes, with the aim of enhancing innovation, competitiveness, and sustainability. Initiatives associated with the smart city concept are prominent in the political and academic domains. The integration of the smart city perspective is facilitated by the tourism activity, leading to the emergence of the concept of Smart Tourism Destination. The incorporation of this concept into tourism is deemed suitable, as it combines strategic planning, technology advancement, sustainability policies, and innovation. Additionally, there is an increasing body of research that establishes a connection between the smart city concept and tourism (Soares & Conceição, 2016; Gusakov et al., 2020).

Tourist cities are being urged to reassess their strategy in order to sustain their appeal and enhance their reputation in the virtual realm as well. Conversely, tourists have become increasingly aware and engaged in their role as visitors and users of the city (La Rocca, 2014; Khan et al., 2017). Currently, there is a growing demand for a city model that prioritises efficiency, resilience, sustainability, and social fairness, known as the "smart city" paradigm. The concept of sustainability necessitates a shift or, at least, a re-evaluation of the current socio-economic growth models, which are fundamentally unsustainable. The notion of a "smart city", while relatively new, is equally contentious as the concept of sustainability (Jasrotia & Gangotia, 2018). This aims to expand the implementation of sustainability principles to enhance urban competitiveness, encompassing the utilisation of information and communication technologies (ICTs) as well as the quality of "social capital". Undoubtedly, the existence of a significant amount of social capital of superior quality is a key determinant of territorial competitiveness and appeal (Nam et al., 2021).

In recent years, startups have emerged as a prominent phenomenon in the Indian marketplace. Consequently, there has been a proliferation of domestically produced unicorns throughout the nation. One of the primary factors that has significantly contributed to this advancement is the substantial financial investment that has been allocated to the majority of these unicorns throughout the timeframe spanning after 2015 (Vargas-Sanchez, 2023). This has been consistent with the prevailing global trend in the field. Even the aspiring unicorns have experienced a successful era during this time, despite the typically challenging challenge of securing investors. Investment patterns indicate a desire among investors to participate as early investors, even prior to the establishment of the company. India appears to be a prosperous consumer-driven market that has not been fully penetrated, but has the potential for significant expansion. The widespread adoption of the internet and its growing significance will propel the majority of enterprises. Due to the customer demographics, India presents the most lucrative investment potential globally, surpassing China. Notwithstanding the numerous operational, regulatory, and taxation challenges that encompass the business operating landscape in India (Al-Jubari et al., 2019; Sharma & Goyal, 2023).

Artificial Intelligence (AI) has brought about a significant transformation in various industries globally, by replicating human intelligence in machines to perform tasks such as problem-solving and decision-making. AI revolutionises trip planning, experiences, and reflections in the tourist industry. Artificial intelligence examines data to provide tailored suggestions, improves service through chatbots, optimises pricing, and forecasts travel patterns. The Fourth Industrial Revolution is characterised by recent progress in artificial intelligence (AI), which is driven by enhancements in algorithms, processing capabilities, and massive data management. Artificial intelligence (AI) applications are undergoing advancements in various sectors of the tourist industry, encompassing personalisation, travel assistants, robots, predictions, language translation, voice recognition, and natural language processing. The incorporation of artificial intelligence (AI) holds the potential to optimise tourism operations, augment client pleasure, and ensure the long-term prosperity of the sector. Tourists partake in decision-making procedures pertaining to forthcoming excursions, encompassing determinations regarding destination selection, transit options, hotel arrangements, and activities, so exerting an impact on their total contentment with their travel encounters (Sharma & Goyal, 2023).

The need to compare our existing development strategy in order to guarantee a superior standard of urban living is clearly apparent. Yet, the practicality of adopting the "smart city" concept seems to mostly rely on the capacity to fundamentally alter the behaviours and habits of both administrators and users. This article aims to examine the connection between tourism and cities, emphasising the crucial role of startups, based on a comprehensive approach to urban development, should have in coordinating and integrating urban policies aimed at creating a Smart City by innovative start up in tourism industry.

REVIEW OF LITERATURE

Joss et al. (2017) emphasises the widespread existence of the smart city in literature, but admit a lack of agreement on its exact description. The concept of smart cities is praised in academic literature as the use of the Internet of Things (IoT) in conjunction with the collection and analysis of large amounts of data, resulting in data-driven government (Chourabi et al., 2012; Harrison & Donnelly, 2011; Nam &

Pardo, 2011) The smart city paradigm is widely recognised as highly applicable to the best practises in urban management (Chourabi et al., 2012). Proposals for digitally-enhanced cities are being presented as exemplary answers to the current problems faced by urban areas. These proposals aim to inspire urban people to strive for the creation of more sustainable and liveable cities (Dabeedooal et al., 2019; Mitra et al., 2023).

The way people travel has been transformed by innovation (Plug and Play Travel accelerator, 2019; Pavlatos, 2021) and one of the key players in this case are travel startups. For instance, in 2014, Airbnb's 155 million guest stays were 22% more than Hilton Worldwide's (Pricewaterhouse Coopers, 2014). Venture capital firms have also shown interest in travel and tourism start-ups. Venture capital firms have invested over $1 billion into the travel industry in the past five years (Techcrunch, 2018; Pavlatos, 2021). Apps pertaining to travel and tourism, software platforms for travel, leisure, or hospitality, and short-term rental start-ups like Airbnb are the primary types of tourism start-ups (Techcrunch, 2018; Pavlatos, 2021). Unlike other early-stage/startup enterprises, platform organisations and mobile applications like Uber and Airbnb constitute a novel organisational structure (Kornberger et al., 2017). According to Kornberger et al. (2017), these groups are becoming more common in the economy.

The existing body of research on smart tourist destinations demonstrates that these destinations utilise information and communication technology (ICT) to improve and facilitate the growth and implementation of tourism activities (Wang et al., 2013; Jasrotia & Gangotia, 2018). In their 2014 article titled "Smart tourism destinations," Buhalis and Amaranggana emphasised the need to connect stakeholders through a shared platform in order to make tourism destinations smarter. According to Guo et al., (2014), Wang et al., (2013), and Zhu et al., (2014), smart tourism destinations are described as locations that make use of available technology to collaboratively produce value, enjoyment, and experiences for tourists. Hence, smart tourism destinations must actively involve local stakeholders in order to guarantee community participation. Smart tourism destinations are advantageous for the tourism sector as they enable the interchange of information between tourism organisations and tourists via a centralised platform (Presenza et al., 2020). Smart Tourism Destinations have the potential to get valuable information regarding customers' genuine needs and preferences. Facilitating meaningful interaction between tourists and service providers is crucial in order to effectively deliver products that cater to the tourists' needs (Chenhall and Moers, 2015). This will ultimately facilitate the comprehension of tourists' needs by service providers, enabling them to deliver novel and enhanced offerings (Schaffers et al., 2011; Jasrotia & Gangotia, 2018).

Innovation can be classified into three main categories: disruptive/radical, gradual, or open. These concepts can be defined as follows: (i) disruptive/radical innovation refers to the creation of new products that completely replace existing ones, leading to significant changes in the market and society, (ii) incremental innovation involves making improvements and enhancements to existing goods or services, either by adapting, refining, or enhancing them, and (iii) open innovation refers to a collaborative network that connects different stakeholders in the innovation process, which can be either incremental or radical (Gretzel et al., 2016; Alvares & Soares, 2021). In this particular context, startups arise, which are endeavours characterised by scalable and replicable business models, where the innovation component plays a crucial role. A key attribute of startups is their capacity to rapidly achieve scalability. Startups can emerge from diverse areas and sectors of the economy, with a predominant focus on technology (Alvares & Soares, 2021).

Trips to nearby countries and regions are experiencing substantial growth compared to more distant destinations. Experts attribute this trend to the increasing global terrorism threat, rising number of annual trips, expanding availability of holidays, and various other factors. The economic advantages arising from tourism are becoming more evident, and countries are adopting a more favourable stance towards tourism, as seen by the substantial elimination of various barriers on their part (Trzmielak et al., 2021). This facilitates the expansion of tourist numbers in the future and reinforces the ongoing process of globalisation. The ongoing increase in competition, whether from inside or beyond the region, compels the top tourism companies to adopt comprehensive and assertive strategies to consistently promote their products. The rise of urbanisation and densely populated areas has greatly fostered the development of many forms of tourism, such as village tourism, short-term vacations, year-round holidays, non-active forms of tourism, hotel-free tours, eco-tourism, and hunting, among others. Due to the implementation of information technology and advancements in tourist operators' services, the global population has gained access to more knowledge, resulting in a more comprehensive understanding of tourism. This trend will continue to evolve, leading to a new phenomenon of venturing to obscure and challenging destinations in search of distinctive amusement and indelible encounters (Trzmielak et al., 2021).

The marketing of innovative tourism practices involves the use of novel methods and techniques, together with the implementation of steps to promote the creation of an appealing and favourable image of a country's tourist sector within the global community. These efforts must be methodical in nature, characterised by qualitative innovation, resulting in positive advancements, and ensuring the stable establishment and growth of the industry. This may involve modifications in procedures, structure, advertising, products, and other aspects, but it will ultimately enhance socio-economic progress. Significant material and financial investments are necessary for advancements in tourism, thus requiring state assistance (Trzmielak et al., 2021; Ghouse & Chaudhary, 2024).

Another notable trend in tourism is associated with sustainable development. Increasingly, there is a growing popularity in travelling to remote and less frequented destinations, away from the main tourist attractions of a particular country. These trips offer the opportunity to experience tranquilly, alone, and a deep connection with the natural environment. There is a noticeable increase in the current trend of engaging in local tourism. Recently, there has been a growing trend in travelling to unconventional destinations, such as houses floating on lakes or flats located in trees. Websites are being developed with databases including distinctive accommodations, catering to individuals seeking a higher level of comfort and uniqueness. One additional trend in the sustainable tourism sector, particularly in Poland, is the arrangement of specialised trips that often incorporate physical activities. These activities may encompass bicycle tours, family survival camps, culinary excursions, self-improvement workshops, yoga retreats, sports trips, and multi-day canoeing expeditions (Trzmielak et al., 2021).

India holds the highest position among South Asian nations on the Global Travel Development Index. Tourism firms are providing appealing all-inclusive packages, enticing discounts, programmes, and bundled offers to meet the demands of this substantial sector, which is seeing rapid expansion due to good travel attitudes (Filieri et al., 2021). Curiously, the pattern of travel purchases has experienced a notable change in the era after the pandemic. Although individuals desire to allocate more funds towards travel, they also have a strong inclination to economise. Currently, individuals are inclined towards a payment method that allows them to make installment payments or pay in a staggered manner, rather than spending money all at once. Consequently, the travel-now-pay-later (TNPL) services are experiencing a rapid and intense boom. In addition to offering convenient credit access and cost-effective travel choices, they also have a transformational impact, particularly in light of our progressively digitalized society (Kapur, 2022)

OBJECTIVE OF THE STUDY

This paper aims to analyse creative activities in Eastern India that promote entrepreneurs, recognising the crucial role played by startups in the process of innovation in smart destinations. In order to achieve this goal, the following precise objectives have been established: 1. Determine the programmes associated with innovation and entrepreneurship in India. 2. To examine particular undertakings pertaining to startup ventures in the eastern region of India's tourist sector. 3. To ascertain the primary goals of the innovation-related activities in the eastern region of India's tourist sector.

METHODOLOGY

A qualitative study was done to explore and describe the subject matter. The information was curated, focusing solely on news articles that featured practical instances of innovation in the tourism industry, such as startup success stories, awards, and effective initiatives by both public and private entities. It is crucial to emphasise that additional searches were conducted to acquire comprehensive information and confirm their current operational status. The news data were transcribed and subjected to a descriptive analysis.

RESULTS

The study examined the programmes and initiatives associated with innovation and entrepreneurship in Eastern India. Regarding the promotion of innovation and entrepreneurship, programs/actions primarily focused on promoting entrepreneurship were highlighted. Emphasis was placed on the investigation of programmes associated with a public sector entity.

India has significant geographical diversity and presents a multitude of civilizations, each accompanied by unique experiences. Consequently, it has emerged as a prominent nation in terms of international tourism expenditure. According to the report on the Growth of Tourism and Hospitality Industry by the Investment Bank of India (IBEF), the travel and tourism sectors in India are among the most significant industries, collectively contributing approximately US$ 178 billion to the nation's Gross Domestic Product (GDP). The nation's extensive coastline is adorned with numerous captivating beaches. By the Financial Year 2027, it is estimated that the travel market in India will attain a value of US $125 billion (Yadav, 2024). By 2028, the number of international tourists is projected to reach 30.5 million. Indian enterprises have been utilising technology as a crucial catalyst for growth in the industry for more than ten years, much like in other industries. The travel business has experienced substantial innovation, ranging from search engines and global distribution system (GDS) services to online travel agencies, and there is yet potential for more advancements. The use of cloud solutions and the development of Software as a Service (SaaS) technologies are key factors contributing to the growth of travel and hospitality enterprises in the technology sector. India boasts a substantial market for the travel and tourism industry. The company provides a wide range of specialised tourism offerings, including cruises, adventure, medical, wellness, sports, MICE, eco-tourism, film, rural, and religious tourism. India has gained recognition as a prominent destination for both domestic and foreign tourists seeking spiritual tourism experiences (Yadav, 2024).

Given the multitude of reasons of diversity, it is imperative for Indian tourism to prioritise its ability to cater to a diverse range of individuals across various categories and budgetary constraints. This may be achieved through the provision of customised experiences, luxury spa sessions, rare animal sanctuaries, religious pilgrimage trips, and even extreme Himalaya tours. India can be experienced from various perspectives, including India on a budget, India in opulence, the royal India, urban India, the common man's India, historical India, and more. The tourist sector has the potential to undergo significant changes through the provision of accessible locations and the implementation of environmentally sustainable hotel construction in coastal areas and wildlife reserves. A growing trend in the hospitality industry is the concept of 'conscious luxury', exemplified by the emergence of small, intimate hotels such as palaces, plantation retreats, and jungle lodges. These establishments prioritise transformative travel experiences that aim to educate, enrich, and promote a digital detox when desired, while still allowing connectivity when necessary. Ensuring the sustainable progress of tourism is crucial, and it is now essential for all parties involved to actively adopt proactive measures in this regard.

Nevertheless, the sector encounters some obstacles, including inadequate infrastructure such as access roads, electricity, water supply, sewerage, and telecommunication. Additionally, factors such as limited access and accessibility to new destinations, as well as the exploration of niche segments, pose significant problems. Additional concerns encompass insufficient marketing and promotional efforts, regulatory challenges pertaining to visa and internal permits, human resource management, service quality, taxation, and security measures. In response to these issues and upon recognising the tourism industry's potential within the country, the Indian Government has implemented various measures aimed at positioning India as a prominent worldwide tourism destination. Prime Minister Mr. Narendra Modi, in his Independence speech from Red Fort, called upon individuals to visit 15 domestic tourist destinations in India by 2022 in order to stimulate tourism. The primary objective of the Draught National Tourism Policy 2022 is to establish Tourism as a National Priority, bolster its competitiveness as a tourism destination, and develop top-tier infrastructure worldwide.

The tourism marketing campaign, initiated in 2019 by the Ministry of Tourism, Government of India (MoT, GoI), is primarily focused on enhancing the quality of domestic and international tourism, which has been a long-standing priority. These activities, including "Dekho Apna Desh", "Swadesh Darshan Scheme", "Pilgrimage Rejuvenation and Spiritual Heritage Augmentation Drive" (PRASHAD), were part of the second phase of "the Incredible India" initiative. This initiative aimed to not only prioritise the number of visitors, but also to improve the overall tourist experience and provide sustainable employment prospects. These projects were established in 2019 with the intention of capitalising on significant prospects within the Indian Travel, Tourism, and Hospitality (TTH) ecosystem. However, their progress was hindered by the outbreak of COVID-19. However, the situation of "unlocking" allowed the exhausted Indian population to take advantage of vacation chances in challenging conditions. TTH's new vocabulary of terminology includes references to "staycations" and "workcations" (Trzmielak et al., 2021; Ghouse & Chaudhary, 2024).

India is experiencing a surge of innovative start-up ideas across all sectors of the economy, including the Travel & Tourism business. According to the National Association of Software and Services Companies (NASSCOM), there are currently over 3,100 start-ups in India. According to a NASSCOM survey in 2014, it is recognised as the fastest growing and third largest start-up ecosystem worldwide. India witnesses a yearly influx of around 800 newly established start-ups. India provides a favourable environment for numerous startup concepts due to a multitude of factors. Indian entrepreneurs are prepared to capitalise on the vast market size, economic growth, and government initiatives aimed at fostering business (van den Berg, 2016).

Prominent international start-ups like Airbnb, Expedia, and Zostel have already established their presence in the Indian market. However, the indigenous Indian corporations have successfully introduced concepts that might captivate individuals with certain inclinations, as well as those who are simply seeking something intriguing. Indian consumers have been exposed to a variety of unconventional travel concepts, including backpacking, couch surfing, food tourism (India Food Tour), and fishing tourism (Otter Reserves). Certain companies develop groundbreaking travel solutions, while others streamline everyday travel tasks. For example, TravelKhana.com is a platform that accepts meal orders from those who are travelling great distances by rail and arranges for the delivery of these meals through eateries located along the route (Khan & Maria, 2022).

The Department for the Promotion of Industry and Internal Trade (DPIIT) acknowledged more than 26,000 startups in 2022. Since 2016, enterprises in India's startup sector have been proliferating at a rapid pace. The government of India established the Startup India programme to encourage and facilitate its expansion. Official recognition from DPIIT for 92,683 startups was extended in February 2023[1]. These startups include organisations that offer platforms for planning and booking travel services, as well as those that provide technology solutions to travel service providers. This encompasses organisations that provide services facilitating consumers in finding and reserving travel-related services, such as transportation, lodging, facility management, tours, ticketing, and activities, using online platforms (Khan & Maria, 2022).

Ecotourism has the capacity to simultaneously provide advantages to the indigenous people and save the abundant cultural heritage and ecosystem of the host region. The tourism potential of the Northeast remains untapped. This region, sometimes referred to as an "unexplored paradise," has been seeing significant growth, and future estimates indicate that this tendency will persist. The region possesses abundant and varied natural beauty, including diverse flora and wildlife, as well as unusual cultural and ethnic diversities (Ghouse & Chaudhary, 2024). These untapped resources offer great potential for the development of ecotourism (McPhee et al., 2016; Sharma, 2000). The Indian Government acknowledges that tourism can play a significant role in driving socio-economic and infrastructure development in this region. The North Eastern states have begun to play a significant part in the implementation of the Look East policy, which is contributing to the development of the region. The Look East Policy (LEP) in the northeast region is poised to embark in a new phase of progress through comprehensive expansion encompassing a network of pipelines, well-built roads, efficient trains and air connectivity, as well as effective channels for communication and trade. According to the Annual Report 2015-2016, NEC has built an eco-tourism park at Langkawet, located in the east Khasi Hills District of Meghalaya. Additionally, they have established an adventure tourism camping and recreation site in Huto village, Doimukh, as well as other locations in Arunachal Pradesh. Nevertheless, there exist certain obstacles that must be resolved before to engaging in any significant endeavours (Sundaram, 2013). The North-East States possess abundant ecotourism resources, although they suffer from a deficiency of essential infrastructure and a lack of strategic view and planning. The region's tourism business is underutilised given its significant potential. Hence, it is imperative for the North-Eastern States to recognise the current necessity of pursuing sustainable tourism development as a crucial marketing strategy, with eco-tourism playing a pivotal role in attaining this objective. In addition, there must be effective collaboration among all players involved in the tourism industry. The utilisation of the public-private partnership approach will enhance the results of ecotourism. Furthermore, it is imperative to have an all-encompassing tourism development policy that actively fosters and motivates individuals' engagement in the sector (Filieri et al., 2021; Khan & Maria, 2022).

The influential Shukla Commission has already suggested the formation of a tourist development corporation for the northeast. Das, (2013) and Duarah and Mili (2013) state that the corporation's primary focus will be on increasing aviation services to encourage tourism in the region. The aforementioned research makes it clear that the northeastern states are ripe with potential for ecotourism. If some things are fixed, this might be used. Despite the opportunity, there are a few obstacles that can be overcome with improved communication and management. In certain regions, the green economic theory can be applied to make money without harming the local ecology (Bertasini, 2020). If promoting ecotourism is the goal, then the participation of the people is the most sought-after. People have learned about the conservation and financial benefits of ecotourism. Every step of the policymaking and implementation processes should involve the people. Thorough three-dimensional evaluations have revealed that eco-friendly management practices are the answer to tourism centred on sustainable development (Filieri et al., 2021).

The primary demand for help is government assistance, primarily in two areas: providing tax exemptions and Promotion of tourism at the government and federal levels (Bertasini, 2020). This initiative would enhance the value of the travel industry by providing Indians with a wide range of travel options and trip packages that cater to various budgetary constraints. Gaining a deeper comprehension of customers is an ongoing process, and the travel industry should be vigilant about the specific methods of cancellation that customers are expecting (Rodriguez-Sanchez et al., 2019). During the shutdown in India, numerous flights were cancelled, and obtaining refunds proved to be challenging. Even well-known e-commerce platforms like MakeMyTrip (MMT) and Yatra.com displayed hesitancy when it came to cancellations (Khan & Maria, 2022). However, understanding this scenario has resulted in the reorganisation of cancellation procedures and the provision of vouchers for future travel. After the initial round of "unlocking" was announced, the Indian domestic market surprisingly started visiting ecotourism destinations amidst the pandemic. Travellers sought information regarding the certification of their resorts and properties by an ecological authority. As a result, resorts and hotels began pursuing eco-label certification to market themselves as sustainable institutions and destinations (Khan & Maria, 2022). The Responsible Tourism Society of India (RTSOI), acknowledged as the national authority for responsible tourism, has become a crucial element in the self-certification process of the tourism industry. The Global Sustainable Tourism Council (GSTC) is presently engaged in promoting the adoption of eco-labelling as a prominent practice in India. The Indian travel industry has acknowledged that giving priority to domestic tourism is of greatest importance. Government regulations effectively supported the travel industry, encompassing airlines and hotels, by making internal travel essential for its survival during the phased reopening of the epidemic. Both e-commerce businesses and brick-and-mortar tour operators and travel agencies significantly rely on domestic tourism (Khan & Maria, 2022).

DISCUSSIONS

The research findings clearly indicate the existence of special standards associated with startups, particularly in the tourism industry. Nevertheless, there exists a propitious environment for innovation in the nation, facilitated by various initiatives undertaken by private enterprises, public organisations, and universities. These include the establishment of incubators, accelerators, programmes to foster startups, competitions, and solicitations for proposals. In India, it is crucial to acknowledge the availability of European financial programmes. The identified initiatives encompass the objectives of commercialization, management, innovation promotion, experience enhancement, cultural valorisation, environmental preservation, accessibility, promotion, exchange of experiences, translation, transportation, safety, collaborative economy, solidarity tourism, and commercialization of handicrafts and small businesses.

CONCLUSION

According to the data from Startup India, the travel and tourism business consists of over 1500 startups. These firms offer platforms that facilitate the planning and booking of travel services, as well as give technological solutions to travel service providers. This includes enterprises that provide services facilitating users in exploring and reserving travel-related services, such as transportation, lodging, facility administration, guided tours, tickets, and recreational activities, via digital platforms. The perspectives on the ideas of smart city and smart tourism destinations vary across cities and countries, influenced by factors such as their degree of development, policies, and available resources. Tourism destinations encompass a combination of tourism products and services, and comprehending and overseeing these systems can be challenging. Hence, it is crucial to establish clear definitional borders in order to provide guidance to cities in this regard.

Smart tourism destinations refer to urban areas or locations that effectively employ technological tools, innovations, and strategies to enhance the enjoyment and experiences of tourists while also generating financial gains for both the organisations and the destinations themselves. Smart cities serve as a platform for developing intelligent tourism destinations. Smart tourism destinations refer to urban areas that employ information technology and innovative solutions to enhance the enjoyment and satisfaction of tourists. Therefore, it is evident that smart tourism is an essential component of smart cities. In the contemporary era, there has been a notable surge in the prevalence of smart cities and smart tourism destinations. Hence, it is imperative in the present era to comprehend these principles and formulate and implement enduring strategies for the advancement of intelligent urban areas, which will finally pave the path towards the establishment of intelligent tourism destinations in the future.

LIMITATIONS AND FUTURE RESEARCH

A noteworthy drawback of the research is the inability to gather all available experiences. However, a substantial sample has been acquired, which enables the characterization of the innovation environment in the analysed nations. For future studies, it is recommended to focus on various areas of development. These include conducting in-depth surveys and evaluations of novel activities in tourism, as well as analysing cities that are implementing policies for conversion in sustainable tourism development (STD).

It is crucial to highlight that there are significant disparities between conventional destinations and intelligent destinations. Hence, it is imperative to implement strategic tourism planning that is founded on the principles of Sustainable Tourism Development (STD), alongside focused investment, promotion of market knowledge, and engagement of tourism stakeholders. The purpose is to ensure that tourism locations are progressively sustainable, well-connected, easily accessible both physically and digitally, autonomously administered by local or regional governing authorities, and primarily serve as platforms for promoting remarkable tourism experiences.

REFERENCES

Abbate, T., Accordino, P., Coppolino, R., Tiziana La Rocca, E., & Rupo, D. (2019). *Innovative Tourism Startups: An Explorative Analysis. Knowledge—Economy—Society: Contemporary Trends and Transformations of Economies and Enterprises*. Polonia.

Al-Jubari, I., Bahari, S. B. S., Kamarudin, N. I. H. B., & Fadzli, A. D. B. M. (2019). Examining attitudinal determinants of startup intention among university students of hospitality and tourism. *International Journal of Human Potentials Management, 1*(2), 33–42.

Alvares, D. F., & Soares, J. C. (2021). Innovation in tourism and startups in Brazil, Spain and Portugal. *Smart Tourism, 2*(2).

Bertasini, M. (2020). *Startups value proposition in the tourism and art sector: an empirical analysis of digital and innovative trends.*

Chenhall, R. H., & Moers, F. (2015). The role of innovation in the evolution of management accounting and its integration into management control. *Accounting, Organizations and Society, 47*, 1–13. doi:10.1016/j.aos.2015.10.002

Chourabi, H., Nam, T., Walker, S., Gil-Garcia, J. R., Mellouli, S., Nahon, K., . . . Scholl, H. J. (2012, January). Understanding smart cities: An integrative framework. In *2012 45th Hawaii international conference on system sciences* (pp. 2289-2297). IEEE.

Dabeedooal, Y. J., Dindoyal, V., Allam, Z., & Jones, D. S. (2019). Smart tourism as a pillar for sustainable urban development: An alternate smart city strategy from Mauritius. *Smart Cities, 2*(2), 153–162. doi:10.3390/smartcities2020011

Das, D. (2013). Tourism Industry in North-East Indian States: Prospects and Problems. *Global Research Methodology Journal, 2*(7), 1–6.

Duarah, I., & Mili, B. (2013). Tourism Potentiality in North East India. *International Journal ofScience and Research (IJSR), 2*(10), 1-3.

Filieri, R., D'Amico, E., Destefanis, A., Paolucci, E., & Raguseo, E. (2021). Artificial intelligence (AI) for tourism: An European-based study on successful AI tourism start-ups. *International Journal of Contemporary Hospitality Management, 33*(11), 4099–4125. doi:10.1108/IJCHM-02-2021-0220

Ghouse, S. M., & Chaudhary, M. (2024). Artificial Intelligence (AI) for Tourism Start-Ups. In Innovative Technologies for Increasing Service Productivity (pp. 161-178). IGI Global. doi:10.4018/979-8-3693-2019-8.ch010

Gretzel, U., Zhong, L., & Koo, C. (2016). Application of smart tourism to cities. *International Journal of Tourism Cities, 2*(2). Advance online publication. doi:10.1108/IJTC-04-2016-0007

Guo, Y., Liu, H., & Chai, Y. (2014). The embedding convergence of smart cities and tourism internet of things in China: An advance perspective. [AHTR]. *Advances in Hospitality and Tourism Research*, *2*(1), 54–69.

Gusakov, A. A., Haque, A. U., & Jogia, A. V. (2020). Mechanisms to support open innovation in smart tourism destinations: Managerial perspective and implications. *Polish Journal of Management Studies*, *21*(2), 142–161. doi:10.17512/pjms.2020.21.2.11

Harrison, C., & Donnelly, I. A. (2011, September). *A theory of smart cities.* In *Proceedings of the 55th Annual Meeting of the ISSS-2011*, Hull, UK.

Jasrotia, A., & Gangotia, A. (2018). Smart cities to smart tourism destinations: A review paper. *Journal of tourism intelligence and smartness, 1*(1), 47-56.

Joss, S., Cook, M., & Dayot, Y. (2017). Smart cities: Towards a new citizenship regime? A discourse analysis of the British smart city standard. *Journal of Urban Technology*, *24*(4), 29–49. doi:10.1080/1 0630732.2017.1336027

Kapur, S. K. (2022, December 19). *Dr Samir Kapur in Voices.* TOI, India. https://timesofindia.indiatimes. com/blogs/voices/innovations-in-tourism-industry-to-attract-travellers/

Khan, M. S., Woo, M., Nam, K., & Chathoth, P. K. (2017). Smart city and smart tourism: A case of Dubai. *Sustainability (Basel)*, *9*(12), 2279. doi:10.3390/su9122279

Khan, S., & Freeda Maria, S. M. (2022). What innovations would enable the tourism and hospitality industry in India to re-build? *Worldwide Hospitality and Tourism Themes*, *14*(6), 579–585. doi:10.1108/ WHATT-05-2022-0053

Korinnyi, S. O., & Tsyhanok, K. (2020). Current State of Tourism Business in European Countries and Its Trends. *Bulletin of Zaporizhzhia National University: Economic Sciences*, *2*(46), 65–70. doi:10.2478/ minib-2021-0011

Kornberger, M., Pflueger, D., & Mouritsen, J. (2017). Evaluative infrastructures: Accounting for platform organization. *Accounting, Organizations and Society*, *60*, 79–95. doi:10.1016/j.aos.2017.05.002

La RoccaR. A. (2014). The role of tourism in planning the smart city. *TeMA-Journal of Land Use, Mobility and Environment, 7*(3), 269-284. DOI: doi:10.6092/1970-9870/2814

McPhee, C., Guimont, D., & Lapointe, D. (2016). Innovation in tourism. *Technology Innovation Management Review*, *6*(11), 3–5. doi:10.22215/timreview/1029

Mitra, S., Kumar, H., Gupta, M. P., & Bhattacharya, J. (2023). Entrepreneurship in smart cities: Elements of start-up ecosystem. *Journal of Science and Technology Policy Management*, *14*(3), 592–611. doi:10.1108/JSTPM-06-2021-0078

Nam, K., Dutt, C. S., Chathoth, P., & Khan, M. S. (2021). Blockchain technology for smart city and smart tourism: Latest trends and challenges. *Asia Pacific Journal of Tourism Research*, *26*(4), 454–468. doi:10.1080/10941665.2019.1585376

Nam, T., & Pardo, T. A. (2011, June). Conceptualizing smart city with dimensions of technology, people, and institutions. In *Proceedings of the 12th annual international digital government research conference: digital government innovation in challenging times* (pp. 282-291). ACM. 10.1145/2037556.2037602

Pavlatos, O. (2021). Drivers of management control systems in tourism start-ups firms. *International Journal of Hospitality Management, 92*, 102746. doi:10.1016/j.ijhm.2020.102746

Pohuda, N. V., & Rozmetova, O. H. (2018). *Sluchasnyi stan turistichnogo rynku Ukraiyiny: Ocenka ta perspektyvy rosvitku.* Efektivna Ekonomika. doi:10.2478/minib-2021-0011

Presenza, A., Abbate, T., Meleddu, M., & Sheehan, L. (2020). Start-up entrepreneurs' personality traits. An exploratory analysis of the Italian tourism industry. *Current Issues in Tourism, 23*(17), 2146–2164. doi:10.1080/13683500.2019.1677572

Rodriguez-Sanchez, I., Williams, A. M., & Brotons, M. (2019). The innovation journey of new-to-tourism entrepreneurs. *Current Issues in Tourism, 22*(8), 877–904. doi:10.1080/13683500.2017.1334763

Sharma, N. N. (2000). Ecotourism in North East India–A marketing Alternative in the next millennium. *Management and Labour Studies, 25*(3), 177–190. doi:10.1177/0258042X0002500303

Sharma, S., & Goyal, D. P. (2023). Startup-India: An exploratory analysis of issues, challenges, and the road ahead. *International Journal of Entrepreneurship and Small Business, 49*(2), 246–262. doi:10.1504/IJESB.2023.132442

Soares, J. C., & Conceição, R. B. (2016). A aplicação do conceito de cidade inteligente no turismo. *Ponta de Lança: Revista Eletrônica de História. Memória & Cultura, 10*(19), 128–145.

Sundaram, A. (2013). Look east policy. *International Journal of Advancements in Research & Technology, 2*(5), 169–185.

Techcrunch, (2018). Travel Start-ups an Taking Off. *Tech Crunch.* https://techcrunch. com/2018/11/11/travel-startups-are-taking-off/

Trzmielak, D. M., Shonia, D., & Skoneczna, M. (2021). Marketing, Start-Ups and Innovation: A Framework for Understanding the Possibilities for Harnessing Technological Innovations in Tourism (Based on the Example of the Georgian Tourism Sector and Russian Start-Ups). *Marketing of Scientific and Research Organizations, 40*(2), 93–113. doi:10.2478/minib-2021-0011

van den Berg, G. (2016). *The unfolding of innovation processes by start-ups in the tourism and service industry.*

Vargas-Sanchez, A. (2023). Toward a circular tourism industry: The importance of a start-up ecosystem. *Worldwide Hospitality and Tourism Themes, 15*(6), 625–632. doi:10.1108/WHATT-09-2023-0111

Wang, D., Li, X. R., & Li, Y. (2013). China's "smart tourism destination" initiative: A taste of the service-dominant logic. *Journal of Destination Marketing & Management, 2*(2), 59–61. doi:10.1016/j.jdmm.2013.05.004

Zhu, W., Zhang, L., & Li, N. (2014). Challenges, function changing of government and enterprises in Chinese smart tourism. *Information and communication technologies in tourism, 10*, 553-564.

ENDNOTE

[1]   https://www.statista.com/topics/4839/startups-in-india/

Chapter 7
Performance of ESG Funds Under the Shadow of Climate Policy Uncertainty:
The Sustainable Outline of India

Raktim Ghosh
 https://orcid.org/0000-0002-9595-9964
Maharaja Srischandra College, India

Biswajit Paul
University of Gour Banga, India

Bhaskar Bagchi
University of Gour Banga, India

ABSTRACT

This study empirically investigates the effects of the climate policy uncertainty (CPU) on the BSE 100 ESG during the study period December 2017 to August 2023 in the backdrop of the application of ESG reporting that was introduced in India in December 2009 with the voluntary guidelines issued by the Ministry of Corporate Affairs (MCA), Government of India. To address the objectives of the study, different econometric tools namely the FIGARCH model, Wavelet Coherence Analysis, Johansen Co-integration test, Wald test, and Philips-Perron unit root test, along with descriptive statistics are used. The study reveals a noteworthy volatility effect and the variability in the volatility on the BSE 100 ESG from the CPU index. Johansen's co-integration test confirms the presence of a long-run association between the select variables. However, the Wald test suggests the absence of short-run association. Furthermore, the FIGARCH model confirms the lack of a long-memory effect but there exists a substantial impact of CPU on the BSE 100 ESG established by the results of the Wavelet Coherence test.

DOI: 10.4018/979-8-3693-2197-3.ch007

INTRODUCTION

Climate change is one of the foremost problems the world is currently experiencing. Without significant action to reduce greenhouse gas (GHG) emissions, it is anticipated that the negative effects of climate change will worsen, increasing the risk of shattering outcomes, predominantly in developing nations where the poorest segments of society are expected to suffer the most. With limited resources for preventing climate-related disasters, adapting to them, and recovering from them, climate change thus poses a threat to the triumph of international poverty reduction and progress. Following such a circumstance, the Government of different nations makes necessary changes in their climatic policies to cater to the issues of sustainable development goals (SDGs).

Therefore, according to academics, the idea of sustainable development should be put into practice in order to address environmental problems (Zhou et al., 2023). As a result, using renewable energy has elevated to the top of the priority list. Many nations currently promote the use of clean, low-carbon energy to address environmental. As a result, it is frequently believed that in order to ensure environmental sustainability on a global scale, traditional fossil fuel-intensive energy sectors need to switch to renewable energy (Zhou et al., 2023).

Therefore, in the modern context, moving away from dependence on fossil fuels and towards dependence on renewable energy sources has been regarded as a feasible action plan for lowering the catastrophic environmental footprints linked to energy consumption (Zhou et al., 2023). The ratio of renewable energy use to total energy consumption is far from adequate, nevertheless. Furthermore, this scenario of low renewable energy is seen in both developed and developing countries (Zhou et al., 2023). Less than 10% of the world's energy supply in 2018 was derived from renewable energy, according to the International Energy Agency (IEA). Thus, a key component of the present economic development is increasing the use of renewable energy (Zhou et al., 2023).

Likewise, Environmental, Social, and Corporate Governance, or ESG is a crucial intangible assessing element for investors who are socially conscious and responsible. ESG reporting is no longer viewed as a cheap alternative. As they work to uphold the integrity of their commitments, trust, and duties both inside and throughout the extended company, organizations are putting more and more emphasis on ESG. Investors have depended on standardized and transparent financial reporting standards for many years to evaluate the performance of businesses, and now that possibility is being broadened to include financial plans. ESG approach. The governance, social, and environmental practices of the corporation are subjects of comprehensive disclosure requests from investors who place money in ESG outlay vehicles (Pandey et al., 2023). In making investment decisions and evaluating investments, consideration is being given to the sustainability of investments and compliance with environmental, social, and governance (ESG) standards. There is always a decision between chances for direct profit maximization and those where ESG is incorporated. ESG investing, usually referred to as socially responsible investing, has grown significantly since the start of the twenty-first century. The United Nations (UN) was at the forefront of the first activities in this field, which laid the foundation for ESG investment in 2004 (Pandey et al., 2023).

The MacKenzie quotation demonstrates how important ESG problems are in influencing company performance and reporting (Adams, 2017). This shift is important because, according to more than 50% of participants in a recent global study, "capitalism, as it exists today, does more harm than good in the world" (Edelman, 2020). ESG problems like poverty and climate change are at the core of this harm, and the United Nations encourages everyone to take action on these problems, including corporations, through the Sustainable Development Goals (United Nations Development Programme, 2015). The

COVID-19 crisis's effects have a negative influence that makes these issues worse (Wood, 2020). The world has fundamentally altered; thus, businesses must prepare for and respond to future ESG challenges.

Investors have become more proactive in recent years, concentrating on these non-financial concerns of social and environmental issues as part of their study to find niche investments with development potential and pinpoint significant dangers related to the choices (Seth et al., 2021).

The rest of the paper is structured as follows: section 2 presents the brief results of the existing studies along with the research gaps and objectives of the study; Section 3 discusses the research methodology; Section 4 confers the data analysis along with the corresponding discussions; Section 5 presents the significance of the study and Section 6 highlights the concluding observations.

REVIEW OF LITERATURE

The extant studies in the relevant area that are pertinent enough have been studied minutely and some fascinating results are prominent that are summarized below. Nonetheless, it needs to be mentioned that there is a dearth of literature in this particular area, so, the authors decided to consider literature belonging to environmental, social, and governance (ESG), climate policy uncertainty (CPU), and appropriate tools and techniques to be applied.

Mallek et al. (2024) look at the linear and non-linear effects of the ESG components on bank stock returns. It also looks into how bank size affects the relationship between bank stock performance and ESG. Applying generalized quantile regression to a sample of 59 banks from the 12 MENA nations between 2010 and 2021, findings point to a non-linear link between bank stock returns and ESG factors. Put otherwise, there may be a U-shaped, an inverted U-shaped, or no relationship at all between the ESG components and stock market results. Furthermore, the authors discover that the relationship between bank stock returns and the ESG pillars is influenced by size.

De Melo Neto & Fontgalland (2023) studied the returns and performances by comparing using the average return, and the risk measurement metrics—variance, standard deviation, volatility, and value at risk — as well as the computation of covariance, correlation, beta, and drawdown by using data from the MSCI ESG Leaders index. Since the average profitability of the ESG indices was greater in all nations over the study period compared to the broad index, the authors can corroborate the idea of long-term profits. The findings supported the idea that bigger organizations face more risks than ESG companies in terms of volatility risk metrics.

Hewa et al. (2023) intend to investigate how much Australian businesses react to the legal, physical, and economic risks brought on by climate change. It also looks at how much stakeholder pressure and the corporate governance system affect how much business reacts to risks by collecting 120 top-risk executives of Australian concerns. According to their study, corporations react to regulatory risks more so than physical and market hazards. In terms of the influence of stakeholder pressure, the findings demonstrate that pressure from the government, non-governmental organizations, rival businesses, and the media is generally favorably and substantially related to how businesses respond to climate change risk. Disaggregated analyses reveal variations in how the influence of specific stakeholder groups influences the company's reaction to physical dangers. In terms of corporate governance, the findings show that having a climate change risk committee and having female participation on the board of directors both help businesses respond to climate change risks more quickly.

Liu et al. (2023) using data from 1990 to 2020, explores the correlation between CO_2 and coal efficiency, climate policy uncertainty, green energy, and green innovation. They further investigated these relationships using wavelet cohesion, wavelet correlation, wavelet coherence, and the unique causality in continuous wavelet transform to assist policymakers in creating sustainable energy policies at various periods. The findings of wavelet coherence and wavelet cohesion showed that while climate policy uncertainty affects CO_2 emissions over the long run, coal efficiency helps to decrease CO_2 emissions at different frequencies and timeframes. Green energy use and innovation also enhance ecological quality by lowering CO_2 throughout the short- and medium-term. Additionally, wavelet causality analysis showed that all indicators were capable of forecasting CO_2 emissions at various frequencies and time scales. Based on the overall results of our study, we advise policymakers in the US to embrace energy efficiency and green energy efforts as the most efficient means of lowering CO_2 and addressing other serious climate challenges.

Savio et al. (2023) in order to comprehend what the academics uncovered, they intend to present a comprehensive literature review that can investigate the interaction between the ESG and COVID-19 epidemic. Eighty-five studies underwent a thorough assessment. They employed a systematic literature review method, which may guarantee that all pertinent information from the subject of the inquiry is taken into account. This method is regarded as the most thorough and rigorous since it enables the generation of new information about a particular issue. In order to accommodate the key subjects discussed in the literature (investment and stock returns, ESG in particular industries, ESG grading, gender studies, ESG reporting, and others), the authors defined five classes plus a residual one. The study shows that only a small number of studies have been devoted to the other subjects, while the majority of studies have been concentrated on the foremost three themes, often coming to contradictory or divergent conclusions. The necessity for more study into the ESG/COVID-19 combo in the areas of gender variety and ESG reporting, as well as additional research able to comprehend the various findings of the other three indicated subjects, is thus stated.

Broadstock et al. (2021) examine how ESG performance fared throughout the global financial crisis as a result of the occurrence of the COVID-19 pandemic. It was observed that during a crisis, ESG performance reduces financial risk. Moreover, portfolios with a high ESG performance typically beat ones with a low ESG performance.

Gavriilidis, K. (2021) establishes a new metric for climate policy uncertainty based on information from significant US newspapers. The Climate Policy Uncertainty (CPU) index increases in the vicinity of significant advances in climate policy, including new emission regulations, worldwide climate change protests, and presidential pronouncements. According to the study, CO_2 emissions are strongly and negatively impacted by the uncertainty of climate policy.

Fuss et al. (2008) examine the effects of knowing that the government is committed to a climate policy regime in the context of genuine alternatives. Market-determined price instability about a mean price and diverging price trails simulating uncertainty about shifting policy regimes are two distinct forms of uncertainty considered in this study. They observed that the producer invests in carbon-saving equipment earlier than if the real price trend had been known beforehand when faced with market uncertainty regarding CO_2 costs. However, policy uncertainty makes the producer wait to see if the government would continue to support climate policy. This waiting effect has genuine options i.e. if learning about government assurance is more important than investing in mitigation technologies right away, the investment will be delayed since the option value is greater than the value of the technology. Supply issues and a slow spread of lower carbon-concentrated know-how might result from this.

After a minute examination of the existing literature, it is witnessed that studies in the Indian context are hard to find. Moreover, studies belonging to the relatable area in the other countries are theoretical in nature. Furthermore, it is worth mentioning that none of the authors have made any endeavor to empirically inspect the effects of the climate policy uncertainty on the Indian Environmental, Social, and Governance or ESG funds. These can be enlisted as the research gap within the prevailing works.

The above-mentioned research lacunas allow the authors to finalize the objectives of the present study to understand the performance of ESG funds in India following the effect of climate policy uncertainty. So, the authors decided first, to study the dynamic relationship between climate policy uncertainty and ESG funds, second, to study the long-run causality between climate policy uncertainty and ESG funds, third, to study the short-run causality between climate policy uncertainty and ESG funds and finally, to study the long-memory effect of the climate policy uncertainty on the ESG funds in the Indian context.

RESEARCH METHODOLOGY

The application of ESG reporting was first introduced in India in December 2009 with the voluntary guidelines issued by the Ministry of Corporate Affairs (MCA), Government of India on Corporate Social Responsibility (https://www.mca.gov.in/Ministry/latestnews/National_Voluntary_Guidelines_2011_12jul2011. pdf) but, SEBI's guidelines required the top 100 publicly traded companies to file a BRR and added the requirement for ESG reporting (https://www.mca.gov.in/Ministry/pdf/BRR_11082020.pdf).

We consider the monthly data of S&P BSE 100 ESG from December 2017 to August 2023 due to the unavailability of data from 2012. Furthermore, the climate policy uncertainty index developed by Konstantinos Gavriilidis in "Measuring Climate Policy Uncertainty" is considered the proxy for climate policy uncertainty and is included as a variable in this study. All the data are converted into corresponding natural logarithmic returns to eliminate the innate disadvantages associated with time series data.

To address the objectives of the study, the Philips-Peron unit root test, Johansen Co-integration test, Wald tests, FIGARCH (1,d,1) model as well as Wavelet Coherence method along with descriptive statistics are used.

The unit root test will be able to identify the existence of any stationarity within the time series dataset. Likewise, the Johansen Co-integration test will allow us to measure the long-run causality within the select variables. Moreover, the Wald test captures the existence of any short-run causality, the FIGARCH model helps to capture the long-memory effects within the dependent variable over a specific period, and finally, the Wavelet Coherence method will enable to capture the co-movements of the variables along with the effects graphically.

Variables of the Study

The methodology presented in "Measuring Economic Policy Uncertainty" by Scott R. Baker, Nicholas Bloom, and Steven J. Davis is adhered to by Gavriilidis. To create the Climate Policy Uncertainty index, he searches for articles from April 1987 onwards in eight of the top US newspapers that contain the terms "uncertainty" or "uncertain" and "carbon dioxide" or "climate" or "climate risk" or "greenhouse gas emissions" or "greenhouse" or "CO_2," or "emissions" or "global warming" or "climate change" or "green energy" or "renewable energy" or "environmental" and "regulation" or "legislation" or "White House" or "Congress" or "EPA" or "law" or "policy" (including variants like "uncertainties", "regulatory", "policies", etc.). The Wall Street Journal, USA Today, the New York Times, the Tampa Bay Times, the Los Angeles Times, the Miami Herald, the Boston Globe, and the Chicago Tribune are the eight newspapers. He divides the monthly total of relevant articles for each newspaper by the total number of articles published in that same month. These eight series are then averaged across newspapers by month after being standardized to have a unit standard deviation. Lastly, a mean value of 100 is assigned to the averaged series covering the period from April 1987 to August 2022 (https://www.policyuncertainty. com/climate_uncertainty.html).

The S&P BSE 100 ESG Index is a market capitalization (FMC) weighted index that is adjusted for flotation. Its purpose is to quantify the exposure to stocks that satisfy sustainability investing standards while preserving a risk and return profile akin to that of the S&P BSE 100 (the "underlying index"). Using an S&P DJI Environmental, Social, and Governance (ESG) score as the defining characteristic, the index aims to capture 75 per cent of the float-adjusted market capitalization of each Global Industry Classification Standard (GICS) Industry Group within the relevant underlying index. Additionally, the index applies exclusions based on a company's enactment against the philosophies of the United Nations Global Compact, its involvement in pertinent ESG controversies, and its involvement in particular business activities (https://www.spglobal.com/spdji/en/documents/methodologies/methodology-sp-bse-100-esg-index.pdf).

Philips-Peron (PP) Unit Root Test

Phillips and Perron (1988) propose an alternative (non-parametric) method of controlling for serial correlation when testing for a unit root. To mitigate the impact of serial correlation on the test statistic's asymptotic distribution, the PP method computes the non-augmented DF test equation and modifies the coefficient's ratio. The PP test is based on the following statistics:

$$\tilde{t}_\alpha = t_\alpha \left(\frac{\gamma_0}{f_0} \right)^{1/2} - \frac{T(f_0 - \gamma_0)(se(\hat{\alpha}))}{2f_0^{1/2}s} \dots \tag{1}$$

Where s is the test regression standard error, $\hat{\alpha}$ is the estimate, and t_α the ratio of α is the coefficient standard error. A consistent estimate of the error variance is also provided γ_0, and it is computed as (T – k) s^2/T, where k is the number of repressors. An estimator of the residual band at frequency zero is found in the remaining term, f_0.

The authors consider this study to be noteworthy and unique of its kind. The reasons are several. Firstly, in order to provide a thorough knowledge of how policy uncertainty affects ESG investing, this study looks at how uncertainty in climate policy impacts each of the three factors. Secondly, investors and policymakers can better navigate a landscape that is rapidly changing by understanding how these uncertainties distress ESG funds, ensuring that investments are in line with sustainable goals despite political unpredictability. Moreover, studying how climate policy uncertainty affects ESG funds reveals how long-term investment objectives are impacted by short-term policy swings, offering insights into the adaptability and durability of sustainable investing strategies. Additionally, it needs to be mentioned that ESG portfolio risk management strategies and the capacity to reduce market risks brought on by regulatory uncertainty can both be evaluated by looking at how ESG funds react to these uncertainties. Uncertainty around climate policy affects sustainable economic growth and has larger economic ramifications. Examining how it affects ESG funds enables one to gauge the potential contribution of sustainable investments to economic growth and stability in the face of changing policies.

Johansen Co-Integration Test

The Co-integration test propounded by Johansen measures the long-run causality between the select variables within a time series model. Johansen's approach begins with the vector autoregression (VAR) of order p provided by:

$$y_t = \mu + A_1 y_{t-1} + \ldots + A_p y_{t-p} + \varepsilon_t \ldots \tag{2}$$

Where y_t is an n*1 vector of first-order integrated variable noted by I(I) and ε_t is the vector of innovation of n*1 innovation. The VAR can be denoted as:

$$\Delta y_t = \mu + \Pi y_{t-1} + \sum_{i=1}^{p-1} \Gamma_i \Delta y_{t-i} + \varepsilon_t \ldots \tag{3}$$

Where,

$$\Pi = \sum_{i=1}^{p} A_i - I \text{ and } \Gamma_i = -\sum_{j=i+1}^{p} A_j \ldots \tag{4}$$

The alternative hypothesis of n co-integrating vectors is tested against the null hypothesis of r co-integrating vectors using the trace test. Conversely, the maximum eigenvalue test verifies the null alternative hypothesis of r + 1 co-integrating vectors against the hypothesis of r co-integrating vectors. Asymptotic critical values are provided by most econometric software packages and can be found in Johansen and Juselius (1990); neither of these test statistics generally follows a chi-square distribution. When the variables in the system are near unit root processes, the critical values used for the maximum eigenvalue and trace test statistics which are predicated on a pure unit root assumption will no longer hold true. Johansen (1995) asserts that there is a minute need to pre-test the variables in the arrangement to establish their order of integration, even though his methodology is usually applied in a setting where all of the system's variables are I(1). Nevertheless, having stationary variables in the system is theoretically not a problem. The presence of a single variable that is I(0) rather than I(1) will be shown by a co-integrating vector whose space is traversed by the single stationary variable in the framework (https://www.imf.org/external/pubs/ft/wp/2007/wp07141.pdf).

The Johansen Co-integration test is widely applied in studies Kaur and Dhiman (2024), Zorgati et al. (2024), Mohnot et al. (2024), and Raphael (2024) to determine the long run association in stock markets.

Wald Test

The Wald test captures the short-run causality between the select variables within a time series framework. The Wald test is typically predicated on an asymptotically normal estimator i.e., $\hat{\theta}$ where the null hypothesis fulfils the property:

$$\hat{\theta} \xrightarrow{d} N(\theta_0, \sigma_0^2) \dots \tag{5}$$

Where, σ_0^2 under the null, is the estimator's variance.

It may be noted that if the parameters associated with any variables are not zero the variables should be included in the model if the Wald test is significant for an explanatory variable or group of related explanatory variables. These explanatory variables can be removed from the model if the Wald test results show that they are not significant. In the case of a single explanatory variable, Altman (1991) employs a t-test to determine the significance of the parameter. The Wald statistic is simply the t-statistic squared for a single parameter, so the results are the same (https://www.blackwellpublishing.com/specialarticles/jcn_10_774.pdf).

Recent studies by Hong et al. (2024), Kurtoglu and Durusu-Ciftci (2024), Simran and Sharma (2024), and Chatterjee et al. (2024) have used the Wald test to determine the short-run association among the stock markets.

Fractionally Integrated GARCH (FIGARCH) Model

Baillie, Bollerslev, and Mikkelsen (1996) presented the fractionally integrated generalized autoregressive conditional heteroscedasticity (FIGARCH) model. We omit some details by closely adhering to their model specification.

The effect of the lag squared innovations (unexpected return shocks) on the conditional variance declines at a slow, hyperbolic rate according to the FIGARCH model. Consequently, in contrast to the IGARCH model, the FIGARCH model can arrest long-memory effects while still permitting the shocks to decay. We examine the FIGARCH (p,d,q) model to gain a better understanding. In this model, p governs the number of AR lags (GARCH effect), and q determines the number of MA lags (ARCH effect). It is significant to note that, unlike in the simple GARCH model, the coefficient of the ARCH effect in the FIGARCH model is ϕ rather than α. However, it will still be interpreted similarly, that is, as the impact of the unexpected shocks and, consequently, as the ARCH parameter (Mensi et al., 2019). The process exhibits long memory for the conditional variance when $0 < d < 1$, but it will eventually die out (Mensi et al., 2019). The FIGARCH model's memory increases as the fractional differencing parameter d approaches 1 (Ghalanos, 2020). Moreover, the FIGARCH meets the IGARCH model at $d = 1$ and collapses to a basic GARCH at $d = 0$. Constructing an ARMA $(1,1)$ process model for the return series:

$$r_t = \mu + \vartheta r_{t-1} + n_t + \zeta n_{t-1} \dots \tag{6}$$

enables us to include an AR and an MA effect in the mean equation already, where the unpredicted return shock (error term) is represented by ηt. Assuming ηt is a real-valued stochastic process with discrete time:

$$n_t \equiv \varepsilon_t \sigma_t \dots \tag{7}$$

Where, $\varepsilon t \sim (0,1)$ and $\eta t \sim (0, \sigma t\, 2)$

The conditional variance series can be modelled as a FIGARCH $(1,d,1)$ process, where σt is a time-varying function that represents the presented information set at time $t-1$.

The following equation can be used to display a FIGARCH (p,d,q) process:

$$\varphi(L)(1-L)^d n_t^2 = \omega + [1 - \beta(L)]v_t \dots \qquad (8)$$

Where L is the backshift operator defined to lag the coefficients:

$$\varphi(L) = [1 - \alpha(L) - \beta(L)](1-L)^{-1} \dots \qquad (9)$$

$$\alpha(L) = \alpha_1 L + \alpha_2 L^2 + \dots + \alpha_q L^q \dots \qquad (10)$$

$$\beta(L) = \beta_1 L + \beta_2 L^2 + \dots + \beta_p L^p \dots \qquad (11)$$

The following is the fractional differencing operator:

$$(1-L)^d = \sum_{k=0}^{\infty} \frac{\Gamma(d+1)}{\Gamma(k+1)\Gamma(d-k+1)} L^k \dots \qquad (12)$$

In which $\Gamma(z)$ outlines the gamma function:

$$\Gamma(z) = \int_{x=0}^{x=\infty} x^{z-1} e^{-x} dx \dots \qquad (13)$$

Rearranging equation (8) as:

$$v_t = n_t^2 - \sigma_t^2 \dots \qquad (14)$$

Produces the following expression for the FIGARCH (p,d,q):

$$[1 - \beta(L)]\sigma_t^2 = \omega + [1 - \beta(L) - \varphi(L)(1-L)^d]n_t^2 \dots \qquad (15)$$

Next, we get the conditional variance of the random process ηt, which is as follows:

$$\sigma_t^2 = \omega[1 - \beta(L)]^{-1} + \{1 - [1 - \beta(L)]^{-1}\varphi(L)(1-L)^d\}n_t^2 \dots \qquad (16)$$

We think that by using this method, we can accurately simulate the dynamics without having to make ad hoc parameter choices. We manually equate the conditional volatility series from each subseries with the sample volatility series and the conditional volatility series of the entire data set to see if the corresponding parts resemble each other to validate our obtained results (Chen and Ulmer, 2021).

Wavelet Coherence (WTC) Analysis

This study measures the dynamic relationship along with the co-movements of the select variables namely BSE 100 ESG and CPU under the framework of bivariate Wavelet Coherence (WTC) modelled by Torrence and Compo (1998) where the idea of Wavelet Coherence Analysis is used to enable the cross-wavelet transformations of two-time series x(t) and y(t). The model equation can be framed as:

$$W_{xy}(u,s) = W_x(u,s) \; W_y^*(u,s) \; \dots\dots\dots\dots\dots\dots \tag{17}$$

Where, $W_x(u,s)$ and $W_y(u,s)$ are the continuous wavelet transforms of x(t) and y(t), respectively; u represents the position index and s the scale; while a composite conjugate is indicated by the symbol *. The cross-wavelet transform $\left|W_{xy}(u,s)\right|$ makes it simple to calculate the cross-wavelet power. The cross-wavelet power, which quantifies the local covariance between the time series at each scale, identifies regions in the time-frequency space where the time series shows a high common power. The time series under examination may exhibit co-movement in specific regions of the time-frequency space; however, this co-movement does not necessarily have a significant common power. We define the squared wavelet coherence coefficient as follows, following the methodology of Torrence and Webster (1999):

$$R^2(u,s) = \frac{\left|S(s^{-1}W_{xy}(u,s))\right|^2}{S(s^{-1}\left|W_x(u,s)\right|^2)S(s^{-1}\left|W_y(u,s)\right|^2)} \; \dots\dots \tag{18}$$

S functions as a smoothing operator in this case. The squared wavelet coherence coefficient ranges in the following manner $0 \leq R^2(u,s) \leq 1$. Numbers near zero suggest a weak link, whereas numbers near one indicate a significant correlation. Thus, the squared wavelet coherence, which is the same as the squared correlation coefficient in linear regression, quantifies the local linear correlation between two stationary time series at each scale.

Nevertheless, the use of wavelets raises the issue of controlling boundary conditions on a finite-length dataset. This is a typical issue with transformations based on filters. In our study, we tackle this problem by following Grinsted et al. (2004) and appropriately increasing the number of zeroes in the time series. The zone of influence, as defined by Grinsted et al. (2004), is the region where errors or edge effects resulting from discontinuities in wavelet transforms cannot be disregarded. The effect cone is enclosed by a cone with a thin black line.

RESULTS AND DISCUSSIONS

Descriptive Statistics

Table 1. Descriptive statistics results of BSE 100 ESG and CPU

	BSE 100 ESG	**CPU**
Mean	0.0094	0.0011
Median	0.0083	-0.0004
Maximum	0.1519	1.2326
Minimum	-0.2661	-0.9438
Std. Dev.	0.0554	0.3511
Skewness	-1.5176	0.3001
Kurtosis	10.5905	4.2441
Jarque-Bera	189.3485	5.4065
Probability	0.00*	0.0669***
Sum	0.6446	0.0781
Sum Sq. Dev.	0.2059	8.261
Observations	68	68

(* indicates significance at 1% level, *** indicates significance at 10% level)

Table 1 displays the results of the descriptive statistics of the select variables namely BSE 100 ESG and CPU with 68 sample observations.

Figure 1. QQ Plot of BSE 100 ESG and CPU

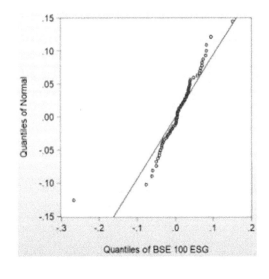
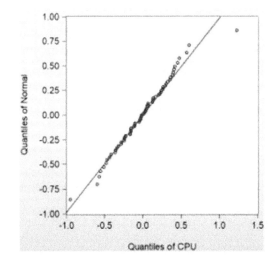

It is observed that both the variables are non-normal in nature at 1 per cent and 10 per cent levels respectively confirmed by the results of the Jarque-Bera test along with the QQ plot in Figure 1. BSE 100 ESG increases to the highest of 0.1519 and reduces to the lowest of -0.2661 with a mean value of 0.0094. Likewise, CPU increases to 1.2326 and declines to -0.9438 with an average of 0.0011. Skewness is within the allowable range and the standard deviation is also significantly less.

This implies that the mean for BSE 100 ESG is relatively tiny, and there is a significant variation. The CPU exhibits a significant range with a near-zero mean. A much lower standard deviation suggests that there is comparatively little variety, with the data points being grouped around the mean.

Philips-Peron (PP) Unit Root Test

Table 2. Philips-Peron unit root test results of the select variables

Variables	At Level		At First Difference	
	Adj. t-Stat	Prob.*	Adj. t-Stat	Prob.*
BSE 100 ESG	-5.9182	0.00*	-34.6957	0.0001*
CPU	-2.1401	0.5144	-92.1626	0.0001*

(* indicates significance at 1% level)

Table 2 signifies the results of the PP unit root test where it is observed that the BSE 100 ESG index is significant at 1 per cent level at both levels and the first difference indicates the non-existence of unit root. On the contrary, the CPU index is insignificant at the level but significant at first difference indicating the existence of unit root at the level but free from unit root problem at first difference.

Lag Selection Criteria

Table 3. Optimal lag length

Lag	LogL	LR	FPE	AIC	SC	HQ
0	65.6137	NA	0.0004	-2.0520	-1.8652	-1.9903
1	70.2052	8.7386	0.0004*	-2.0711*	-1.9834*	-2.0251*
2	72.5365	4.2865	0.0004	-2.0173	-1.6742	-1.8826
3	74.4855	3.4578	0.0004	-1.9511	-1.4708	-1.7625
4	78.2097	6.3672	0.0004	-1.9422	-1.3246	-1.6997
5	82.2849	6.7043	0.0004	-1.9446	-1.1898	-1.6483
6	88.9791	10.5811*	0.0004	-2.0315	-1.1395	-1.6813

(* indicates optimal lag length)

The optimal lag length is selected as 1 considering the results of the lag selection criteria table denoting 1 as the optimal lag as per FPE, AIC, SC, and HQ.

Johansen Co-Integration Test

Table 4. Johansen co-integration test results of the select variables

Hypothersized No. of CE(s)	Eigenvalue	Trace Statistics	0.05 Critical Value	Max Eigen Statistics	0.05 Critical Value	Prob.**
None **	0.4213	55.8136	15.4947	35.5607	14.2646	0.00*
At most 1 **	0.2677	20.2528	3.8414	20.2528	3.8414	0.00*

(* indicates significance at 1% level)
(** indicates 2 co-integrating equations)

Table 4 portrays the results of the Johansen Co-integration test which captures the long-run association among the select variables BSE 100 ESG index and the CPU index. Both the trace statistics and the max-eigen statistics indicate the long-run association between the BSE 100 ESG index and the CPU index. The p-value is significant at a 1 per cent level with a 99 per cent confidence interval confirming the long-run co-movements.

This indicates that there is a fundamental relationship or underlying economic equilibrium between the CPU index and the BSE 100 ESG index. The BSE 100 ESG index's incorporation of ESG criteria suggests that environmental, social, and governance factors are relevant. The stock market and technology businesses may be impacted by adjustments in investor preferences toward socially accountable financing or changes in corporate governance procedures. Moreover, events in one market might have repercussions in other markets within a globally interconnected financial system. Global factors that are common to both the CPU index and the BSE 100 ESG index may have an impact over a long-run time horizon (https://www.indexologyblog.com/2020/04/28/the-sp-bse-100-esg-index-a-socially-responsible-investment-strategy/).

Wald Test

Table 5. Wald test results of the select variables

C(1) = 0			
Test Statistic	**Value**	**df**	**Probability**
t-statistic	-0.1756	67	0.8611
F-statistic	0.0308	(1, 67)	0.8611
Chi-square	0.0308	1	0.8606

Table 5 demonstrates the results of the Wald statistics where it is observed that there is no association between the select variables BSE 100 ESG index and the CPU index over a short-run time period due to an insignificant p-value. There are several reasons behind such performance. First, some of the BSE 100 listed industries might be more resilient to policy uncertainty in the near term because of their diverse business methods or due to their environmental effect are less susceptible to sudden changes in regulations. This may be a factor in the absence of a direct correlation with ESG scores. Second, ESG metrics reporting timelines might not coincide with transient variations in the unpredictability of climate policy. Businesses may publish ESG reports annually or on a quarterly basis, and these reports may not update instantly to reflect changes brought on by ambiguous policies. Finally, momentary or alterable policy changes may be linked to short-term variations in climate policy uncertainty. Businesses may take a wait-and-see stance in the hopes that policy uncertainty will be cleared up or stabilized soon, which would cause an impact on ESG scores to be postponed.

Fractionally Integrated GARCH (FIGARCH) (1,d,1) Model

Table 6. FIGARCH (1,d,1) results of BSE 100 ESG

Dependent Variable: BSE 100 ESG					
Independent Variable	**Parameters**	**Coefficient**	**Std. Error**	**z-Statistic**	**Prob.**
CPU	Constant (ω)	0.0065	0.0098	0.6654	0.5058
	ARCH (α)	0.5351	0.2579	2.0749	0.038**
	GARCH (β)	-0.3462	0.0801	-4.3221	0.00*
	Long Memory (d)	-0.0106	0.2519	-0.0422	0.9663
	$\alpha+\beta$		0.1889		

(* indicates significance at 1 per cent level, ** indicates significance at 5 per cent level)

The above table 6 embodies the results of the FIGARCH model where it is observed that there exists a significant volatility on BSE 100 ESG due to the effect of CPU. Moreover, the β term confirms the variability of the volatility in BSE 100 ESG which is also noteworthy. However, it is also relevant to mention that the coefficient of the ARCH term is positive indicating positive volatility whereas the coefficient of the GARCH term is negative indicating a negative variability in volatility. A negative coefficient indicates that the volatility of the present is tempered by past forecast errors. Decisions made on climate policy can have a big impact on businesses, especially those that prioritize the social, environmental, and governance aspects. The d term is insignificant confirming the absence of a long-memory effect within BSE 100 ESG. The $\alpha+\beta$ term is also very small indicating a quick decay of the volatility over time. This suggests that shocks have a comparatively short-subsisted impact on volatility since their impact fades quickly.

The authors consider the novelty of the study conducted by Cochran et al., (2012) that made to apply the FIGARCH model.

Wavelet Coherence (WTC) Analysis

Figure 2. Heatmap of wavelet coherence analysis between CPU and S&P BSE 100 ESG

CPU vs S&P BSE 100 ESG

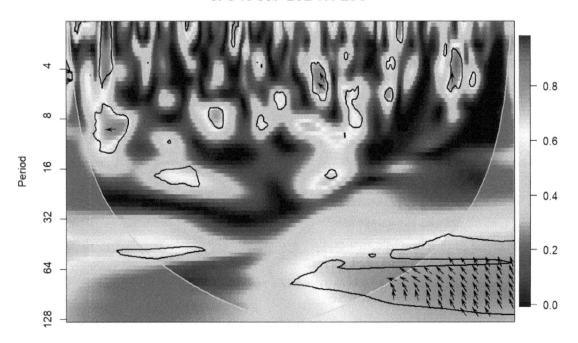

The above figure 2 outlays the heatmap of the bivariate Wavelet Coherence (WTC) Analysis between CPU and S&P BSE 100 ESG index during the study period December 2017 to August 2023. The significant effect of CPU is noted within BSE 100 ESG throughout the study period. This effect is confirmed by the red and the yellow patches within the contour inside the black cone. However, it is noteworthy to mention that the effect is greater during the initial part of the study period although the effect is also evident in the later months. There remains a negative effect of the CPU on the BSE 100 ESG confirmed by the leftward arrows (←) and the northwest arrows (↖) within the effect patches throughout the study period. This negative effect might be due to several reasons. Companies listed in the BSE 100 ESG may face regulatory risks due to the ambiguity surrounding climate policy. Businesses and industries that depend largely on environmental regulations or are heavily regulated may find it difficult to adjust to changing regulatory environments. Moreover, prices of the stock and ESG behavior may suffer if investors become wary of businesses operating in industries that are vulnerable to climate-related laws. Furthermore, uncertain rules may make it difficult for businesses to validate an obligation to environmental sustainability, which may make it difficult for them to draw in environmentally sensitive investors and customers (Settembre-Blundo et al., 2021).

The blue patches within the contour inside the cone indicate a comparatively cooler zone having no effect on the CPU on the BSE 100 ESG. Furthermore, it needs to be mentioned that the yellow and red patches also appear outside the cone indicating a spillover effect for a prolonged time.

SIGNIFICANCE OF THE STUDY

There is several relevance of this present study. First, this study adds new and innovative findings to the body of the existing literature gathered from the FIGARCH model and the Wavelet Coherence Analysis which are unique of its kind in terms of methodology. Second, uncertainty surrounding climate policy can have a big influence on the investing landscape, particularly for ESG funds that give environmental concerns priority. For investors who base their decisions on sustainability criteria, it is imperative to comprehend how these funds operate in such an unstable environment. Third, this study sheds light on ESG funds' risk management tactics in the face of ambiguous climate policies. Investment returns may be impacted by financial market volatility brought on by policy changes. For risk-averse investors, it is critical to comprehend how ESG funds handle this volatility. Finally, a global priority is matching investments to sustainable development objectives. The study's conclusions can help us comprehend how ESG funds assist SDGs in the framework of India, a nation that places a high priority on sustainable development.

CONCLUSION

This study has shed light on the performance of the BSE 100 ESG of India amid encounters postured by the CPU. The dataset can be identified as non-normal during the study period that outlines long-run relationships among themselves. However, it is also significant to note that there is no short-run relationship between the variables. A positive volatility is noted in BSE 100 ESG as a result of CPU against a negative variance in volatility. This indicates that the CPU is sufficient enough to affect the BSE 100 ESG and make its performance much more volatile. On the contrary, there is no long-memory effect that is in line with moral and environmental principles, sustainable investing has the potential to be a strong investment strategy that reduces risk to some extent in the face of unforeseen circumstances. The study has also emphasized how crucial it is to incorporate ESG considerations into strategic asset allocation, as doing so may help investors as well as the larger financial ecosystem. Wavelet coherence establishes the effect of CPU on BSE 100 ESG graphically through a heatmap identified by different colors across time and periods.

The goal of Indian policymakers should be to create a coherent and a uniform framework for climate policy. Investors may become confused by unclear climate policy, which could negatively impact the performance of the ESG funds. A stable regulatory framework would help investors make better judgments, which would lead to the expansion of the ESG industry. Furthermore, necessary impetus can be provided for attracting investments in the ESG.

There is ample scope to conduct further research on the area by studying the switching behaviour of the ESG funds in India in the backdrop of CPU. Moreover, switching GARCH model can also be used to study the switching volatility across different regimes.

The limitation of the study lies in using the monthly data. Daily or weekly data would have provided greater sample size with better results. Moreover, the application of tools like MS GARCH along with the DCC-MGARCH model would have provided some more interesting outcomes.

Author Contribution Statement

Conceptualization, BB and RG; Methodology, BB and RG.; Software, BB and BP; Validation, BB and BP; Formal Analysis, BB and BP; Investigation, BB and RG; Resources, BB and BP; Data Curation, RG; Writing—Original Draft Preparation, RG; Writing—Review and Editing, BB; Visualization, BP; Supervision, BB. All authors have read and agreed to the published version of the manuscript.

Funding

This research received no external funding.

Data Availability Statement

We used data to support the results of the findings in our study, which are included in Section 4, with the analysis and findings of the manuscript. The datasets used and/or analyzed during the current study are available from the corresponding author upon reasonable request.

Conflict of Interest

The authors declare that there are no conflicts of interest in this present article.

ACKNOWLEGEMENT

The authors make an honest effort to express their deep sense of gratitude towards the esteemed editors and the anonymous referees for their valuable suggestions that have helped to complete this study. The authors also sincerely acknowledge the kind and invaluable suggestions of Dr. Ashish Kumar Sana, Professor, Department of Commerce, University of Calcutta that have helped to give shape to the present article.

REFERENCES

Adams, C. A. (2017). Conceptualizing the contemporary corporate value creation process. *Accounting, Auditing & Accountability Journal, 30*(4), 906–931. doi:10.1108/AAAJ-04-2016-2529

Altman, D. G. (1991). *Practical Statistics for Medical Research*. Chapman & Hall. https://books.google. co.in/books?hl=en&lr=&id=Y5ebDwAAQBAJ&oi=fnd&pg=PP1&dq=Altman,+D.+G.+(1991).+Pr actical+Statistics+for+Medical+Research.+Chapman+%26+Hall,+London&ots=iohvI168Qk&sig=k xPmZ5AEgUXmKcyb35ZgON_h-wI&redir_esc=y#v=onepage&q&f=false

Baillie, R. T., Bollerslev, T., & Mikkelsen, H. O. (1996). Fractionally integrated generalized autoregressive conditional heteroskedasticity. *Journal of Econometrics*, *74*(1), 3–30. doi:10.1016/S0304-4076(95)01749-6

Broadstock, D. C., Chan, K., Cheng, L. T., & Wang, X. (2021). The role of ESG performance during times of financial crisis: Evidence from COVID-19 in China. *Finance Research Letters*, *38*, 101716. doi:10.1016/j.frl.2020.101716 PMID:32837385

Chatterjee, T., Bhattacharjee, K., & Das, R. C. (2024). Long-run and Short-run Dynamic Linkages Among Capacity Utilization, Inflation and Per Capita Income: Theoretical and Empirical Enquiries for Panel of Countries. *Global Business Review*, *09721509231219318*, 09721509231219318. Advance online publication. doi:10.1177/09721509231219318

Chen, L., & Ulmer, J. (2021). Volatility and Risk – FIGARCH Modelling of Cryptocurrencies, https://lup.lub.lu.se/luur/download?func=downloadFile&recordOId=9050072&fileOId=9050077

Cochran, S. J., Mansur, I., & Odusami, B. (2012). Volatility persistence in metal returns: A FIGARCH approach. *Journal of Economics and Business*, *64*(4), 287–305. doi:10.1016/j.jeconbus.2012.03.001

de Melo Neto, J. J., & Fontgalland, I. L. (2023). The BRICS in the sustainable agenda: Performance analysis of ESG indices in the financial markets in Brazil, China, India and South Africa. *International Journal of Business, Economics and Management, 10*(1), 1-11. https://ideas.repec.org/a/pkp/ijobem/v10y2023i1p1-11id3325.html

Edelman. (2020). Washington, DC: Depicting trans spatialities. In *Transvitalities* (pp. 30–56). Routledge. doi:10.4324/9781351128025-3

Fuss, S., Szolgayova, J., Obersteiner, M., & Gusti, M. (2008). Investment under market and climate policy uncertainty. *Applied Energy*, *85*(8), 708–721. doi:10.1016/j.apenergy.2008.01.005

GavriilidisK. (2021). Measuring Climate Policy Uncertainty. SSRN. https://ssrn.com/abstract=3847388 doi:10.2139/ssrn.3847388

Ghalanos, A. (2020). *Introduction to the rugarch package*. (Version 1.4-3). Cran R Project. https://cran.r-project.org/web/packages/rugarch/vignettes/Introduction_to _the_rugarch_package.pdf

Grinsted, A., Moore, J. C., & Jevrejeva, S. (2004). Application of the cross wavelet transform and wavelet coherence to geophysical time series. *Nonlinear Processes in Geophysics*, *11*(5/6), 561–566. doi:10.5194/npg-11-561-2004

Hewa, S. I., Chen, J., & Mala, R. (2023). Corporate responses to climate change risks: Evidence from Australia. *Australasian Journal of Environmental Management*, *30*(2), 1–27. doi:10.1080/14486563.2023.2220297

Hong, Y., Zhang, R., & Zhang, F. (2024). Time-varying causality impact of economic policy uncertainty on stock market returns: Global evidence from developed and emerging countries. *International Review of Financial Analysis*, *91*, 102991. doi:10.1016/j.irfa.2023.102991

Johansen, S. (1988). Statistical Analysis of Cointegration Vectors. *Journal of Economic Dynamics & Control*, *12*(2–3), 231–254. doi:10.1016/0165-1889(88)90041-3

Johansen, S., & Juselius, K. (1990). Maximum Likelihood Estimation and Inference on Cointegration– with Applications to the Demand for Money. *Oxford Bulletin of Economics and Statistics, 52*(2), 169–210. doi:10.1111/j.1468-0084.1990.mp52002003.x

Kaur, G., & Dhiman, B. (2024). Co-integration and Causal Relationship between Energy Commodities and Energy Stock Index: Empirical Evidence from India. In *BIO Web of Conferences* (*Vol. 86*, p. 01053). EDP Sciences. 10.1051/bioconf/20248601053

Kurtoglu, B., & Durusu-Ciftci, D. (2024). Identifying the nexus between financial stability and economic growth: the role of stability indicators. *Journal of Financial Economic Policy.* doi:10.1108/JFEP-09-2023-0260

Liu, X., Adebayo, T. S., Ramzan, M., Ullah, S., Abbas, S., & Olanrewaju, V. O. (2023). Do coal efficiency, climate policy uncertainty, and green energy consumption promote environmental sustainability in the United States? An application of novel wavelet tools. *Journal of Cleaner Production, 417,* 137851. doi:10.1016/j.jclepro.2023.137851

Mallek, S., Albaity, M., Ur-Rehman, I., & Thangavelu, S. (2024). *The puzzle of convex/concave ESG returns and large banks in MENA region countries.* Borsa Istanbul Review. doi:10.1016/j.bir.2024.03.007

Mensi, W., Al-Yahyaee, K. H., & Kang, S. H. (2019). Structural breaks and double long memory of cryptocurrency prices: A comparative analysis from Bitcoin and Ethereum. *Finance Research Letters, 29,* 222–230. doi:10.1016/j.frl.2018.07.011

Mohnot, R., Banerjee, A., Ballaj, H., & Sarker, T. (2024). Re-examining asymmetric dynamics in the relationship between macroeconomic variables and stock market indices: Empirical evidence from Malaysia. *The Journal of Risk Finance, 25*(1), 19–34. doi:10.1108/JRF-09-2023-0216

Pandey, A., Tiwari, D., & Singh, R. (2023). Environmental Social and Governance Reporting in India: An Overview. *EPRA International Journal of Multidisciplinary Research (IJMR), 9*(8), 47-51. https://www.eprajournals.net/index.php/IJMR/article/view/2554

Raphael, G. (2024). Causality between Financial Development and Foreign Direct Investment: Evidence from Tanzania. *International Journal of Business, Law, and Education, 5*(1), 158–176. doi:10.56442/ijble.v5i1.242

Savio, R., D'Andrassi, E., & Ventimiglia, F. (2023). A Systematic Literature Review on ESG during the COVID-19 Pandemic. *Sustainability (Basel), 15*(3), 2020. doi:10.3390/su15032020

Seth, R., Gupta, S., & Gupta, H. (2021). ESG investing: a critical overview. *Hans Shodh Sudha, 2*(2), 69-80. https://hansshodhsudha.com/volume2-issue2/October_December%202021_%20article%207.pdf

Settembre-Blundo, D., González-Sánchez, R., Medina-Salgado, S., & García-Muiña, F. E. (2021). Flexibility and resilience in corporate decision making: A new sustainability-based risk management system in uncertain times. *Global Journal of Flexible Systems Managment, 22*(S2, Suppl 2), 107–132. doi:10.1007/s40171-021-00277-7

Simran, & Sharma, A. K. (2024). Asymmetric nexus between economic policy uncertainty and the Indian stock market: Evidence using NARDL approach. *The Quarterly Review of Economics and Finance, 93*, 91-101. doi:10.1016/j.qref.2023.11.006

Torrence, C., & Compo, G. P. (1998). A practical guide to wavelet analysis. *Bulletin of the American Meteorological Society, 79*(1), 61–78. doi:10.1175/1520-0477(1998)079<0061:APGTWA>2.0.CO;2

Torrence, C., & Webster, P. J. (1999). Interdecadal changes in the enso-monsoon system. *Journal of Climate, 12*(8), 2679–2690. doi:10.1175/1520-0442(1999)012<2679:ICITEM>2.0.CO;2

Wood, J. (2020). Why this moment could be decisive for tackling climate change: Report, https://www.weforum.org/agenda/2020/07/how%20covid-19-could-spark-climate-change-recovery-sustainability/

Zhou, D., Siddik, A. B., Guo, L., & Li, H. (2023). Dynamic relationship among climate policy uncertainty, oil price, and renewable energy consumption—Findings from TVP-SV-VAR approach. *Renewable Energy, 204*, 722–732. https://www.mca.gov.in/Ministry/latestnews/National_Voluntary_Guidelines_2011_12jul2011.pdf. doi:10.1016/j.renene.2023.01.018

Zorgati, I., Albouchi, F., & Garfatta, R. (2024). Financial contagion during the COVID-19 pandemic: The case of African countries. *International Journal of Accounting. Auditing and Performance Evaluation, 20*(1/2), 23–42. doi:10.1504/IJAAPE.2024.135531

Chapter 8

Problems and Prospects of Social Entrepreneurship:
A Study in Singur Block, Hooghly, West Bengal

Jyotirmoy Koley

https://orcid.org/0009-0001-5184-9587

Hooghly Mohsin College, India

ABSTRACT

The emergence and success of entrepreneurship contribute to the economic growth and development of a nation. Social entrepreneurship primarily focuses on social or environmental issues. It is derived from social innovation to find solutions to social or environmental challenges. They provide quality and affordable products and services to serve the community, especially underserved and marginal sections of the society. Out of this, social entrepreneurship generates revenues, to be financially sustainable so that it can invest the same in further social programmes. The present has attempted to analyze the challenges and prospects of social entrepreneurship. It further aims to explore the societal need factors and motivational factors for the emergence of social entrepreneurship. The study reveals that finance, family support, and awareness are the major challenges, whereas opportunities for personal welfare and social transformation, integration of marginalized groups, and excellent mobilization of social capital are the major prospects for social entrepreneurship in the study area.

INTRODUCTION

Entrepreneurship defines and determines the economic development and growth of any nation. Entrepreneurship is of two types. Economic entrepreneurship primarily focuses on the profits and wealth sides by fulfilling the needs of the society. The social entrepreneurship primarily focuses on the social and environmental issues. They provide quality and affordable products and services to serve the community especially underserved and marginal sections of the society. Out of this, social entrepreneurship generates

DOI: 10.4018/979-8-3693-2197-3.ch008

revenues, with the objective of being financially sustainable so that it can invest the same in further social programmes. By addressing gaps and unmet needs, social entrepreneurs create dramatic transformations in society and the economy. They increase output, add value, and generate wealth. Social firms prioritize both financial success and positive social and environmental effects. Instead of focusing on maximizing profits, wealth creation should be done to help target populations become self-sufficient. The target communities are not wealthy customers and are under-served, ignored, or underprivileged. According to the Impact Investors Council (IIC), presently, estimated 2 million social entrepreneurs are working and serving over 500 million lives across India*. The primary aim of the paper is to analyze the challenges and prospects of social entrepreneurship in the area of Singur block, Hooghly, West Bengal, India.

CONCEPTUAL FRAMEWORK

Social Entrepreneurship

It focuses on the identification of social or environmental problems and tries to overcome the issue by using the available social resources. The basic components of social entrepreneurship include the following:

1. It is undertaken by a special group of people referred to as social entrepreneurs whose prime focus is on social innovations for prevailing social problems.
2. It is situated where social issue is identified and solved using entrepreneurial principles.
3. It stands with the main objective of social changes, rather than making individual profits and the unquantifiable social impacts.

Social Entrepreneur

Social entrepreneurs develop a mission and vision to bring change in society, especially in the marginalized section of society. They primarily bring innovative solutions to social problems at an affordable cost with the aim of social development with less focus on the return or profits. The individual entrepreneur's personal traits, creativity, and innovation are the key to the success of social entrepreneurship. Social entrepreneurs are those people who come up with new innovative ideas to address major social issues. They execute their works with mainly not-for-profit motives. The primary motive of a social entrepreneur should be social growth and development and the return or profit is exclusively a secondary aim.

Examples of Some Social Entrepreneurs in India

1. **Nikhil Singh:** He is one of the top social entrepreneurs in India. He is the founder and general sectary of Sai Seva Sansthan Trust. The trust was set up in 2020. The primary objective of the trust is to provide necessities such as agriculture, water sanitation, and nutrition to make the lives of rural people easier and better. On behalf of the trust, more than 100 people are working for the education of rural people by reaching out to their households.
2. **Hanumappa Sudarshana:** He is the founder of Karuna Trust in healthcare services. He was awarded as the top Indian social entrepreneur of the year 2014.

3. **Shaheen Mistri:** She is an Indian social activist, educator, and social entrepreneur. She founded the Akanksha Foundation in 1989. The organization aims to provide a quality education to the children of marginal sections of the society. She also set up the Teach for India Foundation in 2008. More than 700 students have been placed in various schools across India.

. 4. **Olivia Deka:** She is a gender equality advocate and social entrepreneur. She is the founder and CEO of the Evangelist organization, set up in 2019.

It is a community-powered and led feminist organization that advocates gender equality. It aims to assist Indian women and girls to gain access to health services and education.

5. **Agnishwar Jayaprakash:** He is a dynamic youth leader and founder of Lgnite-India Trust. The organization was set up in 2014. It focuses on helping the underprivileged citizens of India by providing quality education so that they can accomplish their dreams. The organization provides educational opportunities and scholarships to students. To date, it has extended its hand to the students at over 7000 educational institutions across the nation.

Focus Areas of Social Entrepreneurship in India

Following are the prominent areas where social entrepreneurs can venture into and contribute to resolving the issues of society using the principles of Entrepreneurship.

1. Upliftment of the weaker sections of the society.
2. Agriculture and sustainable farming.
3. Skill development.
4. Creating a digitally empowered society
5. Increasing access and quality of healthcare.
6. Climate changes

Roles and Responsibilities of Social Entrepreneurs

1. Identification of social problems is the initial role of social entrepreneurs.
2. Their innovative products can influence society and social problems can be solved by using the resources depending upon social innovations.
3. Reaching out to every section of society and serving them positively is one of the main roles of social entrepreneurs.
4. Their unique approaches are supposed to provide employment. The biggest accountability of a social entrepreneur is to offer services to a resident possessing optimum skills and credentials.
5. Making evident changes in Indian society with the approach of social balance is an important role of social entrepreneurs.

Characteristics of Social Entrepreneurship

The social entrepreneurship has the following characteristics:

1. Social entrepreneurship has risk risk-taking capacity like any other branch of entrepreneurship. It takes risks and uncertainties in setting up social entrepreneurs.
2. Social entrepreneurship has vision and foresightedness. It sees the problems and finds a solution that nobody can imagine.
3. Social entrepreneurship provides leadership and direction to people who are working in social enterprises to achieve a common goal.
4. Social entrepreneurship has unique creativity. It overcomes the social problems with creative solutions.

How to Face Challenges Effectively

1. The government should set up proper training and development institutions for the systematic development of social entrepreneurship like economic entrepreneurship.
2. The social entrepreneurship subject should be included in the course curriculum of higher education to the awareness among students about social entrepreneurship.
3. With the help of Media and other vehicles, the government should organize a mass awareness programme about social entrepreneurship among the general public to make them aware of social entrepreneurship and remove the confusion between social entrepreneurship and social work.
4. The government and other stakeholders must provide infrastructure and basic facilities for social entrepreneurship.

Qualities of Social Entrepreneurs

1. **Ambitious:** Social business individuals handle significant public problems, from growing the varsity mobilization pace of low-pay entities to battling neediness. They add association in a nursing array of collaborations: creative, non-profit seeking, social cause adventures, and links that merge parameters of selfless and profit-oriented associations.
2. **Motion Driven:** Producing social worth not abundance is that the central objective of an efficient social trade person. Whereas abundance creation can be essential for the series, it's something associated with the nursing finish in itself. The continuing foundational social amendment is the real aim.
3. **Strategic:** Like business enterprise, social business observes and tracks what others overlook., for instance, to advance frameworks, create coming up with and develop new ways for special worth.
4. **Resourceful:** As social business individuals work inside the social scene instead of the business world, they need restructured entry to capital and conservative market sensitivity encouraging networks. Afterward, social business individuals ought to be precocious at the aggregation of human, financial, and political possessions.
5. **Result-Oriented:** Social business individuals aim to deliver positive returns. These results alter existing real factors and open new dimensions for the undervalued loaded and unharnessed society's potential to affect social amendment.

Problems of Social Entrepreneurship

1. **Lack of Awareness:** It is one of the major challenges of social entrepreneurship. Lack of awareness among the general people of society about social entrepreneurship. Most people do not about what social entrepreneurship means, or what for they are set up.

2. **Lack of Education about Social Entrepreneurship:** Lack of knowledge about social entrepreneurship is another major problem. It creates obstacles to discovering the capable promoters for social entrepreneurship.

3. **Lack of Financial Aid:** Financial problem is the major difficulties of social entrepreneurs. They mostly run their business activities with their fund. Sometimes, they arrange funds from local money lenders. But that creates a heavy interest in their soldiers. It is a great hindrance to the growth of social entrepreneurship.

4. **Social Work and Confusion:** Sometimes, social entrepreneurship is being considered as social work. There is a huge confusion among the people of the society. This results in various stakeholders considering working in and with such organizations as more voluntary work and thus compromising on the inputs and expectations from such enterprises. It is a challenge for social entrepreneurship.

5. **Issues of Creativity:** Lack of creativity is the next level of problem for social entrepreneurship. Creativity is the prime and crucial thought behind social entrepreneurship. Social entrepreneurship aims to find solutions to problems at grassroots levels which have existed for years. Often it is challenging to find innovative and creative solutions to the problems that have plagued society over the years. The social entrepreneurs find it challenging to think out of the box to be able to address these issues.

6. **Lack of Structure and Planning:** Lack of proper planning for social entrepreneurship may lead to a collapse of business activities. For the smooth and hassle-free functioning of social entrepreneurship, appropriate planning regarding business operations is the foremost need.

7. **Lack of Commercial Supposition:** Lack of focus on commercial viability is the biggest challenge. It distorts the development of social entrepreneurship in India.

8. **Shortage of Skilled Workforces:** Hiring skilled workforces is another challenge in social entrepreneurship. Here, skilled shortage and lack of employability skills is a major problem. Searching for skilled and talented employees for social entrepreneurship is another challenging task. Social entrepreneurship cannot provide high salaries to the employees due to a limited focus on profits. That is why; social entrepreneurship cannot attract and retain talented workforces in their enterprise. It is a major problem for social entrepreneurship.

9. **Social and Cultural Problems:** The social and cultural aspects of any country define the attributes of its people. These social and cultural aspects may act as hindrances and pose issues for the initiation and development of social entrepreneurship. Indians are found to be risk averse and this is one of the major challenges for social entrepreneurship. Social entrepreneurship works for the betterment of society and offers low-cost solutions to social problems with limited returns for the business. It makes social entrepreneurs less financially motivated and more risky. It leads many of them to not opt for a venture into the field of social entrepreneurship.

Prospects of Social Entrepreneurship

1. **Opportunities for Social Transformation and Personal Welfare:** Social transformation is the main objective of social entrepreneurship. Welfare, personal education, creation of job opportunities, and all-round development of the economy are the primary emphasis of social entrepreneurship.

2. **Marginalized Groups and Integration:** The upliftment of the society is the focus of social entrepreneurship It fulfills the requirements of the bottom of the pyramids in the market through the collaboration of the marginalized section of the society.

3. **Social Capital Mobilization and Excellence:** Creation and mobilization of social capital is the major contribution of social entrepreneurship.

4. **Government Collaborative and Participation:** Social entrepreneurship has opened a wide scope for Government collaboration to address the major social issues. It is a great opportunity for the growth and development of social entrepreneurship in the upcoming days.

LITERATURE REVIEW

Several studies have been conducted by many academicians and researchers on the different challenges and prospects of social entrepreneurship in India. Some of them are highlighted below.

Panda et al. (2023) have analyzed the various issues and challenges faced by social entrepreneurship in India from different aspects. They have measured the performance of social entrepreneurship in terms of social value creation by applying the components of the balance scorecard technique. It has presented a clear stand and position of social enterprises.

Jarakunti (2023) studied the emerging trends of social entrepreneurship in developing countries like India and its prospects and challenges. She shed light on how the development of social entrepreneurship can solve the problems of society that are ignored by commercial and government enterprises.

Pawni and Sailaja (2022) studied the basic framework of social entrepreneurship including their roles and responsibilities in Indian society. They found that social entrepreneurship is a unique combination of entrepreneurial traits and philanthropy. They suggested that social entrepreneurship should use a networking approach with other social enterprises to avail themselves of market opportunities.

Akhtar and Anjum (2022) highlighted on how the advancement of social business enterprise could take care of the issues of society which was disregarded by business and government undertakings. They made a connection with rising patterns of social enterprise in creating nations like India and its prospects and difficulties. They also distinguished what decides social entrepreneurial achievement factors and the difficulties for social business visionaries of Uttar Pradesh. They found that social business has risen to a more prominent degree and is very much valued.

Kaur (2021) has examined the development patterns of social business in India and the new activities taken by different social business visionaries. She has elaborated on the meaning of social entrepreneurship and discussed the foremost challenges being faced by social entrepreneurship in India.

Suhashini et al. (2021) have studied the objectives of social entrepreneurship that to focus the social needs. They have found that social entrepreneurship has increased its scope and importance in recent years. They have also studied how social entrepreneurship can change or impact the social setup and social fiber in India, especially in the developing nations which are at the bottom of the pyramid level.

Khosla (2021) aimed to understand the term social entrepreneurship and explored the factors that have contributed to the emergence of social entrepreneurship in India. He also discussed the current challenges that social entrepreneurship confronts in the current Indian context. He suggested prominent areas where social entrepreneurs can set up their ventures and contribute to national well-being.

Gupta (2021) provided a comprehensive examination of social entrepreneurship, covering its conceptual foundation and operations. They showed how social entrepreneurship may change or influence the social system and social fibers in India and other developed countries at the bottom of the pyramid.

Pandey and Shukla (2021) analyzed the impact of social entrepreneurship in India along with problems, prospects, and recent growth trends. They revealed that a plethora of opportunities were awaited despite facing various challenges in social entrepreneurship in India.

Kamalaveni and Buvaneswaran (2019) have discussed the marketing problems of social entrepreneurs in Tamilnadu. They found that the state of Tamilnadu has a high potential for developing social entrepreneurship which is determined by the share of educated people and the potential of unemployed individuals who can work as well as the inability of the government to tackle all socio-economic problems.

Meghna and Arya (2019) have attempted to understand the concept of social entrepreneurship, prospects, and challenges of social entrepreneurship. They have revealed that proper adoption of appropriate measures may reduce the challenges of social entrepreneurship which has led to the acceleration in the popularity of social entrepreneurship in this modern era.

Rawal (2018) made a detailed study on a variety of topics related to social entrepreneurship, including their various challenges, conceptual framework, and process of social entrepreneurship. She also discussed the similarity and contrast between social and economic entrepreneurship along with explaining the traits of a social entrepreneur. How social entrepreneurship can change or impact the setup and social fiber in India and other developed nations, especially at the bottom of the pyramid level has also been underlined by the author.

Bulsara et al. (2015) have studied the growing trends of social entrepreneurship in India and the new initiatives taken by various social entrepreneurs. They have tried to give a brief idea of different theories of social entrepreneurship. They have also provided information relating to activities of social entrepreneurship and social entrepreneurial ventures in India.

Singh (2012) attempted an analytical, critical, and synthetic examination of social entrepreneurship in India. He found that India has been experiencing an increase in social entrepreneurship and attempts by social entrepreneurs to find affordable solutions to various social problems of the society. He suggested that with the changes in technology and increasing competition, social entrepreneurs have to become more dynamic.

RESEARCH GAP

From the above review of various literatures, it has been observed that no such seminal work has been conducted on the challenges and prospects of social entrepreneurship in the block of Singur, Hooghly, West Bengal. The present study has tried to highlight this untouched area.

NEED OF THE STUDY

The social entrepreneurship is a very important concept to address on social and environmental issues. It primarily focuses on the sustainable solution to social problems rather than profit earnings. The study aims to analyze the problems and prospects of social entrepreneurship along with the identification of the societal need factors and the motivational factors for social entrepreneurship in the block of Singur, Hooghly, West Bengal, India.

OBJECTIVES OF THE STUDY

The objectives of the study are (i) to analyze the challenges and prospects of social entrepreneurship (ii) to study the societal need factors for social entrepreneurship (iii) to identify the motivational factors for social entrepreneurship in the block of Singur, Hooghly, west Bengal, India.

RESEARCH METHODOLOGY

Database

The study is analytical in nature and mainly based on the primary data. Some secondary data have been used in the study which has been collected from various research-based articles, journals, and publications. The primary data have been collected from the field survey through a structured questionnaire. The present study has been conducted in the block of Singur, Hooghly, West Bengal. The purposive sampling technique has been applied to select and interview the respondents to the questionnaire during the months from October to December 2023. Finally, 155 people responded to the questionnaire.

Methodology

The questionnaire has two sections; the first section consists of seven demographic questions and the second section consists of five subsections of technical questions relating to the challenges and prospects of social entrepreneurship in the block of Singur, Hooghly, West Bengal. The internal consistency of the questionnaire has been tested by using Cronbach's alpha test, which has given a result of 0.917. Usually, a reliability coefficient above 0.60 is considered to be satisfactory in social science research. Therefore, it can be said that the measures used in this study are valid and reliable. The frequency tables, percentageand various statistical tools like the chi-square test and one sample t-test have been used to analyze the data to achieve the research objective and draw a logical conclusion. The processing and analysis of data have been done with the help of a statistical package (SPSS-20.0 version).

HYPOTHESIS

Six sets of hypotheses have been formulated to achieve the research objectives. There are shown below:
   Hypothesis-1:

H_0: There is no relation between social worker and social entrepreneur or willing to be a social entrepreneur

H_1: There is a relation between social worker and social entrepreneur or willing to be a social entrepreneur

Hypothesis-2:

H_0: There is no association between social entrepreneur or willing to be a social entrepreneur and lack of financial resources

H_1: There is an association between social entrepreneur or willing to be a social entrepreneur and lack of financial resources

Hypothesis-3:

H_0: There is no association between social entrepreneur or willing to be a social entrepreneur and lack of family/social support

H_1: There is an association between social entrepreneur or willing to be a social entrepreneur and lack of family/social support

Hypothesis-4:

H_0: There is no connection between social entrepreneur or willing to be a social entrepreneur and opportunity for personal welfare & social transformation

H_1: There is a connection between social entrepreneur or willing to be a social entrepreneur and opportunity for personal welfare & social transformation

Hypothesis-5:

H_0: There is no difference between the averages of societal need factors for social entrepreneurship

H_1: There is a difference between the averages of societal need factors for social entrepreneurship

Hypothesis-6:

H_0: There is no difference between the averages of motivational factors for social entrepreneurship

H_1: There is a difference between the averages of motivational factors for social entrepreneurship

ANALYSIS AND DISCUSSIONS

The primary data collected from the field survey through the structured questionnaire have been analyzed to achieve the research objectives. The analysis has been divided into three parts. The first part isconsiders the demographic aspects of the respondents. The second part is concerned with the technical aspects of social entrepreneurship. Whereas, the last part is taking care of the hypothesis testing. The details are shown below:

Demographic Aspects

Gender of Respondent

Table 1. Gender of respondent

Gender	Frequency	Percent
Male	83	53.5
Female	72	46.5
Total	155	100.0

(Source: Primary Data)

Observation: From the above Table 1, it has been observed that 53.5 percent of the respondents are male whereas 46.5 percent of the respondents are female.

Age Group of Respondent

Table 2. Age group of respondent

Age Group	Frequency	Percent
18Yrs-25Yrs	32	20.6
26Yrs-35Yrs	62	40.0
36Yrs-50Yrs	40	25.8
Above 50Yrs	21	13.5
Total	155	100.0

(Source: Primary Data)

Observation: From the above Table 2, it has been seen that 40.0 percent of the respondents fall in the age group between 26 Yrs-35 Yrs whereas 13.5 percent of the respondents fall in the age group above 50 Yrs.

Educational Qualification of Respondent

Table 3. Educational qualification of respondent

Educational Qualification	Frequency	Percent
Illiterate	10	6.5
Primary	63	40.6
High School	72	46.5
UG	10	6.5
PG	0	0
Total	155	100.0

(Source: Primary Data)

Observation: From the above Table 3, it has been found that 46.5 percent of the respondents have passed high school whereas 6.5 percent of the respondents are Illiterate.

Occupation of Respondent

Table 4. Occupation of respondent

Occupation	Frequency	Percent
Govt. Service	42	27.1
Private Service	62	40.0
Business	41	26.5
Student	0	0
Retired	0	0
Others	10	6.5
Total	155	100.0

(Source: Primary Data)

Observation: From the above Table 4, it has been seen that 40.0 percent of the respondents are in private service whereas 6.5 percent of the respondents are involved in other occupation like self employment.

Technical Aspect

The technical questions covered under the structured questionnaire have been analyzed and discussed in this section including five different sub classes.

Inclination to Work for Societal Cause

Whether You are Social Worker

Table 5. Whether you are social worker

Whether You are Social Worker	Frequency	Percent
Yes	32	20.6
Undecided	62	40.0
No	61	39.4
Total	155	100.0

(Source: Primary Data)

Observation: From the above Table 5, it has been observed that 39.4 percent of the respondents are not social worker whereas 20.6 percent of the respondents are social worker.

Table 6. Whether you are social entrepreneur or willing to be

Whether You are Social Entrepreneur or Willing to be	Frequency	Percent
Yes	71	45.8
Undecided	54	34.8
No	30	19.4
Total	155	100.0

(Source: Primary Data)

Whether You are a Social Entrepreneur or Willing to be

Observation: From the above Table 6, it has been seen that 45.8 percent of the respondents are social entrepreneur or willing to be social entrepreneur whereas 19.4 percent of the respondents are not social entrepreneur or willing to be social entrepreneur.

Societal Need Factors for Social Entrepreneurship

Unaddressed Societal Problems

Table 7. Unaddressed societal problems

Unaddressed Societal Problems	Frequency	Percent
Agree	82	52.9
Neutral	53	34.2
Disagree	20	12.9
Total	155	100.0

(Source: Primary Data)

Observation: From the above Table 7, it has been identified that 52.9 percent of the respondents agree with the unaddressed societal problems that government is not able to combat whereas 12.9 percent of the respondents disagree with the said matter.

Inefficiency in Social System

Table 8. Inefficiency in social system

Inefficiency in Social System	Frequency	Percent
Agree	85	54.8
Neutral	40	25.8
Disagree	30	19.4
Total	155	100.0

(Source: Primary Data)

Observation: From the above Table 8, it has been observed that 54.8 percent of the respondents agree with the inefficiency in social system whereas 19.4 percent of the respondents disagree with the same.

Fulfillment of Self Actualization Need

Table 9. Fulfill self actualization need

Fulfillment ofSelf Actualization Need	Frequency	Percent
Agree	85	54.8
Neutral	50	32.3
Disagree	20	12.9
Total	155	100.0

(Source: Primary Data)

Observation: From the above Table 9, it has been observed that 54.8 percent of the respondents agree with the fulfillment of self actualization need whereas 12.9 percent of the respondents disagree with the same.

Motivational Factors for Social Entrepreneurship

Consciousness towards Social Needs

Table 10. Consciousness towards social needs

Consciousness towards Social Needs	Frequency	Percent
Agree	95	61.3
Neutral	40	25.8
Disagree	20	12.9
Total	155	100.0

(Source: Primary Data)

Observation: From the above Table 10, it has been seen that 61.3 percent of the respondents agree with the consciousness towards social needs whereas 12.9 percent of the respondents disagree with the issue.

Empathy or Passion

Table 11. Empathy or passion

Empathy Or Passion	Frequency	Percent
Agree	84	54.2
Neutral	51	32.9
Disagree	20	12.9
Total	155	100.0

(Source: Primary Data)

Observation: From the above Table 11, it has been seen that 54.2 percent of the respondents agree with the empathy or passion whereas 12.9 percent of the respondents disagree with the matter.

Personal Goals

Table 12. Personal goals

PersonalGoals	Frequency	Percent
Agree	74	47.7
Neutral	71	45.8
Disagree	10	6.5
Total	155	100.0

(Source: Primary Data)

Observation: From the above Table 12, it has been seen that 47.7 percent of the respondents agree with the personal goals whereas 6.5 percent of the respondents disagree with the matter.

Personal Support or Environment

Table 13. Personal support or environment

Personal Support Or Environment	Frequency	Percent
Agree	84	54.2
Neutral	41	26.5
Disagree	30	19.4
Total	155	100.0

(Source: Primary Data)

Observation: From the above Table 13, it has been found that 54.2 percent of the respondents agree with the personal support or environment whereas 19.4 percent of the respondents disagree with the issue.

Feelings of Self Worth

Table 14. Feelings of self worth

Feelings of Self Worth	Frequency	Percent
Agree	68	43.9
Neutral	57	36.8
Disagree	30	19.4
Total	155	100.0

(Source: Primary Data)

Observation: From the above Table 14, it has been observed that 43.9 percent of the respondents agree with the feelings of self worth whereas 19.4 percent of the respondents disagree with the same.

Challenges of Social Entrepreneurship

Lack of Financial Resources

Table 15. Lack of financial resources

Lack of Financial Resources	Frequency	Percent
Agree	76	49.0
Neutral	64	41.3
Disagree	15	9.7
Total	155	100.0

(Source: Primary Data)

Observation: From the above table-15, it has been found that 49.0 percent of the respondents agree with the lack of financial resources whereas 9.7 percent of the respondents disagree with the issue.

Lack of Infrastructure

Table 16. Lack of infrastructure

Lack of Infrastructure	Frequency	Percent
Agree	61	39.4
Neutral	64	41.3
Disagree	30	19.4
Total	155	100.0

(Source: Primary Data)

Observation: From the above Table 16, it has been found that 39.4 percent of the respondents agree with the lack of infrastructure whereas 9.7 percent of the respondents disagree with the matter.

Lack of Knowledge

Table 17. Lack of knowledge

Lack of Knowledge	Frequency	Percent
Agree	44	28.4
Neutral	91	58.7
Disagree	20	12.9
Total	155	100.0

(Source: Primary Data)

Observation: From the above Table 17, it has been found that 58.7 percent of the respondents are neutral about the lack of knowledge whereas 12.9 percent of the respondents disagree with the matter.

Lack of Social or Family Support

Table 18. Lack of social or family support

Lack of Social or Family Support	Frequency	Percent
Agree	88	56.8
Neutral	52	33.5
Disagree	15	9.7
Total	155	100.0

(Source: Primary Data)

Observation: From the above Table 18, it has been observed that 56.8 percent of the respondents agree with the lack of social or family support whereas 9.7 percent of the respondents disagree with the issue.

Lack of Time

Table 19. Lack of time

Lack of Time	Frequency	Percent
Agree	63	40.6
Neutral	52	33.5
Disagree	40	25.8
Total	155	100.0

(Source: Primary Data)

Observation: From the above Table 19, it has been observed that 40.6 percent of the respondents agree with the lack of time whereas 25.8 percent of the respondents disagree with the topic.

Lack of Confidence or Self Efficacy

Table 20. Lack of confidence or self efficacy

Lack of Confidence or Self Efficacy	Frequency	Percent
Agree	43	27.7
Neutral	72	46.5
Disagree	40	25.8
Total	155	100.0

(Source: Primary Data)

Observation: From the above Table 20, it has been observed that 46.5 percent of the respondents are neutral about the lack of confidence or self efficacy whereas 25.8 percent of the respondents disagree with the same.

Lack of Govt. Support

Table 21. Lack of govt. support

Lack of Govt. Support	Frequency	Percent
Agree	68	43.9
Neutral	72	46.5
Disagree	15	9.7
Total	155	100.0

(Source: Primary Data)

Observation: From the above Table 21, it has been found that 46.5 percent of the respondents are neutral about the lack of govt. support whereas 9.7 percent of the respondents disagree with the subject.

Lack of Awareness

Table 22. Lack of awareness

Lack of Awareness among the General Public	Frequency	Percent
Agree	75	48.4
Neutral	60	38.7
Disagree	20	12.9
Total	155	100.0

(Source: Primary Data)

Observation: From the above Table 22, it has been found that 48.4 percent of the respondents agree with the lack of awareness among the general public whereas 12.9 percent of the respondents disagree with the topic.

Prospects of Social Entrepreneurship

Opportunity of Personal Welfare and Social Transformation

Table 23. Opportunity of personal welfare and social transformation

Opportunity of Personal Welfare and Social Transformation	Frequency	Percent
Agree	96	61.9
Neutral	35	22.6
Disagree	24	15.5
Total	155	100.0

(Source: Primary Data)

Observation: From the above Table 23, it has been observed that 61.9 percent of the respondents agree with the opportunity of personal welfare and social transformation whereas 15.5 percent of the respondents disagree with the same.

Integration of Marginalized Groups

Table 24. Integration of marginalized groups

Integration of Marginalized Groups	Frequency	Percent
Agree	91	58.7
Neutral	54	34.8
Disagree	10	6.5
Total	155	100.0

(Source: Primary Data)

Observation: From the above Table 24, it has been observed that 58.7 percent of the respondents agree with the integration of marginalized groups whereas 6.5 percent of the respondents disagree with the issue.

Excellent Mobilization of Social Capital

Table 25. Excellent mobilization of social capital

Excellent Mobilization of Social Capital	Frequency	Percent
Agree	95	61.3
Neutral	36	23.2
Disagree	24	15.5
Total	155	100.0

(Source: Primary Data)

Observation: From the above Table 25, it has been observed that 61.3 percent of the respondents agree with the excellent mobilization of social capital whereas 15.5 percent of the respondents disagree with the matter.

Collaborative Participation with Government

Table 26. Collaborative participation with government

Collaborative Participation with Government	Frequency	Percent
Agree	65	41.9
Neutral	70	45.2
Disagree	20	12.9
Total	155	100

(Source: Primary Data)

Observation: From the above Table 26, it has been seen that 45.2 percent of the respondents are neutral about the collaborative participation with government whereas 12.9 percent of the respondents disagree with the topic.

Hypothesis Testing

Chi-Square Test

The chi-square test of independence is used in the present study to examine whether two categorical variables are independent of each other.

Hypothesis-1

H_0: There is no relation between social worker and social entrepreneur or willing to be a social entrepreneur

H_1: There is a relation between social worker and social entrepreneur or willing to be a social entrepreneur

Table 27. Cross tabulation between social worker and social entrepreneur or willing to be a social entrepreneur

			Social Worker			Total
			Yes	Undecided	No	
Social Entrepreneur or Willing to bea social entrepreneur	Yes	Number	24	5	42	71
		% of Total	15.5%	3.2%	27.1%	45.8%
	Undecided	Number	5	45	4	54
		% of Total	3.2%	29.0%	2.6%	34.8%
	No	Number	3	12	15	30
		% of Total	1.9%	7.7%	9.7%	19.4%
Total		Number	32	62	61	155
		% of Total	20.6%	40.0%	39.4%	100.0%

(Source: Compiled by researcher)

Table 28. Chi-Square tests

	Value	df	Asymp. Sig. (2-sided)
Pearson Chi-Square	77.563	4	.000
Likelihood Ratio	88.041	4	.000
Linear-by-Linear Association	.054	1	.815
No of Valid Cases	155		

(Source: Compiled by researcher)

Interpretation: From the cross tabulation in Table 27, it is found that 39.4 percent of the surveyed respondents are not social worker and 45.8 percent of the respondents are social entrepreneur or willing to be a social entrepreneur. The above Table28 exhibits that the Pearson Chi-Square or P-value of the test at the 1 percent level of significance is 0.000 which is less than 0.01. So, the null hypothesis is rejected and the alternative hypothesis is accepted. Therefore, it can be concluded that there is a relationship between social worker and social entrepreneur or willing to be a social entrepreneur.

Hypothesis-2

H_0: There is no association between social entrepreneur or willing to be a social entrepreneur and lack of financial resources

H_1: There is an association between social entrepreneur or willing to be a social entrepreneur and lack of financial resources

Table 29. Cross tabulation between social entrepreneur or willing to be a social entrepreneur and lack of financial resources

			Lack of Financial Resources			Total
			Agree	Neutral	Disagree	
Social Entrepreneur or Willing to bea social entrepreneur	Yes	Number	20	47	4	71
		% of Total	12.9%	30.3%	2.6%	45.8%
	Undecided	Number	45	8	1	54
		% of Total	29.%	5.2%	0.6%	34.8%
	No	Number	11	9	10	30
		% of Total	7.1%	5.8%	6.5%	19.4%
Total		Number	76	64	15	155
		% of Total	49%	41.3%	9.7%	100.0%

(Source: Compiled by researcher)

Table 30. Chi-Square tests

	Value	df	Asymp. Sig. (2-sided)
Pearson Chi-Square	62.921	4	.000
Likelihood Ratio	58.489	4	.000
Linear-by-Linear Association	.033	1	.856
No of Valid Cases	155		

(Source: Compiled by researcher)

Interpretation: From the cross tabulation in Table 29, it is found that 49 percent of the surveyed respondents face the challenge of lacking in financial resources and 45.8 percent of the respondents are social entrepreneur or willing to be a social entrepreneur. The above Table 30 shows that the Pearson Chi-Square or P-value of the test at the 1 percent level of significance is 0.000 which is less than 0.01. So, the null hypothesis is rejected and the alternative hypothesis is accepted. Therefore, it can be concluded that there is an association between social entrepreneur or willing to be a social entrepreneur and lack of financial resources.

Hypothesis-3

H_0: There is no association between social entrepreneur or willing to be a social entrepreneur and lack of family/social support

H_1: There is an association between social entrepreneur or willing to be a social entrepreneur and lack of family/social support

Table 31. Cross tabulation between social entrepreneur or willing to be a social entrepreneur and lack of family/social support

			Lack of Family/Social Support			Total
			Agree	Neutral	Disagree	
Social Entrepreneur or Willing to bea social entrepreneur	Yes	Number	48	15	8	71
		% of Total	31.0%	9.7%	5.2%	45.8%
	Undecided	Number	23	29	2	54
		% of Total	14.8%	18.7%	1.3%	34.8%
	No	Number	17	8	5	30
		% of Total	11.0%	5.2%	3.2%	19.4%
Total		Number	88	52	15	155
		% of Total	56.8%	33.5%	9.7%	100.0%

(Source: Compiled by researcher)

Table 32. Chi-Square tests

	Value	df	Asymp. Sig. (2-sided)
Pearson Chi-Square	17.299	4	.002
Likelihood Ratio	17.248	4	.002
Linear-by-Linear Association	1.880	1	.170
No of Valid Cases	155		

(Source: Compiled by researcher)

Interpretation: From the cross tabulation in Table 31, it is found that 56.8 percent of the surveyed respondents face the problem of lack of family/social support and 45.8 percent of the respondents are social entrepreneur or willing to be a social entrepreneur. The above Table 32 reveals that the Pearson Chi-Square or P-value of the test at the 1 percent level of significance is 0.002 which is less than 0.01. So, the null hypothesis is rejected and the alternative hypothesis is accepted. Therefore, it can be concluded that there is an association between social entrepreneur or willing to be a social entrepreneur and lack of family/social support.

Hypothesis-4

H_0: There is no connection between social entrepreneur or willing to be a social entrepreneur and opportunity for personal welfare & social transformation

H_1: There is a connection between social entrepreneur or willing to be a social entrepreneur and opportunity for personal welfare & social transformation

Table 33. Cross tabulation between social entrepreneur or willing to be a social entrepreneur and opportunity for personal welfare and social transformation

			Opportunity for Personal Welfare & Social Transformation			Total
			Agree	Neutral	Disagree	
Social Entrepreneur or Willing to be a social entrepreneur	Yes	Number	62	8	1	71
		% of Total	40.0%	5.2%	.6%	45.8%
	Undecided	Number	28	23	3	54
		% of Total	18.1%	14.8%	1.9%	34.8%
	No	Number	6	4	20	30
		% of Total	3.9%	2.6%	12.9%	19.4%
Total		Number	96	35	24	155
		% of Total	61.9%	22.6%	15.5%	100.0%

(Source: Compiled by researcher)

Table 34. Chi-Square tests

	Value	df	Asymp. Sig. (2-sided)
Pearson Chi-Square	94.81	4	.000
Likelihood Ratio	80.388	4	.000
Linear-by-Linear Association	61.790	1	.000
No of Valid Cases	155		

(Source: Compiled by researcher)

Interpretation: From the cross tabulation in Table 33, it is found that 61.9 percent of the surveyed respondents agree on the opportunity for personal welfare & social transformation and 45.8 percent of the respondents are social entrepreneur or willing to be a social entrepreneur. The above Table 34 shows that the Pearson Chi-Square or P-value of the test at the 1 percent level of significance is 0.000 which is less than 0.01. So, the null hypothesis is rejected and the alternative hypothesis is accepted. Therefore, it can be concluded that there is a connection between social entrepreneur or willing to be a social entrepreneur and opportunity for personal welfare & social transformation.

One Sample t-test

The one sample t- test has been used in the present study to compare the mean of categorical variables of each other of the same sample.

Hypothesis-5

H_0: There is no difference between the averages of societal need factors for social entrepreneurship

H_1: There is a difference between the averages of societal need factors for social entrepreneurship

Table 35. One-Sample test

Societal Need Factors for Social Entrepreneurship	t	df	Sig. (2-tailed)	Mean Difference	95% Confidence Interval of the Difference	
					Lower	Upper
Unaddressed Societal Problems that the Government is not Able to Combat	28.134	154	.000	1.60000	1.4877	1.7123
Inefficiency in Social/Working System	26.012	154	.000	1.64516	1.5202	1.7701
Fulfill Self Actualization Need	27.697	154	.000	1.58065	1.4679	1.6934

(Source: Compiled by researcher)

Interpretation: From the above Table 35, it is observed that the P-value of the test at the 1 percent level of significance is 0.000 which is less than 0.01. So, the null hypothesis is rejected and the alternative hypothesis is accepted. Therefore, it can be concluded that there is a difference between the averages of societal need factors for social entrepreneurship.

Hypothesis-6

H_0: There is no difference between the averages of motivational factors for social entrepreneurship
H_1: There is a difference between the averages of motivational factors for social entrepreneurship

Table 36. One-Sample test

Motivational Factors for Social Entrepreneurship	t	df	Sig. (2-tailed)	Mean Difference	95% Confidence Interval of the Difference	
					Lower	Upper
Consciousness towards Societal Needs	26.403	154	.000	1.51613	1.4027	1.6296
Empathy/Passion	27.840	154	.000	1.58710	1.4745	1.6997
Personal Goals (Employment, income, status)	32.316	154	.000	1.58710	1.4901	1.6841
Personal Support Or Environment	26.154	154	.000	1.65161	1.5269	1.7764
Feelings of Self Worth	28.790	154	.000	1.75484	1.6344	1.8753

(Source: Compiled by researcher)

Interpretation: From the above Table 36, it is found that the P-value of the test at the 1 percent level of significance is 0.000 which is less than 0.01. So, the null hypothesis is rejected and the alternative hypothesis is accepted. Therefore, it can be concluded that there is a difference between the averages of motivational factors for social entrepreneurship.

FINDINGS OF THE STUDY

Some of the most important findings from the above analysis are shown below:

1. Lack of financial resources, lack of social/family support, lack of awareness, and lack of time are found to be the major challenges for social entrepreneurship.
2. Opportunity for personal welfare & social transformation, integration of marginalized groups, and excellent mobilization of social capital are observed to be the major prospects for social entrepreneurship.
3. There is a relationship between social worker and social entrepreneur or willing to be a social entrepreneur.
4. There is an association between social entrepreneur or willing to be a social entrepreneur and lack of financial resources.
5. There is an association between social entrepreneur or willing to be a social entrepreneur and lack of family/social support.
6. There is a connection between social entrepreneur or willing to be a social entrepreneur and opportunity for personal welfare & social transformation.
7. There is a difference between the averages of societal need factors for social entrepreneurship.
8. There is a difference between the averages of motivational factors for social entrepreneurship.

CONCLUSION

From the above study on social entrepreneurship, it is very clear that the social entrepreneurship has a great positive impact on the social or environmental issues. These social entrepreneurs are working a lot for the community. They are facing some major challenges like finance, family support, awareness, etc. but these problems could be sorted out or managed over time with the support of the general public and government by conducting more awareness programmes about social entrepreneurship. The prospects of the social entrepreneurship are very bright at present. These are also very important needs of the current socio-environmental context. At this conjecture, the societal need factors and motivational factors for building more and more social entrepreneurship should be the top most priority to present a better society to the next generation.

REFERENCES

Akhtar, M., & Anjum, U. (2022). Problems and Prospects of Social Entrepreneurship in Uttar Pradesh. *International Journal of Research Publication and Review*, *3*(6), 353–359.

Bulsara, H. P., Gandhi, S., & Chandwani, J. (2015). Social Entrepreneurship in India: An Exploratory Study. *International Journal of Innovation*, *3*(1), 7–16. doi:10.5585/iji.v3i1.20

Gupta, S. (2021). A Review on Social Entrepreneurship and Challenges in India. [IJIREM]. *International Journal of Innovative Research in Engineering & Management*, *8*(6), 298–301.

Jarakunti, T. (2023). Social Entrepreneurship – Prospects and Challenges. *Iconic Research and Engineering Journals*, *6*(12), 663–668.

Kamalaveni, R., & Buvaneswaran, V. (2019). A Study on Problems and Prospects of Social Entrepreneurs in Tamilnadu. *CIKITUSI Journal for Multidisciplinary Research*, *6*(4), 392–400.

Kaur, K. (2021). Social Entrepreneurship: Major Challenges Faced by Social Entrepreneurs in India. [IJCRT]. *International Journal of Creative Research Thoughts*, *9*(4), 1738–1741.

Khosla, A. (2021). Social Entrepreneurship in India: Scope and Challenges. *PalArch's Journal of Archaeology of Egypt/Egyptology (AJAEE),* 18(10), 385-391.

Meghna, C. K., & Arya, S. P. (2019). Social Entrepreneurship: Prospects and Challenges. *International Journal of Scientific and Engineering Research*, *10*(3), 211–213.

Pandey, P., & Shukla, R. (2021). The Process of Social Entrepreneurship: Opportunities and Challenges. *Emerge Managing Innovation and Entrepreneurship in New Normal*, *1*, 97–103.

Pansa, L. (2023). Social Enterprises in India: The Issues, Challenges and Its Performance Measurement. *International Journal of Current Research*, *15*(01), 23587–23595.

Pawni, B. and Sailaja, V. (2022). Social Entrepreneurship in India: Opportunities and Challenges. *International Journal of Advanced Research in management (IJARM), 13*(1), 237-245.

Rawal, T. (2018). A Study of Social Entrepreneurship in India. [IRJET]. *International Research Journal of Engineering and Technology*, *5*(1), 829–837.

Singh, P. (2012). Social Entrepreneurship: A Growing Trend in Indian Economy. [IJIET]. *International Journal of Innovations in Engineering and Technology*, *1*(3), 44–52.

Suhashini, S. (2021). A Study of Social Entrepreneurship in India. [IJCRT]. *International Journal of Creative Research Thoughts*, *9*(10), 164–168.

Chapter 9

Reshaping Futures:
The Impact of CSR Investment in Health and Education on Poverty and HDI in India

Subrata Halder

https://orcid.org/0009-0002-4048-2756

Fakir Chand College, India

ABSTRACT

This study comprehensively explores corporate social responsibility (CSR) in India over eight years (2014-15 to 2021-22), analyzing trends, regional variations, and the socio-economic impact. It uncovers intriguing patterns in CSR engagement and emphasizes the widening gap in spending between top and bottom states. Using regression models, the study quantitatively assesses the influence of CSR investments in health and education on poverty and human development. Results highlight the pivotal role of CSR in health, education, poverty reduction, and overall human development. The empirical dimension deepens the understanding of CSR dynamics in India, contributing significantly to academic literature and offering practical insights for policymakers. This multi-level examination, covering expenditure trends and socio-economic outcomes, enriches the discourse on CSR in India, providing a holistic perspective for comprehensive comprehension and strategic decision-making.

INTRODUCTION

In a country like India, every policy must undergo scrutiny through the lens of development. Put simply, the prevailing development discourse has established a framework where policies are expected to align with the nation's predefined development objectives. Consequently, governmental and corporate actions alike are expected to conform to the contemporary development discourse.

Now, the pertinent question arises: what constitutes the contemporary development discourse of the country? Answering this question succinctly proves challenging. Since independence, policymakers have implemented various strategies aimed at advancing the welfare of the nation's citizens. However,

DOI: 10.4018/979-8-3693-2197-3.ch009

these policies cannot be categorized as purely indigenous; rather, they are often crafted in accordance with the global development discourse.

At the core of this dominant development discourse lies the imperative of poverty eradication. Both national and international policymakers formulate strategies with the overarching goal of addressing poverty. Sustainable Development (SD) and Human Development (HD) have emerged as the prevailing concepts in this domain. Consequently, every policy must be crafted in a manner that not only aligns with SD and HD principles but also contributes effectively to poverty eradication.

Corporate Social Responsibility (CSR) originated as a voluntary practice among corporations in developed nations of Europe and America during the 1950s. In our country, the adoption of the Western concept of CSR began following the liberalization of the economy. The Companies Act of 2013, specifically Section 135, now mandates that certain companies allocate a minimum of 2% of their average profits from the past three years towards CSR activities. Additionally, the Act delineates the specific areas in which these funds are to be utilized, aligning closely with Sustainable Development (SD) goals.

This chapter aims to analyze the effectiveness of the 2013 Corporate Social Responsibility (CSR) policy as a developmental instrument, specifically exploring its impact on the interplay between CSR initiatives, poverty alleviation, and human development. The objective is to assess how CSR practices contribute to addressing social and economic disparities, particularly in the context of poverty reduction and the advancement of human development. By delving into the multifaceted aspects of CSR, this examination seeks to provide insights into its role as a strategic tool for fostering sustainable development and improving the overall well-being of communities.

The initial section of the chapter delves into the genealogy of the contemporary development discourse. Following that, the subsequent section explores CSR as a developmental instrument. The third section comprehensively examines the mandatory CSR regime in India. Trends pertaining to CSR in India are scrutinized in the fourth section. The fifth section elucidates the data and methodology employed in this study. Subsequently, the sixth section presents the results and initiates discussion. Finally, the chapter concludes with a summary of findings and implications.

Genealogy of the Development Discourse

Development is a ubiquitous term in our daily lives, yet its interpretation lacks a universally agreed-upon meaning, context, or program of action within the social sciences. This ambiguity is compounded by the fact that the definition of 'development' varies depending on factors such as time, space, context, and the professional or organizational interests of the definer. Over time, the meaning of development has undergone a significant transformation, evolving from the Enlightenment concept of 'Progress' to encompass a diverse array of human needs (Herath, 2009).

The roots of the doctrine of development can be traced back to a colonial legacy, with the term's semantic history intricately tied to the British Development Act of 1929 (Sanyal, 2014). Classical economists, in conjunction with the Marxist school, conceptualized development as an inherent process of societal change, where the economy naturally evolves over time. In stark contrast, within the colonial context, the British Development Act envisioned development as a "discrete structural change in the economy to be brought about by purposeful intervention" (Sanyal, 2014, p.105).

The structured or organized shape of the colonial notion of development took form during the 1950s amid the decolonization and geopolitical tension between two global powers, the USA and the USSR. In his 1949 inaugural speech, marking the beginning of a new era, President Harry Truman presented his vision for a global "fair deal," stressing the importance of addressing the challenges confronted by underdeveloped regions across the world. This speech marked a significant juncture in global affairs, with a focus on less economically advanced nations. Truman aspired to usher in an era where these nations could emulate the characteristics of advanced societies, including heightened industrialization, urbanization, technological advancements in agriculture, increased material production, elevated living standards, and widespread adoption of contemporary education. Key to Truman's vision were the essential elements of capital, science, and technology, considered crucial for achieving a transformative global revolution and extending the American dream of peace and prosperity to all (Escobar, 1995).

The fundamental distinction between the colonial and the President Truman's post-war development discourse is that Truman's project emerged as inherently positive, progressive, and humanitarian, in contrast to Britain's colonial project being perceived as bad, exploitative, and oppressive (Kothari, 2011).

The discourse surrounding decolonized nations has classified them under various labels like underdeveloped, less developed, developing, the Third World, and the South (Naz, 2006). This discourse has prescribed specific practices aimed at transforming these nations into developed entities, with a primary focus on addressing mass poverty. Escobar (1995) notes that the development discourse and strategy emerged in the post-World War II period, primarily driven by the problematization of poverty during that era.

In 1948, the World Bank classified nations with an annual per capita income below $100 as impoverished, a category into which many newly decolonized nations fell (Arndt, 1987). To address absolute poverty and foster the transformation of underdeveloped economies into developed ones, two primary development theories emerged in the 1950s: modernization theory and dependency theory. Modernization theory proposed that reducing poverty in underdeveloped countries could be achieved by providing developed nations greater access to their resources and markets. It emphasized fostering the continuous growth of international capital, anticipating that this progress would uplift less-developed regions globally. In contrast, Dependency theory, rooted in Marxist analysis, argued that the international capitalist system perpetuates economic dominance, with the 'core' (Western centers of power) maintaining control over the 'periphery' (former colonies). It advocated for developing countries to sever ties with Western capitalism and pursue an independent path, often based on socialist principles, to address global economic inequalities (Du Pisani, 2006).

However, by the late 1960s, there was a significant shift in the modernization theory, specifically in terms of the objectives of development, emphasizing ends rather than means. This marked the emergence of new dimensions in development, including a shift towards social development, employment orientation, equity, and the eradication of poverty (Arndt, 1987).

In the 1970s, the discourse on development underwent a transformation, shifting from a narrative centered around capitalist transformation to one focused on "development as improvement" (Sanyal, 2014). During this period, a novel development approach known as the "basic needs approach" gained prominence, garnering attention from both national and international development practitioners, with support from the International Labour Organization (ILO). This approach, an extension of the subsistence concept, went beyond mere material needs for an individual's survival. It advocated for essential facilities and services such as sanitation, education, and healthcare.

In the 1980s, Dr. Amartya Sen introduced a ground-breaking alternative model of progress and development. Sen challenged the conventional understanding of poverty, asserting that constructing an overall picture of poverty required moving beyond merely identifying the poor (Sen, 1982). The concept of entitlement formed the analytical foundation of Sen's theory, where entitlement refers to the ownership that connects one set of ownership to another through certain rules of legitimacy (Sen, 1982). Sen identified various types of entitlement relationships, including trade-based, production-based, own-labor-based, and inheritance and transfer-based entitlements. He argued that the root cause of poverty lies in the failure of entitlement rather than the availability of commodities (Sen, 1982).

Subsequently, Sen refined and transformed the idea of entitlement into the capability approach. He contended that the standard of living is a matter of functioning and capability, emphasizing that a person's capability is the freedom to achieve various lifestyles. Sen defined functioning as "the various things a person may value doing or being" and capability as the ability to achieve these alternative combinations of functioning (Sen, 2000, p.75). According to Sen, capability deprivation is the fundamental cause of poverty, and capability failure results from a lack of freedom. Therefore, he argued that the primary goal of development should be the expansion of freedom (Sen, 2000).

This approach gained acclaim and recognition from international organizations and various fields of knowledge, including welfare economics, philosophy, sociology, and development economics. The United Nations Development Programme (UNDP) embraced this idea, publishing the Human Development Report in 1990, marking a paradigm shift in development practices. In this report Human Development (HD) was defined as:

Human Development is a process of enlarging people's choices. In principle, these choice can be infinite and change over time. But at all levels of development, the three essential ones are for people to lead a long and healthy life, to acquire knowledge and to have access to resources needed for a decent standard of living. If these essential choices are not available, many other opportunities remain inaccessible (UNDP, 1990, p.10).

Mahbub ul Haq (1995), the chief architect of Human Development Report, outlined the fundamental principles of the human development paradigm.

- Development must put people at the centre of its concerns.
- The purpose of development is to enlarge all human choices, not just income.
- The human development paradigm is concerned both with building up human capabilities (through investment in people) and with using those human capabilities fully (through an enabling framework for growth and employment).
- Human development has four essential pillars: equity, sustainability, productivity and empowerment. It regards economic growth as essential but emphasizes the need to pay attention to its quality and distribution, analyses at length its link with human lives and questions its long-term sustainability.
- The human development paradigm defines the ends of development and analyses sensible options for achieving them (Haq, 1995, p.21).

Thus, while recognizing the critical role of economic growth, the paradigm underscores the importance of its quality and fair distribution. It meticulously scrutinizes the impact of economic growth on human lives and raises questions regarding its long-term sustainability. Beyond delineating the ultimate objectives of development, this paradigm also evaluates practical options for achieving them.

Apart from the effort to alleviate poverty, a different approach emerged that examined the interplay among the economy, environment, and society. In the 1960s, impactful scientific revelations in books such as "The Silent Spring," "The Population Bomb," "A Blueprint for Survival," and "Small is Beautiful" highlighted how human activities were negatively affecting the natural environment. This led to heightened awareness through various media channels, including films, TV, and music, warning about an impending ecological crisis. The inception of Earth Day in 1970 marked the commencement of the Green Movement, giving rise to the formation of the first environmental groups like Greenpeace and Friends of the Earth. The momentum continued after UN-led conferences in 1972 and 1974, prompting the establishment of the Brundtland Commission by the UN. In 1987, the commission presented the "Our Common Future" report, emphasizing the need for global fairness by redistributing resources to support economic growth in less affluent nations, with the goal of meeting everyone's basic needs. The report advocated for the simultaneous pursuit of social equity, economic growth, and environmental conservation, coined as the triple bottom line. It recognized the tension between economic development and environmental protection, urging a shift toward environmentally friendly 'sustainable development,' particularly in the developing world (Du Pisani, 2006).

Brundtland Commission (1987) defined sustainable development as "development that meets the needs of the present without compromising the ability of future generations to meet their own needs". The report further stated that at the core of development lies the fundamental aim of meeting human needs and aspirations. Regrettably, in numerous developing nations, a substantial segment of the populace faces challenges in accessing basic necessities like food, clothing, shelter, and employment. Beyond these essential requirements, individuals possess legitimate aspirations for an elevated quality of life. It is essential to acknowledge that a world characterized by enduring poverty and inequality remains vulnerable to ecological and other crises. Achieving sustainable development necessitates a concerted effort to fulfill the basic needs of every individual and guarantee that everyone has the chance to pursue their aspirations for a better life (Brundtland, 1987).

Perceiving human development and sustainable development as conflicting choices is a misconception. Development, as an ongoing process enhancing capabilities, must benefit both present and future generations. Development inherently implies sustainability, with human development incorporating sustainable principles. Sustainable development prioritizes environmental concerns and inter-generational aspects within the broader human development framework (Griffin & McKinley, 1994). According to Haq (1995), Sustainability goes beyond renewing natural resources; it centers on preserving human opportunities. This involves sustaining various forms of capital - physical, human, financil, and environmental. Depleting any capital jeopardizes sustainable development, compromising future generations' options. The key strategy is to replenish and regenerate all forms of capital.

The evolution of development theories, from colonial intervention to the contemporary human development paradigm and sustainable development principles, marks a significant global trajectory. India, actively engaging in this discourse, prioritizes human-centric, equitable, and sustainable progress. Development is a cornerstone of Indian policies, emphasizing meeting diverse needs and aspirations. The nation's commitment to fostering human capabilities, ensuring social equity, and embracing environmentally sustainable practices showcases its dedication to global contributions. This dual focus underscores India's proactive stance in addressing socio-economic challenges while positively influencing the global developmental landscape.

Corporate Social Responsibility (CSR) and Development

Historically, both development and CSR discourse have evolved in parallel. Similar to development, the concept of CSR has gained recognition as an academic discipline following World War II, particularly in the 1950s, and, much like development, it lacks a singular, universally accepted definition. Notably, in each phase of a paradigm shift in development discourse, CSR discourse has been subject to modification and enrichment, incorporating a variety of liberal and sophisticated ideas. Although these two discourses initially evolved independently, over time, the gap between them has gradually diminished, and they are now perceived as complementary to each other.

The origins of the concept of Corporate Social Responsibility (CSR) extend back to the pre-capitalist era, but the academic discourse gained momentum in the 1950s with the publication of Howard Bowen's seminal work, "Social Responsibility of Business." Bowen's influential book marked the beginning of a formal discussion on CSR. According to Bowen, businesses were not only economic entities but were also expected to contribute to social goods such as higher standards of living, widespread economic progress and security, order, justice, freedom, and the development of the individual person (May, Cheney, & Roper, 2007). In the 1960s, CSR literature, mainly driven by academics like Davis, Frederick, McGuire, and Walton, witnessed significant development (Carroll, 1999). CSR gained significant traction in both corporate and academic circles during the 1970s (Kahraman Akdoğu, 2017).

The 1970s marked the initiation of a debate centered on the relationship between business and society. During this period, scholars across various disciplines engaged in a discourse responding to the fundamental question: Does business bear social responsibility? In 1970, he distinguished economist Milton Friedman contended that a business's primary objective is profit generation within legal boundaries. According to Friedman, the responsibility of a business lies in the efficient utilization of its investors' or shareholders' funds, emphasizing a commitment to profitability (Friedman, 1970). In contrast, scholars including Archie Carroll (1979), Thomas M. Jones (1980), R. Edward Freeman (1984), and others, not only recognized the profit motive of corporations but also broadened their perspective on responsibilities to include a more extensive array of stakeholders. This expanded view encompassed employees, customers, suppliers, distributors, competitors, and communities. They advocated for a conception of Corporate Social Responsibility (CSR) that goes beyond the narrow focus on the economic bottom line and legal compliance. Instead, they emphasized addressing a spectrum of contemporary social issues that might be of concern to the public at any given historical moment (May, Cheney, & Roper, 2007).

Archie Carroll, a prominent scholar in Corporate Social Responsibility (CSR), outlined diverse CSR concepts, spanning economic, legal, and voluntary dimensions. These include profit-centric focus (Friedman), extending beyond profit (Davis, Backman), surpassing economic and legal obligations (McGuire), voluntary actions (Manne), a combination of economic, legal, and voluntary efforts (Steiner), concentric circles representing widening responsibilities (CED, Davis, and Blomstrom), broader social system concern (Eells and Walton), and addressing social issues (Hay, Gray, and Gates) (Carroll, 1979, p.498-99). Carroll (1979) proposed shifting towards "social responsiveness," asserting that "the social responsibility of business encompasses the economic, legal, ethical, and discretionary expectations that society has of organizations at a given point in time" (Carroll, 1979, p.500).

Carroll's model has been influential in shaping the discourse around corporate responsibility. Its significance lies in offering a comprehensive framework that guides businesses toward responsible practices, considering economic, legal, ethical, and discretionary dimensions. This holistic approach contributes to building trust, enhancing reputation, and fostering sustainable business practices. It is one of the more popular constructs of CSR that has been used in the literature and practice for several decades (Carroll, 2016).

In the 1980s, the Reagan and Thatcher administrations ushered in a new political ideology centered on alleviating pressure on corporations and tackling high inflation in the USA and the UK. This era saw the introduction of neoliberal economic policies, which, unfortunately, led to adverse social consequences for third-world countries. These repercussions included escalating unemployment rates, a widening wealth gap, and environmental degradation resulting from unethical corporate practices in these nations. Thomas M. Jones played a pivotal role during this period by introducing CSR as a decision-making process influencing corporate behavior. His contribution gave way to a new area of debate around CSR which focused more on its operationalization than on the concept itself. This marked a shift towards operationalizing CSR, giving rise to frameworks like Tuzzolino and Armandi's need-hierarchy model, Strand's systems model, and Cochran and Wood's exploration of the CSR and financial performance link and so on. The operationalization of CSR in the 1980s was influenced by emerging societal concerns. This era witnessed pivotal events reflecting the international community's stance on sustainable development and corporate behaviour. The shift towards operational frameworks and models during this period was a response to these evolving global perspectives (Latapí Agudelo et al., 2019). The World Business Council for Sustainable Development (WBCSD) views CSR as the third pillar of sustainable development (Yakovleva, 2017).

Throughout the 1990s, sustainable development and corporate behavior remained central themes in the CSR discourse. The downsides of globalization, coupled with a rise in corporate scandals and growing societal dissatisfaction, prompted a re-evaluation of corporate conduct. Previously perceived as a societal benefit, economic growth now posed potential threats to development. Activists and international development agencies actively sought solutions to align corporate behavior with development goals. Key players such as the World Bank, United Nations, Business for Social Responsibility (BSR), European Commission (EC), and Department for International Development (DFID) worked towards institutionalizing CSR, aiming for poverty reduction and sustainable business practices (Newell & Frynas, 2007; Latapí Agudelo et al., 2019).

The CSR agenda has traditionally focused on core development issues such as labor standards, human rights, education, health, child labor, conflict, and transparency in government natural resource revenues. However, the business community has often avoided addressing the poverty agenda directly, preferring to frame discussions in terms of wealth creation and livelihoods. Efforts are emerging to bridge the business agenda with poverty reduction, notably through initiatives like the World Business Council for Sustainable Development's 'Sustainable Livelihoods' and the UN Global Compact/UNDP's 'Growing Sustainable Business.' Yet, there's a need for further initiatives targeting smaller enterprises, examining economic power within supply chains, and ensuring equitable standards and practices to truly align CSR with development goals (Fox, 2004). Akdoğu (2017) argued that the emergence of CSR discourse can be viewed as a response to sustainable development, and the integration of CSR initiatives into core business strategies profoundly influences sustainable development.

Various studies affirm the positive impact of Corporate Social Responsibility (CSR) on poverty reduction. For instance, Schölmerich (2013) utilizes a conceptual framework in Cambodia, suggesting that CSR measures integrated into a company's core business have more significant effects on poverty reduction than measures outside core business activities (Schölmerich, 2013). Wuttke & Vilks (2014) explore CSR strategies in India's construction industry, emphasizing the need for core business alignment to improve housing conditions for the poor, proposing industry-specific CSR guidance (Wuttke & Vilks, 2014). Jing et al. (2023) examined the relationship between China's Targeted Poverty Alleviation (TPA) strategy and corporate value. The findings suggest that corporate participation in TPA has a dual impact: it directly benefits individuals and communities by lifting them out of poverty, while also positively influencing corporate value and economic development (Jing et al., 2023). Umar et al. (2023) revealed that significant CSR contributions towards UN SDGs, focusing on sectors such as education, health, environment, disaster relief, and support for micro/small businesses to alleviate poverty (Umar et al., 2023). (Ventura & Jauregui, 2023) found that the CSR strategies used by the companies directly and indirectly contribute toward a reduction in rural poverty in Peru (Ventura & Jauregui, 2023).

In Indian context, Choudhary & Singh (2020) report positive impacts of Tata Steel's CSR initiatives in Odisha, India, indicating potential effectiveness in achieving development goals and reducing poverty. Gautam et al., (2023) found that CSR funding plays a positive role in India's sustainable development, particularly in the sectors of education and environment. Furthermore, it highlights that the interaction of poverty, total CSR funding, and CSR funding in education has a positive impact on sustainable growth, whereas the influence of CSR funding for environmental activities on India's sustainable development is not significant when moderated by poverty scores. Kulkarni & Aggarwal, (2023) examined whether CSR funds can address SDG challenges by analyzing 60 Indian companies' prescribed vs. actual CSR expenditure, thematic focus, geographical distribution, and compliance with the Companies Act. Findings revealed increased business awareness of SDGs post-2014, with a narrow focus on education, healthcare, hunger, and poverty alleviation, limited geographical spread, and improvements in reporting quality, though compliance with the Act remains a challenge. Kulkarni & Aggarwal (2024) Despite government efforts to broaden CSR initiatives in India, there remains a predominant emphasis on four thematic areas: education, healthcare, hunger, and poverty alleviation.

Corporate Social Responsibility (CSR) has become a vital tool for fostering development, especially in poverty reduction. Its evolution within the realm of development responds to the imperative of sustainable development. Integrating CSR initiatives into core business strategies has demonstrated positive impacts on poverty reduction, as evidenced by various studies across the globe. The multifaceted nature of CSR, extending beyond profit motives to encompass social and environmental considerations, positions it as a dynamic force for positive change in the global effort to combat poverty. As CSR evolves, its role as a development tool gains prominence, emphasizing the need for inclusive practices to bridge the gap between business objectives and poverty reduction. The alignment of CSR with broader sustainable development goals reflects a growing recognition of its potential to contribute to societal well-being. In this trajectory, CSR remains a powerful and dynamic force, capable of driving positive change and promoting inclusive development in the corporate sphere.

Mandatory CSR Model in India

India's corporate philanthropy has a longstanding history influenced by Gandhi's Trusteeship philosophy. However, a significant transformation occurred with the introduction of the Companies Act in 2013, marking a paradigm shift in the country's approach to Corporate Social Responsibility (CSR) since its independence. The economic landscape, initially dominated by the Soviet-inspired five-year plans and Public Sector Units (PSUs), posed challenges to the growth of private capital. PSUs, operating under a stringent legal framework, controlled key business areas with a prioritization of social interests over economic gain or profit. Despite objections citing violations of labour rights, environmental damage, and human rights issues within PSUs, they remained a dominant force.

The scenario changed with the deregulation of the economy, paving the way for the rapid growth of the private sector. The subsequent influx of capital, technology, information, labour, and cultural influences reshaped the business landscape. This shift led to the emergence of new business models, ideas, and global practices, influencing domestic investors, regulators, and entrepreneurs. Consequently, the traditional practices of social obligations were gradually replaced by CSR practices aligned with those of developed countries.

The neoliberal economic policy has indeed ushered opulence for a segment of the population, but concurrently, it has marginalized millions, pushing them to the brink of survival. This poses a significant challenge for development planners and policymakers to legitimize the chariot of economic growth. Despite the implementation of numerous schemes for the subsistence of the marginalized, the conditions have not witnessed substantial improvement. Since 2004, a new model of rights-based development practice has emerged in the country.

Parliament has enacted several legislations, such as the Right to Information Act, 2005, the Mahatma Gandhi National Rural Employment Guarantee Act, 2005, and the Right to Education Act, 2009, reflecting a paradigm shift that views development as a human right. In this trajectory, Section 135 of the Companies Act, 2013, which mandates CSR practices, represents an extension of the notion of rights-based development discourse. This provision has transformed the Western notion of CSR as a business tool into CSR as a development tool.

The foundation of Section 135 lies in the "Corporate Social Responsibility Voluntary Guidelines (CSRVG), 2009" and "Guidelines on Corporate Social Responsibility for Central Public Sector Enterprise (GCSRCPSE), March 2010." The preamble of the CSRVG explicitly asserts that CSR is not merely "philanthropy" (Ministry of Corporate Affairs, GOI,2009, p.10), while Para 1.3 of the GCSRCPSE emphasizes that "corporate social responsibility is a company's commitment to operate in an economically, socially, and environmentally sustainable manner, recognizing the interests of its stakeholders. This commitment goes beyond statutory requirements and is closely linked with the practice of Sustainable Development" (Department of Public Enterprises, GOI, 2010, p.3). The core principles articulated in these documents found their way into the Companies Bill, 2011, and were subsequently sanctioned by the Parliament as Section 135, Schedule VII under the Companies Act, 2013 (Mitra & Schmidpeter, 2017). The Section 135 of the Companies Act, 2013 mandates that:

- Every company having net worth of rupees five hundred crore or more, or turnover of rupees one thousand crore or more or a net profit of rupees five crore or more during any financial year shall constitute a Corporate Social Responsibility Committee of the Board consisting of three or more directors, out of which at least one director shall be an independent director [Section 135(1)].
- The CSR Committee is empowered to (a) formulate and recommend to the Board, a Corporate Social Responsibility Policy which shall indicate the activities to be undertaken by the company as specified in Schedule VII; (b) recommend the amount of expenditure to be incurred on the activities referred to in clause (a); and (c) monitor the Corporate Social Responsibility Policy of the company from time to time [Section 135(3)].
- The Board of every company referred to in sub-section (1), shall ensure that the company spends, in every financial year, at least two per cent. of the average net profits of the company made during the three immediately preceding financial years, in pursuance of its Corporate Social Responsibility Policy [Section 135 (5)]. (Indian Companies Act 2013, 2022)

The Schedule VII of the act outlines the specific areas in which companies are obligated to allocate funds for their CSR activities. These include addressing extreme hunger and poverty, promoting education, supporting gender equality and women's empowerment, reducing child mortality, improving maternal health, ensuring environmental sustainability, and enhancing vocational skills for employment. These areas closely align with the Sustainable Development Goals (SDGs) set by the United Nations (UN) in 2015 (Mishra, 2021).

In conclusion, India's approach to Corporate Social Responsibility (CSR) reflects a distinctive trajectory shaped by historical influences, legislative interventions, and evolving development paradigms. The transformation from traditional philanthropy to the legislated CSR model under Section 135 of the Companies Act in 2013 signifies a profound shift. Unlike the European or American notions of CSR, India's CSR framework is mandatory for qualifying companies, underscoring a statutory commitment rather than a voluntary business decision. Moreover, the emphasis on addressing specific societal issues aligns with a rights-based development discourse, viewing CSR as a tool for holistic and sustainable development, going beyond mere philanthropy. This departure from Western models highlights India's unique integration of CSR into a broader human rights and sustainable development agenda, creating a distinctive paradigm in the global CSR landscape.

Trend in CSR Expenditure in India

Figure 1. CSR engagement among PSU and Non-PSU Firms

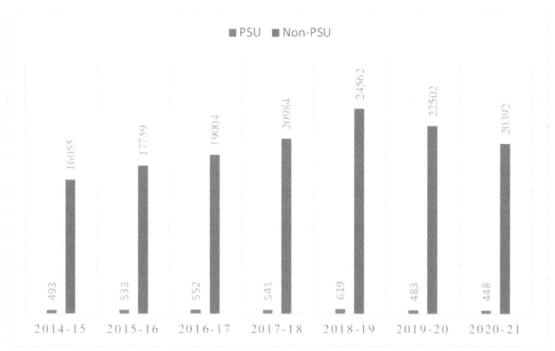

Source: GOI

Figure 1 provides an overview of Corporate Social Responsibility (CSR) engagement among Public Sector Undertakings (PSUs) and non-PSUs in India from 2014-15 to 2020-21. The total number of companies engaged in CSR programs has consistently increased, with a notable rise in both PSU and non-PSU categories. While PSUs have shown a slight decline in the number of companies from 619 in

2018-19 to 448 in 2020-21, non-PSUs exhibit a relatively steady increase from 24,562 in 2018-19 to 20,392 in 2020-21.

Figure 2. Average CSR expenditure per company

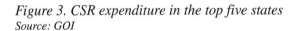

Source: GOI

Figure 2 reveals the average expenditure per company, indicating a substantial difference between PSUs and non-PSUs. PSUs consistently allocate a higher average expenditure per company, ranging from 5.71 to 10.01, compared to non-PSUs, which range from 0.45 to 1.07. This discrepancy underscores variations in CSR commitment and financial allocations between the two sectors, reflecting diverse approaches and priorities in fulfilling corporate social responsibilities.

Figure 3. CSR expenditure in the top five states
Source: GOI

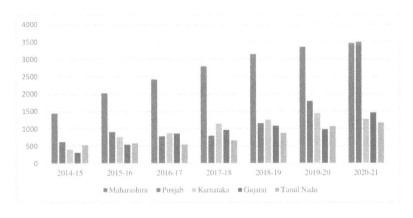

Figure 4. CSR expenditure in the bottom five states

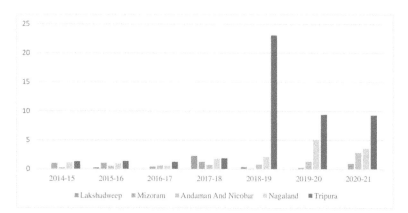

Figure 3 and 4 outline the Corporate Social Responsibility (CSR) expenditure in the top five and bottom five states of India from 2014-15 to 2020-21. Maharashtra consistently leads in CSR expenditure among the top five states, reaching 3,464.80 in 2020-21. Punjab, Karnataka, Gujarat, and Tamil Nadu also show varying levels of CSR spending, with notable increases in Punjab and Gujarat over the years. In contrast, the bottom five states, including Lakshadweep, Mizoram, Andaman and Nicobar, Nagaland, and Tripura, exhibit considerably lower CSR expenditures.

Figure 5. Expenditure gap between the top five and bottom five states

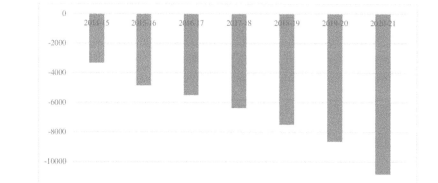

The gap between the top five and bottom five states widens significantly each year, with the difference reaching -10,852.90 in 2020-21. This disparity emphasizes regional imbalances in CSR spending, indicating a need for targeted initiatives to ensure more equitable distribution and fulfillment of corporate social responsibilities across diverse states in India.

Figure 6. Total CSR expenditure (2014-15 to 2021-22

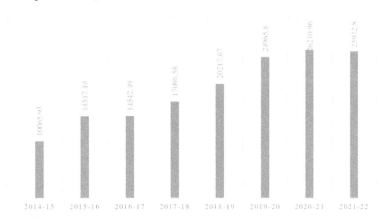

The total Corporate Social Responsibility (CSR) expenditure in India has shown a consistent upward trend over the years, reflecting a growing commitment from companies towards social initiatives. Starting at 10,065.93 in 2014-15, the CSR expenditure has steadily increased, reaching 26,210.96 in 2020-21. The subsequent year, 2021-22, witnessed a slight dip to 25,932.80. This overall positive trajectory underscores a recognition among companies of their role in contributing to societal well-being. The increasing CSR expenditure indicates a heightened awareness of corporate social responsibility and a willingness to invest in various projects and initiatives aimed at fostering sustainable development and addressing societal challenges across different sectors.

Figure 7. Distribution of CSR expenditure

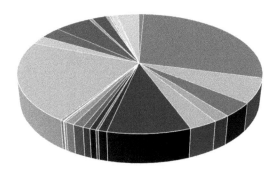

- Conservation Of Natural Resources
- Environmental Sustainability
- Art And Culture
- Rural Development Projects
- Slum Area Development
- Swachh Bharat Kosh
- Women Empowerment
- Clean Ganga Fund
- Health Care
- Other Central Government Funds
- Animal Welfare
- Senior Citizens Welfare
- Setting Up Orphanage
- Special Education

- Education
- Livelihood Enhancement Projects
- Prime Minister'S National Relief Fund
- Safe Drinking Water
- Socio-Economic Inequalities
- Training To Promote Sports
- Armed Forces, Veterans, War Widows/ Dependants
- Gender Equality
- Nec/ Not Mentioned
- Poverty, Eradicating Hunger, Malnutrition
- Sanitation
- Setting Up Homes And Hostels For Women
- Agro Forestry
- Technology Incubators

The Corporate Social Responsibility (CSR) expenditure reflects a diverse and comprehensive commitment by companies towards addressing various societal issues. Education emerges as a significant focus with a substantial allocation of 43,296.23, emphasizing the importance of investing in educational initiatives. Health care is another prominent sector receiving substantial attention, with an allocation of 33,182.91, showcasing the commitment to the well-being of communities. Rural development projects (14,119.78) and livelihood enhancement projects (5,771.06) underscore efforts towards inclusive development and poverty alleviation. Environmental sustainability (10,190.38) and conservation of natural resources (1,139.78) signify a commitment to ecological responsibility. The allocation to gender equality (501.93), women empowerment (1,563.91), and socio-economic inequalities (1,109.64) highlights a focus on fostering inclusivity and addressing social disparities. Other key areas include sanitation (3,494.83), poverty eradication (8,589.38), and technology incubators (228.97), indicating a holistic approach to CSR that aligns with the broader goals of sustainable development. The diverse range of sectors addressed in the CSR expenditure underscores a multifaceted commitment to social and environmental well-being.

From the above analysis it has been observed that corporations in India directing approximately 50% of their total expenditure over an eight-year period (2014-15 to 2021-22) towards the health and education sectors. This substantial investment underscores a strategic emphasis on fundamental elements contributing to human development. Universally health and education are both recognized as direct components of human well-being and a form of human capital that increases an individual's capabilities (Bloom & Canning, 2003; Gounder & Xing, 2012).

This allocation pattern reflects a conscientious effort by corporations to enhance foundational capabilities, grounded in the belief that progress in health and education is instrumental in elevating the overall well-being of the nation. By prioritizing these sectors, businesses signal a commitment to fostering positive change, aligning their efforts with broader developmental objectives. Against this backdrop, the chapter endeavors to examine the impact of CSR investment in education and health on poverty and human development.

DATA AND METHODOLOGY

Secondary data has been collected from the official websites of the Government of India (GOI), the World Bank (WB) and the United Nations (UN) over a period of 8 years commencing from 2014 to 2021. The collected data has been normalized using the following technique.

X= (Actual Value – Minimum Value) / (Maximum Value – Minimum Value)

Table 1. Description of the variables used in this study

Variable	Type	Description	Data Source
Poverty	Dependent	Poverty headcount ratio at $2.15: the percentage of the population living on less than $2.15 a day at 2017 international prices.	WB
CSR Expenditure on Health and Education (CSREHE)	Independent	Total expenditure incurred by all the companies falling under the purview of Section 135 of the Companies Act, 2013	GOI
Human Development Index (HDI)	Independent/ Dependent	Human Development Index of India	UN
Employment	Independent	Employment to population ratio, 15+, total (%) (modeled ILO estimate)	WB
Foreign Direct Investment (FDI)	Independent	Foreign direct investment, net (BoP, current US$): net inflows of investment to acquire a lasting management interest (10 percent or more of voting stock) in an enterprise operating in an economy other than that of the investor.	WB
Health	Independent	Life Expectancy at Birth (years)	UN
Education	Independent	Expected Years of Schooling (years)	UN

Regression Model:

$$\text{Poverty} = \beta_0 + \beta_1 \text{CSREHE} + \beta_2 \text{HDI} + \beta_3 \text{Employment} + \beta_4 \text{FDI} + \varepsilon \ \ldots\ldots \tag{1}$$

$$\text{HDI} = \beta_0 + \beta_1 \text{CSR} + \beta_2 \text{Poverty} + \beta_3 \text{ Health} + \beta_4 \text{Education} + \beta_5 \text{ Employment} + \varepsilon \ \ldots\ldots \tag{2}$$

Where, ε stand for error term

Results and Discussion

Table 2. Regression Output Model-I

HDI	Coef.	St.Err.	t-value	p-value	Sig
CSREHE	-0.61	0.175	-3.49	0.04	**
HDI	-31.545	6.712	-4.7	0.018	**
FDI	-0.954	0.19	-5.02	0.015	**
Employment	0.261	0.248	1.05	0.37	
Constant	21.291	4.381	4.86	0.017	**
Mean dependent var	0.502	SD dependent var			0.415
R-squared	0.96	Number of obs			8
F-test	18.059	Prob > F			0.019
Akaike crit. (AIC)	-8.209	Bayesian crit. (BIC)			-7.811

*** p<.01, ** p<.05, * p<.1

The results of the regression analysis, represented in Table 2, indicate a well-fitted model, as evidenced by the statistically significant F-statistic ($F(4, 3) = 18.06$, $p = 0.0194$). The model accounts for a substantial proportion of the variance in the dependent variable, with an R-squared of 0.9601, reflecting a strong goodness of fit. Examining the individual predictors, the CSR Expenditure on Health and Education (CSREHE) exhibits a significant negative relationship with poverty ($\beta = -0.610$, $t = -3.49$, $p = 0.040$), implying that an increase in CSR expenditure in health and education corresponds to a decrease in poverty. Similarly, the Human Development Index (HDI) and Foreign Direct Investment (FDI) both demonstrate highly significant negative associations with poverty ($\beta = -31.545$, $t = -4.70$, $p = 0.018$; $\beta = -0.954$, $t = -5.02$, $p = 0.015$, respectively), indicating that improvements in human development index and increased foreign direct investment are linked to substantial reductions in poverty. Conversely, Employment (employment) does not show a significant association with poverty ($\beta = 0.261$, $t = 1.05$, $p = 0.370$).

In summary, the model demonstrates a robust fit, and individual predictors such as CSR expenditure in health and education, HDI, and FDI significantly contribute to explaining variations in poverty levels. The findings suggest that efforts in CSR in health and education, improvement in human development, and increased foreign direct investment are associated with reduced poverty levels.

Table 3. Regression Output Model-II

	Coef.	**St.Err.**	**t-value**	**p-value**	**Sig**
CSREHE	0.021	0.004	5.91	0.027	**
Poverty	-0.014	0.002	-7.37	0.018	**
Health	0.029	0.003	10.75	0.009	***
Education	0.018	0.003	6.73	0.021	**
Employment	0.012	0.003	3.36	0.078	*
Constant	0.599	0.006	104.83	0	***
Mean dependent var		0.637	SD dependent var		0.009
R-squared		0.993	Number of obs		8
F-test		60.447	Prob > F		0.016
Akaike crit. (AIC)		-81.346	Bayesian crit. (BIC)		-80.87

*** p<.01, ** p<.05, * p<.1

The results of the regression analysis, presented in Table 3, reveal a well-fitted model for predicting the Human Development Index (HDI), as evidenced by the statistically significant F-statistic ($F_{(5, 2)}$ = 60.45, p = 0.0164). The model explains a substantial proportion of the variance in the dependent variable, with an impressive R-squared of 0.9934, indicating a strong goodness of fit. Exploring the individual predictors, the CSR Expenditure on Health and Education (CSREHE) demonstrates a significant positive relationship with HDI (β = 0.021, t = 5.91, p = 0.027), suggesting that an increase in CSR expenditure in health and education is associated with higher levels of human development. Additionally, Poverty exhibits a significant negative association with HDI (β = -0.014, t = -7.37, p = 0.018), indicating that lower poverty levels are linked to higher human development. Furthermore, Health and Education both show highly significant positive associations with HDI (β = 0.029, t = 10.75, p = 0.009; β = 0.018, t = 6.73, p = 0.021, respectively), emphasizing the importance of investments in health and education for overall human development. However, Employment does not exhibit a statistically significant association with HDI (β = 0.012, t = 3.36, p = 0.078).

In short, these findings underscore the crucial role of CSR initiatives in health and education, poverty reduction, and investments in health and education for fostering higher levels of human development.

Table 4. Multicollinearity

Model-I			**Model-II**		
Variable	**VIF**	**1/VIF**	**Variable**	**VIF**	**1/VIF**
Employment	2.76	0.362	CSREHE	5.61	0.178
CSREHE	1.75	0.571	Employment	4.24	0.236
HDI	1.71	0.585	Health	2.62	0.382
FDI	1.51	0.662	Education	2.11	0.474
			Poverty	2.09	0.478
Mean VIF		1.93	Mean VIF		3.33

In both models, the Variable Inflation Factor (VIF) values for all variables are below the commonly accepted threshold of 10. Additionally, the mean VIF, which is also low in both models, further supports the conclusion that multicollinearity is not a concern.

Table 5. Breusch-Pagan / Cook-Weisberg test for Heteroskedasticity

Ho	Model-I Constant variance	Model_II Constant variance
Variables	Fitted values of Poverty	Fitted values of HDI
chi2(1)	0.08	0.75
Prob > chi2	0.7732	0.3852

The Breusch-Pagan/Cook-Weisberg test for heteroskedasticity assesses whether there is a constant variance in the residuals related to the fitted values of dependent variable. For Model-I, the chi-squared test statistic is 0.08 with a p-value of 0.7732. Since the p-value is greater than the typical significance level of 0.05, we fail to reject the null hypothesis (Ho) of constant variance. This suggests that there is no significant evidence of heteroskedasticity in the residuals of Model-I concerning the fitted values of Poverty.

Similarly, for Model-II, the chi-squared test statistic is 0.75 with a p-value of 0.3852. As the p-value exceeds 0.05, we do not reject the null hypothesis (Ho) of constant variance. This implies that there is no substantial indication of heteroskedasticity in the residuals of Model-II concerning the fitted values of HDI. Both test results suggest that the assumption of constant variance holds for the respective models.

Table 6. Shapiro-Wilk W test for normality of residuals

Model	Variable	Obs	W	V	Z	Prob>z
Model-I	Residu1	8	0.91982	1.117	0.18	0.42843
Model-II	Residu2	8	0.94674	0.742	-0.463	0.67831

For Model-I, the Shapiro-Wilk W test assesses the normality of residuals (Residu1). The test statistic is 0.91982, and the p-value associated with the Z statistic is 0.42843. With a higher p-value, there is insufficient evidence to reject the null hypothesis of normality. Therefore, the residuals in Model-I can be considered approximately normally distributed.

The test statistic is 0.94674, and the p-value associated with the Z statistic is 0.67831 for Model-II. Similar to Model-I, the higher p-value suggests that there is no significant departure from normality in the residuals of Model-II. Consequently, the residuals in Model-II can be considered to follow an approximately normal distribution.

The results of the statistical analysis reveal significant insights into the relationship between various factors and poverty, as well as predictors of the Human Development Index (HDI). Both models exhibit a robust fit, supported by noteworthy F-statistics and high R-squared values, indicating their effectiveness in explaining variance in the dependent variables. In the poverty analysis (Model-I), CSR Expenditure on Health and Education (CSREHE) exhibits a negative relationship with poverty, emphasizing the importance of corporate social responsibility in health, education, and foreign investment for poverty reduction. Conversely, the non-significant association of Employment with poverty suggests its limited role as a predictor in this context. Transitioning to the HDI analysis (Model-II), a positive relationship between CSREHE and HDI, along with a significant negative association of Poverty with HDI, underscores the vital role of corporate social responsibility in health and education for overall human development. The absence of a significant association with Employment in HDI highlights its lesser impact in this model. The low VIF values, confirmation of constant variance, and normality of residuals further support the robustness and validity of the models. In conclusion, the study emphasizes the pivotal roles of CSR initiatives in health and education, alongside poverty reduction efforts, in influencing both poverty levels and the Human Development Index, offering valuable insights for policymakers and practitioners aiming to enhance human development and alleviate poverty through strategic interventions. Thus, the findings of the study support the notion of CSR as development tool.

This study contributes significantly to the understanding of Corporate Social Responsibility (CSR) dynamics in India through a multi-faceted approach. Firstly, it presents a detailed analysis of CSR trends in both Public Sector Undertakings (PSUs) and non-PSUs, unraveling nuanced patterns in expenditure and sectoral preferences. The examination of regional CSR spending disparities, particularly the widening gap between top and bottom states, sheds light on the need for targeted interventions to ensure more equitable distribution. The study's revelation of an upward trajectory in India's total CSR expenditure over seven years provides a valuable snapshot of the evolving landscape of corporate philanthropy. Furthermore, the exploration of the impact of CSR investments on poverty and human development, employing regression models, adds a quantitative dimension to the research, contributing empirical evidence to the broader discourse on CSR. In summary, this study's multi-level analysis, ranging from expenditure trends to socio-economic impact, makes substantial original contributions to the literature on CSR in India, providing insights valuable for both academia and practical policy considerations.

CONCLUSION

The comprehensive analysis of Corporate Social Responsibility (CSR) expenditure in India reveals notable trends and patterns in the period from 2014-15 to 2021-22. The increasing engagement of companies, particularly the consistent rise in non-Public Sector Undertakings (non-PSUs), underscores a growing commitment towards fulfilling corporate social responsibilities. However, a significant difference in average expenditure per company between PSUs and non-PSUs suggests variations in CSR commitment and financial allocations, highlighting diverse approaches in meeting social responsibilities. State-wise disparities in CSR spending are evident, with Maharashtra leading among the top five states, while the bottom five states witness considerably lower expenditures. The widening gap between these states emphasizes the need for targeted initiatives to promote more equitable CSR distribution across regions in India.

The overall upward trend in CSR expenditure indicates a positive recognition among companies of their role in contributing to societal well-being. Education and health emerge as predominant areas of focus, reflecting a strategic emphasis on fundamental elements crucial for human development. This strategic allocation aligns with global understanding, emphasizing health and education as vital components of human well-being and capital.

The statistical models further elucidate the relationships between CSR expenditure, poverty, and the Human Development Index (HDI). The findings indicate that CSR initiatives in health and education, coupled with poverty reduction efforts, significantly influence poverty levels and contribute to higher HDI. These insights are valuable for policymakers and practitioners seeking effective strategies for poverty alleviation and human development.

Despite the robustness of the statistical models, certain limitations need consideration. The study relies on aggregate CSR expenditure data, and a more granular analysis at the company level could provide deeper insights. Additionally, the analysis does not account for the qualitative aspects of CSR initiatives, and a qualitative assessment could enhance the understanding of the impact of specific projects.

The study contributes to the existing literature on CSR by providing a detailed analysis of trends, sectoral allocations, and the impact on poverty and human development. The insights into state-wise disparities and the predominant focus on education and health have practical implications for policymakers, allowing them to tailor interventions for more equitable outcomes. The findings also offer guidance to businesses aiming to align their CSR initiatives with societal needs.

Future research could delve into a longitudinal analysis of specific CSR projects to assess their long-term impact on poverty and human development. Exploring the effectiveness of different CSR strategies and initiatives in diverse contexts would provide nuanced insights. Additionally, investigating the role of regulatory frameworks and policy changes in shaping CSR practices could contribute to a more comprehensive understanding of the factors influencing corporate social responsibility in India.

REFERENCES

Akdoğu, S. (2017). *The Link Between CSR and Sustainable Development in a Global Economy.*, doi:10.1007/978-3-319-35083-7_13

H. W. Arndt. (1987). *ECONOMIC DEVELOPMENT THE HISTORY OF AN IDEA.* The University of Chicago Press Chicago and London. doi:10.4324/9781315774206-29

Bloom, D., & Canning, D. (2003). The Health and Poverty of Nations: From theory to practice. *Journal of Human Development*, 4(1), 47–71. doi:10.1080/1464988032000051487

Brundtland, G. H. (1987). *Our Common Future World Commission On Environment And Developement.*

Carroll, A. B. (1979). A Three-Dimensional Conceptual Model of Corporate Performance. *Academy of Management Review*, 4(4), 497–505. doi:10.2307/257850

Carroll, A. B. (1999). Corporate Social Responsibility: Evolution of a Definitional Construct. *Business & Society*, 38(3), 268–295. doi:10.1177/000765039903800303

Carroll, A. B. (2016). Carroll's pyramid of CSR: Taking another look. *International Journal of Corporate Social Responsibility*, 1(1), 3. doi:10.1186/s40991-016-0004-6

Choudhary, A., & Singh, V. (2020). In N. Capaldi, S. O. Idowu, & R. Schmidpeter (Eds.), *Exploring the Impact of Corporate Social Responsibility on Poverty Reduction BT - Responsible Business in a Changing World: New Management Approaches for Sustainable Development (B. Díaz Díaz* (pp. 329–338). Springer International Publishing., doi:10.1007/978-3-030-36970-5_18

Department of Public Enterprises. (2010). Guidelines on Corporate Social Responsibility for CPSES. In *Corporate Social Responsibility for Central Public Sector Enterprises.* http://pib.nic.in/newsite/erelease. aspx?relid=68604

Du Pisani, J. A. (2006). Sustainable development – historical roots of the concept. *Environmental Sciences (Lisse)*, *3*(2), 83–96. doi:10.1080/15693430600688831

Dynamic CSR Report. (n.d.). CSR. https://www.csr.gov.in/content/csr/global/master/home/ExploreCsrData/dynamic-csr-report-search.html

Employment to population ratio, 15+, total (%) (modeled ILO estimate) - India. (n.d.). World Bank. https://data.worldbank.org/indicator/SL.EMP.TOTL.SP.ZS?locations=IN

Escobar, A. (1995). Encountering Development. In Encountering Development. doi:10.1515/9781400839926

Fox, T. (2004). Corporate Social Responsibility and Development: In quest of an agenda. *Development*, *47*(3), 29–36. doi:10.1057/palgrave.development.1100064

Friedman, M. (n.d.). A Friedman doctrine-- The Social Responsibility of Business Is to Increase Its Profits. *The New York Times.* https://www.nytimes.com/1970/09/13/archives/a-friedman-doctrine-the-social-responsibility-of-business-is-to.html

Gautam, R. S., Bhimavarapu, V. M., Rastogi, S., Kappal, J. M., Patole, H., & Pushp, A. (2023). Corporate Social Responsibility Funding and Its Impact on India’s Sustainable Development: Using the Poverty Score as a Moderator. In Journal of Risk and Financial Management (Vol. 16, Issue 2). doi:10.3390/jrfm16020090

Gounder, R., & Xing, Z. (2012). Impact of education and health on poverty reduction: Monetary and nonmonetary evidence from Fiji. *Economic Modelling*, *29*(3), 787–794. doi:10.1016/j.econmod.2012.01.018

Griffin, K., & McKinley, T. (1994). Human Development and Sustainable Development BT - Implementing a Human Development Strategy (K. Griffin & T. McKinley (Eds.); pp. 96–102). Palgrave Macmillan UK. doi:10.1007/978-1-349-23543-8_6

Haq, M. U. (1995). Reflections On Human Development. In Reflections On Human Development. doi:10.1093/oso/9780195101911.001.0001

Herath, D. (2009). The Discourse of Development: Has it reached maturity? *Third World Quarterly*, *30*(8), 1449–1464. doi:10.1080/01436590903279216

Indian Ministry Of Corporate Affairs, & Werner, W. J. (2009). Corporate Social Responsiblility Voluntary Guidelines. *Journal of Health Population and Nutrition, 27*(4), 545–562. http://www.ncbi.nlm.nih.gov/pubmed/20304693%5Cnhttp://www.mca.gov.in/Ministry/latestnews/CSR_Voluntary_Guidelines_24dec2009.pdf

Jing, J., Wang, J., & Hu, Z. (2023). Has corporate involvement in government-initiated corporate social responsibility activities increased corporate value?—Evidence from China's Targeted Poverty Alleviation. *Humanities & Social Sciences Communications*, *10*(1), 355. doi:10.1057/s41599-023-01869-7

Kahraman Akdoğu, S. (2017). In S. Vertigans & S. O. Idowu (Eds.), *The Link Between CSR and Sustainable Development in a Global Economy BT - Corporate Social Responsibility: Academic Insights and Impacts* (pp. 223–240). Springer International Publishing. doi:10.1007/978-3-319-35083-7_13

Kothari, U. (2011). History, time and temporality in development discourse. *History, Historians and Development Policy: A Necessary Dialogue*, 65–70.

Kulkarni, V., & Aggarwal, A. (2023). Assessing synergies and challenges between CSR and SDG with evidence from India. *International Journal of Indian Culture and Business Management*, *28*(4), 425–441. doi:10.1504/IJICBM.2023.130091

Kulkarni, V., & Aggarwal, A. (2024). Business response to mandatory corporate social responsibility with evidence from India. *Business Strategy & Development*, *7*(1), e323. doi:10.1002/bsd2.323

Latapí Agudelo, M. A., Jóhannsdóttir, L., & Davídsdóttir, B. (2019). A literature review of the history and evolution of corporate social responsibility. *International Journal of Corporate Social Responsibility*, *4*(1), 1. doi:10.1186/s40991-018-0039-y

May, S. K., Cheney, G., & Roper, J. (2007). The debate over corporate social responsibility (J. May, S. K., Cheney, G., & Roper (Ed.)). Oxford University Press.

Mishra, L. (2021). Corporate social responsibility and sustainable development goals: A study of Indian companies. *Journal of Public Affairs*, *21*(1), e2147. doi:10.1002/pa.2147

Mitra, N., & Schmidpeter, R. (2017). The why, what and how of the CSR mandate: The India story. *Corporate Social Responsibility in India: Cases and Developments after the Legal Mandate*, 1–8.

Nations, U. (n.d.). *Human Development Index*. Human Development Reports. https://hdr.undp.org/data-center/human-development-index#/indicies/HDI

Naz, F. (2006). Arturo Escobar and the development discourse: An overview. *Asian Affairs*, *28*(3), 64–84.

Newell, P., & Frynas, J. G. (2007). Beyond csr? Business, poverty and social justice: An introduction. *Third World Quarterly*, *28*(4), 669–681. doi:10.1080/01436590701336507

Poverty headcount ratio at $2.15 a day (2017 PPP) (% of population) - India | Data. (n.d.). World Bank. https://data.worldbank.org/indicator/SI.POV.DDAY?locations=IN

Sanyal, K. (2014). *Rethinking Capitalist Development Primitive Accumulation, Governmentality and Post-Colonial Capitalism-Routledge India*. Routledge India. doi:10.4324/9781315767321

Schölmerich, M. J. (2013). On the impact of corporate social responsibility on poverty in Cambodia in the light of Sen's capability approach. *Asian Journal of Business Ethics*, *2*(1), 1–33. doi:10.1007/s13520-012-0016-6

Sen, A. (1982). *Poverty and famines: an essay on entitlement and deprivation*. Oxford university press.

Sen, A. (2000). *Develeopment as freedom*. Anchor Books.

Umar, U. H., Besar, M. H. A., & Abduh, M. (2023). Compatibility of the CSR practices of Islamic banks with the United Nations SDGs amidst COVID-19: A documentary evidence. *International Journal of Ethics and Systems*, *39*(3), 629–647. doi:10.1108/IJOES-12-2021-0221

UNDP. (1990). *Human Development Report 1990. UNDP*. United Nations Development Programme.

Ventura, J., & Jauregui, K. (2023). Poverty Reduction through Corporate Social Responsibility: Case Study of Peruvian Rural Families. In Sustainability, 15(2). doi:10.3390/su15021256

Wuttke, M., & Vilks, A. (2014). Poverty alleviation through CSR in the Indian construction industry. *Journal of Management Development*, *33*(2), 119–130. doi:10.1108/JMD-11-2013-0150

Yakovleva, N. (2017). *Corporate social responsibility in the mining industries*. Routledge. doi:10.4324/9781315259215

Chapter 10
Role of Media and Communication on Sustainable Entrepreneurship

Nidhi Agarwal

https://orcid.org/0000-0002-1590-9888

Lincoln University College, Malaysia

Ekansh Agarwal

https://orcid.org/0000-0001-5497-8838

NMIMS University, India

Jocelyn B. Hipona

La Consolacion University, Philippines

ABSTRACT

This chapter presents a comprehensive examination of the role that media and communication play in the development and promotion of sustainable business practises. This study analyses how communication and media affect sustainable business in different ways. This study focuses on how media affects public views and understanding of sustainable practises, influencing consumer behaviour and market needs. This study also explores how successful sustainable firms use various media platforms to communicate their sustainability initiatives, build brand equity, and engage stakeholders. The relationship between media coverage and green company practises is examined in this study. This programme seeks to illuminate the shifting relationship between media, communication, and sustainable enterprise. A careful review of relevant scholarly articles and empirical studies will achieve the goal. This chapter seeks to identify optimal, strategic, and promising research areas in media and communication to create a more sustainable corporate ecosystem.

DOI: 10.4018/979-8-3693-2197-3.ch010

INTRODUCTION

Entrepreneurship is essential to the advancement of society and the emergence of new opportunities in today's interconnected world. Particularly popular is the concept of sustainable entrepreneurship, which places equal importance on a company's financial success and its positive environmental, social, and economic effects on the world (Punla, 2022). The media and communication industries have also undergone profound changes, maturing into potent instruments for distributing data, moulding public opinion, and influencing institutional norms and procedures. This study delves into the complicated web of connections between media, communication, and eco-friendly business practises, illuminating how the media may encourage, assist, and even discourage the quest for environmental responsibility among businesses. This study examines the significance of media and communication in influencing and bolstering environmentally responsible business practises in today's dynamic global economy.

Sustainable entrepreneurship, defined as an all-encompassing strategy that prioritises financial growth with social and environmental improvement, has emerged as a potent agent of change. The media's ability to reach wide audiences through a variety of mediums gives it considerable sway in the dissemination of information, the elevation of consciousness, and the moulding of public opinion. In this context, the study analyses the symbiotic link between media and sustainable business, emphasising both the benefits and problems this partnership brings. Dwivedi et al. (2022), Nishant et al. (2020), and Pan et al. (2022) agree that sustainability and digitalization are two of the most pervasive concepts directing modern social, political, and scientific discussions. Grand social and environmental concerns, such as climate change and yawning inequality, are coming into sharper focus, and initiatives like the United Nations' Sustainable Development Goals reflect this.

Some major points of interest are:

- By increasing people's understanding of environmental and social problems (Dwivedi, 2022), the media can help spur the growth of sustainable businesses by expanding demand for their goods and services.
- In its educational capacity, the media helps to disseminate information about sustainable business practises and encourages their adoption.
- To advocate for legislation that promote sustainability and to encourage enterprises adhering to sustainable principles, the media plays a crucial role. They highlight cutting-edge approaches to business sustainability.
- The media encourages openness by holding companies responsible for their sustainability claims and actions.

The study also recognises difficulties, such as the inherent biases and potential conflicts in media coverage. Sustainable entrepreneurs face the double-edged sword of media criticism and the need for transparency from news organisations that may be biased or motivated by financial interests in how they report on the topic. This study attempts to provide a thorough understanding of how media and communication may be used to further the goals of sustainable entrepreneurship through the use of case studies, surveys, and content analysis. This provides helpful information for those interested in using the media to inspire social and environmental good and ethical corporate practises. Finally, this article offers a nuanced perspective on a dynamic and vital interaction in today's business scene, adding to the current discourse on the nexus of media, entrepreneurship, and sustainability (Lizarondo, 2023).

PURPOSE

Our goal is to better understand the ways in which media and communication affect, promote, and challenge the pursuit of sustainable business practises by analysing and shedding light on this complex relationship. We're committed to learning more about how the media can help achieve sustainable goals including public engagement, policy change, and corporate responsibility.

We strive to provide valuable insights and knowledge to entrepreneurs, businesses, policymakers, and the general public by conducting extensive research, analysing data, and presenting studies. This enables these groups to make informed decisions that have a positive impact on the economy, society, and the environment as a whole. It will include:

- Inspiring ethical, ecologically friendly (Bhati, 2021), and socially responsible business models by demonstrating the potential of the media to bring attention to sustainable practises and innovations.
- To discourage "greenwashing" and encourage greater openness and credibility in the pursuit of sustainability, we strive to ensure that corporations are held accountable for their sustainability claims.
- In order to facilitate the sharing of knowledge and best practises, our research and findings provide a forum for conversation among business owners, journalists, policymakers, and the general public.
- Our goal is to improve the conversation about sustainable entrepreneurship, the influence of the media on this field, and the opportunities and difficulties that arise from this interplay. As a result, the business community as a whole becomes more knowledgeable, ethical, and long-term sustainable.

NEED AND SIGNIFICANCE

1. When it comes to global issues like climate change, resource depletion, and social inequality, sustainable business is more important than ever. The dissemination of information, the impetus for collective action, and the influence on corporate and consumer decisions are all facilitated by the media and communication.
2. Businesses that want to survive in a world of ever-shifting consumer tastes and regulatory mandates would do well to study the media's impact on sustainable entrepreneurship. To better match their actions with sustainability aims, entrepreneurs should leverage the power of media.
3. Mass Media Is a Crucial Educational and Informational Resource. Media outlets can influence the entrepreneurial landscape for the better by spreading awareness of sustainable practises among entrepreneurs, corporate leaders, and the general public through their reporting and messaging.
4. Media serves as watchdog, holding companies accountable for sustainability claims and practises through increased transparency. The study of media's role in this accountability process can assist identify areas where firms need to improve their transparency and authenticity.
5. The media's ability to educate the public about pressing environmental and social problems presents a promising window of opportunity. Entrepreneurs looking to break into emerging countries would do well to study the impact media has on consumer tastes and habits.

6. The media often promotes sustainable policies and laws. By analysing this phenomenon, we can learn more about how business owners can influence legislators and win public support for their initiatives through the media.

7. The relevance of ethical and responsible business practises has been highlighted by research on the impact of the media on sustainable entrepreneurship. These practises are vital to maintaining a positive image for a company's brand and ensuring its long-term success.

8. Sharing knowledge and best practises is essential as sustainable enterprise develops. This study provides a forum for exchanging ideas and information that can improve the awareness of sustainable business amongst the general public.

9. To further our understanding of the complex interaction between media and sustainable entrepreneurship, this area of study presents a fertile ground for academic research and intellectual contributions.

10. Because it promotes economic growth while also addressing environmental and social concerns, sustainable entrepreneurship has the potential to have a global influence. The media's position as a powerful force on a global scale means that this effect might be greatly magnified, making the investigation of this connection of paramount importance.

Platforms, blockchain, AI, VR, and IoT, among other digital technologies, have revolutionised many sectors (e.g., hospitality, agriculture, transportation) by giving businesses access to previously unimaginable efficiencies and fresh avenues for expansion (Nambisan, 2017; von Briel et al., 2018). Dwivedi et al. (2022) and Papagiannis's and Marikyan (2022) are only two examples of recent works that highlight the potential of digital technologies in mitigating and counteracting some of the world's most pressing environmental and social challenges. A rise in the number of patents for digital sustainability and a rise in venture capital investments are more evidence in favour of this theory (Anderson & Caimi, 2022).

The research on the significance of media and communication in environmentally responsible business is crucial. It might have far-reaching effects for entrepreneurs, businesses, legislators, businesses, consumers, and the general public. We can create a better, more sustainable future where enterprises thrive while contributing to the well-being of the earth and its inhabitants if we learn how the media can both catalyse and challenge sustainable entrepreneurship.

CONCEPTUAL FRAMEWORK

It is possible to construct a conceptual framework for the function of media and communication in sustainable entrepreneurship by focusing on several essential components, including the following aspects:

Influence of Media Towards Sustainability: The influence of the media on creating views and attitudes towards sustainability is at the heart of the framework. This influence is one of the most important aspects of the framework. Through the use of conventional, digital, and social media, this component investigates the ways in which different types of media platforms contribute to the formation of public perceptions, the influence of consumer behaviour, and the promotion of awareness among the audience regarding sustainable practises.

Strategies for Entrepreneurial Communication: This section focuses on the strategic communication tactics that are utilised by entrepreneurs who are committed to sustainability. It involves the manner in which business owners make use of various media platforms in order to successfully communicate their sustainability activities, develop brand identity, engage stakeholders, and differentiate themselves in the market based on their commitment to sustainability.

Impact on Enterprise and Media Coverage: This aspect evaluates the reciprocal relationship that exists between media coverage and sustainable enterprise. It investigates the ways in which the portrayal of sustainable enterprises in the media, whether favourable or bad, can have an effect on the visibility, credibility, and resource accessibility of these endeavours. In addition to this, it investigates the ways in which the actions of business owners have an impact on the coverage of sustainability issues in the media.

Innovation and Digital Media: The focus of this component is on the role that digital media and developing communication technologies play in the overall process. This article sheds light on the significance of various platforms, including social media, online communities, and digital storytelling, in terms of their ability to facilitate stakeholder participation, develop networks, and advocate for sustainable business models.

Changes in the Nature of Media, Communication, and Sustainable Entrepreneurship: This section captures the changing nature of media, communication, and sustainable entrepreneurship. This article investigates the probable future trends, difficulties, and opportunities that are associated with utilising media for sustainable self-employment. Moreover, it highlights the importance of continuously adapting to new circumstances, being innovative, and working together in this ever-changing environment.

The purpose of this conceptual framework is to provide a thorough guide for understanding the complex relationship that exists between sustainable business, communication tactics, and the media. For the purpose of analysing, implementing, and further exploring the multifaceted relationship between media and the promotion of sustainable entrepreneurial endeavours, it offers a systematic strategy that can be utilised by researchers, practitioners, and stakeholders.

RESEARCH METHODOLOGY

The research on the impact of media and communication on sustainable entrepreneurship encompassed a sample size of 100 participants, consisting of 50 small and medium-sized enterprise (SME) stakeholders and 50 media executives. A series of questionnaires was developed to assess the constructs of systematic strategy (SS), communication tactics (CT), media (M), and sustainable business (SB), specifically focusing on the perceived influence of media on sustainable entrepreneurship (Valdez, 2023). The study participants were chosen using a convenience sampling procedure. The data were encoded and underwent data cleansing before to analysis using SPSS.

ANALYSIS

The advent of internet access and the subsequent growth of social media have brought about a shift in how consumers acquire information regarding products and services. Therefore, previously, organisations relied on conventional methods of communication and enlisted the assistance of marketing and public relations agencies to create their messages and act as intermediaries between the organisation and the media (Cahapin, 2022; Khedhiri, 2022). However, nowadays, business agencies have the capability to independently create their own messages and possess a wide array of tools and methods to effectively disseminate their message to the public.

The traditional method of commercial organisations disseminating their message to consumers, without providing them with a direct means of response, is obsolete. In the present era, social media serves as a platform for businesses and customers to engage in communication, allowing both parties to be aware that their voices are being heard (Cruz, 2022).

The shift in consumer behaviour, with a decline in reliance on traditional media such as print and television, and a growing preference for social networks, blogs, and online forums for information consumption, necessitates a change in communication and business strategies for organisations (Clemente, 2023). To enhance consumer reach, commercial organisations must transition from only transmitting messages to implementing methods that provide customers with timely and relevant information, regardless of their location or time.

Like any type of communication, including online platforms, the information and messages conveyed through social media are intended for an audience (Austin, 2023). The primary benefit of social media is the active and direct response from the audience, allowing corporate organisations to promptly tailor their messages to meet client demands. Simultaneously, information pertaining to consumers' behaviour, desires, and habits is increasingly pertinent and readily accessible.

In order for organisations to effectively promote their goods and services, it is crucial to have a well-targeted audience. The organization's messaging might be directed towards either an internal audience (comprising employees and shareholders) or an external audience (including consumers, investors, clients, distributors, and suppliers).

Distributors engage in the process of market prospecting to identify new products for sale, whereas consumers are individuals who express a desire to purchase such products. Social media, aided by technological advancements,

At their platforms, manufacturers showcase their products & services, providing an initial opportunity for potential customers to familiarise themselves with what the manufacturer offers. For employees & shareholders, social media may act as a very efficient platform for disseminating pertinent information about organisations. Simultaneously, it can serve as both an educational instrument and a means to train internal staff.

These elements can form a community on social media, which the organisation can leverage to cultivate and sustain a profitable business (Kumar, 2023). The group that connects with the organization's beliefs and ideals and utilises its products and services is referred to as such. Therefore, the individuals who establish this group play a crucial role in the organisation as they have the ability to convey their emotions to others, thereby contributing to the development of the online community centred around the organisation. In order to maintain the vitality of such a group, trust is crucial. Therefore, it is imperative that the information conveyed is precise and the tone used is amicable, rather than formal or condescending.

A community remains vibrant as long as it engages in communication, articulates its opinions, offers critiques or compliments regarding the organization's products and services. The community's members must experience a sense of being heard and included, as if they are part of a cohesive one. It is vital to motivate them to actively participate, as they may contribute valuable suggestions that can drive the advancement of new products and services, as well as enhance the present ones.

In order to achieve success, a corporate organisation must prioritise the identification of pertinent information that can enhance the innovation process. Additionally, it should emphasise the sharing of information and expertise within the organisation, as well as the ability to innovate and extract crucial information from the external world. Both within and outside a corporate organisation, there are knowledge resources that, if not utilised, can result in decreased productivity, loss of competitiveness, and ultimately, market failure. This data, disseminated through social media, is a highly valuable knowledge resource. Harnessing and leveraging this data can potentially result in the creation of new products and services, and can foster innovation within organisations and the broader economic landscape.

Social media can significantly influence the innovation process within business organisations by facilitating more efficient communication and utilisation of knowledge both within and outside the organisation. Additionally, it presents new opportunities for the emergence and growth of innovative potential.

Table 1. Stakeholders responses on media and communication for sustainable business

SYSTEMATIC STRATEGY (SS)	Weighted Mean	Interpretation
SS1. Integrating media and communication strategies within the systematic planning significantly enhances sustainable business objectives.	3.45	Agree
SS2. A structured approach to integrating media and communication consistently supports the systematic efforts towards sustainable business practices.	4.15	Strongly Agree
SS3. Systematically embedding media and communication planning into the sustainable business framework ensures better alignment with long-term sustainability goals	3.37	Agree
COMMUNICATION TACTICS (CT)		
CT1. Tailored communication tactics are pivotal in effectively promoting the sustainable business initiatives through diverse media channels.	2.16	Disagree
CT2. The success of our sustainable business goals heavily relies on the implementation of well-thought-out communication tactics through media outreach.	4.31	Strongly Agree
CT3. Adopting successful communication tactics used in other sustainable business models could significantly enhance the media-driven sustainability efforts.	3.32	Agree
MEDIA (M)		
M1. Different media platforms play varying roles in influencing perceptions and encouraging adoption of sustainable practices within the business.	3.61	Agree
M2. Innovative or emerging media shapes perceptions and drives action towards sustainable business development more effectively than traditional media.	2.7	Disagree
M3. Leveraging various media types strategically is essential to maximize the impact of our sustainable business messaging and initiatives.	3.3	Agree
SUSTAINABLE BUSINESS (SB)		
SB1. Effective media and communication significantly influence stakeholders' perception of our commitment to sustainable business practices.	4.12	Strongly Agree
SB2. A well-thought-out communication strategy through media channels contributes significantly to the scalability and replication of our sustainable business model.	4.30	Strongly Agree
SB3. Integrating media and communication into our sustainable business framework amplifies our social and environmental impact while ensuring business growth and stability.	3.33	Agree

Source: Compiled by the Researchers

On the subject of sustainable corporate success, stakeholders place a strong emphasis on the significant role that structured media integration (SS2) plays, as well as the deep impact that successful communication strategies (CT2) have. The media plays a vital role in creating perceptions (SB1) and scaling sustainable models through strategic communication (SB2), which is aligned with the concept of finding consensus. It becomes clear that there is a divergence of opinion over the necessity of personalised strategies (CT1) and the efficiency of new media (M2). In general, stakeholders recognise the significance of the media in sustainability (M1, M3); nonetheless, these variances underscore the necessity of developing tailored strategies that take into account a variety of perspectives. Incorporating media in a strategic manner appears to be of utmost importance; yet, specific strategies and preferences about media should be investigated further in order to develop holistic and impactful sustainable projects.

Table 2. Media executive's responses on media and communication for sustainable business

SYSTEMATIC STRATEGY (SS)	Weighted Mean	Interpretation
SS1. Implementing a systematic media and communication strategy is crucial for effectively aligning sustainable business objectives with broader organizational strategies.	2.65	Disagree
SS2. A well-defined systematic approach to media and communication enhances the consistency and coherence of sustainable business messaging across various platforms.	4.36	Strongly Agree
SS3. Integrating media planning within systematic business strategies significantly contributes to the long-term success of sustainability initiatives.	4.10	Agree
COMMUNICATION TACTICS (CT)		
CT1. Tailoring communication tactics specifically for diverse media channels is pivotal for effectively highlighting a company's sustainable business practices.	3.85	Agree
CT2. The success of sustainable business goals heavily depends on the strategic implementation of communication tactics through media platforms.	4.25	Strongly Agree
CT3. Leveraging innovative communication tactics plays a vital role in increasing audience engagement and buy-in towards sustainable business messaging.	2.00	Strongly Disagree
MEDIA (M)		
M1. Various media platforms wield different influences on how sustainability initiatives are perceived and embraced by audiences.	3.45	Agree
M2. Emerging media platforms have a greater potential to amplify the impact of sustainable business messaging compared to traditional media.	2.80	Disagree
M3. Strategically using a mix of media types is essential to maximize the reach and effectiveness of sustainable business communication.	3.80	Agree
SUSTAINABLE BUSINESS (SB)		
SB1. Effective media and communication significantly shape stakeholders' perception of a company's commitment to sustainable business practices.	4.50	Strongly Agree
SB2. A robust communication strategy through media channels is crucial for scaling up and replicating successful sustainable business models.	4.25	Strongly Agree
SB3. Integrating media and communication into the core of sustainable business frameworks amplifies social and environmental impact while fostering business growth and stability.	3.65	Agree

Source: Compiled by the Researchers

The feedback from Media Executives demonstrates agreement on the strategic incorporation of media into sustainable plans, highlighting the vital importance of well-organized media strategies (SS2) and recognising its influence on stakeholder perception (SB1). Discrepancies occur in the preferred methods of communication (CT1, CT3) and the possibilities of new media (M2), emphasising the need for flexible approaches that include a range of perspectives. Executives prioritise nuanced media use (M3) and acknowledge the impact of various media on perception (M1, M2), highlighting the necessity for advanced methodologies. In general, Media Executives give high importance to carefully designed, flexible media strategies that are in line with different media environments and stakeholder viewpoints in order to effectively support long-lasting business initiatives.

Table 3. Mean, variances, and standard deviation of stakeholders

CONSTRUCTS	ITEM	N	Mean	Std Deviation
SYSTEMATIC STRATEGY (SS)	SS 1	50	3.45	0.0858
	SS 2	50	4.15	
	SS 3	50	3.37	
COMMUNICATION TACTICS (CT)	CT 1	50	2.16	0.2152
	CT 2	50	4.31	
	CT 3	50	3.32	
MEDIA (M)	M 1	50	3.61	0.0925
	M 2	50	2.7	
	M 3	50	3.3	
SUSTAINABLE BUSINESS (SB)	SB 1	50	4.12	0.1032
	SB 2	50	4.30	
	SB 3	50	3.33	

Source: Compiled by the Researchers

Table 4. Mean, variances, and standard deviation of media executives

CONSTRUCTS	ITEM	N	Mean	Std Deviation
SYSTEMATIC STRATEGY (SS)	SS 1	50	2.65	0.1843
	SS 2	50	4.36	
	SS 3	50	4.10	
COMMUNICATION TACTICS (CT)	CT 1	50	3.85	0.240
	CT 2	50	4.25	
	CT 3	50	2.00	
MEDIA (M)	M 1	50	3.45	0.1015
	M 2	50	2.80	
	M 3	50	3.80	
SUSTAINABLE BUSINESS (SB)	SB 1	50	4.50	0.0874
	SB 2	50	4.25	
	SB 3	50	3.65	

Source: Compiled by the Researchers

FINDINGS

There are a number of themes that have been recognised, one of which is the importance of media and communication in terms of achieving value for both society and the environment. It has been argued in the literature that the particularities and affordances of digital technologies make it possible for entrepreneurial activity to be taken, which in turn facilitates sustainability.

It is the social factors that are the primary focus of attention when considering the role that digital technologies play in enabling sustainability. Through the application of sociological viewpoints, for example, academics have begun conversations on the question of whether or not digital technologies may play a role in reducing inequality (Dale & Kyle, 2016). The body of research suggests that there is a strong connection between the rise of Media and Communication and the well-being of individuals (Torres & Augusto, 2020). According to Gino and Staats (2012) and Mora et al. (2021), the findings shed light on the potential of technologies to improve the quality of life and contribute to the reduction of poverty. For instance, business models that make use of digital technologies make it possible to easily follow and monitor individuals who are affected during times of crisis, and then provide assistance to meet their requirements (Ibáñez et al., 2021). To be more specific, crowd-based digital technologies are being proposed as potential ways to alleviate suffering in this area (Majchrzak & Shepherd, 2021). One of the most important concepts that may be utilised to bring about positive social change is the concept of technologically enabled inclusion. The concept of digital inclusiveness encompasses the act of connecting individuals who are disadvantaged through entrepreneurial endeavours. This involves providing them with access to innovations (Ibáñez et al., 2021), services (Srivastava & Shainesh, 2015), education (Torres & Augusto, 2020), or government information (Goyal, Agrawal, & Sergi, 2020) that would otherwise be unavailable to them. According to Torres and Augusto's research from 2020, it is of utmost significance to take this action in areas where the overall adoption of Media and Communication is inadequate. As a result of the fact that ventures aim to enable individuals to participate in democratic processes (Arora, 2016, Calzada, 2020), engage with new work opportunities (Soltysova & Modrak, 2020), or become entrepreneurial (Langley et al., 2017, Pankaj and Seetharaman, 2021, Pazaitis et al., 2017), the value of inclusiveness is further connected to the empowerment of individuals.

A lesser amount of emphasis has been paid to minimising adverse effects on the environment. The promise of digital solutions for environmental sustainability is discussed in a number of articles (Pierce et al., 2017, Suseno and Abbott, 2021, Zeng, 2018), as is the importance of large-scale data analysis in informing environmentally friendly outcomes (Mora et al., 2021). Additionally, digital entrepreneurial solutions have the potential to lessen the amount of space required for travel and living, as well as to promote environmental education (Devereaux, 2021). De Bernardi et al. (2019) and Soltysova and Modrak (2020) suggest that digital technologies are a driver for a larger transformation of the economy, which involves alternate forms of consumption to lessen negative environmental impact. According to these researchers, digital technologies are a driver for this transition.

The various affordances that digital technologies offer are also believed to be essential for scaling the business as well as the impact that it has. Increasing reach through digital means is a central point in this context. This enables sustainable entrepreneurs to improve geographical access, overcome preconditions of spatial proximity, and, as a result, reach other markets and target groups that were not previously served (Goyal et al., 2020; Parthiban et al., 2020; Srivastava and Shainesh, 2015). The importance of digital technology in efficiently scaling the venture's desired impact is elaborated upon by academics. (Gregori and Holzmann, 2020; Majchrzak and Shepherd, 2021; Pankaj and Seetharaman, 2021) The socioenvironmental impact can be scaled up and intensified through the generativity of digital solutions, which link numerous forms of value and include persons who are touched by the situation. Digital technologies have the potential to not only have the impact that is sought, but also to stimulate the development of the venture itself. The publications that were examined, for example, describe the utilisation of digital technologies as an effective method to adhere to and put into practice lean principles for the purpose of scaling and expanding (Cabrera and Byrne, 2021; Carroll and Casselman, 2019).

CONCLUSION

When media, communication, and sustainable entrepreneurship are brought together, a dynamic landscape emerges, in which one component has a substantial impact on the others (Yadav, 2021). The conclusion that was reached as a result of the exhaustive research highlights the crucial part that the media and communication play in forming, supporting, and advancing sustainable entrepreneurship (Agarwal, 2022 & Agarwal, 2023).

Measure of Influence of Media: The influence of the media on public views and behaviours in the direction of sustainability is significant because the media acts as a potent channel for affecting public perceptions and behaviours. It has the capacity to raise awareness, educate people, and encourage them to adopt sustainable practises, which will ultimately in turn influence the choices that consumers make and the demands that the market places.

Strategic Communication for Impact: Successful entrepreneurs who are committed to sustainability make strategic use of communication channels in order to convey their sustainability activities. Not only does this increase the value of their brand, but it also attracts stakeholders, such as investors, customers, and partners whose values are congruent with their own.

Relationship Between Media Coverage and Sustainable Business: The symbiotic relationship between media coverage and sustainable business is readily apparent. Media visibility and entrepreneurial impact are two aspects that are closely related. The exposure and legitimacy of sustainable initiatives are increased when they receive positive media attention, which in turn enables these ventures to gain access to resources and cultivate collaborations. Concurrently, actions related to entrepreneurship contribute to the formation of narratives in the media regarding challenges related to sustainability.

Innovation and Digital Media: The emergence of digital media and new communication technologies brings with it a number of opportunities as well as obstacles. The use of social media and other online platforms provides opportunities for participation, the development of communities, and lobbying for environmentally responsible business models. In order for entrepreneurs to successfully drive their sustainability agendas, it is essential for them to strategically leverage these platforms (Weller, 2022 & Northup, 2022).

As a conclusion, the synergy that exists between sustainable enterprise, communication, and the media is an essential component in the process of cultivating a sustainable future. Stakeholders need to deliberately leverage the power of the media and apply creative communication tactics in order to amplify the impact of sustainable entrepreneurship on a global scale. This is because the landscape is continuing to shift. Furthermore, continual research and collaboration efforts are required in order to investigate and capitalise on the ever-changing dynamics in this domain, which will ultimately pave the way for an entrepreneurial environment that is more responsible and sustainable.

REFERENCES

Agarwal, A., Kumar, R., & Agarwal, S. (2022). Impact of Media on Society. *IJCRT*, *10*(6), a956–a965.

Agarwal, N. (2023). Strength of distributed web page management system within the space of online e-learning administration in a contextualized group of science teachers. *European Chemical Bulletin*, *12*(4), 144–155. doi:10.31838/ecb/2023.12.4.010

Antolin-Lopez, R., Martinez-del-Rio, J., & Cespedes-Lorente, J. J. (2019). Environmental entrepreneurship as a multi-component and dynamic construct: Duality of goals, environmental agency, and environmental value creation. *Business Ethics (Oxford, England)*, *28*(4), 407–422. doi:10.1111/beer.12229

Bhati, Dr. Bharat. (2021). An Empirical Study on Environmental Seriousness and Green Product Purchasing. *Cosmos An International Journal of Management*, *10*(2), 22–29. doi:10.46360/cosmos.mgt.420211005

Cahapin, E. L., Malabag, B. A., Samson, B. D., & Santiago, C. S. Jr. (2022). Stakeholders' Awareness and Acceptance of The Institution's Vision, Mission and Goals and Information Technology Program Objectives in A State University in The Philippines. *Globus Journal of Progressive Education*, *12*(1), 51–60. doi:10.46360/globus.edu.220221006

Clemente, Paul Timothy A. (2023). Operations Strategy of Air Bed and Breakfast (AIRBNB): Basis for An Enhanced Business Model. *Globus An International Journal of Management & IT, 14*(2), 06-25. doi:10.46360/globus.mgt.120231002

Dwivedi, M. C. (2022). Assessing The Socioeconomic Implications of Climate Change. *Cosmos An International Journal of Art & Higher Education*, *11*(2), 20–23. doi:10.46360/cosmos.ahe.520222004

Dwivedi, Y. K., Hughes, L., Kar, A. K., Baabdullah, A. M., Grover, P., Abbas, R., Andreini, D., Abumoghli, I., Barlette, Y., Bunker, D., Chandra Kruse, L., Constantiou, I., Davison, R. M., De', R., Dubey, R., Fenby-Taylor, H., Gupta, B., He, W., Kodama, M., & Wade, M. (2022). Climate Change and COP26: Are digital technologies and information management part of the problem or the solution? An editorial reflection and call to action. *International Journal of Information Management*, *63*, 102456. doi:10.1016/j.ijinfomgt.2021.102456

Goyal, S., Agrawal, A., & Sergi, B. S. (2020). Social entrepreneurship for scalable solutions addressing sustainable development goals (SDGs) at BoP in India. *Qualitative Research in Organizations and Management*, *16*(3/4), 509–529. doi:10.1108/QROM-07-2020-1992

Gregori, P., & Holzmann, P. (2020). Digital sustainable entrepreneurship: A business model perspective on embedding digital technologies for social and environmental value creation. *Journal of Cleaner Production*, *272*, 122817. doi:10.1016/j.jclepro.2020.122817

Holzmann, P., Breitenecker, R. J., Schwarz, E. J., & Gregori, P. (2020). Business model design for novel technologies in nascent industries: An investigation of 3D printing service providers. *Technological Forecasting and Social Change*, *159*, 120193. doi:10.1016/j.techfore.2020.120193

Khedhiri, M. (2022). Empowering The Saudi's Higher Education System: Real Strategies Towards A World-Class Status. *Globus Journal of Progressive Education*, *12*(2), 82–87. doi:10.46360/globus.edu.220222013

Kumar, P., & Diego, M. C. (2023). Understanding the Dynamics of Economic Development in Developing Countries. Handbook of Research on Bioeconomy and Economic Ecosystems. IGI Global. doi:10.4018/978-1-6684-8879-9.ch020

Langley, D. J., Zirngiebl, M., Sbeih, J., & Devoldere, B. (2017). Trajectories to reconcile sharing and commercialization in the maker movement. *Business Horizons*, *60*(6), 783–794. doi:10.1016/j. bushor.2017.07.005

Markman, G. D., Waldron, T. L., Gianiodis, P. T., & Espina, M. I. (2019). E pluribus unum: Impact entrepreneurship as a solution to grand challenges. *The Academy of Management Perspectives*, *33*(4), 371–382. doi:10.5465/amp.2019.0130

Mora, H., Morales-Morales, M. R., Pujol-López, F. A., & Mollá-Sirvent, R. (2021). Social cryptocurrencies as model for enhancing sustainable development. *Kybernetes*, *50*(10), 2883–2916. doi:10.1108/K-05-2020-0259

Muñoz, P., & Cohen, B. (2018). Sustainable entrepreneurship research: Taking stock and looking ahead. *Business Strategy and the Environment*, *27*(3), 300–322. doi:10.1002/bse.2000

Nambisan, S. (2017). Digital Entrepreneurship: Toward a Media and Communication Perspective of Entrepreneurship. *Entrepreneurship Theory and Practice*, *41*(6), 1029–1055. doi:10.1111/etap.12254

Nishant, R., Kennedy, M., & Corbett, J. (2020). Artificial Intelligence for Sustainability: Challenges, Opportunities and A Research Agenda. *International Journal of Information Management*, *53*, 102104. doi:10.1016/j.ijinfomgt.2020.102104

Northup, T., Santana, A. D., Choi, H., & Puspita, R. (2022). Personality traits, personal motivations, and online news and social media commenting. *Journal of Media and Communication Studies*, *14*(3), 68–78. doi:10.5897/JMCS2022.0775

Pan, S. L., Carter, L., Tim, Y., & Sandeep, M. S. (2022). Digital Sustainability, Climate Change, and Information Systems Solutions: Opportunities for Future Research. *International Journal of Information Management*, *63*, 102444. doi:10.1016/j.ijinfomgt.2021.102444

Pankaj, L., & Seetharaman, P. (2021). The balancing act of social enterprise: An IT emergence perspective. *International Journal of Information Management*, *57*, 102302. doi:10.1016/j.ijinfomgt.2020.102302

Papagiannidis, S., & Marikyan, D. (2022). Environmental Sustainability: A Technology Acceptance Perspective. *International Journal of Information Management*, *63*, 102445. doi:10.1016/j.ijinfomgt.2021.102445

Pazaitis, A., Kostakis, V., & Bauwens, M. (2017). Digital economy and the rise of open cooperativism: The case of the Enspiral Network. *Transfer: European Review of Labour and Research*, *23*(2), 177–192. doi:10.1177/1024258916683865

Pierce, P., Ricciardi, F., & Zardini, A. (2017). Smart cities as organizational fields: A framework for mapping sustainability-enabling configurations. *Sustainability (Basel)*, *9*(9), 1506. doi:10.3390/su9091506

Saebi, T., Foss, N. J., & Linder, S. (2019). Social entrepreneurship research: Past achievements and future promises. *Journal of Management*, *45*(1), 70–95. doi:10.1177/0149206318793196

Shepherd, D. A., & Patzelt, H. (2022). A call for research on the scaling of organizations and the scaling of social impact. *Entrepreneurship Theory and Practice*, *46*(2), 255–268. doi:10.1177/1042258720950599

Soltysova, Z., & Modrak, V. (2020). Challenges of the sharing economy for SMEs: A literature review. *Sustainability (Basel)*, *12*(16), 6504. doi:10.3390/su12166504

Terán-Yépez, E., Marín-Carrillo, G. M., del Pilar Casado-Belmonte, M., & de las Mercedes Capobianco-Uriarte, M. (2020). Sustainable entrepreneurship: Review of its evolution and new trends. *Journal of Cleaner Production*, *252*, 119742. doi:10.1016/j.jclepro.2019.119742

Umali, R. J., Alba, D., Alinapon, R. J., Calara, J. R., Lizarondo, M., & Miguel, R. A. (2023). The Effectivity of The Development Plan of Malolos LGU to The Small Businesses at Malolos Convention. *Cosmos An International Journal of Management, 12*(2), 84-92. 10.46360/cosmos.mgt.420231010

Valdez, D., & Nunag, R. (2023). The Research and Creative Works Colloquium and Its Effect on Research Performance. *Cosmos Journal of Engineering & Technology*, *13*(1), 57–69. doi:10.46360/cosmos.et.620231006

Weller, K., & Holaschke, M. (2022). Whose stream is this anyway? Exploring layers of viewer-integration in online participatory videos. *Journal of Media and Communication Studies, 14*(1), 17-32. IJCRT22A6128.pdf

Zeng, J. (2018). Fostering path of ecological sustainable entrepreneurship within big data network system. *The International Entrepreneurship and Management Journal*, *14*(1), 79–95. doi:10.1007/s11365-017-0466-3

Chapter 11
Sustainability in the Indian Banking Industry:
An Analysis of Top 10 Commercial Banks in India

Payel Roy
Umeschandra College, India

ABSTRACT

In this volatile world where sustainability is a major concern, the growing importance of the backbone of the economies, the financial sector, is inevitable. This chapter tries to seek the factors responsible for the changes in the financial performance of the commercial banks in Indian banking sector. The secondary data related to selected key performance indicators (KPI) are selected for the top ten banks for the years 2018-19 to 2022-23. These also include the ESG risk rating of these banks that gives an idea of the overall performance of the banks in the long run. The chapter further tries to forecast a trend of the selected KPIs. The results of the exploratory factor analysis followed by dependency tests proved that there is considerable impact of net non-performing assets, current account savings account, and the ratio of fixed assets to total assets on profitability of the banks.

INTRODUCTION

Though the harsh realities like pollution and climate change attract our attention towards the degradation of environment and biodiversity caused by unsolicited human behavior and unnatural haste in industrialization, still we often fail to understand the inter dependency with the connected areas. The co-existence of the environment, economy and society in harmony is a difficult goal to achieve but inevitable for the all-round development. It is true that without paying heed to the environmental issues, simply focusing on economic growth cannot render the expected quality of life (Kumar P., UNEP, February 2022), but it is equally important to understand the threats and opportunities faced by the factors having impact on the environmental issues directly or indirectly. Finance, being the lifeline of the overall growth and development of all allied areas of this co-existence, plays a crucial role in integration and channelization

DOI: 10.4018/979-8-3693-2197-3.ch011

of various resources towards the achievement of economic goals without hampering the ecological balance. Financial Institutions are the organizations that help in such activities. They deal with transactions related to investments, loans, deposits etc. (Economic Survey, 2008-09)

Background

The banking sector, a part of the financial sector of any economy, is responsible for accumulation and application of funds (Prabhavati and Dinesh, August 2018) towards the suitable, prudent, and economically viable projects which can contribute to the development of the economy. This industry is not only essential for the creation of employment opportunities, unlocking of wealth etc. but it also provides a formal system for both individuals and businesses to be a part of Global Economy (Douglas. J.L, June 2008). Like any other business organization, the banks are also inclined to have a part in the social responsibility. In addition to providing loans at lower rates to underprivileged sections of society, the institutions extend their support to financial literacy, financial inclusion and many environment friendly activities and events. Though it is not so popular in India as in other countries to have the concept of Green Banking (United States Environment Protection Agency, October 2023) in all the segments of Banking Industry but there are many projects initiated by various banks in India. The first bank to invest in wind farm project is SBI (Sharma and Choubey, May 2021). Thus, it is correct to announce that the banks are coming in the forefront in reaching the Sustainable Development Goals (SDGs) set by United Nations (Innig.C, April 2021). The increase in digitization drive like paperless transactions, use of blockchain technology etc. resulting into less use of non-renewable resources and increased use of modern methods in their daily operations has brought a major change in their Corporate Social Responsibility. Today, the CSR activities are not restricted to contribution of money towards the events dedicated for environment protection only. It has extended to the various issues related to Society and Governance also. Thus, ESG scores (ESG The Report, 2021) are an important indicator of non-financial performance. Supporting the great cause of conserving nature is possible only if the existence and development of these institutions supporting it is feasible.

This chapter puts emphasis on the various performance indicators related to the sustainability of the Banking sector. The research first depicts the status of the financial and non-financial performances of this sector depending on the major Key Performance Indicators (KPIs) (Daryakin et al. 2019) of selected commercial banks from Indian Banking Sector. For this, the top 10 Indian Banks based on Market Capitalization are selected. The KPIs are considered to depict both financial and non-financial performances. Next, the level of credibility of such banks and the reasons for the changes in the financial performance of the banks over the years are studied. Further, this chapter has also tried to forecast the potential for growth of this sector based on the selected banks. This empirical research is based on secondary data that has been collected from the Banking websites and common data sources. The collected data are analyzed using software like MS Excel, IBM SPSS and the findings are interpreted and represented in tabular form. Exploratory Factor analysis is used for the study along with related statistical tools for data analysis. This study is divided into five main sections namely, Introduction, Literature Review, Research Methodology, Analysis & Findings and Conclusions and Scope for further research.

OBJECTIVES

1. To present a descriptive analysis of 13 KPIs (both Financial and Non-financial) of top 10 Banks in India (Public and Private banks) over the last 5 years (2018-19 to 2022-23).
2. To identify the factors responsible for the change in profitability of the selected banks over the last 5 years.
3. To forecast the potential for growth of Banking sector in India based on the selected banks.

LITERATURE REVIEW

There are many studies done on exploring reasons behind the changes in the financial performances of Banking sector throughout the world. Since this sector holds an important position in the economies of almost all the countries, the researchers are interested to know the causes of the variability in their performance. 16 commercial banks of Albania are studied to establish the impact of four internal factors on their performances in 2010 to 2013. The bank's profitability is measured by ROA and the internal factors are size age liquidity and capital adequacy. In this study the size is measured by the total assets, capital adequacy is measured by total equity by total assets measured by total loans to total assets and each being the number of years of difference between the foundation of the banks to the recent year. It has been found that both size and age have no proper significance in the performance related to profitability, but liquidity and capital adequacy have (Cekrezi, 2015). There are a variety of indicators considered by different researchers to understand the association between them. In a study on Indonesian commercial banks, few financial performance indicators such as capital adequacy ratio, non-performing loans, return on assets, net interest margin and loan to deposit ratio in this study the factors influencing financial performance of the selected banks, studied with finding the most dominant factor influencing the financial performance of all the selected banks. The author used regression analysis, ANOVA and T test to conclude that though the financial performance is dependent on the independent variables selected but non-performing loans are the most dominant factor among the rest (Fibryanti and Nurcholidah, 2020). In most of the studies the findings regarding factors affecting profitability are common. This study of 16 listed banks of China chooses 11 financial indicators to measure 4 dimensions of performance namely market share capability, size, profitability and operation capacity, safety and growth. Using factor analysis this study identified three main factors. The first one of them is named as factor of bank scale and market share capacity, the second one is named as factor of safety and growth and the third one is named as profitability factor. The variance contribution rates of each factor are calculated along with the total variance contribution rates of the three factors and after waiting and summarizing of this the proportion is found and composite score is calculated based on that (Du and Chen, 2015). Similarly, the study on 6 Moroccan banks selected return on asset and return on equity as the indicator of banks, performance and for this, the financial performance were selected during the period of 2010 to 2016. Here, panel data analysis was used to analyze the effect of some selected variables on the performance of these banks. It was found that the operating management efficiency indicated by cost to income ratio has a high impact and is negatively related to banks' performance on the other hand the size of the banks is also having some impact on ROA but is positive related to it (Jaouad. E and Lahsen. O, 2018). In some studies the profitability is taken as independent variable to explore the dependency of any other indicator of performance on profitability. 43 banking firms of Indonesia listed in IDX were studied over 11 years ending on 2020 to understand the effects of affordable funds and profitability on the market ratio that is Price to Book Value (PBV) of Banking sector. The Current Account Savings Account (CASA) and Net Profit Margin (NPM) are considered as independent variables, some variables like Return on Equity (ROE) etc. are taken as controlled variables to measure the extent of dependency through regression analysis. It was found that both NPM and CASA have a positive and significant impact on the dependent variable (Jennifer et al, 2022). Sometimes, new ratios are formed to analyze the financial indicators in a different way which are calculated by the authors. One of such studies calculated variables like Growth Ability and Profitability to evaluate the financial performance of 36 listed Commercial Banks in China in the year 2018 through factor analysis. The results identified that the development of the Banks under study are unbalanced in all aspects (Qin et al, 2020).

On the contrary, number of studies on the sustainability of Banking sector is less. Most of the studies relate to the CSR activities and the monetary contribution of the Banking sector towards protection of sanctity of the Environment. The research on the sustainability of Banking sector in alliance with its contribution towards the overall sustainability of the earth is lesser. With United Nations' 17 Sustainable Development Goals (UNSDGs, 2023), it becomes a mandate that all the activities happening around the world are intertwined. The 8th Goal of UN which is Decent work and Economic Growth paves the way for overall development of all the sectors in the economy and thus gives an opportunity for the research and development to concentrate on unexplored areas of the evaluation of performance of these sectors. There is a research gap where this chapter tries to fit in. Here, along with financial indicators, Environment, Social and Governance Risks are also evaluated. Further, there are a few uncommon areas of financial information that are studied to understand the overall performance of the Commercial Banking sector in India and ultimately, forecasts are made for few KPIs.

RESEARCH METHODOLOGY

Source Of Data

Secondary sources are used to collect data for this analysis. The top 10 commercial banks operating in India are selected as published by forbesindia.com based on their Market capitalization on October 4th, 2023 (Forbes India, 2023). The list included four Public Sector Banks (PSBs) namely, State Bank of India (SBI with Market Cap of Rs.5.22 lakh crores), Bank of Baroda (BOB with Market Cap of Rs.1.09 lakh crores), Punjab National Bank (PNB with Market Cap of Rs.0.877 lakh crores) and Union Bank (with Market Cap of Rs.0.807 lakh crores) with six Private Sector Banks (PvtSBs) namely, Housing Development Finance Corporation (HDFC with Market Cap of Rs.11.61 lakh crores), Industrial Credit and Investment Corporation of India (ICICI with Market Cap of Rs.6.52 lakh crores), Kotak Mahindra Bank (with Market Cap of Rs.3.43 lakh crores), AXIS Bank(with Market Cap of Rs.3.05 lakh crores), IndusInd Bank (with Market Cap of Rs.1.08 lakh crores), and Industrial Development Bank of India (IDBI with Market Cap of Rs.0.747 lakh crores) respectively. The relevant Key Performance Indicators are collected from the respective Banks' websites and the free database named moneycontrol.com. For financial performance of the banks, KPIs depicting Profitability, Capital Adequacy, Asset Quality, Operational Efficiency, Earning Capability, Prudent interest expense management and Valuation Ratios are selected while for non-financial performances, Current ESG Risk Ratings (Sustain Analytics, 2023) are considered. The KPIs that were not available in the Financial Statements and Reports are calculated as required.

Software and Tools Used

The collected data is summarized and analyzed with the help of MS Excel and IBM SPSS Statistics 29 software. Few of the descriptive data are represented in tabular and graphical forms. Apart from calculation of various ratios and averaging the data values for determination of the trend and overall analysis of performance of the Indian Banking sector, the data is analyzed using Exploratory Factor Analysis along with Regression Analysis and ANOVA for determination of level and direction of association between the Profitability and Asset Quality of the selected banks.

ANALYSIS OF DATA

This study is divided into 3 main sections. In the first section, descriptive analysis of the selected KPIs involving both financial and non-financial performance are studied. In the second section, dependency test of Profitability on Asset Quality of these banks are studied and the third section consists of forecast of data values of the selected KPIs depending on the trend of the past 5 years.

Descriptive Analysis

For the first objective, a descriptive analysis is done for the KPIs of the selected banks in which financial KPIs depicting six dimensions of performance are studied with two indicators in each dimension. Capital Adequacy is assessed through Capital Adequacy Ratio (CAR%) and the ratio of Tier 1 and Tier 2 Capital (T1/T2). This ratio of two types of Capital is calculated to understand the strength of the Capital structure. Asset Quality is measured with Percentage of Gross Non-performing Assets (GNPA%) and Ratio of Net Non-performing Assets and Total Advances expressed in percentages (NNPA/TADV%). Here, the ratio of NNPA with Total Advance is calculated to depict the proportion of the Advances being non-performing after provisions are made. The Operational Efficiency of these banks is assessed through Net Interest Margin (NIM) and Operating Profit Margin (%) (OPM). Both these indicators show the managerial skills to utilize the core areas of operation of the banks in earning revenues. Earning capability is studied through Return on Assets (ROA%) and Return on Capital Employed (ROCE%). Though in most of the studies earlier, Return on Equity (ROE) is considered by in this study intentionally the Operating Profit is given importance over Net Profit. The Prudent interest expense management is measured with Current Account Savings Account (CASA%) and Interest Expended/ Total Assets (IE/TA%). CASA% defines the percentage of funds procured through Current and Savings Account is the cheapest source of funds (Jennifer et al, 2022) and denotes that bank's capacity to raise funds at low cost while IE/TA expresses the percentage of interest expenses that the banks bear out of Fixed Assets valuation. Both indicators show how the banks are utilizing their prudency to manage the interest expenses. Finally, the Valuation dimension is measured through Price to Book Value (P/B) and Earning Yield ratios (E/P). In this category, if the P/B ratio is stronger, the total value of performance in this dimension will be high since higher P/B ratio indicates a high Market Price of the shares compared to the Book Value and the

E/P ratio will be lower because of high P. In addition, the ESG Risk Rating of these banks is considered as non-financial KPI for this study.

The average values of the indicators selected under each of the categories are presented per year with the help of Clustered Bar Figures.

The Capital Adequacy position (Figure 1) is best for the ICICI and Kotak Mahindra Bank currently but in case of the later, it is showing a declining trend which is not good. It means that either CAR or the portion of Tier 1 Capital in Total Capital is decreasing. The worst result is shown by PNB but the positive side is that unlike many others in this group, it is improving in this dimension over the years. IDBI is also showing an increasing trend over the years.

Figure 1. Capital adequacy over the last five years
Source: Calculation is done by the Author.

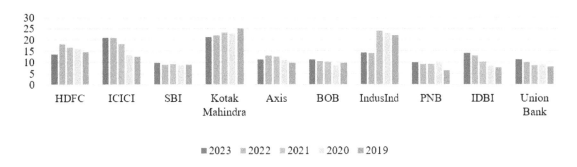

For Asset Quality indicators (Figure 2), both the indicators determine the negative sides of the assets, one being GNPA another being NNPA_TADV. So, the lesser value shows better position of the assets. In this dimension, all the banks are improving their positions every year, IDBI being the leader in such improvement. Currently PNB is having the worst position followed by Union Bank. The best one of them is HDFC having a low trend throughout.

Figure 2. Asset quality over the last five years
Source: Calculation is done by the Author.

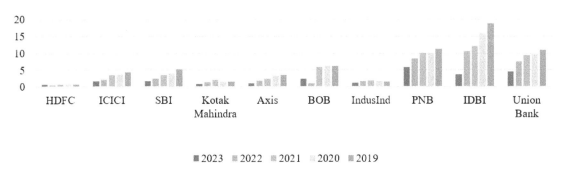

In Operational Efficiency (Figure 3), most of the banks fail to show good results. Both ICICI and Kotak Mahindra are in comparative better positions than other banks, ICICI being the trend setter in improving from negative to positive values over the last 5 years which is closely followed by SBI, BOB and IndusInd Bank. The worst result is perceived for IDBI. This bank has also improved which is good. HDFC Bank has shown a moderate results through the years.

Figure 3. Operational efficiency of the last five years
Source: Calculation is done by the Author.

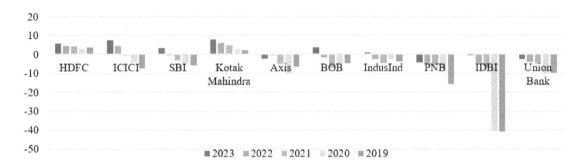

The current Earning Capacity (Figure 4) of Kotak Mahindra is the best closely followed by ICICI. HDFC Bank is also in a good position but there happens to be declining trend since 2021. Comparatively, IndusInd bank is improving. The worst performer in this dimension is PNB and the surprisingly IDBI has bounced back from having a huge loss entering into a high profit zone.

Figure 4. Earning capacity over the last five years
Source: Calculation is done by the Author.

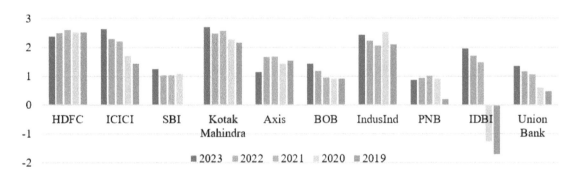

In showing prudency in management of interest expense (Figure 5), this study has taken two indicators, one shows the percentage of low interest carrying deposits another is showing the percentage of Total assets being exepended as interest. Since the stronger indicator will take the average value to the upper or lower level, so, it can be well understood that in case of Kotak Mahindra or IDBI Banks, the interest expenses are quite high and these banks are not able to procure low interest bearing funds. On the other hand, the lower average values of Union Bank and Bank of Baroda shows that these banks do not have to spend much amount as interest expenses. This is quite evident from the results of Operational Efficiency where one of the indicators was Net Interest Margin (NIM).

Figure 5. Prudent interest expense management over the last five years
Source: Calculation is done by the Author.

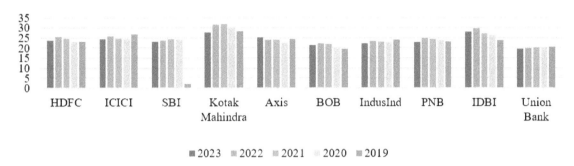

For Valuation indicators (Figure 6), P/B ratio and E/P ratio are showing the opposite results like the previous category of indicators. Thus, it is evident from the Earning Capability Indicators that for Kotak Mahindra Bank, ROA and ROCE were more than the other banks and hence its E/P ratio is stronger than P/B ratio. So, this bank has undervaluation of its stock price which is actually creating good investment opportunity for the investors. On the other hand, the Market price of the shares are less than the Book value since P/B ratio should be weaker for Kotak Mahindra Bank. This may cause from over valuation of Assets in the books. In this dimension too, HDFC and ICICI are close contenders.

Figure 6. Valuation indicators over the last five years
Source: Calculation is done by the Author.

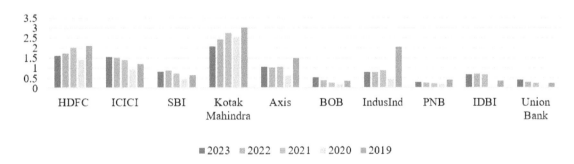

When the overall results of the industry based on the top 10 banks are studied (Figure 7), it is found that the Earning Capability and Operational Efficiency are of major concern, mainly because total earning is associated with the core activities and operational efficiency is measuring that. Since it has been showing negative results till 2022, it is unlikely that the banks can earn profits without managing its core operations effectively and efficiently.

Figure 7. Financial key performance indicators of the top ten banks over the last five years
Source: Calculation is done by the Author.

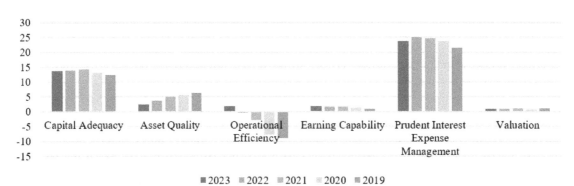

After Financial indicators, the ESG Risk Ratings are studied for the selected banks. This rating agency, Sustain Analytics by Morning Star segregates the Ratings under 5 categories: 0 to 10 Negligible, 10 to 20 Low, 20 to 30 Medium, 30 to 40 High and Above 40 Severe. Table 1 shows the top 10 banks of India based on their Market Capitalization as of October 2023 along with their ESG risks and ESG Risk Ratings collected from the database of Sustain Analytics. It is found that 5 out of the top 10 banks in the industry have high risk in managing their ESG related issues (as shown in Table 1). This poses a threat for the endeavor towards the sustainability goals. Only Kotak Mahindra Bank among the top 10 banks is having low risk.

Table 1. ESG risk and ESG risk ratings of the top ten (based on Market Cap) banks in India

Ranking in India (Market Cap)	Name of the Banks	ESG Risk	ESGR Ratings	Market Cap (Rs. in Lakh Crores)
1	HDFC	High	30.8	11.61
2	ICICI	Medium	23.3	6.52
3	SBI	Medium	26.8	5.22
4	Kotak Mahindra	Low	18.8	3.43
5	Axis	Medium	23.5	3.05
6	BOB	Medium	22.4	1.09
7	IndusInd	High	30.1	1.08
8	PNB	High	37.5	0.877
9	IDBI	High	32.5	0.747
10	Union Bank	High	34.2	0.807

Source: Sustainanalytics by Morning Star

Environmental, Social and Governance Risks for the banking sector deal with a range of risks beginning from Physical and Transition risks in the Environment part, non-compliance of labor and safety standards in Social Risks and tax rules, corruption, data protection and management issues in

Governance Risks (ESG Risks in Banks, KPMG International, 2021). In the current scenario, the bank with the highest Market Capitalization (Rs. 11.61 lakh cores), is under high risk with 4 other banks that belong to the list of top 10 Indian Banks. The riskiest one is the Punjab National Bank with a score of 37.5. This is quite evident from the results of descriptive analysis mentioned in the first section where PNB failed to show satisfactory results.

Dependency Test of Profitability on Asset Quality

Since quality of the assets pave the way for prudent utilization of the available resources and converting them into revenues, to understand the factors responsible for the changes in profitability, the KPIs denoting Asset Qualities are considered for the analysis. In the first stage of this analysis, five KPIs depicting Profitability and five KPIs depicting the Asset Quality are considered namely, Operating Profit Margin % (OPM), ROA % (ROA), ROCE % (ROCE), Net Interest Margin (NIM) and Net Profit Margin (NPM) for Profitability whereas GNPA (%) (GNPA), NNPA to ADV % (NNPA_ADV), CASA, FA/TA % (FA_TA) and NNPA % (NNPA) for Asset Quality of the banks. The average of the data of individual banks over the last five years is calculated (Appendix Table 8 and Table 9). The ratio of Fixed Assets and Total Assets expressed in percentage (FA/TA%) defines the percentage of the Total assets being stuck in fixed form.

Next, data reduction is conducted through Factor Analysis using IBM SPSS 29. Here, the Principal Component Analysis method is applied for extraction of main factors followed by Direct Oblimin Rotation. This Rotation method is applied because the factors may have correlation between them. The following two Principal components (Table 2) are identified with an Eigen value greater than 1 that can explain almost 90% of the variance in the data set.

Table 2. Identification of principal factors

	Total Variance Explained						
Component	**Initial Eigenvalues**			**Extraction Sums of Squared Loadings**			**Rotation Sums of Squared Loadings**
	Total	**% of Variance**	**Cumulative %**	**Total**	**% of Variance**	**Cumulative %**	**Total**
1	7.094	70.942	70.942	7.094	70.942	70.942	6.657
2	1.859	18.586	89.529	1.859	18.586	89.529	3.465
3	0.622	6.215	95.744				
4	0.297	2.970	98.714				
5	0.092	0.924	99.637				
6	0.024	0.238	99.875				
7	0.008	0.076	99.951				
8	0.005	0.049	100.000				
9	3.416E-05	0.000	100.000				
10	1.964E-16	1.964E-15	100.000				

Source: Calculation is done by the Author.

After identification of two components comprised of the financial indicators, the individual indicators identified under each component were to be shown. Table 3 shows the structure of the two Principal factors. It clearly separates two sets of variables, OPM, ROA, ROCE, NIM and NPM are in a group while GNPA, NNPA_ADV, CASA, FA_TA and NNPA are in another group.

Table 3. Structure of the components

Structure Matrix		
	Component	
	1	**2**
OPM	0.955	0.202
ROA	0.975	0.429
ROCE	0.563	0.851
NIM	0.680	0.880
NPM	0.976	0.409
GNPA	-0.985	-0.260
NNPA_ADV	-0.805	-0.629
CASA	0.041	0.853
FA_TA	-0.875	0.084
NNPA	-0.821	-0.614

Source: Calculation is done by the Author.

As the first five variables load together, all these variables can be considered for measuring Profitability. While the correlation between the variables in Set 1 is studied (Table 4), the least association is observed between OPM and ROCE. Correlation coefficient (r) between OPM and NIM is not significant either. Since the banks are selected based on their Market Capitalization, ROCE is considered important to determine profitability. Also, during the last 5 years, it has been found that 8 out of 10 top banks excluding HDFC and Kotak Mahindra are having average negative OPM. This is alarming since these banks are not able to generate enough revenues to cover even their variable costs. On the contrary, NIM is positive for all the banks for all the years under study. Thus, both ROCE and OPM are considered as significant indicators of profitability for this study.

Table 4. Correlation among the Indicators in set one

r	OPM	ROA	ROCE	NIM	NPM
OPM	1	.954**	0.446	0.589	.965**
ROA	.954**	1	.673*	.780**	.997**
ROCE	0.446	.673*	1	.930**	.639*
NIM	0.589	.780**	.930**	1	.754*
NPM	.965**	.997**	.639*	.754*	1

Source: Calculation is done by the Author.
Note: Correlation is significant at 0.05 (*) and at 0.01 (**) levels respectively.

But in the second set of variables (Table 5), CASA does not load with other variables. Also, the r is not significant between FA_TA and other variables in this set except GNPA. Both GNPA and NNPA show high correlation with other variables while NNPA_ADV is highly correlated with GNPA and NNPA, not with FA_TA and CASA. Since NNPA is more accurate measure of NPA burden for the banks (Alice Blue, 2023), so NNPA is taken as one of the indicators of Asset Quality for this study. The other two variables taken out of these selected set of 5 are CASA and FA_TA to avoid multicollinearity in this model. Thus, the independent variables chosen from Set 2 are NNPA, CASA and FA_TA.

Table 5. Correlation among the Indicators in set two

r	GNPA	NNPA_ADV	CASA	FA_TA	NNPA
GNPA	1	.825**	0.001	.859**	.847**
NNPA_ADV	.825**	1	-0.278	0.447	.997**
CASA	0.001	-0.278	1	0.188	-0.266
FA_TA	.859**	0.447	0.188	1	0.475
NNPA	.847**	.997**	-0.266	0.475	1

Source: Calculation is done by the Author.
Note: Correlation is significant at 0.05 (*) and at 0.01 (**) levels respectively.

The impact of Asset Quality on Profitability of the banks is analyzed with the help of Regression done through IBM SPSS 29. For this the following hypotheses are formulated:

H_0: There is no dependency of Profitability on Asset Quality of the banks.

H_1: There is dependency of Profitability on Asset Quality of the banks.

To understand the data type, the Normality Test is done. The P-P Plots (Appendix Figure 14 and Figure 15) show the data sets being normal so, the two Linear Regression Equations are formed as follows:

$$OPM_i = f\{(NNPA*\beta_1) + (CASA* \beta_2) + (FA\_TA* \beta_3)\} + \varepsilon_i \dots\dots\dots\dots\dots\dots\dots 1$$

$$And\ ROCE_i = f\{(NNPA*\beta_1) + (CASA* \beta_2) + (FA\_TA* \beta_3)\} + \varepsilon_i \dots\dots\dots\dots\dots\dots 2$$

where the dependent variables are OPM and ROCE with independent variables being NNPA, CASA and FA_TA, β represents the unknown parameters and ε denotes the Error terms. The regression analysis along with ANOVA by using IBM SPSS 29 resulted in Table 6 for Equation 1 and Table 7 for Equation 2.

Table 6. Dependency of OPM on independent variables

Regression Analysis between OPM and Independent variables			
R	R Square	F	Sig.
.931	0.866	12.952	.005

Source: Calculation is done by the Author.

Table 7. Dependency of ROCE on independent variables

Regression Analysis between ROCE and Independent variables			
R	**R Square**	**F**	**Sig.**
.800	0.639	3.547	.087

Source: Calculation is done by the Author.

It is found that both the indicators of Profitability i.e. OPM and ROCE are strongly associated with the independent variables NNPA, CASA and FA_TA respectively. The changes in OPM can be explained by the independent variables as far as 86% whereas these can explain the changes in ROCE to the extent of 63%. For the test of dependency of OPM on independent variables, the F value denotes that there is lower variance between the samples compared to the test of dependency of ROCE on independent variables. This makes p value significant for the dependency test of OPM. Thus, from the present analysis, it can be said that OPM is a better indicator of profitability than ROCE.

Forecast of The KPIs Depending on The Trend

When the trend of Financial KPIs indicating the six dimensions in the descriptive analysis are studied over the last 5 years for the selected banks, the forecast shows a positive result in almost all dimensions of this study. This is done with the help of forecasting technique provided by MS Excel. Capital Adequacy (Figure 8) and Earning Capability (Figure 11) indicators show an upward trend along with Operational Efficiency (Figure 10) in which the individual banks showed a not so good performance. There is not much movement for the curve in future with respect to Prudent Interest Expense Management (Figure 12). But Asset Quality (Figure 9) is showing a downward movement in future, which is not a good sign for the sustainability of this sector. For Valuation Indicators (Figure 13), there is an interesting trend perceived. In 2024, there will be a dip but in 2025, it will rise again. It means that there is a chance the Market Price of shares will first fall in 2024 as compared to 2023 and then go up in 2025.

Figure 8. Forecast of Capital Adequacy till 2025
Source: Calculation is done by the Author.

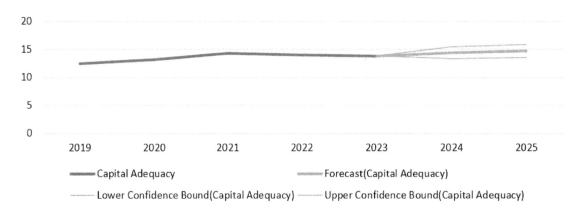

Figure 8 depicts the forecast of Capital Adequacy that generously shows that there is overall a similar level of adequacy to be maintained in future as well. This is a positive thing to ponder as Capital being the lifeline of these institutions would stick to a satisfactory level even in case of lower confidence level.

Figure 9. Forecast of Asset Quality till 2025
Source: Calculation is done by the Author.

The forecast for Asset Quality as depicted in Figure 9 is constantly falling. In the current study, it is a positive result since the measures of Asset Quality here being GNPA (%) (GNPA), NNPA to ADV % (NNPA_ADV), CASA, FA/TA % (FA_TA) and NNPA % (NNPA). Over the years, the GNPA, NNPA etc. in relation with the Total Advances are encouraged to decline to improve the usefulness of the Assets owned by the institutions.

Figure 10. Forecast of Operational Efficiency till 2025
Source: Calculation is done by the Author.

Figure 10 shows the increasing trend of Operational Efficiency which is definitely a good sign in the future performance of the banks considered for the study. This shows skills in managing the expenses to increase the profit percentage of the concerns. Even for the lower confidence level, the trend line is upward moving.

Figure 11. Forecast of Earning Capability till 2025
Source: Calculation is done by the Author.

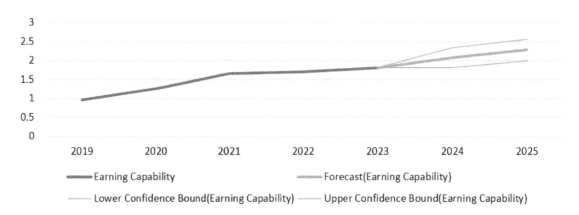

The forecast for Earning Capability as depicted in Figure 11 also shows a positive result since the upward curve is resulted from an enhancement of Returns of Assets and Capital Employed over the years. This proves a long term sustainability in the earning of these banks.

Figure 12. Forecast of Prudent Interest Expense Management till 2025
Source: Calculation is done by the Author.

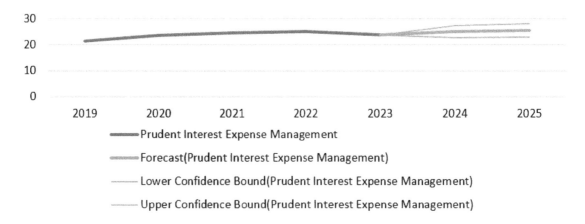

Figure 12 shows the forecast for the Prudent Interest Expense Management measured through the percentage of Current Account and Savings Account and percentage of Interest expended out of Total Assets. The continuity of prudence is depicted through the trend line here even when the lower confidence limit is considered.

Figure 13. Forecast of Valuation Indicators till 2025
Source: Calculation is done by the Author.

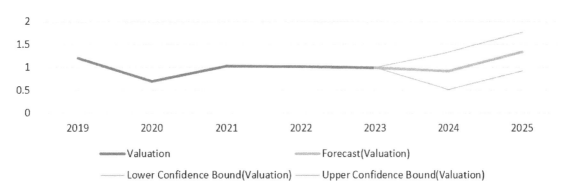

The forecast for the Valuation Indicators in Figure 13 shows a mixed result. When Price to Book Value (P/B) and Earning Yield ratios (E/P) are taken as measures of Valuation Indicator, the slightly upward trend is observed depicting that Earning Yield ratio is the driving factor here and Earning is stronger than the Price which creates a scope for undervaluation of stock and investment opportunities for the potential investors.

CONCLUSION AND SCOPE FOR FURTHER RESEARCH

In brief, among the top 10 banks in Commercial Banking Industry in India, though HDFC leads in Market Capitalization but in terms of both financial and non-financial performance Kotak Mahindra Banks is the best. In most of the financial indicators, HDFC fails to prove better than Kotak Mahindra Bank though in many dimensions it is better than the rest. But the alarming thing is that HDFC faces high ESG Risks whereas Kotak Mahindra Bank has low ESG Risk. Further, in the case of Valuation indicators, the results showed a chance of undervaluation of stock prices in the market that may give Kotak Mahindra Bank an extra edge over others in getting more investors. Since in the identification of factors and dependency tests it is found that the quality of the assets of the banks has high impact on their Profitability, the industry should be prioritizing in improving their Asset Quality rather than only depending on their Capital Adequacy and Market Capitalization. In respect of forecasting of the Key Performance Indicators, it is found that Capital Adequacy (Figure 8) and Earning Capability (Figure 11) indicators show an upward trend along with Operational Efficiency (Figure 10) in which the individual banks showed a not so good performance. There is not much movement for the curve in future with respect to Prudent Interest Expense Management (Figure 12). But Asset Quality (Figure 9) is showing a downward movement in future, which is not a good sign for the sustainability of this sector. For Valuation Indicators (Figure 13), there is an interesting trend perceived. In 2024, there will be a dip but in 2025, it will rise again. It means that there is a chance the Market Price of shares will first fall in 2024 as compared to 2023 and then go up in 2025.

This chapter tries to strike a balance between the feasible methods to enhance the most appropriate use of resources available and the Sustainable Development Goals. To achieve economic development, all the sectors are required to grow and Banking industry, playing a pivotal role in the financial sector of the economy can contribute largely to this process. Unless the said sector is not strong enough to sustain and prosper, it cannot prove to be instrumental in the sustainability of its associated areas. In this study, only 14 Financial and 1 Non-financial indicators are studied, in case the number of KPIs are increased to cover the other dimensions of performance of these banks, the results may occur different. Similarly, the forecast is made based on the last 5 years' data, a greater number of previous years included in the study gives the more accurate data values. Further, the study limits itself to the top 10 commercial banks of India, the greater number of banks may produce a different scenario of the Indian Banking sector. There is scope for further research on this.

REFERENCES

Aliceblueonline (2023). *Gross vs Net NPA*. Alice in Blue. https://aliceblueonline.com/gross-vs-net-npa/

Cekrezi, A (2015), Factors Affecting Performance of Commercial Banks in Albania, *The European Proceedings of Social & Behavioral Sciences EpSBS*, eISSN: 2357-1330, 2015. doi:10.15405/epsbs.2015.05.3

Daryakin, A. A., Sklyarov, A. A., & Khasanov, K. A. (2019). *Nº 04 - Ano 2019* (Special Edition, Vol. 8). The role of Key Performance Indicators (KPI) in Banking Activities, Periódico do Núcleo de Estudos e Pesquisas sobre Gênero e Direito Centro de Ciências Jurídicas - Universidade Federal da Paraíba. doi:10.22478/ufpb.2179-7137.2019v8n4.48458

Douglas, J. L. (2008), The Role of a Banking System in Nation-Building, *Maine Law Review*, 60. https://digitalcommons.mainelaw.maine.edu/mlr/vol60/iss2/14

Du, X. L., & Chen, S. J. (2015), The application of factor analysis method in performance evaluation of listed banking business, *Proceedings of the 2015 International Conference on Education, Management, Information and Medicine, Advances in Economics, Business and Management Research*. Atlantis. https://www.atlantis-press.com/proceedings/emim-15/21527 doi:10.2991/emim-15.2015.156

ESG. (2021). *How to Calculate an ESG Score for a Bank*. ESG. https://www.esgthereport.com/how-to-calculate-an-esg-score-for-a-bank/

Fibryanti, Y. V., & Nurcholidah, L. (2020), Analysis of Factors that affect the Financial Performance of the Banks, *Proceedings of the 3rd Green Development International Conference (GDIC, 2020) Advances in Engineering Research*, Atlantis press. DOI:10.2991/aer.k.210825.087

Innig, C. (April 9, 2021). *In Banking, sustainability is the new digital, now what?* Banking Blog. https://bankingblog.accenture.com/banking-sustainability-new-digital-now-what

Jaouad, E., & Lahsen, O. (2018), Factors Affecting Banks Performance: Empirical Evidence from Morocco, European Scientific Journal, 14. doi:10.19044/esj.2018.v14n34p255

Jennifer, & Radianto, W. & Kohardinata, C. (2022). Determinant Effect of CASA and NPM on Market Ratio of Banks Listed In IDX. *Business and Finance Journal, 7*(2). . DOI: https://www.researchgate.net/publication/368776396_DETERMINANT_EFFECT_OT_CASA_AND_NPM_ON_MARKET_RATIO_OF_BANKS_LISTED_IN_IDX doi:10.33086/bfj.v7i2.3490

KPMG International. (2021) *Effective Strategies to use opportunities and mitigate risks, ESG risks in Banks.* KPMG International. https://assets.kpmg.com/content/dam/kpmg/xx/pdf/2021/05/esg-risks-in-banks.pdf

Kumar, P. (February 7, 2022). *Beyond GDP: making nature count in the shift to sustainability.* UNEP https://www.unep.org/news-and-stories/story/beyond-gdp-making-nature-count-shift-sustainability

Prabhavati, K., & Dinesh, G. P. (2018), Banking: D definition and evolution, *International Journal of scientific and engineering research, 9*(8). https://www.ijser.org/researchpaper/Banking-Definition-and-Evolution.pdf

Qin, Lv., Wang, Y., Zhang, D., Yang, M., & Zheng, Y. (2020), Performance evaluation of commercial banks based on factor analysis, *E3S Web Conf. 2020 International Conference on Energy Big Data and Low-carbon Development Management (EBLDM 2020).* IEEE. 10.1051/e3sconf/202021402017

Sharma, M., & Choubey, A. (2022). Green banking initiatives: A qualitative study on Indian banking sector. *Environment, Development and Sustainability, 24*(1), 293–319. doi:10.1007/s10668-021-01426-9 PMID:33967597

United States Environment Protection Agency. (October 31, 2023) *Green Banks, Energy Resources for State and Local Governments.* EPA. https://www.epa.gov/statelocalenergy/green-banks

UNSDGs. (2023) *Take action for the Sustainable Development Goals.* UN. https://www.un.org/sustainabledevelopment/sustainable-development-goals/

APPENDIX

Table 8. Average of last five years' Profitability KPIs of selected banks

Name of the Banks	Profitability Indicators				
	OPM	**ROA**	**ROCE**	**NIM**	**NPM**
HDFC	4.954	1.748	3.256	3.65	25.222
ICICI	-3.168	1.206	2.896	3.252	18.516
SBI	-6.78	0.474	1.288	2.472	8.056
Kotak Mahindra	5.654	1.846	3.006	3.928	26.394
Axis	-12.38	0.646	2.324	2.892	10.402
BOB	-8.49	0.336	1.824	2.52	5.778
IndusInd	-8.664	1.228	3.304	3.678	15.042
PNB	-17.384	-0.13	1.706	2.248	-1.754
IDBI	-39.798	-1.33	2.182	2.7	-18.498
Union Bank	-14.87	0.05	1.806	2.262	1.186

Figure 15. P-P plot for dependency test of ROCE on NNPA, CASA, and FA_TA

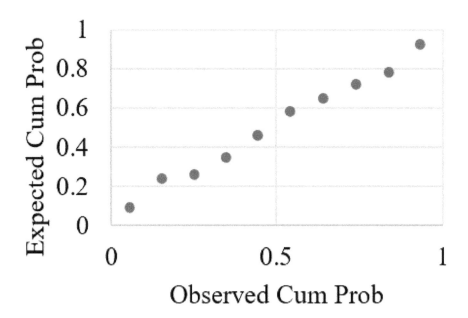

210

significant amount of study and practice has contributed to the implementation of urban sustainability in certain areas, the practice of urban planning on a daily basis rarely combines its multiple dimensions. More specifically, this is the case with regard to accessibility as well as the efficient combination of land use and transportation (Cheng et al., 2007). According to Li and Liu (2017), one of the most discussed and investigated themes in the field of urban studies is job access. As an integrated perspective of urban sustainability, it has a wide range of effects, including the protection of the environment (Stokes and Seto, 2018), the expansion of the economy (Kim and Jin, 2019), and the promotion of social fairness (Zhao and Howden-Chapman, 2010; Stokes and Seto, 2018). On the other hand, the trade-offs associated with job access are not sufficiently investigated, notably the latter two contributions. In light of the fact that it boosts the location premium in property prices and the mobility of urban residents, both of which are substantially related to individual welfare (Stokes and Seto, 2018), this aspect should be emphasised as being both vital and urgent. For urban residents who have more access to employment possibilities, there are more options for commuting and reduced costs associated with commuting (Kim et al., 2005). Additionally, there are more opportunities for employment and income (Andersson et al., 2018). These benefits, however, are not spread in an equitable manner among the various population generations. According to Yeganeh et al. (2018), higher property costs, which are related with employment access, frequently price out the disadvantaged, with the result of isolating people of colour and communities that are already disadvantaged. Furthermore, individuals who have increased access to employment opportunities are typically in a stronger position in the labour market, which tends to exacerbate urban inequality and poverty. Firstly, the majority of the research that has been done in recent times has concentrated on the relationship between the use of renewable energy and the environment. However, this study has not acknowledged the ways in which a green economy might bridge the gap between economic activity and sustainable development in Saudi Arabia. As far as we are concerned, to the best of our knowledge, there are just a handful of studies that have investigated the integration of the two primary frameworks of the green economy and sustainable development in Saudi Arabia (Al-Arjani et al., 2021; Albanawi, 2015; Alwakid et al., 2020). Second, this study uses a novel index system technique that evaluates the performance of green economic growth and reflects the attainment of sustainable development goals for the instance of Saudi Arabia. This is done from an empirical perspective and is compared to other studies that have been conducted.

Here there is a need to understand about sociology, political science, and technological factors with various aspects. These factors provide unique viewpoints on sustainable development, with each discipline offering vital insights into its social, political, & technological aspects. Sociology investigates the impact of social structures, institutions, including cultural norms on sustainability practices, such as consumption habits, environmental views, and social disparities. Political science examines the impact of governments, policies, including international organizations on the development of sustainability agendas, governance architectures, and tactics for implementing policies. Technology studies examine the interaction between technological advancements, goals related to sustainability, and socio-political circumstances. They investigate the possible benefits and drawbacks of technologies in advancing sustainable development. Collectively, these fields of study offer a comprehensive comprehension of sustainable development, emphasizing the interdependence of social, political, as well as technological elements and the necessity for multidisciplinary methods to tackle global sustainability issues.

Sociological Viewpoint

1. This enfolds the impact of social institutions, cultural norms, including collective behavior on sustainable development.
2. This study examines the patterns of consumption, production, & distribution within society and how they affect the environment.
3. Sociological research emphasizes the influence of social disparities, power dynamics, including cultural values on the development of sustainability practices.
4. Comprehending social aspects is essential for tackling concerns like environmental justice, community resilience, including social fairness in sustainable development endeavors.

Political Science Viewpoint

1. This enfolds the involvement of governments, policies, & organizations in advancing sustainable development.
2. This study examines the development, execution, and application of environmental policies at the local, national, and global scales.
3. Political scientists analyze the relationship between politics and sustainability, specifically focusing on the impact of entrenched interests, lobbying, including global governance institutions.
4. Gaining a comprehensive understanding of political processes and the intricate interplay of power dynamics is crucial in order to make progress in implementing effective policy solutions & reaching a consensus on sustainability objectives.

Technological Studies Viewpoint

1. This explores the relationships between technology advancements and the goals of sustainable development.
2. The text examines how technical solutions might reduce environmental consequences, improve resource efficiency, and encourage the use of renewable energy.
3. Technology researchers analyze the societal, economic, and environmental consequences of emerging technologies, including artificial intelligence, biotechnology, and renewable energy.
4. Incorporating technological viewpoints into discussions about sustainability is crucial for recognizing potential advantages, mitigating risks, and promoting creativity in the pursuit of sustainable development objectives.

Practical Examples and Case Studies

1. **The Payment for Ecosystem Services (PES) Program in Costa Rica:** Costa Rica's government has created a Payment for Ecosystem Services (PES) program with the dual purpose of safeguarding its unique rainforests and fostering economic development and social fairness. Through this initiative, landowners are compensated for their efforts in preserving and rehabilitating forests,

which in turn contribute to the provision of ecosystem services like carbon sequestration, watershed protection, including biodiversity conservation.

The program serves the dual purpose of conserving vital habitats and mitigating climate change, while also generating revenue for rural communities. This fosters social fairness by offering alternative livelihoods and lowering poverty. Costa Rica's PES program exemplifies a successful strategy for sustainable development by effectively harmonizing economic incentives, environmental conservation, and social benefits.

2. **The transition to renewable energy in Germany:** The Energiewende initiative in Germany seeks to transition from fossil fuels to renewable energy sources, while simultaneously promoting economic growth, environmental preservation, and social equality.

Germany has significantly increased its renewable energy capacity, namely in wind and solar power, by implementing policies such as feed-in tariffs, renewable energy objectives, and community ownership programs. The transformation has resulted in the creation of numerous environmentally-friendly employment opportunities, a decrease in the release of harmful gases that contribute to global warming, and an enhancement of the stability and reliability of energy sources, all of which have positively impacted both the economy and the environment. Furthermore, renewable energy initiatives driven by the community have given local inhabitants more influence, encouraged a fair distribution of clean energy advantages, and promoted energy democracy.

3. **Overview of Fair-Trade Certification for the Coffee Industry:** The objective of Fair Trade accreditation in the coffee business is to advance social fairness among smallholder producers, while simultaneously guaranteeing environmental sustainability & economic viability. Coffee growers must comply with social and environmental requirements, including fair salaries, safe working conditions, including sustainable farming practices, in order to meet Fair Trade standards. Certified producers can enhance the well-being of farmers and their families by utilizing the revenue from selling their coffee at a justifiable price to fund community development initiatives, including education, healthcare, and infrastructure.

Fair Trade also promotes sustainable methods, like organic farming & agroforestry, that safeguard ecosystems, preserve biodiversity, and lessen the effects of climate change.

There is lot of researches done till date but there is a requirement to more work and researches to interconnect these parameters. This chapter is organised in the following manner for the remaining sections: In the second segment, mission is provided on the subject of considering the significance of sustainable development and the green economy. The literature review is conducted that utilised in this study are presented in the third section of the report. The discussion part of this investigation provided in the fourth section of the report. The study concluded in the final section, along with some policy implications that were suggested.

Research Gap

Although there has been considerable advancement in comprehending the ideas and significance of sustainable development, there is still a noticeable lack of research in determining successful techniques and frameworks for attaining the intricate equilibrium of economic viability, environmental preservation, and social equality. Although there are many case studies and examples that demonstrate effective initiatives in certain situations, there is a dearth of comprehensive research that methodically assesses the trade-offs, synergies, & unintended consequences of sustainability efforts across many industries and countries.

1. Research on comprehensive strategies that take into account the interdependence of social, environmental, and economic problems in sustainable development is lacking and should be prioritized. Contemporary research frequently concentrates on a single element independently, disregarding the many interconnections and reciprocal influences that determine sustainable results.
2. Current studies frequently depend on traditional economic metrics, like GDP growth, to evaluate advancements towards sustainable development objectives. Nevertheless, there is a dearth of agreement over comprehensive measurements and indicators that encompass the multifaceted aspects of sustainability, such as social welfare, environmental excellence, and economic robustness.
3. Although numerous studies propose policy recommendations for attaining sustainability objectives, there is a scarcity of research on the efficacy of policy implementation tactics in real-life situations. Gaining a comprehensive understanding of the obstacles, motivators, and systems of control that either support or impede sustainable development strategies is crucial for informing decision-making based on factual evidence.
4. The convergence of sustainability with fairness and justice is a subject that necessitates additional examination. Research frequently neglects to include the distributional consequences of sustainability programs, such as the effects of policies on marginalized communities, indigenous peoples, particularly vulnerable populations.
5. As the world becomes more globalized and interconnected, there is a rising demand for research that focuses on global sustainability concerns, including climate change, biodiversity loss, & resource depletion. Nevertheless, there exists a lack of comprehension regarding the extent to which local and national initiatives contribute to global sustainability objectives and vice versa.
6. Engaging stakeholders and local people in sustainable development processes through participatory approaches is essential for promoting ownership, inclusivity, & legitimacy. However, there is a scarcity of research on participatory methodologies that enable a wide range of voices and viewpoints to have influence in decision-making processes.

To fill these gaps in research, it is necessary to have collaboration amongst different disciplines, use creative methods, and have a comprehensive understanding of the many factors that influence sustainable development. By closing these disparities, scientists may contribute to more efficient, fair, and robust strategies for sustainability that are advantageous to both current and future generations.

Mission

Our goal is to promote sustainable development principles, which include a healthy equilibrium between economic growth, environmental preservation, and social justice. We are dedicated to conducting research, encouraging dialogue, and giving practical insights to address the important concerns of our day. Our work is driven by the conviction that ensuring the success of future generations depends on ensuring the success of the present one. Our mission is to:

- We're devoted to digging deep into the dynamics of sustainable development to figure out how the economy, environment, and society all fit together. The results of our study will hopefully provide actionable advice for policymakers and other stakeholders.
- Create a forum for the exchange of information and ideas regarding sustainable development is an overarching goal. We hope to reach many people by publishing, holding conferences, and participating in the local community.
- In order to achieve sustainable development, we must work together as governments, corporations, and members of civil society. To tackle the complex problems in this area, we advocate for increased collaboration and partnership.
- We see it as part of our purpose to promote changes in policy and practise that will have a positive impact on the environment. Our goal is to encourage responsible policymaking by increasing public understanding of the connection between sustainable development, environmental protection, and social equity.
- Motivate people to take positive steps towards a better world is one of our top priorities. Our mission is to encourage people and institutions to adopt sustainable behaviours and make well-informed decisions that improve the quality of life for future generations.

REVIEW OF LITERATURE

Akhter (2024) has examined the notion of achieving a harmonious equilibrium between economic expansion, societal fairness, and ecological preservation within the framework of sustainable development economic strategies. The conceptual framework emphasized the interconnectedness and compromises between these dimensions. The case studies of inclusive growth in Nordic countries, sustainable tourism in Costa Rica, & South Korea's green growth policy exemplified successful economic policies that effectively balanced growth, social fairness, and environmental conservation. The challenges that were discovered highlighted the necessity for integrated strategies and efficient governance systems to tackle the intricate problems linked to sustainable development. The research highlights the significance of implementing well-rounded economic strategies in order to attain sustainable growth. The pursuit of economic growth should be conducted in a manner that upholds environmental boundaries, fosters social fairness, and protects natural resources for the benefit of future generations. For attaining this balance, it is necessary to incorporate sustainability goals into economic policy frameworks, encourage green and inclusive growth methods, reinforce social safety nets, improve environmental legislation, and establish effective institutional structures. This research offers valuable insights into the importance of economic policies in achieving a balance between growth, social fairness, and environmental conservation. However, there are some areas that require more investigation. Moreover, gaining insight into the interplay between local and international environments when adopting sustainable economic strategies would be advantageous.

Hariram and others (2023) explores the complex idea of sustainability, including its development, regulations, principles, and the various areas and difficulties associated with attaining it in today's society. Despite the historical utilization of capitalism, socialism, and communism, these economic systems have not effectively addressed the overall needs of sustainable development. Thus, it is imperative to adopt a comprehensive approach that serves as the foundation for a novel development paradigm known as sustainalism. This study presents a novel socio-economic theory called sustainalism, which places emphasis on enhancing quality of life, promoting social equity, preserving culture, fostering world peace, ensuring social justice, and promoting overall well-being. This paper delineates the six principles of sustainalism and characterizes sustainalists as persons who wholeheartedly accept these novel concepts. This study also examines the means of achieving sustainability in the contemporary world through a sustainable revolution, which signifies a significant progression towards a sustainable period.

Royal et al (2023) investigates the correlation between economic openness, development, and urbanization in sustainable ecosystems. The analysis relies on the use of balanced panel data for QUAD countries spanning from 1991 to 2019. This research examines the relationship between sustainability and openness using the PMG-ARDL methodology. The published findings suggest a positive correlation between sustainability and urbanization in both Australia and India. All panels had a negative and significant ECT value, which confirms the presence of short-term association as well. The granger causality analysis indicates that there was a reciprocal causal relationship between sustainability and urbanization in the United States and India. Although governments are already committed to the "Kyoto Protocol and Paris Agreement," it is still important to maintain and enhance efforts to promote sustainability and raise awareness about the importance of achieving sustainable ecosystems. Furthermore, it is advisable to implement subsidizing schemes and raise awareness through programs, such as providing incentives for sustainable urban design and encouraging the adoption of green power purchase agreements. Additionally, the use of green bonds for energy infrastructure needs should be promoted.

Brown, K. & Corbera, E. (2003) There have been statements made that are quite ambitious regarding the development advantages of market-based policy instruments for climate mitigation. Within the context of many dimensions of fairness and sustainable development, we investigate the implications that forest carbon initiatives potentially have. In order to investigate the many stakeholders, their responsibilities, interests, and points of view, we apply a stakeholder multi-criteria evaluation to a case study that is located in Mexico. Access to markets and forests, as well as legitimacy in decision-making and institutions, are two aspects of equality that are covered in this article. The establishment of robust institutional frameworks that span several scales is essential in order to guarantee that the goals of equitable and sustainable development are achieved, and that existing marginalised segments of society are not barred from participation. In the process of their development, these institutions are still in the process of developing, and their establishment brings together a wide variety of stakeholders from the corporate sector, the government, and civil society. In spite of this, it is possible that the nature of the market itself will ultimately be a limiting factor in the capacity of the "new carbon economy" to deliver tangible benefits for sustainable development. Numerous research that investigate the relationship between mining and sustainable development have highlighted the importance of establishing a balance between economic, environmental, and social objectives. This is something that has been emphasised in a number of these studies. The research conducted by Y. Li and Umair in 2023 focused on sustainable mining and brought attention to the necessity of striking a balance between economic, environmental, and social concerns in order to achieve long-term growth and prosperity. The importance of integrated techniques that take into consideration economic, environmental, and social problems was also discovered in a study of the literature on sustainable development and mining that was carried out by (Xiuzhen et al., 2022). These studies demonstrate that the mining industry is becoming increasingly aware of the importance of striking a balance between social, environmental, and economic goals. Mining practices that are less harmful to the environment are gaining more and more significance, but there are still a lot of obstacles to overcome. The conflict that arises from the need to preserve both society and the environment while simultaneously expanding the economy is a big obstacle. In addition, the mining industry suffers from a lack of accountability and transparency, which makes it difficult to assess and apply practices that are sustainable for mining. According to Sachs et al.'s research from 2020, these problems highlight the necessity of determining how to strike a balance between social, environmental, and economic expectations in the mining industry. Zhanbayev, R.A., Irfan, M., Shutaleva, A.V., Maksimov, D.G., Abdykadyrkyzy, R. & Filiz, Ş. (2023) In the context of contemporary society, the purpose of this study is to investigate a demoethical paradigm for sustainable development. The proposal suggests a strategy that centres on the organisation of activities with the goal of enhancing sustainable development. To be more specific, it provides a demoethical model that is applicable to enterprises that are part of the Industry 5.0 and Society 5.0. The purpose of this endeavour is to define the demoethical principles that have the potential to propel sustainable development in this age of digitalization. This study outlines major components of the demoethical model by doing a literature review and analysis. Additionally, it offers recommendations that can be put into practice by stakeholders who are participating in digital transformation. The examination of demoethical norms and phenomena, such as education, nurturing, mind, knowledge, science, and honest work, has made it possible to identify values that are congruent with the concept of sustainable growth in society. According to the findings of the research, the concept of a demoethical foundation for sustainability has its origins in the idea of spirituality serving as the foundation for a new scenario of societal growth and its connection to the natural world. According to the findings of the study, concepts on the demoethical foundation of sustainability are founded on the premise that spirituality should be given importance as the foundation for a new scenario for the growth of society. Additionally, the study demonstrates that system-wide modelling should incorporate demographic, socio-economical, and ecological components.

The importance of sustainable development in the mining industry has been highlighted in a number of studies that have been conducted in recent times. According to Taghizadeh-Hesary and Yoshino's research (2019), environmentally responsible mining practices lead to improvements in economic development, social benefits, and environmental performance. There are a number of obstacles that limit the widespread implementation of sustainable mining practices, despite the fact that their understanding is growing. According to Mononen et al. (2023), sustainable mining operations in underdeveloped nations have a number of challenges, including difficulty in acquiring more money, infrastructure, and technology. It has been suggested by Taghizadeh-Hesary et al. (2019) that the absence of robust laws and enforcement mechanisms may also be a barrier to the implementation of environmentally responsible mining methods.

According to Dehghani et al. (2021), in order to address these challenges, it is necessary to develop new approaches and regulate mining practices that promote environmental responsibility. Make the case that market-based rules, such as tariffs and tradable licences, could be used to encourage mining companies to utilise techniques that are less harmful to the environment. Life cycle assessment is another method that might be utilised to encourage environmentally responsible practices in the mining industry, as suggested by Li et al. (2022). As the demand for natural resources continues to rise, the mining industry has come under increasing scrutiny for the negative impact it has on the environment and the people living in the surrounding areas. Mining companies are coming under growing pressure to find a middle ground between making a profit and ensuring that their growth is sustainable. One of the ways in which the mining sector has responded to this issue is by using sustainable mining technologies. In an effort to decrease the impact that mining has on the environment and to enhance ethical behaviour, several strategies were developed. Mining companies have the potential to assist local communities by fostering economic growth and safeguarding cultural heritage places. Additionally, mining companies have the ability to implement cutting-edge technologies in order to reduce their energy footprint and emissions of greenhouse gases (Yoshino et al., 2021). However, there are other challenges involved in putting sustainable mining techniques into practice with mining operations. A significant barrier is presented by the high expense of implementing such procedures, which is especially problematic for mining businesses that are not as big. In the lack of clearly defined legislation and rules for sustainable mining, it may be challenging for firms to determine the criteria that they should be meeting in order to avoid any potential problems. In spite of these challenges, a rising number of people believe that environmentally responsible mining methods are necessary for the continued success of the mining industry (Le et al., 2019).

According to Chen (2023) Despite the fact that equity is a fundamental principle for the area of public administration and for the development of sustainability, it is disproportionately and considerably underrepresented and underprioritized in the sustainability priorities of local governments in the United States. When it comes to sustainability, equity is considered to be one of the three important "Es" that are essential, along with the environment and the economy. Ever since the very first Minnowbrook Conference, which took place in 1968, promoting social justice has arisen as one of the most important objectives of public administration. This is because equity has emerged as one of the four "Es" that are associated with the field, along with economy, efficiency, and effectiveness. In light of this, to what degree do the concerns and efforts of public administrators have an impact on the process of accepting and furthering social fairness in sustainable development? This study provides a unique knowledge of the tiered realisation of sustainability priorities by localities, as well as elements that are connected with ascending upwards through the tiered pathway of prioritising sustainability orientation. This understanding is based on the results of the 2015 Local Government Sustainability Practices Survey conducted by the International Council of Municipalities (ICMA). Chaaben, N., Elleuch, Z., Hamdi, B. & Kahouli, B. (2022) The Kingdom of Saudi Arabia, which is a member of the United Nations, is working towards the goal of achieving the Sustainable Development Goals of the 2030 Agenda and making its economy more environmentally friendly. There are three elements of sustainable development: economic, social, and environmental. The green economy is a catalyst for sustainable development in all three of these dimensions, with the goal of enhancing human well-being and social fairness while simultaneously lowering environmental dangers. The relevant prior research, on the other hand, did not take into account the role that a green economy plays in producing sustainable development for Saudi Arabia. In light of this, the purpose of this research is to investigate the degree to which the kingdom is environmentally friendly and to evaluate its progress towards sustainable development from the years 2015 to 2020. For this reason, we have decided to implement the EEPSE Green Economy Index, which is a composite index that incorporates educational, economic, political, societal, and environmental variables that are related with the pillars of the Quintuple Helix Innovation Model. According to the findings of this research, this index is made up of 42 different variables that are associated with sustainable growth and the green economy. Based on the empirical findings, it appears that Saudi Arabia has had a substantial improvement in its EEPSE grade equivalent index score. In addition, the data provide evidence that the performance of the kingdom in terms of the green economy is impacted as a result of the COVID-19 dilemma. The purpose of this study is to present policymakers with creative views that will stimulate the transition to a green economy, which is the primary locomotive that will lead to the achievement of economic, social, and environmental sustainability for the kingdom.

POLICIES AND GOVERNANCE STRUCTURES RELATED TO SUSTAINABLE DEVELOPMENT: EFFECTIVENESS AND CHALLENGES

Policies and governance structures are essential in directing and executing sustainable development at several levels, including global, regional, national, & local. These structures comprise legal frameworks, regulations, policies, and systems that strive to achieve a harmonious balance between economic development, environmental preservation, and social fairness. The efficacy of governance and policy structures pertaining to sustainable development differs significantly, contingent upon their design, implementation, and adaptability to evolving circumstances. The challenges encompass guaranteeing consistent and unified strategies, involving relevant parties, obtaining essential resources, and sustaining adaptability. Notwithstanding these difficulties, these frameworks are vital in directing worldwide, regional, national, & local endeavors towards attaining a more sustainable and fair world. Here, I present a summary of these governance and policy systems, including their efficacy and difficulties.

Global Governance Structures

a. The United Nations Framework Convention on Climate Change (UNFCCC) and its Paris Agreement have the objective of mitigating climate change by imposing restrictions on the increase in global temperatures. Countries pledge to nationally determined contributions (NDCs) in order to decrease the amount of greenhouse gas emissions.

Effectiveness: It has successfully generated worldwide efforts to address climate change, but encounters difficulties in achieving the agreed-upon goals.

Challenges: Ensuring universal compliance with Nationally Determined Contributions (NDCs) and meeting the financial requirements of poor nations.

b. The Sustainable Development Goals (SDGs) are a collection of 17 interconnected objectives that were accepted by member states of the United Nations. These goals are designed to tackle many global concerns such as poverty, inequality, climate change, and environmental degradation, with the aim of achieving significant progress by the year 2030.

Effectiveness: They offer a comprehensive framework for promoting sustainable development, fostering action across all sectors.

Challenges: The progress made towards achieving goals and improving different regions is not constant, and there is a lack of enough finance.

c.   The Convention on Biological Diversity (CBD) seeks to preserve biological diversity, encourage the sustainable utilization of its constituents, and guarantee equitable distribution of benefits derived from genetic resources.

Effectiveness: It has successfully increased awareness and resulted in the development of national policies to preserve biodiversity.

Challenges: The rate of biodiversity loss remains concerning, in part because it has not been well included into wider land and sea use policy.

Regional and National Governance Structures

a.   The European Union (EU) Green Deal is a comprehensive collection of policy initiatives implemented by the EU with the primary objective of achieving climate neutrality in Europe by the year 2050. Effectiveness: It signifies a substantial dedication to promoting environmental sustainability and facilitating economic transformation. Challenges: Involves a significant financial commitment, and there are apprehensions over the societal and economic effects on many industries and areas.

b.   National Development Plans encompass the formulation of individualized policies and strategies by countries, with the aim of achieving sustainable development in accordance with their own economic, social, and environmental circumstances. As an illustration, let's consider the National Decarbonization Plan of Costa Rica. Effectiveness: Can achieve significant results when tailored to local requirements and capabilities. Challenges may arise in the form of political, financial, and technological obstacles that could hinder the successful implementation of the project.

Challenges

1.   The implementation gap refers to the common issue of translating policy aspirations into action on the ground. This gap is often caused by insufficient financing, limited technical skills, or a lack of political will.

2.   Coherence and integration refer to the challenge of ensuring that policies across various sectors and levels of government are aligned and work together effectively.

3.   Stakeholder Engagement: Successful governance necessitates the participation of diverse stakeholders, such as civil society, the private sector, indigenous peoples, and local communities. Nevertheless, it is difficult to achieve significant involvement and guarantee that these opinions are acknowledged and implemented.

4.   Implementing effective monitoring and accountability systems is essential, but it can be challenging and require significant resources.

5.   Flexibility and resilience are crucial for policies and governance structures to effectively respond to changing conditions, such as emerging scientific evidence, technological advancements, and socio-economic trends.

DISCUSSION

Studying how to maintain a healthy equilibrium among economic growth, ecological preservation, and social justice is crucial in today's world. We can see their significance in the following ways:

Challenges to the Environment

Climate change, deforestation, biodiversity loss, and resource depletion are just a few of the planet's most pressing environmental problems. Finding strategies to minimise these issues and promote ecological sustainability requires extensive research in sustainable development.

The expansion of the world economy is a key factor in the acceleration of human progress. However, this progress is often accompanied by worsening conditions in the natural world and increased social disparity. Maintaining economic security for the long term requires striking a balance between growth and environmentally responsible actions (Sharma, 2023).

When it comes to social conditions, many places of the world still have a long way to go (Agarwal, 2022). To ensure that the advantages of development are shared fairly across all segments of society, it is important to do research into sustainable development that can shed light on policies and practises that promote social equality.

Sustainability is about more than just the environment and society; it affects everyone everywhere. The results of this line of inquiry can be used to develop policies that protect the planet's natural resources for future generations while also raising the standard of living for people everywhere.

Research is used by policymakers as a foundation for making informed decisions. Sustainable development research can help policymakers strike a fair and equitable balance between economic development, environmental protection, and social justice.

Sustainable business practises are becoming widely seen as valuable by corporations. Improved brand reputation and competitiveness may result from this line of inquiry, since it may encourage corporations to implement eco-friendly tactics and embrace corporate social responsibility.

Resilience

Sustainable development contributes to societal and environmental resilience. Long-term stability is fostered while also bolstering the resilience of local communities and ecosystems to survive temporary setbacks like weather events and economic downturns.

Generations to Come

An ethical obligation towards them sustainable development is a moral obligation. Studying this topic makes sure that the future generations won't have their lives and chances hampered by our current decisions.

International Agreements

Many international agreements and goals, such as the United Nations Sustainable Development Goals (SDGs) and the Paris Agreement, emphasise the necessity of sustainable development. Research guides actions taken and measures taken to meet these targets.

Raising public understanding of sustainable development concerns relies heavily on efforts in both research and teaching. Citizens who have more information are more likely to back policies and programmes that put sustainability first.

The term "sustainability" has become the buzzword of the urban planning world. Even while urban sustainability has been put into effect in certain areas thanks to extensive research and practise, its many components are rarely incorporated into daily urban planning practise. Accessibility and the efficient integration of land use and transportation are particularly important factors in this regard (Cheng et al., 2007). In urban studies, job accessibility is a hotly contested and well-researched topic (Bryan, B.A., 2018). An integrated view of urban sustainability shows that it has far-reaching effects on environmental preservation, economic growth, and social fairness (Ejsmont, K., Gladysz, B. & Kluczek, A. (2020).; Zhao and Howden-Chapman, 2010; Stokes and Seto, 2018). However, the costs and benefits of having easier access to jobs, especially the latter two, are not thoroughly investigated. This aspect needs to be emphasised as crucial and time-sensitive since it affects two factors crucial to individual well-being: the location premium in housing prices and the mobility of urban residents (Stokes and Seto, 2018). Greater work availability in cities means more employment and income prospects, as well as more commuting options and lower commuting expenses (Kim et al., 2005; Andersson et al., 2018). However, these advantages do not accrue to all generations of a population in the same way. A lack of affordable housing is a major barrier to economic mobility for people of colour and low-income groups (Yeganeh et al., 2018). Furthermore, those with better access to jobs are in a stronger position in the labour market, which exacerbates urban inequality and poverty.

Environmental Challenges and Social Equity Issues

Sustainable development aims to achieve a harmonious combination of economic growth, environmental preservation, and social fairness. It ensures that the current generation's demands are fulfilled without jeopardizing the ability of future generations to fulfill their own needs.

a. Environmental challenges
    ◦ Climate change is a worldwide problem that causes severe weather events, higher sea levels, and changes in rainfall patterns, which have a significant impact on millions of people around the world. Small island developing nations (SIDS) are confronted with significant risks to their existence due to rising sea levels, while drought-prone regions in Africa are witnessing a rise in food insecurity.
    ◦ Biodiversity loss refers to the swift reduction in the variety of living organisms caused by the destruction of habitats, pollution, climate change, and excessive exploitation. This poses a significant threat to ecosystems. The Amazon rainforest, commonly known as the "lungs of the Earth," is undergoing rapid destruction, which is having a significant impact on global carbon dioxide levels and indigenous people.
    ◦ Pollution, namely air, water, and soil contamination resulting from industrial activity, agricultural runoff, and urbanization, presents significant health hazards and causes environmental harm. The Great Pacific Garbage Patch is a large collection of plastic waste in the ocean that serves as a prime example of the worldwide problem of plastic pollution.
b. Societal disparities in fairness and justice

    ◦   Income inequality refers to the increasing disparity in wealth distribution among individuals and nations, which has detrimental effects on social unity and economic steadiness. In numerous emerging nations, there is a significant disparity in wealth distribution, with a small group of privileged individuals possessing the majority of resources, while the majority of the population faces poverty and limited access to essential services.

    ◦   Disparities in the availability of high-quality education and healthcare services contribute to the continuation of poverty and inequality. Sub-Saharan Africa has substantial obstacles in this aspect, with millions of youngsters not attending school and having restricted availability of healthcare facilities.

    ◦   Gender inequality persists as a significant issue, characterized by the unfair treatment and physical harm inflicted upon women and girls, as well as the unequal access to school, employment, and political involvement. In regions such as South Asia and the Middle East, women's rights and opportunities are greatly restricted due to cultural and legal obstacles.

Technological Innovations and Emerging Economic Models

Sustainable development is a constantly changing area that is influenced by advancements in technology, growing economic models, and shifting challenges and possibilities. Here is an in-depth analysis of these facets:

a.   Technological innovation

    1.   Carbon capture and storage (CCS), advanced renewable energy systems (such as solar photovoltaic panels with improved efficiencies and offshore wind turbines), and battery storage technologies play a vital role in decreasing greenhouse gas emissions and facilitating a shift towards a low-carbon economy.

    2.   Technologies such as smart grids, IoT devices, and intelligent transportation systems can greatly improve urban sustainability by increasing energy efficiency, decreasing traffic congestion, and improving the quality of urban life.

    3.   Precision agriculture is a farming technique that utilizes drones, Internet of Things (IoT) devices, and artificial intelligence (AI) to carefully monitor and optimize farm resources. This technique has the capability to enhance water efficiency, minimize reliance on chemical inputs, and enhance crop yields, thereby promoting the development of more sustainable food systems.

    4.   Advancements in water treatment, such as filters made from graphene or energy-efficient desalination systems, are crucial for tackling water scarcity and guaranteeing universal access to clean water.

b.   Emerging Economic Models

    1.   The Circular Economy concept prioritizes waste minimization and the ongoing utilization of resources. Circular strategies encompass the incorporation of principles such as durability, renewable resources, reusability, repairability, remanufacturing, and recycling. This method not only preserves resources but also creates new business models & economic prospects.

    2.   The sharing economy use digital channels to facilitate the sharing of goods and services, hence minimizing the necessity for ownership. Illustrative instances encompass car-sharing services, co-working facilities, and peer-to-peer lending. This concept has the potential to enhance

        sustainable development through the efficient utilization of resources and the minimization of waste.

3.   Green Finance encompasses financial endeavors that provide support to environmental activities and promote sustainable development. This includes the utilization of green bonds, green banks, including sustainable investment funds. Green finance plays a crucial role in directing both private and public funds towards projects that promote sustainability.

4.   The biobased economy is centered around the manufacturing of products utilizing renewable biological resources, offering an alternative to economies that rely on fossil fuels. This strategy promotes sustainability by minimizing carbon emissions and optimizing resource utilization.

c.   Challenges and Opportunities

1.   Ensuring equal access to technology and promoting fairness in its distribution: Achieving fair and equal availability of sustainable technology in various locations and groups continues to be a difficult task. Tackling this problem provides a chance to promote comprehensive development and decrease inequalities.

2.   As the effects of climate change become more noticeable, the task of creating strong infrastructure and communities that can endure severe weather events and shifting conditions is both a difficulty and a chance for creative solutions.

3.   To address the issue of biodiversity loss, it is necessary to implement creative conservation measures, engage in sustainable land use planning, & undertake restoration initiatives. Advancements in genetic studies and habitat monitoring provide novel instruments for the preservation of biodiversity.

4.   Sustainable urban development is a tremendous challenge as urban populations continue to grow. The task involves creating cities that prioritize good quality of life, efficient transportation systems, and the incorporation of green spaces. Nevertheless, it also gives a chance to reinvent the way people live in cities.

5.   Establishing and executing efficient regulatory & policy frameworks that promote sustainable practices & innovation can be difficult due to conflicting political and commercial interests. However, it is crucial for advancing sustainable development goals.

6.   Education and awareness play a vital role in cultivating a sustainable culture by improving awareness and comprehension of sustainable development challenges. By allocating resources towards education and involvement, individuals and communities can be empowered to make choices that are environmentally and socially sustainable.

Sustainable development is currently at a critical juncture, with obstacles that necessitate inventive resolutions and cooperative endeavors. Advancing towards a more sustainable and equitable world requires technological advancements, evolving economic structures, and a proactive approach to addressing future challenges and utilizing possibilities.

Strategies for Achieving Long-Term, Environmentally-Friendly Progress

1.   Implementing the Paris Agreement involves reducing greenhouse gas emissions, investing in renewable energy, including improving climate resilience. These actions can help to lessen the impacts of climate change. The European Union's Green Deal exemplifies a bold and ambitious approach to addressing climate change.

2. Preserving natural habitats, rehabilitating damaged ecosystems, and advocating for sustainable farming and fishing are essential for the conservation and sustainable utilization of resources, which is vital for maintaining biodiversity. The Convention on Biological Diversity establishes a comprehensive international structure for implementing measures.

3. Policies that foster equitable distribution of economic gains, ensure equal access to healthcare and schooling, and promote gender parity can effectively address social equity concerns. The United Nations Sustainable Development Goals (SDGs) are designed to provide guidance for global endeavors in these fields.

4. International cooperation is necessary to address global challenges effectively. Developing countries can receive help for their sustainability initiatives through multilateral agreements, foreign investment, and technology transfer.

5. Community engagement & empowerment: Grassroots movements & community-led initiatives can offer efficient and culturally suitable resolutions to sustainability concerns at the local level.

To effectively tackle environmental and social equity issues within the framework of sustainable development, it is necessary to adopt comprehensive strategies that take into account the economic, environmental, & social aspects. By fostering international collaboration, implementing effective national policies, and engaging in community initiatives, we may strive towards a more sustainable and just global society.

CONCLUSION

Ultimately, the notion of sustainable development encompasses a comprehensive strategy for societal advancement. This approach acknowledges the interconnectedness of economic well-being, environmental conservation, and social fairness (Pinki, 2021). By fostering a fragile equilibrium among these fundamental principles, we might aspire to a future in which our current activities do not jeopardise the prospects and assets accessible to future generations.

Sustainable development is not merely a lofty concept; it is an essential requirement in practice. It necessitates the collaboration of governments, corporations, communities, and individuals to synchronise their actions and policies in order to achieve a shared objective of guaranteeing a flourishing planet and inclusive societies.

In order to effectively tackle the intricate problems confronting our planet, it is imperative that we wholeheartedly embrace innovation, implement responsible practices, and promote teamwork as we progress. By undertaking this action, we may establish a society that is more resistant to challenges, fairer in its distribution of resources, and more mindful of the environment. This will lead to a sustainable future where economic success, responsible environmental management, and fairness in society can exist together in a balanced and harmonious manner.

Global cooperation: Sustainable development is a worldwide concern that surpasses national boundaries. International cooperation is essential in addressing issues such as climate change, resource depletion, and social inequities (Dwivedi, 2022). Global concerns can be effectively addressed through international agreements, partnerships, and coordinated endeavours (Gupta, 2023).

Education and awareness: This plays a crucial role in promoting sustainable practices. Providing individuals with knowledge about the significance of sustainability enables them to make well-informed decisions, resulting in more conscientious behaviours in their everyday lives, consumption habits, and decision-making processes (Mijares III, 2023).

Resilience and adaptation: Developing the ability to withstand and adjust to environmental changes and unexpected challenges is a crucial element of sustainable development. This entails adjusting to evolving climate patterns, fortifying infrastructure to survive natural calamities, and cultivating resilient communities capable of rebounding and prospering in the midst of hardship (Crescini, 2023).

Long-term thinking: Adopting a long-term perspective is essential for achieving sustainable development, as it involves prioritising lasting advantages over immediate profits. It entails evaluating the consequences of current activities on future generations and making choices that prioritise the welfare of the planet and its inhabitants over immediate financial gains or benefits.

Innovation and green technologies: The use of innovation and the advancement of green technology are crucial in attaining sustainability (Valdez, 2023; Dwivedi, 2022). Allocating resources towards renewable energy, sustainable agriculture, efficient transportation, and waste management technology has the potential to substantially diminish our ecological impact.

Ethical consumption: Promoting ethical consumer habits, such as selecting items from environmentally conscious companies or endorsing fair-trade practices, can foster positive transformation by shaping market expectations and promoting responsible manufacturing methods (Shukla, 2022).

By incorporating these elements into our development strategy, we may progress towards a more equitable, comprehensive, and enduring future for all. The acts of each individual, ranging from personal decisions to contributions to society, collectively determine the trajectory towards a more sustainable world.

EMERGING TRENDS AND FUTURE OUTLOOK ON SUSTAINABLE DEVELOPMENT

The field of sustainable development is always changing due to developments in technology, shifts in social dynamics, and worldwide environmental issues. The future of sustainability is being influenced by emerging trends, which present both new opportunities and problems. Presented below is a comprehensive summary of significant emerging patterns and a prospective analysis of sustainable development.

a. Emerging trends
   1. The transition to renewable energy sources such as wind, solar, and hydroelectric power is gaining momentum. The change is propelled by the declining expenses of renewable technologies, growing recognition of the ecological consequences of fossil fuels, and governmental backing. Projections indicate that there will be a sustained and significant increase in renewable energy capacity worldwide in the coming years. This growth could result in a majority of our energy system being based on renewable sources by the middle of the century.
   2. The circular economy is a departure from the conventional linear economy model of "take, make, dispose." It prioritizes waste reduction, product reuse, and material recycling. This transformation is being facilitated by advancements in material science, waste management, and product design. The shift towards a circular economy is anticipated to expand, propelled by limited resources, customer desire for sustainable products, and regulatory measures.
   3. There is an increasing focus on sustainable agriculture approaches that aim to minimize environmental effect, including regenerative agriculture, precision farming, and agroecology.

In addition, the increasing popularity of plant-based diets and the development of alternative proteins, such as lab-grown meat, effectively tackle issues over the long-term viability of food production. Future advancements are expected to prioritize the enhancement of food security, the mitigation of carbon footprints, and the enhancement of nutrition.

4. The utilization of digital technologies such as artificial intelligence (AI), the Internet of Things (IoT), and blockchain is being employed to tackle sustainability issues. These technologies have the ability to maximize resource utilization, enhance energy effectiveness, and enhance the transparency of supply chains. The continuous process of digital transformation is anticipated to have a crucial impact on the monitoring and administration of sustainable development goals (SDGs).

5. Environmental, Social, and Governance (ESG) criteria are progressively influencing investment choices, directing resources towards sustainable firms. Green bonds and sustainability-linked loans are financial instruments that provide funding for environmental projects. The trajectory towards ESG investing and green finance is expected to persist, propelled by investor demand and regulatory frameworks.

b. Future scope of the study

1. Sustainability is increasingly being included into decision-making processes in various areas, such as banking, healthcare, construction, and transportation. Adopting this comprehensive strategy is crucial for attaining the Sustainable Development Goals (SDGs).

2. Addressing intricate sustainability concerns necessitates collaboration among governments, corporations, civil society, and academics through multi-stakeholder partnerships. Effective collaborations and collaborative solutions will play an increasingly crucial role in achieving future success in sustainable development.

3. Continued innovation and the assimilation of emerging technology will be essential for addressing sustainability challenges. This include progress in renewable energy, eco-friendly materials, and technological innovations for monitoring the environment.

4. Policy and regulatory evolution will be crucial in influencing the trajectory of sustainable development, with governments playing a pivotal role in this process. This include the implementation of carbon pricing mechanisms, the provision of assistance for green technologies, and the enforcement of sustainability requirements.

5. As the general public becomes more cognizant of sustainability concerns, consumer behavior and civic involvement are transitioning towards more environmentally-friendly activities. This tendency is anticipated to expedite, exerting influence on markets, regulations, and social norms.

The future about sustainable development hinges on leveraging innovation, cultivating collaboration, and establishing sustainability as a fundamental concept of societal advancement. Despite the presence of obstacles, the developing patterns present opportunities for achieving a more sustainable, fair, and adaptable world.

REFERENCES

Agarwal, N. (2022). An Analysis of The Socio-Economic Impact of Russia Ukraine War. *Globus An International Journal of Management & IT, 13*(2), 36-39.

Al-Arjani, A., Modibbo, U. M., Ali, I., & Sarkar, B. (2021). A new framework for the sustainable development goals of Saudi Arabia. *Journal of King Saud University. Science, 33*(6), 101477. doi:10.1016/j.jksus.2021.101477

Ali, Mohd Akhter, Kamraju, M. & Sonaji, Devkar Bhausaheb Sonaji (2024). Economic Policies for Sustainable Development: Balancing Growth, Social Equity, and Environmental Protection. *ASEAN Journal of Economic and Economic Education, 3*(1), 23-28.

Alwakid, W., Aparicio, S., & Urbano, D. (2020). Cultural antecedents of green entrepreneurship in Saudi Arabia: An institutional approach. *Sustainability (Basel), 12*(9), 3673. doi:10.3390/su12093673

Baguma, R., Carvalho, J.Á., Cledou, G., Estevez, E., Finquelievich, S., Janowski, T., Lopes, N. and Millard, J. (2016). *Knowledge Societies Policy Handbook.*

Boström, M., Andersson, E., Berg, M., Gustafsson, K., Gustavsson, E., Hysing, E., Lidskog, R., Löfmarck, E., Ojala, M., Olsson, J., Singleton, B., Svenberg, S., Uggla, Y., & Öhman, J. (2018). Conditions for transformative learning for sustainable development: A theoretical review and approach. *Sustainability (Basel), 10*(12), 4479. doi:10.3390/su10124479

Brown, K., & Corbera, E. (2003). Exploring equity and sustainable development in the new carbon economy. *Climate Policy, 3*, S41–S56. doi:10.1016/j.clipol.2003.10.004

Bryan, B. A., Gao, L., Ye, Y., Sun, X., Connor, J. D., Crossman, N. D., Stafford-Smith, M., Wu, J., He, C., Yu, D., Liu, Z., Li, A., Huang, Q., Ren, H., Deng, X., Zheng, H., Niu, J., Han, G., & Hou, X. (2018). China's response to a national land-system sustainability emergency. *Nature, 559*(7713), 193–204. doi:10.1038/s41586-018-0280-2 PMID:29995865

Burck, J., Höhne, N., Hagemann, M., Gonzales-Zuñiga, S., Leipold, G., Marten, F., Schindler, H., Barnard, S., & Nakhooda, S. (2016). *Brown to green: Assessing the g20 transition to a low-carbon economy.* Climate Transparency.

Chaaben, N., Elleuch, Z., Hamdi, B., & Kahouli, B. (2022). Green economy performance and sustainable development achievement: Empirical evidence from Saudi Arabia. *Environment, Development and Sustainability, 26*(1), 1–16. doi:10.1007/s10668-022-02722-8 PMID:36320556

Cheng, B., Ioannou, I., & Serafeim, G. (2007). *Corporate social responsibility and access to finance.* (Harvard Business School Working Paper, No. 09-047). https://doi.org/ doi:10.2139/ssrn.1253170

Cheng, S., & Ali, S. (2023). A tiered pathway toward sustainability: The role of public administrators in advancing social equity in US local governments. *Public Administration Review, 83*(4), 878–894. doi:10.1111/puar.13617

Crescini, C. L., & Avila, E. C. (2023). Perceived Effects of Covid-19 Crisis on Budget Consumption of Filipino Families. *Cosmos An International Journal of Management, 12*(2), 105–115.

D'Amato, D., & Korhonen, J. (2021). Integrating the green economy, circular economy and bioeconomy in a strategic sustainability framework. *Ecological Economics*, *188*, 107143. doi:10.1016/j.ecolecon.2021.107143

Dwivedi, D. M. C. (2022). A Study on Advanced Innovation Managing Risk and Rewards. *Cosmos Journal of Engineering & Technology*, *12*(1), 45–47.

Dwivedi, M. C. (2022). Assessing the Socioeconomic Implications of Climate Change. *Cosmos An International Journal of Art & Higher Education*, *11*(2), 20–23.

Ejsmont, K., Gladysz, B., & Kluczek, A. (2020). Impact of industry 4.0 on sustainability-bibliometric literature review. *Sustainability (Basel)*, *12*(14), 5650. doi:10.3390/su12145650

Gupta, T., & Khan, S. (2023). Education and International Collaboration in The Digital Age. *Globus Journal of Progressive Education*, *13*(1), 79–87.

Hariram, N. P., Mekha, K. B., Suganthan, V., & Sudhakar, K. (2023). An Integrated Socio-Economic-Environmental Model to Address Sustainable Development and Sustainability. *Sustainability (Basel)*, *15*(13), 10682. doi:10.3390/su151310682

Harris, J.M. (2000). Basic principles of sustainable development. *Dimensions of Sustainable Development*, 21-41.

Jan, A. A., Lai, F. W., Asif, M., Akhtar, S., & Ullah, S. (2023). Embedding sustainability into bank strategy: Implications for sustainable development goals reporting. *International Journal of Sustainable Development and World Ecology*, *30*(3), 229–243. doi:10.1080/13504509.2022.2134230

Kim, E. J., & Kim, S. H. (2015). Simplification improves understanding of informed consent information in clinical trials regardless of health literacy level. *Clinical Trials*, *12*(3), 232–236. doi:10.1177/1740774515571139 PMID:25701156

Malik, A., & Gharpe, D. P. S. (2022). Rehabilitation Engineering and its Technological Solutions to Problems Confronted by Engineers. Globus An International Journal of Medical Science. *Engineering and Technology*, *11*(2), 24–27.

Mijares, I. I. I. III, & Benjamin, F. (2023). Development and Validation of a Supplementary learning Material in Earth Science. *Cosmos An International Journal of Art & Higher Education*, *12*(1), 56–76. doi:10.46360/cosmos.ahe.520231005

Pinki. (2021). Environmental Sustainability and Economic Growth during Covid-19 Pandemic. *Cosmos An International Journal of Management, 11*(1), 120-124.

Roseland, M. (2000). Sustainable community development: Integrating environmental, economic, and social objectives. *Progress in Planning*, *54*(2), 73–132. doi:10.1016/S0305-9006(00)00003-9

Royal, S., Chaudhary, N., Dalal, R. C., & Kaushik, N. (2023). A Nexus Between Sustainability, Openness, Development, and Urbanisation: Panel Data Evidence from Quad Nations. [Ikonomicheski Izsledvania]. *Economic Studies Journal*, *32*(3), 178–196.

Sangwan, D. S. (2022). Impact of Russia Ukraine war on Indian Economy. Globus An International Journal of Medical Science. *Engineering and Technology*, *11*(1), 36–39.

Sharma, A., & Sharma, R. P. (2023). A Research Study on Eco-Friendly Green Products: Understanding Consumer Perceptions and Preferences. *Globus An International Journal of Management & IT*, *14*(2), 81–83. doi:10.46360/globus.mgt.120231011

Shukla, D. A. (2022). Urgency of Current Times – Peace and Non-Violence. *Globus Journal of Progressive Education*, *12*(1), 61–63.

Smith, J. (2020). Sustainability and resilience in urban studies: A systematic review. *Journal of Urban Planning*, *15*(3), 170–185.

Stokes, E. C., & Seto, K. C. (2019). Characterizing and measuring urban landscapes for sustainability. *Environmental Research Letters*, *14*(4), 045002. doi:10.1088/1748-9326/aafab8

Toman, M. A. (2017). Economics and "sustainability: Balancing trade-offs and imperatives. In *The Economics of Sustainability* (pp. 145–159). Routledge. doi:10.4324/9781315240084-10

Valdez, D., & Nunag, R. (2023). The Research and Creative Work Colloquium and its Effect on Research Performance. *Cosmos Journal of Engineering & Technology*, *13*(1), 57–69. doi:10.46360/cosmos. et.620231006

Zhanbayev, R. A., Irfan, M., Shutaleva, A. V., Maksimov, D. G., Abdykadyrkyzy, R., & Filiz, Ş. (2023). Demoethical model of sustainable development of society: A roadmap towards digital transformation. *Sustainability (Basel)*, *15*(16), 12478. doi:10.3390/su151612478

Chapter 13
Temporal Dynamics of Capital Inflows, Currency Valuation, and Economic Performance in the Indian Economy:
An Econometric Exploration

Amit Kundu

Cooch Behar Panchanan Barma University, India

Barendra Nath Chakraborty

Cooch Behar Panchanan Barma University, India

ABSTRACT

This chapter investigates the association between FDI inflow, exchange rate and GDP in India for the period 1990-2021. How changes in exchange rate affected the openness measures of India such as FDI and vice versa are the matter of study of this chapter. Cointegration among the three (FDI, exchange rate and GDP) is the prime focus of this investigation. Unit root test, Johansen cointegration test, Granger causality, VAR and variance decomposition are adopted to investigate the relation. Key findings include that, variables are not cointegrated. VAR shows that FDI positively affects GDP from 20 periods ahead forecast. It is found that 40% variance in GDP can be explained by exchange rate and on the other hand 5% forecast error variance in exchange rate can be explained by GDP. Further research direction and policy implications are presented at the end.

DOI: 10.4018/979-8-3693-2197-3.ch013

INTRODUCTION

The majority of the world's economies have greatly benefited from foreign capital's contribution to the economic growth. In the early stages of their economic growth, almost all developed economies relied on foreign investment to supplement their limited domestic savings. Also, if a nation's saving rate is lower than its investment rate, it must find a way to fill the saving gap. In the case of a liquidity crisis in emerging economies, short-term capital inflows—which are mostly made by portfolio investors—may have a negative impact on financial stability. Foreign direct investment (FDI) is a more reliable and preferable way of funding the domestic saving shortfall in this situation. As a result, attracting FDI becomes a priority for emerging nations. The developing nations struggle with a shortage of capital, limited technology, material capability, expertise, etc. These complimentary components, which are extremely important for the growth of the undeveloped nations, are brought with foreign funds in equity form. It is presumable that FDI boosts employees' productivity and introduces new technologies. Foreign investments open up chances for technical education and foster an industrial environment that encourages domestic investment and business. In addition to these benefits, FDI boosts the host nation's balance of payments and generates new job possibilities.

The value of one currency (domestic currency) concerning another (foreign currency) is referred to as the exchange rate. The dynamics of exchange rate level and its volatility is one of the key factors affecting FDI. Investors' hopeful projections for the host country's economy decline as exchange rate volatility rises. A stable exchange rate is sometimes regarded as an indicator of economic strength. It may turn into a sign of national dignity. Investors and entrepreneurs will acknowledge a resilient exchange rate as a sign of prosperous economic environment. In the long run, nations with low inflation frequently experience a high (appreciating) exchange rate, which enhances their competitiveness and boosts their economic performance. In the post-war era, for instance, exchange rates in Japan and Germany steadily increased due to their strong economic success. FDI is a significant source of capital for India's economic growth. Early in the 1990s, when the trade deficit grew as a result of rising oil costs, this exchange rate regime came under an intense amount of pressure. The RBI partially defended the currency by using up its overseas reserves and reducing its depreciation. However, the reserves started getting low in the middle of 1991, which forced the Reserve Bank of India (RBI) to lower the exchange rate of the Indian Rupee by 18–19% in two phases on July 1 and July 3, 1991. Just after the crisis of 1991, India began its liberal economic reforms, and FDI has also steadily expanded ever since. If we analyze the movements of the Rupee-Dollar (INR-USD) exchange rate in the post-liberalization era, we find that it rose from Rs. 31.49 (maximum) in 1993–1994 to Rs. 49.06 in 2003–2004, and then further to Rs. 57.23 in 2012–13. The price of oil and petroleum goods increased, which was the primary reason for these swings (RBI). The rupee's value and foreign exchange reserves have decreased as a result of the 2007–2008 Global Financial Crisis. When the global financial crisis of 2008 hit, the rupee started to fall against the dollar and ranging between Rs. 44 and Rs. 53 per USD. During 2007 and 2008, it was hanging around Rs. 39 to Rs. 40 per USD. Global FDI flows approximately quadrupled between 2003 and 2007. Next a record of US$ 2.1 trillion in 2007, the amount of FDI in the world significantly decreased during the following two years of the global financial crisis. Though the rapid increase in FDI flows in India almost over the past twenty years appears to have been fueled by a liberal policy approach and sound macroeconomic fundamentals, which kept them going even during the global economic crisis of 2008–09 and 2009–10, even while the economy recovered from the financial crisis more quickly, the following reduction in investment flows seems rather enigmatic. Since early May 2013, the value of the rupee has significantly declined, as seen by a record-low rate of Rs. 60 per dollar. Since the early 2013 to 2022 Indian currency have depreciated near about 54.7%. The Indian rupee experienced a significant diminution from the first quarter of 2018 and dropped to an unprecedented low exchange rate of 81.25 per dollar during the post-covid era in September 2022. FDI inflows to India reached $45.15 billion in 2014–15 and have been steadily rising since after. Additionally, overall FDI inflow climbed by 65.3%, from $266.21 billion in 2007–14 to $440.01 billion in 2014–21, whereas FDI equity inflow rose by 68.6%, from $185.03 billion in 2007–14 to $312.05 billion in 2014–21. (2014-21). The very first four months of FY 2021–22 saw an overall FDI inflow of $27.37 billion into India, a 62% increase over the same time in FY 2020–21 ($16.92 billion). With an increase of $84,835 million over the previous year's FDI inflows, India got the largest annual FDI inflows in FY 21-22. Additionally, the FDI equity inflow was $ 59,825 million in FY 2021–22. From 2000-01 to 2021-22, India's FDI inflows have surged 20 times. Between April 2000 and March 2022, India received a total of $847.40 billion in foreign direct investment. India received a total of $22.03 billion in FDI between January and March 2022. In the insurance industry, the government raised the ceiling on foreign investment from 26% to 49%. In September 2014, govt. also unveiled the Make in India program, which further eased FDI restrictions in 25 sectors. Since the "Make in India" initiative's start in April 2015, FDI inflow towards India has surged by 48%. The government boosted FDI from 49% to 74% in May 2020 in defense production using the automated procedure. For years, the Indian government has been liberalizing its FDI regulations in an effort to foster an environment that is favorable to investors. The Indian economy is currently becoming globalized. Multinational corporations in India have been inspired to enter the international market through programs like Make-in-India. Additionally, the convergence of the world's financial markets creates the conditions for this tremendous rise in FDI.

In this study we aim to address research gaps in the literature by conducting an extensive analysis of the interrelationship between FDI inflows, exchange rates, and GDP in the Indian economy. This research paper attempts to bridge the gap by focusing on the unique context of India, exploring the combined impacts of FDI inflows and exchange rates on GDP as well as the multi-directional interconnectedness of these economic variables, and utilizing time series analysis techniques like unit root tests, Johansen cointegration tests, Granger causality, VAR, and Variance Decomposition. The study also addresses the policy ramifications of the FDI, exchange rate, and GDP relationship in India, offering valuable insights for researchers and policymakers to enhance economic growth and attract foreign investment.

REVIEW OF LITERATURE

The correlation between foreign direct investment and economic growth has attracted a significant amount of scientific interest. Through a "contagion" effect induced by the adoption of more sophisticated technology, management techniques, etc. by foreign enterprises, FDI accelerates the rate of technological improvement in the host country (Findlay, 1978). According to (Caves, 1996), the motivation for further attempts to attract more FDI comes from the conviction that FDI has a number of advantageous impacts. Productivity improvements, technological transfers, the adoption of new processes, management knowledge and expertise in the host country's market, capacity building, global production networks, and market access are a few of these. Numerous studies have found empirically that FDI promotes economic growth (Borensztein et al., 1998; Glass and Saggi, 1999). (While De Mello, 1997) demonstrates a positive relationship for a number of Latin American nations, (Dees, 1998) argues that FDI has been crucial in describing China's economic growth. Foreign capital inflows are thought to increase investment levels.

As per (Olofsdotter, 1998), nations with greater levels of institutional strength are more likely to benefit from FDI. Therefore, he underlined how crucial administrative effectiveness is for facilitating FDI benefits. As a whole, the regime may have an impact on the nation's economic growth through the channels of investment, trade, and productivity (Petreski, 2009). In 2023, a study was conducted to investigate the relationship between foreign direct investment (FDI), economic growth, and trade openness in BRICS countries. The study utilized the Bayesian VAR framework and found a significant short-term correlation between FDI and economic growth, but no long-term relationship in BRICS economies (Malik & Sah, 2023). Another study on the interrelationship among foreign aid, foreign direct investment (FDI) and economic growth in South-East Asia (SEA) and South Asia (SA) during 1980-2016, findings of the study suggests that while foreign aid is negatively associated with FDI as well as growth, FDI positively influences growth (Dash et al., 2023). Research on developing economies has shown a positive correlation between the movement of the exchange rate and economic growth, i.e., that undervaluation (high exchange rates) of the exchange rates accelerates economic growth (Rodrik, 2008). The majority of FDI inflows to developed nations are horizontal investments motivated by market-seeking approaches, and they have a tendency to raise the labor intensity of domestic production in the home country (Mariotti et el., 2003).

In the 1970s and 1980s, theories on FDI and exchange rate links first emerged (Kohlhagen, 1977; Cushman, 1985). The United States of America has seen significant changes in the flow of foreign direct investment (FDI) during the 1980s and 1990s. A significant number of theoretical and empirical research, such as that by (Froot & Stein, 1991), (Blonigen, 1997), (Klein & Rosengren, 1994), (Guo & Trivedi, 2002), and (Kiyota & Urata, 2004), attempts to explain those changes largely in terms of the effect of the real exchange rate on FDI (2004). A host country's currency depreciation decreases its manufacturing costs, which is referred to as a relative wage channel. The host country's currency depreciation minimizes the comparative cost of capital, promoting foreign direct investment. Foreign investors can use their current wealth to obtain more capital after depreciation. (Harris & Ravenscraft, 1991); (Froot & Stein, 1991); (Barrel & Pain, 1996); (Swenson, 1994). Furthermore, the appreciation of the home country's currency increases the actual wealth of multinational enterprises, which is known as the relative wealth channel. The more money the company accumulates in the host nation; the more opportunities it has to make more investments. According to (Klein & Rosengren, 1992), the wealth channel was a crucial component in explaining the massive FDI inflows to the USA between 1979 and 1991. Additionally, a surge in volatility increases the risk related to the investment's anticipated returns on the investment (Cushman, 1985). The wealth of foreign investors is supposed to rise when foreign currencies appreciate. A study has investigated the relationship between the real effective exchange rate and foreign direct investment (FDI) in Vietnam from 2005 to 2019. The findings of the study show that, there is a positive causal relationship exists between FDI and Vietnam's real effective exchange rate, economic growth affects real exchange rate but has no significant impact on FDI (Huong et al., 2020). The determinants of FDI inflows in India, factors such as the source country's per capita GDP, FDI openness, gross fixed capital formation, and exports play crucial roles in influencing FDI inflows. This study identifies the negative impact of the source country's per capita GDP and the positive influence of FDI openness, capital formation, and exports on India's FDI (Kaur et al., 2024). According to (Baek & Okawa, 2001), Japanese FDI in Asia is encouraged by a higher yen relative to the dollar and other Asian currencies. A contemporary research has been conducted to analyze the dynamic interactions among foreign direct investment (FDI), economic growth, and real exchange rate in Ghana. The study finds no long-term relationship among the variables but identifies a positive causal impact from both FDI and real exchange rate to economic growth, and a positive response of FDI to shocks in real exchange rate (Arthur & Addai, 2022). According to (Yapraklý, 2006), the exchange rate parameter, which is regarded as a measure of competitiveness in prior research, has an impact on FDI from both an income and cost aspect. The ability to increase domestic input in terms of production, exports, and profits are provided to the investor whose production is export-oriented by depreciation. This is known as the "income effect," and it occurs when a currency's depreciation in the forex markets has a favorable impact on FDI. However, an investor focused on exports may experience a decline in exports and profits if they heavily rely on imported materials and employ them in their manufacturing. This is referred to as the cost effect, and under such circumstances, FDI is adversely impacted by a depreciation of the home currency in the forex markets. Depending on the extent of the income and cost effects, the net impact of foreign currency rates on FDI varies. An increase in the exchange rate has a positive impact on FDI under certain situations, for instance when the income effect is stronger than the cost effect, and a negative impact under the opposite circumstance.

OBJECTIVE OF THE STUDY

(i) To study the relationship between FDI inflows and GDP with respect to exchange rate.
(ii) To study the causal relation between FDI inflows, exchange rate and GDP.

RESEARCH METHODOLOGY

For the empirical investigation three variables are used i.e., GDP, FDI and Exchange Rate over the period of 1990 to 2021. All these data are collected from the World Bank database i.e., World Development Indicator.

The stationery of the data sets is verified by using unit root test, ADF test. Table-4 represents unit root tests. Data sets are stationary 1(1). In the next section we use Johansen cointegration test. We will set up the VAR model for examining the causal relation between the variables concerned. VAR residual portmanteau test for autocorrelation, VAR residual serial correlation LM test, stability of the VAR model will be applied for the better consideration of the VAR model.

Table 1. Descriptive statistics

	LOGGDP	LOGFDI	LOGEXCHANGERATE
Mean	12.06917	9.938478	1.668264
Median	12.07000	10.13354	1.660000
Std. Dev.	0.237113	0.702823	0.124175
Skewness	0.001304	-0.758388	-0.291269
Kurtosis	1.723963	2.787967	2.622517
Jarque-Bera	8.209234	11.43464	2.429292
Probability	0.016496	0.003289	0.296815

Source: Autors' estimation

RESULTS AND DISCUSSION

From Table 1 we can see that, mean and median of the data are approximately equal which means data is symmetric. Skewness of the data is very low identifying transformed data r symmetric. Data should be good and unbiased. Here kurtosis for log GDP, log FDI and log exchange rate are 1.72, 2.78 and 2.62 respectively. Excess kurtosis for log GDP, log FDI and log exchange rate are (1.78-3)=1.22, (2.78-3)=0.22, (2.62-3)=0.32. Here distributions are platykurtic. In the data low frequency of outliers has been found. Jarque-Beras statistics indicate log GDP and log FDI series are not normally distributed but log exchange rate is normally distributed.

Table 2. Outcome of ADF tests

Variable	ADF t Stat	P-values	Lag	Mackinon 1%	Critical 5%	Value 10%
LOGGDP	-1.455	0.839	0	-4.036	-3.447	-3.148
D(LOGGDP)	-11.682	0.000	0	-4.036	-3.448	-3.149
LOGFDI	-2.319	0.419	1	-4.039	-3.449	-3.149
D(LOGFDI)	-5.211	0.0002	0	-4.039	-3.449	-3.149
LOGEXCHANGERATE	-2.566	0.296	4	-4.039	-3.449	-3.149
D(LOGEXCHANGERATE)	-4.241	0.005	3	-4.039	-3.449	-3.149

Source: Autors' estimation

Results of the augmented Dicky-Fuller tests for the presence of unit roots in the series for log GDP, log FDI and log Exchange Rate are being presented in Table 2 and it is observed from the table 4 that all the variables at 1st difference are free from unit roots. Consequently, the series are stationery at 1st difference i.e., I (1).

Table 3. Johansen cointegration test

Trend assumption: Linear deterministic trend (restricted)				
Series: LOGGDP LOGFDI LOGEXCHANGERATE				
Lags interval (in first differences): 1 to 4				
Unrestricted Cointegration Rank Test (Trace)				
Hypothesized		**Trace**	**0.05**	
No. of CE(s)	**Eigenvalue**	**Statistic**	**Critical Value**	**Prob.****
None*	0.206825	40.35453	42.91525	0.0882
At most 1	0.081987	14.40279	25.87211	0.6243
At most 2	0.042139	4.821910	12.51798	0.6221
Trace test indicates no cointegration at the 0.05 level				
* denotes rejection of the hypothesis at the 0.05 level				
**MacKinnon-Haug-Michelis (1999) p-values				
Unrestricted Cointegration Rank Test (Maximum Eigenvalue)				
Hypothesized		**Max-Eigen**	**0.05**	
No. of CE(s)	**Eigenvalue**	**Statistic**	**Critical Value**	**Prob.****
None*	0.206825	25.95174	25.82321	0.0481
At most 1	0.081987	9.580885	19.38704	0.6636
At most 2	0.042139	4.821910	12.51798	0.6221

Max-eigenvalue test indicates no cointegration at the 0.05 level
* denotes rejection of the hypothesis at the 0.05 level
**MacKinnon-Haug-Michelis (1999) p-values
Source: Autors' estimation

It is observed from the Table 3, that

(i)   Trace statistic is less than the critical value.
(ii)   Max-Eigen statistic is also less than critical value.

So, we do not be able to reject H_0 which shows there is no cointegration.

Therefore, trace test as well as Max-Eigen statistic denote rejection of the hypothesis at the 0.05 level showing there is no cointegrating relation among the three variables.

Table 4. Lag selection criterion

VAR Lag Order Selection Criteria						
Endogenous variables: DLOGGDP DLOGFDI DLOGEXCHANGERATE						
Exogenous variables: C						
Sample: 1991Q1 2021Q4						
Included observations: 108						
Lag	LogL	LR	FPE	AIC	SC	HQ
0	1011.913	NA	1.54e-12	-18.68357	-18.60907	-18.65336
1	1130.562	228.5094	2.03e-13*	-20.71411*	-20.41610*	-20.59328*
2	1135.242	8.753277	2.20e-13	-20.63411	-20.11258	-20.42265
3	1143.015	14.10752	2.25e-13	-20.61140	-19.86636	-20.30931
4	1151.139	14.29191	2.29e-13	-20.59517	-19.62662	-20.20246
5	1162.748	19.77747*	2.19e-13	-20.64348	-19.45142	-20.16014
6	1166.088	5.505886	2.44e-13	-20.53867	-19.12311	-19.96471
7	1174.471	13.34946	2.48e-13	-20.52723	-18.88815	-19.86265
8	1181.282	10.46934	2.61e-13	-20.48670	-18.62411	-19.73149
* indicates lag order selected by the criterion						
LR: sequential modified LR test statistic (each test at 5% level)						
FPE: Final prediction error						
AIC: Akaike information criterion						
SC: Schwarz information criterion						
HQ: Hannan-Quinn information criterion						

Source: Autors' estimation

It is observed from Table 4, that

(i)   LR statistics for lag 0 is significant at 5% level.
(ii)   SIC statistics for lag 0 is significant at 5% level.
(iii)   FPE and AIC statistics for lag 1 are significant for VAR specification, we therefore, have followed Enders' method and started with 5 lags. We have then reduced the lags by one and carried out the test, given that the estimated t-stat for the coefficient involved is insignificant. In 2 lag specification of few parameters have been found statistically significant.

VAR is a multi-equation linear model.

VAR model is very important tool in forecasting. VAR explain each variable by its own lagged values and the present and the past values of other variables. Dynamics in multiple time series can be captured by this model. In practice VAR is in reduced form.

Table 5. Outcomes of vector autoregression estimates

Dependent Variable	Independent Variable	Coefficients	Standard errors	't'Stat.
DLOGGDP	Constant	0.0014	(0.0007)	[2.1226]
	DLOGGDP(-1)	0.7675	(0.0690)	[11.114]
	DLOGFDI(-1)	0.0003	(0.0074)	[11.114]
	DLOGEXCHANGERATE(-1)	0.0193	(0.0485)	[0.3979]
R^2= 0.529 F-stat = 41.649 Log likelihood = 485.820 AIC = -8.379				
DLOGFDI				
	Constant	0.0022	(0.0047)	[0.4613]
	DLOGGDP(-1)	0.5073	(0.4746)	[1.0688]
	DLOGFDI(-1)	0.7386	(0.0514)	[14.367]
	DLOGEXCHANGERATE(-1)	-0.2770	(0.3334)	[-0.8309]
R^2 = 0.650 F-stat = 68.867 Log likelihood = 264.137 AIC = -4.524				
DLOGEXCHANGERATE	Constant	0.0018	(0.0010)	[1.8395]
	DLOGGDP(-1)	-0.0996	(0.0989)	[-1.0067]
	DLOGFDI(-1)	0.0107	(0.0107)	[1.0064]
	DLOGEXCHANGERATE(-1)	0.6664	(0.0695)	[9.5879]

R^2 = 0.469 F-stat = 32.757 Log likelihood = 444.468 AIC = -7.660
Source: Autors' estimation

Based on the data presented in Table 5, high t-statistics in absolute values in equation (1) shows that lagged FDI has significant positive impact on current GDP and exchange rate. Regression equations explaining FDI and exchange rate have quite good overall fits but then our lagged values are significant. Exchange rate has insignificant effects in the FDI and GDP.

Table 6. Granger causality test

Pairwise Granger Causality Tests			
Lags: 2			
Null Hypothesis:	Obs	F-Statistic	Prob.
DLOGFDI does not Granger Cause DLOGGDP	114	0.75716	0.4714
DLOGGDP does not Granger Cause DLOGFDI		0.83511	0.4366
DLOGEXCHANGERATE does not Granger Cause DLOGGDP	114	0.60028	0.5505
DLOGGDP does not Granger Cause DLOGEXCHANGERATE		0.64536	0.5265
DLOGEXCHANGERATE does not Granger Cause DLOGFDI	114	0.49518	0.6108
DLOGFDI does not Granger Cause DLOGEXCHANGERATE		0.65699	0.5205

Source: Autors' estimation

Examining the results from Table 6, it is apparent that, when exchange rate is the dependent variable, the null hypothesis that FDI is not its Granger cause cannot be rejected (P = 0.61).

GDP is not the Granger cause of exchange rate can also not be rejected (P = 0.52).

The outcomes depict that GDP and FDI are not Granger cause of each other and exchange rate is not the Granger cause of both GDP and FDI.

The percentile decomposition of variance of GDP representing contributions of shocks, transmitted through the channels of three endogenous variables are given in Table 7.

Table 7. Variance decomposition of DLOGGDP

Period	S.E.	DLOGGDP	DLOGFDI	DLOGEXCHANGERATE
1	0.003604	100.0000	0.000000	0.000000
2	0.004539	99.95207	1.04E-05	0.047921
3	0.005005	99.87980	0.000238	0.119962
4	0.005257	99.80664	0.000944	0.192419
5	0.005398	99.74360	0.002189	0.254208
6	0.005478	99.69416	0.003849	0.301991
7	0.005523	99.65777	0.005708	0.336519
8	0.005549	99.63221	0.007557	0.360233
9	0.005564	99.61487	0.009242	0.375885
10	0.005572	99.60343	0.010676	0.385891
11	0.005577	99.59604	0.011834	0.392123
12	0.005580	99.59135	0.012729	0.395923
13	0.005582	99.58840	0.013397	0.398198
14	0.005583	99.58658	0.013881	0.399541
15	0.005583	99.58545	0.014222	0.400324
16	0.005584	99.58477	0.014459	0.400776
17	0.005584	99.58435	0.014619	0.401034
18	0.005584	99.58409	0.014726	0.401181
19	0.005584	99.58394	0.014796	0.401264
20	0.005584	99.58385	0.014842	0.401311

Source: Autors' estimation

The percentile decomposition of variance of FDI representing contributions of shocks, transmitted through the channels of three endogenous variables are given in Table 8.

Table 8. Variance decomposition of DLOGFDI

Period	S.E.	DLOGGDP	DLOGFDI	DLOGEXCHANGERATE
1	0.024771	8.573448	91.42655	0.000000
2	0.030604	6.888505	92.89435	0.217147
3	0.033312	5.900214	93.57262	0.527171
4	0.034708	5.459831	93.72342	0.816749
5	0.035474	5.385202	93.57376	1.041040
6	0.035914	5.514515	93.29013	1.195351
7	0.036176	5.729987	92.97746	1.292558
8	0.036338	5.958938	92.69158	1.349485
9	0.036440	6.163946	92.45537	1.380679
10	0.036505	6.330760	92.27258	1.396661
11	0.036546	6.458212	92.13755	1.404238
12	0.036573	6.551277	92.04125	1.407473
13	0.036591	6.616932	91.97445	1.408622
14	0.036602	6.662010	91.92913	1.408865
15	0.036609	6.692284	91.89894	1.408771
16	0.036614	6.712251	91.87916	1.408593
17	0.036617	6.725220	91.86635	1.408429
18	0.036618	6.733537	91.85816	1.408304
19	0.036620	6.738812	91.85297	1.408220
20	0.036620	6.742127	91.84971	1.408166

Source: Autors' estimation

The percentile decomposition of variance of exchange rate representing contributions of shocks, transmitted through the channels of three endogenous variables are given in Table 9.

Table 9. Variance decomposition of DLOGEXCHANGERATE

Period	S.E.	DLOGGDP	DLOGFDI	DLOGEXCHANGERATE
1	0.005163	0.295726	0.348702	99.35557
2	0.006230	1.207302	0.246527	98.54617
3	0.006671	2.244011	0.328042	97.42795
4	0.006874	3.166576	0.485296	96.34813
5	0.006973	3.877559	0.649051	95.47339
6	0.007023	4.373988	0.786454	94.83956
7	0.007049	4.696121	0.888673	94.41521
8	0.007062	4.893490	0.958904	94.14761
9	0.007070	5.008853	1.004460	93.98669
10	0.007073	5.073616	1.032738	93.89365
11	0.007075	5.108688	1.049684	93.84163
12	0.007077	5.127056	1.059550	93.81339
13	0.007077	5.136368	1.065156	93.79848
14	0.007077	5.140937	1.068275	93.79079
15	0.007078	5.143103	1.069979	93.78692
16	0.007078	5.144090	1.070895	93.78502
17	0.007078	5.144520	1.071380	93.78410
18	0.007078	5.144697	1.071633	93.78367
19	0.007078	5.144765	1.071764	93.78347
20	0.007078	5.144787	1.071831	93.78338

Source: Autors' estimation

Based on the overview provided in Table 7, Table 8, and Table 9, we can discern, 40% of the forecast error variance in GDP is explained by the exchange rate. From the variance decomposition of FDI it is found that 6.73% variation in FDI is responsible for GDP and more than 91% variation in FDI is responsible for its own shocks.

5.14% variation in exchange rate (forecast error variance) is due to GDP whereas 93.73% variation in the forecast error variance of exchange rate is because of its own shocks.

CONCLUSION

The majority of the world's economies have greatly benefited from foreign capital's contribution to the economic growth. In the early stages of their economic growth, almost all developed economies relied on foreign investment to supplement their limited domestic savings. The Indian government has been liberalizing its FDI regulations in an effort to foster an environment that is favorable to investors. The Indian economy is currently becoming globalized. Multinational corporations in India have been inspired to enter the international market through programs like Make-in-India. Under these circumstances we have tried to find out the causal relationship between FDI inflows, exchange rate and GDP. For the empirical investigation three variables have been used i.e., GDP, FDI and Exchange Rate over the period of 1990 to 2021. The stationarity of the data sets has been verified by using unit root test, ADF test and it is found that the data sets are stationary 1(1). Max-Eigen statistic denoted rejection of the hypothesis at the 0.05 level showing there is no cointegrating relation among the three variables. From the VAR analysis we found that lagged FDI has significant positive impact on current GDP and exchange rate. Exchange rate has insignificant effects in the FDI and GDP. From the variance decomposition analysis, we have found that 40% of the forecast error variance in GDP is explained by the exchange rate. From the variance decomposition of FDI it is also found that 6.73% variation in FDI is responsible for GDP and more than 91% variation in FDI is responsible for its own shocks. 5.14% variation in exchange rate (forecast error variance) is due to GDP whereas 93.73% variation in the forecast error variance of exchange rate is because of its own shocks. Therefore, the prime focus of this article is to find out the relationship among the variables concerned. If the association among exchange rate, FDI and GDP is well managed, policy makers and investors can help decrease exchange rate oscillations to make the economic outlook more steady or predictable to get more paybacks.

REFERENCES

Arthur, B., & Addai, B. (2022). The dynamic interactions of economic growth, foreign direct investment, and exchange rates in Ghana. *Cogent Economics & Finance*, *10*(1), 2148361. doi:10.1080/2332 2039.2022.2148361

Baek, I. M., & Okawa, T. (2001). Foreign exchange rates and Japanese foreign direct investment in Asia. *Journal of Economics and Business*, *53*(1), 69–84. doi:10.1016/S0148-6195(00)00038-2

Barrell, R., & Pain, N. (1996). An Econometric Analysis of U.S. Foreign Direct Investment. *The Review of Economics and Statistics*, *78*(2), 200. doi:10.2307/2109921

Blonigen, B. A. (1997). Firm-Specific Assets and the Link between Exchange Rates and Foreign Direct Investment. *The American Economic Review*, *87*(3), 447–465.

Borensztein, E., De Gregorio, J., & Lee, J.-W. (1998). How does foreign direct investment affect economic growth? *Journal of International Economics*, *45*(1), 115–135. doi:10.1016/S0022-1996(97)00033-0

Caves, R. E. (1996). *Multinational Enterprise and Economic Analysis* (2nd ed.). Cambridge University Press.

Cushman, D. (1985). Real Exchange Rate Risk, Expectations, and the Level of Direct Investment. *The Review of Economics and Statistics*, *67*(2), 297–308. doi:10.2307/1924729

Dash, D. P., Sethi, N., & Barik, P. C. (2023). Dynamics of Foreign Aid and Human Development in South and South-East Asia: Analyzing the Effectiveness of Macro-Institutional Factors. *International Economic Journal*, *37*(4), 646–674. doi:10.1080/10168737.2023.2261011

De Mello, L. R. Jr. (1997). Foreign Direct Investment in Developing Countries and Growth: A Selective Survey. *The Journal of Development Studies*, *34*(1), 1–34. doi:10.1080/00220389708422501

Dees, S. (1998). Foreign direct investment in China: Determinants and effects. *Economics of Planning*, *31*(2/3), 175–194. doi:10.1023/A:1003576930461

Findlay, R. (1978). Relative Backwardness, Direct Foreign Investment, and the Transfer of Technology: A Simple Dynamic Model. *The Quarterly Journal of Economics*, *92*(1), 1–16. doi:10.2307/1885996

Froot, K. A., & Stein, J. C. (1991). Exchange Rates and Foreign Direct Investment: An Imperfect Capital Markets Approach. *The Quarterly Journal of Economics*, *106*(4), 1191–1217. doi:10.2307/2937961

Glass, A. J., & Saggi, K. (1999). Foreign Direct Investment and the Nature of R&D. *The Canadian Journal of Economics. Revue Canadienne d'Economique*, *32*(1), 92. doi:10.2307/136397

Guo, J. Q., & Trivedi, P. K. (2002). Firm-Specific Assets and the Link between Exchange Rates and Japanese Foreign Direct Investment in the United States: A Re-examination. *The Japanese Economic Review*, *53*(3), 337–349. doi:10.1111/1468-5876.00232

Harris, R. S., & Ravenscraft, D. (1991). The Role of Acquisitions in Foreign Direct Investment: Evidence from the U.S. Stock Market. *The Journal of Finance*, *46*(3), 825–844. doi:10.1111/j.1540-6261.1991.tb03767.x

Huong, T. T. X., Nguyen, M. L. T., & Lien, N. T. K. (2020). An empirical study of the real effective exchange rate and foreign direct investment in Vietnam. *Investment Management & Financial Innovations*, *17*(4), 1–13. doi:10.21511/imfi.17(4).2020.01

Kaur, S., Kumar, P., & Ansari, M. A. (2024). An analysis of Indian FDI inflows through an augmented gravity model: Exploring new insights. *International Economics and Economic Policy*, •••, 1–21. doi:10.1007/s10368-024-00594-z

Kiyota, K., & Urata, S. (2004). Exchange Rate, Exchange Rate Volatility and Foreign Direct Investment. *World Economy*, *27*(10), 1501–1536. doi:10.1111/j.1467-9701.2004.00664.x

Klein, M. W., & Rosengren, E. (1994). The real exchange rate and foreign direct investment in the United States: Relative wealth vs. relative wage effects. *Journal of International Economics*, *36*(3-4), 373–389. doi:10.1016/0022-1996(94)90009-4

Kohlhagen, S. W. (1977). Exchange Rate Changes, profitability, and Direct Foreign Investment. *Southern Economic Journal*, *44*(1), 43–52. doi:10.2307/1057298

Malik, A., & Sah, A. N. (2023). Does FDI Impact the Economic Growth of BRICS Economies? Evidence from Bayesian VAR. *Journal of Risk and Financial Management*, *17*(1), 10. doi:10.3390/jrfm17010010

Mariotti, S. (2003). Home country employment and foreign direct investment: Evidence from the Italian case. *Cambridge Journal of Economics*, *27*(3), 419–431. doi:10.1093/cje/27.3.419

Olofsdotter, K. (1998). Foreign direct investment, country capabilities and economic growth. *Weltwirtschaftliches Archiv*, *134*(3), 534–547. doi:10.1007/BF02707929

Petreski, M. (2009). Analysis of exchange-rate regime effect on growth: Theoretical channels and empirical evidence with panel data. *Economics Discussion Paper,* (2009-49). doi:10.2139/ssrn.1726752

Rodrik, D. (2008). The Real Exchange Rate and Economic Growth. *Brookings Papers on Economic Activity*, *2008*(2), 365–412. doi:10.1353/eca.0.0020

Swenson, D. L. (1994). The impact of U.S. tax reform on foreign direct investment in the United States. *Journal of Public Economics*, *54*(2), 243–266. doi:10.1016/0047-2727(94)90062-0

Yapraklý, S. (2006). An Econometric Analysis on the Economic Determinants of Foreign Direct Investments in Turkey. *Dergisi*, *21*(2), 23–48.

APPENDIX

Figure 1. Time plot of log GDP
Source: Author's' estimation

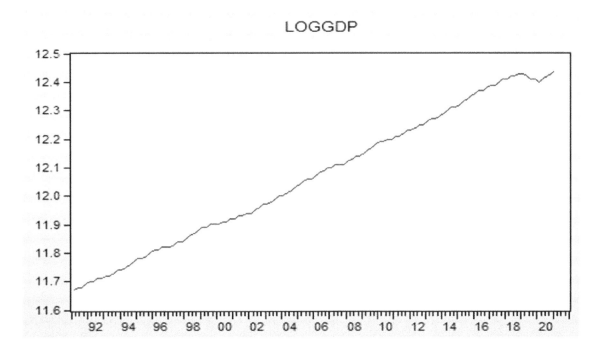

Figure 2. Time plot of log FDI
Source: Author's' estimation

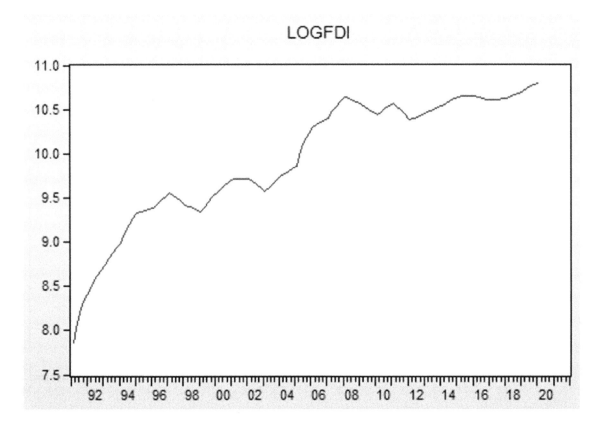

Figure 3. Time plot of log exchange rate
Source: Author's' estimation

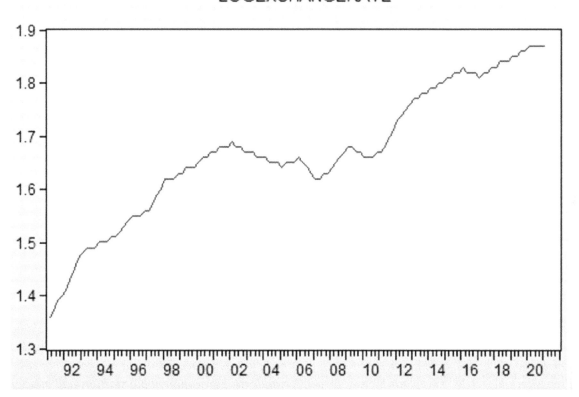

Chapter 14

Willingness Among Students for Startups:
A Ground–Level Analysis on Higher Education Institutes of West Bengal

Nilendu Chatterjee

https://orcid.org/0000-0002-8570-0262

Department of Economics, Bankim Sardar College, India

ABSTRACT

Of late, the concept of startups has become immensely popular among the people entering the labour market. India, being an emerging economy, is not behind - one can say doing exceedingly well with 3rd rank at the global stage. The concept of startup gained currency since 2016 and became a hot cake of discussion since 2018. This study focuses on getting students' perception about startups and analyzing the factors responsible behind their willingness or non-willingness to start a business of their own. The present study is based on the views of 580 students across eight higher educational institutes. Out of these 580 students, 320 are from UG courses and 260 students are from PG courses—all 580 students pursue either formal or non-formal courses which further signifies the relevance of the study. The application of logit model and the high R-square value of the study suggest that the study has immense significance as it gives the ground level view of the next generation.

INTRODUCTION

One can define start-ups as the new businesses operating in the early stages with potential as well as opportunity to grow and financed by a single individual or a group of few individuals or even as a family business with investment from family members. It is nurture and establishment of a business idea that flourishes and takes the form of commercial venture. Hence, these business ventures are very highly scalable where investors or owners foresee new market demand for their service or product, they can also find new market opportunities for existing services or products by means of new business strategies and

DOI: 10.4018/979-8-3693-2197-3.ch014

innovations and thus cut through the existing market and create their own market share or they can even a full new market size for their products or services. In many cases, start-ups use technology in order to capture share in the existing market by differentiating their services or products from the existing ones. Whatever may be the form, start-ups are impactful new avenues for growth of entrepreneurial capability and development of new businesses with employable opportunities for youths (Babu and Sridevi, 2018). Beginning from a mere 29000 startups in 2014, India has 1,12,718 recognized startups in the end of October 2023 and these are spread over 763 districts (Invest India, 2023, Inc 42, 2023). These startups have earned India the second rank as far as innovation in quality is concerned.

India has emerged as one of the pioneer start-up nations in the whole world. Having entered much late compared to the rest of the world or even its developing counterparts, India has been growing exponentially in this field and presently has become the hotspot of start-ups with fouth rank in 2023 and second rank in 2022 (Maradi, 2023). Not only the start-ups have been growing exponentially, at present, three Indian cities have earned places among the top 40 start-up hotspots in the world, namely, Bengaluru, Mumbai and Delhi. Global Start-up Ecosystem Ranking 2023 shows that Bengaluru and Delhi have moved up two places compared to 2022 rankings and presently ranked at 20 and 24, respectively. Mumbai has moved up five places and ranked at 31 in 2023. Such achievements itself are confirmation about the fact that India has been doing well in this field and lots of new ideas, people are coming up with enormous opportunities and business ideas. The number of start-ups in the unicorn club has been rising every year with presently 111 are in the list whose cumulated valuation is around 350 billion US Dollars (Global Start-up Eco system Report, 2023). Unicorn is a startup which is owned privately having a valuation of over 1 billion US Dollars. In the world, we have only 56 companies are enlisted in the Decacorn club out of which 5 are from India. A Decacorn is a startup having valuation of over 10 billion US Dollars. Indian Decacorn companies are Flipkart, BYJU's, Nykaa, Swiggy and Phone Pe (Investment India, 2023). These staggering values speak for themselves because India started emphasizing on this field only in 2016 by means of Government of India's one of the flagship initiatives "Start-up India." This scheme has not only been spread across like fire by means of promotional technology, it has also caught everyone's eyes and won hearts because of its horizon opening abilities and at present the concept of start-up is immensely popular among students and youths for its facilities and opportunities (Gudwani and kaur, 2023). By 'students' we mean who are in the higher education system where the concept of start-up is being mainly highlighted and promoted among the students. The investors from across the globe has been investing in Indian start-ups and such numbers of investors and values of such investment have only been rising over the years - which speak for the growing confidence among the businessmen in the Indian start-ups (Rajani, 2023). Very recent years, India has witnessed significant changes in its growth of start-up journey – it has experienced a change from setting up start-ups to getting investments from foreign investors to changes in its policies as well as infrastructural setting – hence the growth journey has been rapidly changing while being connected with the need of the hour (Babu and Sridevi, 2018). If we look at the world, we can see that USA has been dominating the world stage followed by United Kingdom with holding the top two spots (Global Start-up Ecosystem Ranking, 2023) but the overall phenomenon suggests that around 70% of the start-ups started as home-grown business and over 60% have been using artificial intelligence for the growth of their businesses and around 8% have been performing in the field of fintech (Maradi, 2023). The Indian economy is not only emerging with increasing dominance on the world economy, it has also been emphasizing on several schemes which hovers around entrepreneurial capability development, employment generation, skill development while keeping the basic points of liberalization and inclusive development in focus – flagship programmes like Make in India, Start-up India, MUDRA, etc. are all directed towards achieving such objectives (Pooja, 2017). The rise of entrepreneurs with innovative business ideas and strategies in the recent years has seen an upsurge which has generated hopes and opportunities in front of millions of youths that can take the nation further ahead in near future which could have positive multiplier effects on rest of the sectors of the economy, especially on employment (Institute for Business Value Business Line Bureau, 2018). As a result, in 2023, Indian startups have been serving 56 diverse sectors with 13% focusing on technology, 9% on healthcare and life science related services, 7% in education, 5% each in agriculture, food and beverages, respectively (Invest India, 2023). The mind-boggling jumps of 15 times in the amount of investment, 9 times in the number of investors and 7 times in the number of incubations are self-explaining about the astonishing growth of startups in India (Invest India, 2023). Funding or investment in Indian startups have grown over 8 times in the last 10 years and the figures remained significantly strong even during the Covid - 19 period that tells about the resilience of the Indian labour market and business innovations even during toughest of periods (Inc 42, 2023).

In India, there are certain procedures for a business to be considered as a 'startup'. In the first stage, it has to be either a 'Private Limited Company' or a 'Limited Liability Partnership' or even a simple 'Partnership' firm. In the second stage, the age of the firm should be less than 5 years. In the third stage, the annual turnover of the firm has to be below Rs. 25 Crores. If all these are present, in the fourth stage the firm has to develop an innovative product or service that would add to the value of the customers as well as it should be commercialized. Then, they have to get approval from the Department of Industrial Policy and Promotion (DIPP) about the innovativeness of the firm. If all these are in place, then any one of the following five approvals would allow the business to be considered as a 'startup'. Firstly, it can get recommended by the incubation centre of a Post-Graduate Indian College. Secondly, it can also get recommendation from the incubator which is funded by Government of India. Thirdly, it can also get recommendation of incubator that is recognized by the government. Fourthly, the business could be funded by either an incubation fund or by an angel fund or by private equity fund or by angel network. Fifth and last, if the business holds patent which is granted by Indian patent and trademark office, that will also suffice for the status.

The Indian start-ups, presently, are immensely supported by government initiatives, including financial assistance from the venture capitalists, apart from the fact that incubators and accelerators are always there to help them out. For the purpose of receiving financial assistance, a start-up has to go through several different stages. For developing the product idea, start-ups receive a minimum amount of fund from the venture capitalists, at the first stage, which is also known as the 'seed stage'. This stage is immensely important, for it develops he basic business idea, its future prospects, growth strategies, marketing idea, possible market share and every possible thing that can contribute to the growth and development of a business from its concept-development stage. Then there comes a couple of development stages of the business – identified as series A and series B stages of growth. In the late stage or last stage, start-ups launch their products and services in the market for the commercial business and for acquiring new customers and new market avenues, that is, for the sake of more growth, research and development, they go for acquiring more funds from the market or even venture capitalists. In India, presently, the market is dominated largely by late-stage players who eat up a huge chunk of market investment but new players, new ideas are also coming up and they are also receiving good support, good responses from the market as well as venture capitalists. In this regard, one has to mention popular programmes like 'Shark Tank' which has immensely helped in popularising this concept across India, it has encouraged millions of youths to think about new business concepts, it has funded several new start-ups financially, it has made the concept popular across student fraternity and several institutions have accepted this model of developing new business concepts and pitching it in front of capitalists for financial support. It is a new phenomenon that has been growing like fire among students and management bodies of higher education institutions.

The Indian eco system of start-ups that we have, at present, is still in the transitional phase. It is still developing. There are certain glaring inequalities which have been responsible for its underdevelopment nature – the growth and development of start-ups are hugely limited to few metropolitan cities and hovering around a few business concepts only. In such a vast nation – we need more rapid spread of the concept for its fast development. In the rural or semi-urban cities, there should be enough promotion; encouragement given to the start-ups and existing start-ups should receive promotion across regions which will encourage new entrants. New business concepts should be supported financially so that new people can enter the market, new business ideas can develop. It is a fact that every start-up does not receive financial helping. Since 2014, till 2020 only 6% of the start-ups were financially supported (Inc 42, 2020). Around 2023, these figures have gone up around 10%. Every blooming sector is dominated by a unicorn which is believed to eat up the larger share of the market which prohibits new entry. But, situation is not all gloomy. Despite the existence of Unicorns and Decacorns, new players with new business ideas are coming in the market. Self-funded start-ups are also growing and start-ups from small cities, rural economies are also catching eyes and enjoying market shares. In this respect, role of social media is hugely appreciable along with technology based artificial intelligence which have been helping millions of new businesses to spread across the nation and acquire new customers, find new markets and develop.

The start-ups are the new dimension of business ideas which starts from a seed stage and can flourish to become a market-dominant. In an economy of unemployment but with full of resource, one needs several such start-ups not only to solve the problem of unemployment but also to encourage new generations to be self-sufficient. Developing business ideas, bringing them and presenting them in front of capitalists and pitching for financial support and finally launching own product –are all like dreams becoming reality. New generations have to be encouraged in this field and such encouragement has to be from a very young age and higher education is, perhaps, the best stage for doing so. Indian higher education institutes are not lagging behind in this regard – there are several such institutions, management and technology-based institutes including IITs are forerunners, which have been focusing upon developing several aspects of start-up related behaviour and skill-formation in their students. Few even have incorporated in their curriculum and few have organised for special lecture sessions, competitions among students to develop this concept. Few even have offered financial helps to their students for setting up their own start-up or even developing their business concepts which are at the 'seed' stage, when their early proposals were attractive and praised by the experts. An important helping hand in this regard has been the emphasis on industry-academia interface which has been immensely helpful in nurturing and developing this concept, even breeding new ideas among students.

But, given the unbalanced growth of start-up industries in India, from several aspects –location-wise, funding-wise, promotion wise and industry-wise, etc., the acceptance and growth of start-ups in India, despite having staggering figures in the last decade, is yet to flourish fully and is still developing. The present generation higher education students are the probable owners of developers of start-ups. These students who are pursuing undergraduate and post-graduate degrees are supposed to understand the advantages, drawbacks and various aspects related with start-ups which in fact influence their decision or willingness to undertake, develop a start-up idea or even go into the avenue of forming their own start-ups.

Under this backdrop, we decided to ask the students of undergraduate and post-graduate degrees, including general degree colleges, management degree and technology-based degree, about their views on different aspects of start-ups and ultimately whether they are willing to set up their own start-ups. Based on the views of 580 students, we have applied the logit regression analysis where we have looked to find out as well as analyzed the start-ups related behaviours of the students of higher education who will be the probable future entrepreneurs. We have surveyed students from both non-formal and formal courses and on students of both Undergraduate and Post-Graduate Degrees – this further increases the significance of our study because generally it is believed that students of non-formal courses only have the eagerness or education of starting business of their own. Even if there are few start-ups related analysis in India, most of these are information based or descriptive and there is almost no analysis which considers the views of students of higher education by conducting primary survey on students of all major forms of degree – this study draws its motivation from this lacuna and looks to contribute to the scant of studies on start-ups in India.

Rest of the chapter is organised as follows. Section II discusses about few of the existing literature in this regard followed by section III discussing about few facts and figures of growth and development of start-ups in India. Section IV discusses the data, methodology and discusses about the regression results of the logit analysis. Finally, section V concludes with possible policy suggestions.

LITERATURE REVIEW

Since the concept of start-ups is relatively new in Indian circumstances and business scenarios, there is scant of existing literature in this field, especially in Indian circumstances. But there are few studies related with the field of Indian start-ups, its investment dynamics as well as government initiatives being announced in this regard. Even if the studies are quite limited in numbers, they are generally descriptive. Few of the relevant studies, related with the start-up ecosystem of India, are described here.

Narayan et al. in 2019 conducted a study related with start-up investment in India between 2014-15 and 2018-19. Even if there is general belief that as the start-up grows and requires more financial funding, this study did not find any such relevance in the relationship between these two aspects – stage of growth of a start-up and the level of funding it seeks. Rao and Kumar in 2016 conducted a comparative study between angel investors and other venture capitalists. This study revealed that this company grew fast during these periods and they funded first stage start-ups and therefore they are popular and significantly different from venture capitalists and unlike venture capitalists, angel investors invest in a variety of sectors which is conducive for development of new entrepreneurial ideas, that is, helpful for new start-up to develop and grow. Shetty in 2017 made a comparative analysis between India, China and USA about start-ups and observed that despite the fast catching up by Indian start-up industries, Indian venture capitalists are lagging far behind in investing start-ups, especially the newcomers. But the positive sign is that consumer-based technology sectors in India hugely received investment and that fact is only going to increase in coming days which is a positive fact for both these industries as well as venture capitalists. David et al. in 2020 made a comprehensive study on Indian start-up scenarios – they not only considered the growth of Indian start-ups during 2015-2019 but also explained their stage-wise growth, geographic location wise growth along with sector-specific analysis. The regression analysis conducted in this study revealed the factors significant for growth of start-ups in India, apart from discussing government's initiatives for this sector. Their analysis revealed a cluster sort of outcome, revealing that most of the start-ups, including the big ones are based on big metropolitan cities, where as the small ones have found themselves neglected, investment-wise and location-wise and they are largely based on outside the periphery of metropolitan cities and it is a bit problematic for them to capture market of big cities. Whereas bulk of the studies focused on investment trends in Indian start-ups, David et al. went far ahead and considered the sector specific and location specific concentration of start-ups in India which opened the door for future studies.

Studies highlighting the initiatives of the government in this regard and actually analyzing these schemes with proper criticism are very few. Yet, these studies should be done because they work as eye-openers for all and work as policy improvements for the policy setting bodies which in fact help in the improvement of the government's performance. There are various facilities provided by the government's flagship programme 'start-up India'. These facilities, such as tax-relief or exemption on profits; support for patent filing as well as legal help for incubation, etc., have been discussed in various studies (Mittal and Garg, 2018; Dutta, 2016). There are various schemes undertaken by the government for generating entrepreneurial capabilities in the economy – 'start-up India'; 'stand-up India'; 'make in India'; 'Atal innovation Yojona', etc. all these are helpful for developing entrepreneurship capabilities among the youth and actually results into development of start-ups. These facilities have been discussed elaborately by Jayanthi, 2019. Despite these facilities, start-ups in India do face challenges in the forms of rigid licensing facilities, absence of tax holidays – at least in the early stages, less loanable funding facilities by the banks – all these have been resulting in lack of proper balanced growth in all parts of the nation (Venkatnarayana, 2016). Kshetri (2016) discussed the reasons for slow growth or unbalanced growth of entrepreneurship in India – especially at the start-up level. This study identifies that apart from stringent financial laws and facilities, there are lack of support from the government to all sectors or even to the small start-ups; labour regulation laws are also unfavourable for investors to invest, there is lesser accessibility to the market for start-up investors having origin in the non-metropolitan cities and development of Research and Development (R&D) is also not in favour of Indian start-ups– all these have been holding the growth back and we are remaining far behind than where we should be. Singh in 2020 explained, in detail, about the schemes of the government and analysed their performances with criticism. On one hand the study described all the schemes, their benefits including MUDRA (MUDRA stands for Micro Units Development and Refinance Agency Limited. It funds or provided refinances to the commercial banks, non-bank financial companies, regional rural banks for refinancing or giving credit to the micro units) and on the other hand it examined its successes, failures, possible future plans and possible remedies than can further contribute in the growth of start-ups. Such studies are really missing, even if it is describing in nature. A slightly different study was done by David et al. in 2020 that incorporated data from the government's 'start-up India' website, from responses of Right to Information act and from the ways of funding of 928 start-ups and finally analysed the concentration of investment of start-ups in India by the help of regression analysis and concluded how the government's schemes have been performing in the development and growth of start-ups in India. There are studies that describes not only the effect of start-ups on labour market but also discusses the challenges and problems that lies before this industry (Babu and Sridevi, 2019). Such studies are helpful for improvement of future performances because along with growth performance or positive sides, it brings forward the negative sides as well that tells about the vulnerability of this sector and how future policies can help recover such challenges (Maradi, 2023). Demographic set up of an economy highly influences industrial activities and growth and India, at present, has been enjoying demographic dividend and it will continue to enjoy that at least in the next three to four decades and the economic policies have been banking on this dividend for development of the economy and as a result start-up generally becomes an important aspect of employment creation but with severe challenges from rest of the world and therefore government policies and initiatives are even more crucial (Gudwani and Kaur, 2023). Rajan and Surya in 2019 made an analysis, by describing the pros and cons of start-ups, how far Indian citizens are aware about this industry and how this industry has been flourishing over the years and if such development is actually influencing in the development of awareness in the common youths and set-up of new firms or services in the market. This study describes the positive sides of the awareness build up which is good for the economy.

The above studies show various aspects of start-up industries, present challenges as well as future possibilities but how the present generation is viewing start-ups, how the higher education students of present generation who would be the probable future entrepreneurs of start-ups are viewing start-ups, whether they are willing to enter this industry, which factors they are considering as important, what influence these factors are going to have on their decision-making process – are all missing in the existing set of studies. The present study is influenced by this research gap because in several higher education institutes, this aspect has been getting priority which has been paving the way for rapid growth of start-up in India. This study draws its motivation from this lacuna and contributes greatly to fill it up by applying ground level data analysis along with econometric analysis of logistic regression model.

FEW FACTS AND FIGURES

The ecosystem of start-ups in India has undergone massive changes over the years. It has received over $140 billion, since 2014, grown immensely during even tough periods of COVID-19 during 2020-2022 but witnessed a downfall of 73% in investment in 2023 compared to the 2022 figures - received only S7 billions of investment in 2023 compared to $25 billion in 2022. Even if enormous amount of investment has flown over the years in this sector, there are scarcity of investment in all sectors because of inequal distribution of investment in all sectors or even unbalanced growth of start-up firms. Over 68000 startups have been launched till 2023 but only over 5300 are funded which implies the percentage is below 8%, even though more than 9500 investors are there at present investing in the Indian startup industry and combined valuation of all startups is over $ 450 billion (Inc 42, 2023). The number of startups is projected to go above 1.8 lakhs by 2030, even if over 1200 have exited the industry (Inc 42, 2023). Around 2017, only 2% of the start-ups in India have received over 75% of investment, this skewed behavior of investment has smoothened a bit in the later stage around 2020 but still not all sectors have received funding, even within sectors there is skewed behavior as from healthcare sector only 13% received funding, from fintech only 15% got the funding in 2017 (Inc 42, 2017). The trends of funding over the years – 2014 - 2020 reveal that if we keep aside the Unicorn or big business houses, then average funding received by other startups or average deal size of rest of the startups remained more or less constant or even decreased but with the big players in the scene that figure increased – it shows that bulk of the investment went into the hands of the big players. Another reason for this constancy is that number of deals were more or less constant or not every startup was getting financial backups – both of these appear to be correct when we see the real databases. The incremental investment was flowing to the big houses and they were eating up the market which could have resulted in lesser entry of new firms in the market and also lesser influence of relatively new firms in the market than desired to set up a healthy balanced ecosystem in the startup industry. But the good news is that over 5000 investors are investing in the 'seed' startups, that is, angel investors, which is supposed to help the growth of this industry. The record shows that over the span of 9 years – 2014 to first half of 2023, there were 9560 deals in Indian startup industries but the year wise disaggregation of database reveals that between 2015 to 2020 the number of deals varied between 950 to 1045 but in 2021 and 2022 this number grew by 1584 and 1517, respectively but in the 2023 it fell down to 897 (Inc 42, 2023). Interestingly, 73% of the deals, till 2023, remained below $10 million and 91% deals remained below $50 million of investment (Inc 42, 2023). If we look at the sectoral decomposition of investment of startups in India, the past 10 years record reveals the fact that fintech adaptation rate of Indian citizen is 87% (Inc 42, 2023). The growth and investment have accumulated in those sectors that involves technology as well as ensures fast return. Following diagram shows the sector-wise investment of first 10 sectors followed by first 10 sectors amount of invest-wise, over the period of 2014 – first half of 2023.

Table 1. First ten sectors with highest numbers of deal count & funding (2014-2023 First Half)

Sector with Deal Count	Sector with Funding ($ Bn)
Enterprise tech **1764**	E-Commerce **34**
E-Commerce **1668**	Fintech **29**
Fintech **1451**	Enterprise tech **15**
Health tech **797**	Consumer Services **12**
Consumer Services **783**	Travel tech **12**
Ed tech **717**	Ed tech **11**
Media & Entertainment **686**	Media & Entertainment **9**
Deep tech **512**	Cleantech **7**
Travel tech **672**	Health tech **6**
Cleantech **325**	Logistic **5**

Source: Inc 42, 2023

The above table reveals that technology-based sectors have been garnering more deals and funds over the years, obviously if they have high return chances. E commerce and fintech based businesses, because of having high as well as fast payback probabilities are getting more funds. Health, Education and travelling are those areas where startups have been opened very recently, at least in the post 2014 era, even if they have been performing very well, not all of them are getting the fund. Number of deals in each sector ensures that there are funding opportunities for good performers. The interesting factor that plays the pivotal role is that growth rate of 'seed' stage startups is 66% which way over the growth rates of 'growth' stage startups and 'late' stage startups which are growing at 23% and 7% rates, respectively (Inc 42, 2023). These figures are for the period 2017-2022. One of the reasons for such growth-centric figures could be that most of the 'seed' stage startups belong to the enterprise tech field where as fintech startups and e-commerce startups are in the 'growth' stage and 'late' stage, respectively and India has around 58% investors in the category of 'angel' investors who prefer investing in 'seed' stage firms, compared to 26.3% investors as venture capitalists or private equities and 8.4% as corporate bodies or corporate venture capitalists and the last two forms generally invest in 'growth' and 'late' stage companies (Inc 42, 2023). Next, we shall focus on the region-wise distribution of Indian startups. The following diagrams vividly explain that Bengaluru dominates the list by far with Delhi NCR and Mumbai being ranked at positions 2 and 3, respectively both in the numbers of deal count as well as fund received for the sector. Rest of the cities are lagging far behind with a lot of catching up to be done.

Figure 1. Region wise distribution of Indian startups with amount of funding (2014-2023 first half)
source: Inc 42, 2023

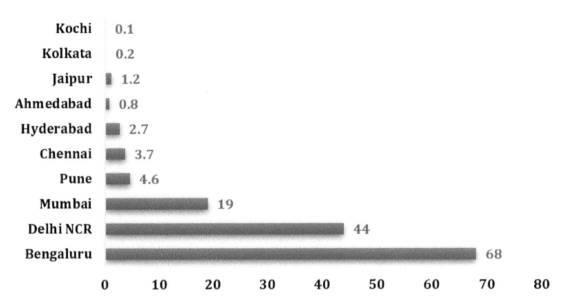

Both figures 1 and 2 reveal satisfying as well as worrying scenarios. Three areas have been growing rapidly and they are ranked among the world leaders in this regard but the worrying side is rest of the cities are far behind and the spread is not only inequal, it is urban centric also. One can see that all the 10 cities are metropolitan ones, yet they have huge differences on both grounds of comparison. There is no rural or semi-urban area that is able to get a position in the figure – which itself speaks about the unbalanced growth structure of this eco-system – a phenomenon that itself asks for policy re-orientation or proper, even distribution of government facilities and business environment across all regions of the economy.

Figure 2. Region wise distribution of Indian startups with deal count (2014-2023 first half)
Source: Inc 42, 2023

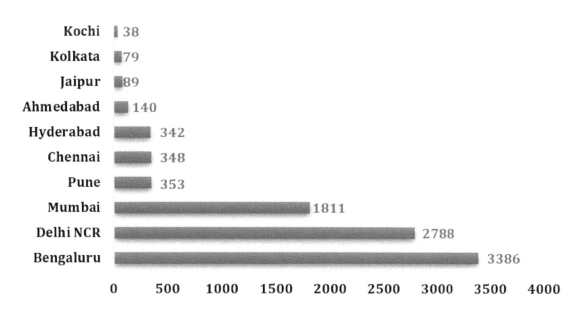

Deal Count

If we look at the gender disparity in this sector, then the situations are really gloomy. Only over 500 startups are women led that has garnered 8.5% of funding or around $12 billion of funding out of $141 billion raised by all. Majority of the women-led business are based on Bengaluru and belong to the E-Commerce category – such gloomy scenarios certainly reveals the policy failure on part of the government and seeks strong action that would ensure the inclusive growth of the industry.

Next, we shall focus on the employment – generating aspect of this industry. Even if overall above 7.68 lakh employment has been generated by this industry between 2017 - 2023, such employment generation has been inequal as well. Not all sectors have been able to generate the desired level of employment and that has inequal spreading as well. The employment generation till 2020 was around 4.65 lakhs (GOI, 2020). So, in the last three years over 3 lakhs employment has been generated but that falls below 2019 and 2020 levels where 1.5 lakhs and 1.7 lakhs employment were generated every year. Hence, post-COVID scenarios are not all well as the growth rate of employment generation has dipped but the sector is recovering since second half of 2022.

DATA AND METHODOLOGY

Here we have collected data from Under Graduate and Post Graduate students of three General Degree Colleges, two Engineering Colleges and three Management Colleges in West Bengal. Hence, we have collected data from students of eight colleges divided into three categories. Hence, it is a study that has covered both forms of students – formal as well as informal - pursuing higher education. The questionnaire was developed and it was shared in the form of google form – hence, absolute randomness of the study was maintained as it was unknown who was replying and who was not. We surveyed 600 students – 200 from each of the three categories.

Students were, first of all, explained about the definition or features of startups that we are using in the present study. Apart from the requirement of fulfilling all the stages set by the government for a business entity to be recognized as a 'startup', we have mentioned certain conditions such as selling goods or services through the online or digital platform – facilitating the both side transactions by online mode, making use of technology on which it enjoys ownership, or even making use of modern-age technology such as internet of things, big data analysis, artificial intelligence and so on. Apart from this, we considered only 'Indian' ownership-based startups having head office or branches in India, secondarily, it may have branches in Foreign Economies. the entity must not have formed after splitting from an existing firm. It should be a new generation firm, that is, formed after 2009 – formed in the era of Industrial Revolution 4.0. It may also be an entity of an existing corporate body but it should be developing goods and services different from its parent company. All such categorization, actually, helped the students to identify the startups, even if it is not so famous or it belongs to their living places or other rural or semi-urban areas and not been able to get the limelight. Having set up these categorizations, we went for the survey where we asked the students, primarily, whether they wanted to develop their own startups in near future and what are the factors they believe are influential behind their willingness or non-willingness. We also asked them what are the challenges, they feel, are there at the present business environment that may be working as drawbacks for encouraging new businesses getting into the market. Brief findings of our survey are given below in the table.

Table 2. Findings of survey

Total Surveyed Students – 580 Male – 321, Female – 259	
Caste	**General- 256 SC- 201 ST- 80 OBC-43**
Total	580
Course	UG – 320, PG - 260
Degrees	General – 250 Management – 180 Engineering – 150
Willing For startup	377
Non-Willing For startup	203

Source: Primary Survey

Even if around 35% of the students were non-willing to form a start-up of their own, they cannot be eliminated from the analysis as their replies are important in getting the overall outcome of the study. (Gupta and Chatterjee, 2021; Chatterjee, 2022). Students were directly asked about their intention or willingness of developing a startup of their own and in reply they had to give direct reply either by stating a 'YES' or a 'NO'. Since, we have covered students from all existing socio-economic categories, we asked several socio-economic related questions which are supposed to influence their decision.

As the received replies were in the form of a direct 'YES' or 'NO', here the response variable is of binary form – we have assigned a '0' for the responses which were 'NO' and '1' for responses with a 'YES' – obviously these responses are in reference to the direct question related with our dependent variable. Hence, applying a logistic regression model is the best econometric methodology to explore and analyse the students' behavior – which we have done. The application of logistic regression model ensures the fact that our dependent variable – whether a student is willing to open a startup of his or own – is the log-odds ratio. The ratio which presents the probability of replying a YES to the question asked and the probability of saying a NO in reply to the question. The econometric build-up of the modelling of logistic analysis is described below.

$$L_n \frac{p_i}{1-p_i} = \theta_0 + \sum_{i=1}^{10} \theta_i Y_i + u_i \tag{1}$$

$$p_i = \frac{e^{\left(\theta_0 + \theta_1 Y_1 + \ldots + \theta_{10} Y_{10}\right)}}{1 + e^{\left(\theta_0 + \theta_1 Y_1 + \ldots + \theta_{10} Y_{10}\right)}} \quad (2) \quad p_i = \frac{e^{\left(\theta Y\right)}}{1 + e^{\left(\theta Y\right)}} \tag{3}$$

$$p_i = \frac{1}{1 + e^{\left(-\theta Y\right)}} \tag{4}$$

In the above equations, p_i is representing the probability of saying a YES – that the student is willing for opening a startup. $(1-p_i)$, consequently, is representing the probability of replying back with a NO, in regard to the question of willingness for opening a startup. The regressors or the independent variables of our analysis are presented by the vector Y which is a set of 10 variables and several of which are socio-economic, including dummies. The effects of these regressors are given by the respective coefficients - Θ_i's. The random term is u_i – representing the unexplained variation.

Just above 65% of our respondents have replied in the 'affirmative' in reply to our prime question and rest have replied in 'negative'. Hence, majority of the students are in favour of having their own startups. Which factors have been influential behind such willingness or non-willingness is to be assessed and analyzed then. The independent variables used in our study is given below.

The set of 10 independent variables as well as attributes of our study are given below.

- Income (Y)– total monthly income (in Indian Currency) of the family of the respondent / student
- Sex (S) – Respondent's Sex (Dummy Variable- 0 for Male; 1 for Female)
- Caste (C) – Caste of the Respondent – (Dummy Variable. 0 for General Caste, 1 for OBC, 2 for SC, 3 for ST)
- Business Idea (BI) – Whether the respondent already possess a Business Idea or in the process of developing one (Dummy Variable. O for Yes, 1 for NO).
- Angel Investors (AI)- Whether it is possible for new startups to get fund from angel investors (Dummy Variable. 0 for high, 1 for Medium, 2 for Bad).

- Knowledge of Internet of Things (IO) – Whether it is essential to have sound knowledge of Internet of Things and Artificial Intelligence (Dummy Variable. 0 for not a problem, 1 for if it is a problem).
- Mentoring throughout the year (MENT.) – If the mentoring facilities throughout the year are helpful (Dummy Variable. 0 for Yes, 1 for No).
- Ease of Doing Business (EDB) – (Dummy Variable. 0 for Very good, 1 for Good, 2 for Medium, 3 for Bad).
- Government Laws (GL) – (Dummy Variable. 0 for Easy, 1 for Not Easy).
- Inspiration from Families / Friends – (IF) – (Dummy Variable. 0 for Yes, 1 for No).

The findings of the logistic regression analysis are given below.

Table 3. Results of logistic regression analysis

Variables	Coefficient	Marginal Effects (dY/dX)
Income (Y)	0.00421*** (8.23)	0.000287*** (7.22)
Sex (S)	- 0.00058** (2.01)	-0.000402** (2.06)
Caste (C)	0.00065 (0.88)	0.00324 (0.70)
Business Idea (BI)	0.00587*** (11.02)	0.00201** (2.09)
Angel Investors (AI)	-0.00489*** (-5.54)	-0.00410*** (-4.21)
Knowledge of Internet of Things (IO)	-0.05001*** (-9.21)	-0.04665*** (-6.24)
Mentoring throughout the year (MENT.)	0.00540*** (7.81)	0.00102*** (2.82)
Ease of Doing Business (EDB)	0.00432*** (3.65)	0.00366*** (2.92)
Government Laws (GL)	- 0.00204*** (5.66)	- 0.00247*** (6.11)
Inspiration from Families / Friends (IF)	0.00229** (2.09)	0.00314** (2.03)
Constant	6.4266*** (6.97)	
Prob> chi-quare	0.000	
Pseudo R^2	0.8323	
Total no. of observations	580	

The values in the parentheses are the t-values.
*** denotes significant at 1% level
** denotes significance at 5% level
Source: Author's Calculation

The above findings of regression analysis are very meaningful. We have found that all the variables are significant at either 5% or 1% level, except 'Caste' – which implies that caste-based division does not have any impact on students' willingness regarding having their own startups. The econometric intuitions behind the significance of rest of the variables are given below.

Both Income and support from the family having positive and significant effects are quite understandable – a student having a high-earning family and correspondingly greater influence in setting up a startup is very reasonable because very often it is found that initial investment for startup is made from the family. Even if the family cannot fund up the business financially, the help they can provide by standing aside the person is immensely important which implies that family's inspiration in every form is important and bears positive impact.

Three important qualitative aspects in any line of business and have more significance in this line - Business Idea, Mentoring throughout the year and Ease of Doing Business – all are positively encouraging. Having a feasible Business Idea already developed always gives a first mover advantage and thus influences positively. Startups are new concepts and therefore require guidance throughout the year – especially when it is in the 'early seed' stage. Several individuals or corporates have been doing that successfully and consistently – the results of which are outstanding, since they have been helping in developing new concepts; modifying the existing ones, helping in crunching stages as well as guiding in the growth. Such facilities are immensely required as far as views of the students are concerned. These facilities have not only helped in the development of new startups, but also have stopped the exit of the existing ones due to lack of guidance during loss or crunch situations. Ease of Doing Business is one such thing that depends on several factors – political stability in the area, corruption, tax payment policies, construction permits, credit availability, etc. One can say that programmes like 'startup India' have been taking care of these aspects because having favourable conditions of these factors actually help the business environment positively which encourages new investment and development of new businesses.

The negatively significant socio-economic aspects are also very meaningful. One can find that females are less willing for having startups - a very common phenomenon witnessed across the nation and it is existent even among students. Internet of things (IOT), Artificial Intelligence (AI) – Industrial Revolution 4.0 have been taking the world by storm and changing the business environments and ideas rapidly and for the sake of coping up with these changes it is almost indispensable to have knowledge of the modern technology and Ai tools – even the students feel so because not having knowledge of these aspects not only reduces the willingness but also worsens the scenario for the owners. Students also believe that if the government laws related with business are stringent, they are only going to make the scenarios tough for development and evolvement of startups across the nation. The findings of our regression deal with serious policy suggestions both for society as well as for the government. We discuss those policy recommendations in the last section.

We have also showed the marginal effects for each variable that show the percentage change in the dependent variable, that is, willingness to have a startup, with respect to percentage change in every dependent variable, keeping the other variables unchanged. So, it shows the partial effects which very much reflect the main findings along with the levels of significance and signs of the coefficients of the independent variables. We have calculated the Variance Inflationary Factors (VIF) for each of the variables that shows how far the independent variables are correlated between themselves. This is also known as the problem of Multicollinearity, severe presence of which asks for re-developing the econometric model. The following table reports the VIF for each and every regressors.

Table 4. Test for multicollinearity

Variables	VIF	1/VIF
Income	2.03	0.492
Sex	3.39	0.294
Caste	1.01	0.990
Business Idea	2.22	0.450
Angel Investors (AI)	3.97	0.251
Knowledge of Internet of Things (IO)	4..01	0.249
Mentoring throughout the year (MENT.)	2.68	0.373
Ease of Doing Business (EDB)	2.88	0.347
Government Laws (GL)	2.67	0.374
Inspiration from Families / Friends (IF)	3.68	0.271
Mean	2.854	

Source: Author's Calculation

The mean VIF is below 5 which is within the tolerable level or permissible level as per rule of thumb. Hence, we accept the given result obtained in table 3 because our model does not suffer from the problem of Multicollinearity.

CONCLUSION WITH POLICY SUGGESTIONS

Our study concentrated on willingness of having a startup among students pursuing higher education in West Bengal. Our focus on probable future entrepreneurs by considering views of higher education students of all forms – Undergraduate, Post Graduate, Non-Professional Courses, Professional Courses – bear more significance and thus this study becomes unique from several aspects. Our findings suggest that several areas are there that need to be taken care off. Female students are less willing – it implies either a change in the social thinking or conservativeness or even more encouragement from all sources so that females feel encouraged to take part in this process. It is a concern nationwide and deserves greater government intervention policy wise that would ensure more female-led startups to usher. Government laws are very much in favour of the startup owners but they need to be more eased, that is, stringency level should be reduced or even more facilities needs to be given for new startups, new business ideas, new people to come in the scenario as well as for ensuring a nationwide balanced spread and growth of startups. Hence, we need an even more business-friendly environment across the nation. The AI education in the era of Industry 4.0 is the need of the hour and that education for all can only be ensured by means of implementing it in the education policy because this is the need of the industries and academia is supposed to back it up. A phenomenon that has already been emphasized in National Education Policy 2020 in India but the spread of AI education needs to be ensured at a very fast pace so that everyone can gain from its benefits (Chatterjee, 2022). Mentoring policy and Angel Investment – these are couple of fields that greatly encourage the development of new startups from the 'seed' stage to get into the 'growth' stage. Hence, it is the business policy, on part of the government, that ensures the existence and fund flow from Angel Investors along with proper guidance from mentoring bodies.

Hence, there are few things that have been influencing positively in the growth of startups in the nation and that have ensured the rapid development of this line of business in India in the last decade. But a lot needs to be done and for that proper policy changes on part of the government and social setup are expected.

REFERENCES

Babu, G. S., & Sridevi, K. (2019). A study on issues and challenges of startups in India. *International Journal of Financial Management and Economics*, *2*(1), 44–48. doi:10.33545/26179210.2019.v2.i1a.16

Chatterjee, N. (2022). Households' Willingness to Pay for Improved Water Supply System in the Dryland areas of West Bengal – an estimation using Double-Bounded Dichotomous-Choice Model. *Economic Affairs*, *67*(5), 787–795. doi:10.46852/0424-2513.5.2022.12

David, D., Gopalan, S., & Ramachandran, S. (2020). *The Startup Environment and Funding Activity in India*. (Working Paper). Asian Development Bank Institute, Tokyo, June.

Dutta, A. (2016). Start-up Initiative. *IOSR Journal of Business and Management*, *15010*(2), 93–97. doi:10.9790/487X-15010020293-97

Gudwani, S., & Kaur, N. (2023). A Study, Challenges and Issues of Indian Startups on Economic Growth. *European Chemical Bulletin*, *12*(S3), 6590–6595.

Gupta, A. C., & Chatterjee, N. (2021). Economic Values for the Environment with special reference to the Contingent Valuation Method, in Environmental Management: Issues and Concerns in Developing Countries, Springer and Capital Publishing Company. doi:10.1007/978-3-030-62529-0_14

Jayanthi, D. (2019). A Study About Entrepreneurship in India and Its Promotion Under 'Startup India' Scheme. *Iconic Research and Engineering Journals*, *2*(11), 118–126.

Kshetri, N. (2016). Fostering Startup Ecosystems in India. *Asian Research Policy*, *7*(1), 94–103.

Maradi, M. (2023). Growth of Indian start-up: A critical analysis. *Journal of Management and Entrepreneurship, 17*(1), II: 181-186.

Mittal, B., & Garg, S. (2018). A Conceptual Study of Startup India-A Rejuvenation. *Journal of Commerce and Trade*, *13*(1), 1–14. doi:10.26703/JCT.v13i1-1

Narayan, M., Mohanty, B., & Kumar, M. (2019). Growth pattern and trends in startup funding in India. *International Journal of Innovative Technology and Exploring Engineering*, *8*(12), 3721–3724. doi:10.35940/ijitee.L2654.1081219

Pooja, H. R. (2019). A descriptive study of opportunities and challenges of Startup India Mission. *International Journal of Advance Research and Innovative Ideas in Education*, *2*(3), 2395–4396.

Rajani, K. (2023). A Study on Opportunities and Challenges of Startups in India. [IJM]. *International Journal of Management, 14*(4), 251–256.

Rao, S. R., & Kumar, L. (2016). Role of Angel Investor in Indian Startup Ecosystem. *FIIB Business Review, 5*(1), 3–14. doi:10.1177/2455265820160101

Shetty, K. K. (2017). A Comparative Study on Impact of Venture Capital Financing on Startups in India. *International Conference on Education, Humanities and Management (ICEHM-17)*, (pp 14-15). Research Gate.

Singh, V. K. (2020). *Policy and Regulatory Changes for a Successful Startup Revolution: Experiences from the Startup Action Plan in India.* (Working Paper 1146). Asian Development Bank Institute, Tokyo, June.

Venkatanarayana, I. (2016). Startups in India Sustainable Development. *International Research Journal of Engineering. IT & Scientific Research, 2*(3), 43–49.

Chapter 15

Women Empowerment as a Tool to Attain Sustainable Development Goals:
A Study of a Remote Area of West Bengal, India

Gopa Ghosh
Umeshchandra College, India

Payel Roy
Umeshchandra College, India

Reuben Das
Umeshchandra College, India

Mercy Hembrom
Umeshchandra College, India

ABSTRACT

This study tries to construct a women empowerment index based on different decision-making areas. For this study, 131 married and unmarried working women from a tribal village of West Bengal, India are surveyed through a structured questionnaire having 34 questions segregated into five dimensions. The responses are coded and converted into binary scores to show more empowered scored as 1 and less or not empowered being scored as 0 to construct a combined composite women empowerment index. The analysis reveals that on average the women studied are moderately empowered with married ones winning over the unmarried. Though there is not much impact of education level is found for the married ones in their empowerment level but for the unmarried women, the more the educational qualification, the more are they empowered.

DOI: 10.4018/979-8-3693-2197-3.ch015

INTRODUCTION

The increasing degradation of the mother nature has opened the opportunity for a comprehensive development of all its associated domains that not only limit to biodiversity and ecological development but also extends to social equity, growth of different forms of organizations and the effects of economic policies on the community. The onus of achieving the three-fold sustainable development goals of Economic Viability, Environmental Protection and Social Equity is on our own behavioral prudency. A sustainable route of development can be reached only when the interests of both men and women are taken into consideration in the allocation of resources by giving women and men the equal possibilities, including in decision-making in all sorts of activities. Amidst the converging crises of COVID-19, the climate catastrophe, and increasing levels of political and economic instability, advancements in gender equality have not only stagnated but have even started to regress. Depending on the employment information and patterns from gender-disaggregated unemployment surveys in the US and India, in the year 2020, McKinsey Global Institute calculates that the global job loss rates for women as a result of COVID-19 are approximately 1.8 times greater than those for males, at 5.7% and 3.1%, respectively (Madgavkar et. al., 2020). The COVID 19 pandemic has extended the time required to reach gender parity from 99.5 years to 135.6 years, according to the Global Gender Gap Report (World Economic Forum, 2021).Thus, it is high time that we realize the importance of striving to accomplish the goal set by The UN Member States as 2030 deadline for achieving gender equality and the empowerment of all women in the Sustainable Development Agenda, which was adopted in 2015(Our World in Data team, 2023).

The empowerment of women is highlighted in this chapter as a crucial step towards achieving gender equality and, consequently, sustainable development. A "multi-dimensional" social process helps people gain control over their own lives and it is the concept of empowerment (Warth, L. and Koparanova, M., 2012). It is a process that helps people develop power—that is, the ability to apply—for use in their own lives, in their communities, and in society by acting on issues that they deem significant. The continuation of women's disadvantage over men serves as the backdrop for this paper's examination of women's empowerment. This drawback is evident in the underprivileged sections of the society residing at Debanandapur village and adjacent areas, a tribal village in the district of Birbhum, West Bengal, India. With a sex ratio of 950 females per 1000 males in the state of West Bengal, India (Census of India, 2011), it is evident that the prosperity largely depends on women population, this chapter wants to analyze in terms of women empowerment which can lead to their sustainable development and their contribution towards the gender equality resulting into overall development of the community.

In their journey some common facility centers, training programmes are set up in association with Backward Classes Welfare Department, Tribal Welfare Department, Govt. of West Bengal to train them for making and promoting handicrafts which also in turn will lead to a sustainable livelihood, economically and socially of those women of this area. This chapter gives an overview of their status in society and in their families and whether they are equipped with the knowledge of health, hygiene, environment protection and sustainability. For this study, a detailed survey of the 150 women in the selected area is done to understand their basic characteristics and how their activities are interconnected with their economic viability, environmental protection, and social equity.

The process of empowering women includes giving them access to a discrimination-free environment as well as enhancing their capacity to take charge of their own lives and actively participate in bringing about the necessary changes in our society. Therefore, the current research wants to calculate multidimensional aspects of women's empowerment using decision-making index to understand the

Table 4. Women empowerment index values for health and education (DS1)

Health and Education (D_{s1})	Married	Unmarried
Do you decide whether you want to pursue your studies?	0.88	0.92
How much benefit do you derive from the training that you receive from here?	0.98	0.98
How much benefit do you expect in future from the training that you receive from here?	1.00	0.98
To what extent you make decisions about education of the children at home?	0.25	0.03
To what extent you make decisions about your Family's health related issues?	0.34	0.14
How are you benefitted by the Government schemes related SC/ST reservations?	0.49	0.59
How often do you visit Doctors' chamber/ Primary Health Centers when any of you family member becomes sick?	0.98	0.98
Average women empowerment	0.70	0.66

Source: Data compiled by the researchers.

However, concerning Table 4, a cause for concern arises as the power of decision-making regarding the education of children at home is notably low for both married women (0.25*) and even lower for unmarried women (0.03*). A similar scenario is observed in decisions related to family health issues. Table 4 also indicates that unmarried women exhibit a higher awareness of government schemes associated with various SC/ST reservations compared to married women, resulting in greater benefits from these programs.

The most pivotal indicators discerned are household income and expenditure, as elucidated in Table 5. The survey outcomes pertaining to women's decisions on household expenses and savings are revealed. In comparison to married women, unmarried women demonstrate a more adept ability to make timely decisions regarding both personal and household spending. Conversely, married women express a greater interest in augmenting their income to support their families.

Table 5. Women empowerment index values for income and expenditures (DS2)

Income and Expenditure (D_{s2})	Married	Unmarried
To what extent do you contribute towards your household expenses?	0.52	0.64
How much of your income can you spend on yourself?	0.51	0.62
To what extent do you decide about increasing your income?	0.74	0.53
How much do you save out of your income?	0.37	0.48
To what extent do you decide about purchasing household furniture?	0.29	0.41
Average women empowerment	0.49	0.54

Source: Data compiled by the researchers.

Referring to Table 5, the overall indices for financial decision-making are 0.49 for married women and 0.54 for unmarried ones. The average value, at 0.51, indicates a relatively low level of empowerment. Both married and unmarried women face limitations in saving, primarily influenced by their family's income level. When it comes to decisions about essential purchases, such as furniture for the home, both groups are in a modest position, displaying limited ability to decide whether to make such purchases.

Table 6 defines the spectrum of family-related decisions that both married and unmarried women can make. Notably, these women have the freedom to allocate their time as they see fit, with single women enjoying a more advantageous position than their married counterparts.

Table 6. Women empowerment index values for family (DS3)

Family (D_{S3})	Married	Unmarried
How can you spend time on the activities that you like?	0.77	0.85
To what extent do you decide about the dishes to be prepared at home?	0.28	0.14
To what extent do you decide about purchasing daily consumables?	0.20	0.03
How do you decide about your children's necessities?	0.83	N.A.
Can you decide about the future of your children?	0.97	N.A.
Average women empowerment	0.61	0.34

Source: Data compiled by the researchers.

While married women in the study region can make decisions regarding their children's essentials and future, women in the study area face limitations in deciding matters related to the health and education of other family members. As depicted in Table 6, women lack agency in determining meal choices and feel less empowered when making purchases of everyday essentials. On average, the index values are 0.61 for married women, 0.34 for unmarried ones, and an overall score of 0.47, reflecting a lower empowerment level.

In Table 7, various decision-making areas in women's daily lives, linked to their happiness, are presented. The overall empowerment index value of nearly 0.99 is promising, indicating that both married and unmarried women in this study have the autonomy to make decisions concerning their happiness. The reactions of family members and neighbours to their work outside the home prompt reflection on their positions within the household and society. Being working women is well accepted by both their families and neighbours, contributing to their happiness. The study also reveals that both married and unmarried women respondents derive immense satisfaction from earning money for their families and enjoy working with others in their workplaces.

married and unmarried women perceived themselves as equals to male family members, expressing satisfaction in their work environments and familial roles. Despite challenges faced by married women in balancing employment and household duties, the overall empowerment index stood notably high at 72.32%. The study underscores the multifaceted nature of women's empowerment, shaped by education, marital status, and societal attitudes. These findings offer valuable insights for policymakers and NGOs seeking to enhance women's empowerment in similar socio-economic contexts. Efforts should prioritize bolstering educational opportunities for women and addressing specific challenges faced by married women in achieving a harmonious balance between work and family responsibilities.

In conclusion, the research positions women's empowerment within the broader framework of sustainable development, highlighting its pivotal role in achieving economic viability, environmental protection, and social equity. This aligns with the growing body of research recognizing the interdependence of gender equality and sustainable development goals. As Nobel Laureate in Economics, Amartya Sen, aptly stated, "development cannot be sustained without the advancement of women." Empowering women creates a virtuous cycle, contributing to the well-being and efficiency of families and communities, ultimately enhancing intergenerational equity.

Moreover, the research emphasizes the positive correlation between educational attainment and women's empowerment levels, reinforcing the connection between gender-responsive education and sustainable development. Investing in girls' education is not only an ethical imperative but also a strategic investment in human capital and the future prosperity of societies. Educated women are better equipped to make informed decisions, contribute to the economy, and advocate for their rights and those of their families. The study acknowledges the multifaceted nature of women's empowerment, influenced by factors such as marital status and societal attitudes. While married women may exhibit significant control over household finances, they may face constraints in other domains, such as family health decisions. This underscores the need for contextualized interventions that address the specific challenges faced by different groups of women within a community.

The conversation above demonstrates how women can be empowered, but they still face a number of challenges, such as a lack of awareness campaigns about various government services, occasionally uncooperative families etc. Thus, this study wants to propose the following some suggestions for the future development of women of the study area and it will be also impacted to long-term sustainability of tribal women empowerment. The suggestions are like that an ongoing effort should be made to motivate, support, foster collaboration, and encourage to women for their desired work, launching several large-scale awareness programmes with the appropriate planning to educate women about the various industries, offering women-specific vocational training besides the traditional training. Thus, to improve the economic development and sustainability, we strongly advise that women be empowered.

REFERENCES

Acharya, D. R., Bell, J. S., Simkhada, P., Teijlingen, E. R. V., & Regmi, P. R. (2010). Women's autonomy in household decision-making: A demographic study in Nepal. *Reproductive Health*, *7*(15), 261–302. doi:10.1186/1742-4755-7-15 PMID:20630107

Ahmed, R., & Hyndman-Rizk, N. (2018). The higher education paradox: Towards improving women's Empowerment, agency development and labour force participation in Bangladesh. *Gender and Education*, *32*(9), 1–19. doi:10.1080/09540253.2018.1471452

Akhtar, M. S., Ayub, A., & Anwar, M. S. M. (2019). An analytical study on women's empowerment regarding decision making: A case study of Pakistan. *The Government-Annual Research Journal of Political Science, 7,* 59-79. https://sujo.usindh.edu.pk/index.php/THE-GOVERNMENT/article/view/213

Asaolu, I., Alaofe, H., Gunn, J. K., Adu, A., Monroy, A., Ehiri, J., Hayden, M. H., & Ernst, K. (2018). Measuring women's empowerment in sub-Saharan Africa: Exploratory and confirmatory factor analyses of the demographic and health surveys. *Frontiers in Psychology*, *9*(994), 1–10. doi:10.3389/fpsyg.2018.00994 PMID:29971030

Banerjee, S., Alok, S., & George, B. (2020). Determinants of women empowerment as measured by domestic decision-making: perspective from a developing economy. *International Symposia in Economic Theory and Econometrics*. In *Advanced Issues in the Economics of Emerging Markets* (Vol. 27, pp. 1–12). Emerald Group Publishing Limited. doi:10.1108/S1571-038620200000027001

Bayeh, E. (2016), The role of empowering women and achieving gender equality to the sustainable development of Ethiopia, *Pacific Science Review B: Humanities and Social Sciences,* 37-42. doi:10.1016/j.psrb.2016.09.013

Biswas, D., Saha, S. K., Sarkar, A. P., Mondal, T., Haldar, D., & Sarkar, G. N. (2020). Participation in household decision-making among married women in rural and urban areas of Bankura, West Bengal: A comparative study. *International Journal of Health & Allied Sciences*, *9*(2), 170–174. doi:10.4103/ijhas.IJHAS_108_19

Dadras, O., & Hazratzai, M. (2023). Survey based women empowerment index for Afghanistan (SWEI A): An explanatory and confirmatory factor analyses. *Social Indicators Research*, *170*(3), 1059–1074. doi:10.1007/s11205-023-03241-3

DamodaranK. (2021). Women in decision making roles in India: An analytical study. *Human Rights International Research Journal*, 9(2): 101-109. doi:10.6084/m9.figshare.20324652

Das, S. (2017). Economic growth and women empowerment through education: A study on santal at Birbhum, West Bengal. *International Journal of Engineering Development and Research*, *3*(5), 392–398. https://www.ijedr.org/papers/IJEDR1703057.pdf

Davis, L. M., Schensul, S. L., Schensul, J., Verma, R., Nastasi, B. K., & Singh, R. (2014). Women's empowerment and its differential impact on health in low-income communities in Mumbai, India. *Global Public Health: An International Journal for Research, Policy and Practice*, *9*(5), 481–494. doi:10.1080/17441692.2014.904919 PMID:24766149

Islam, M. R. (2010), Women's empowerment for sustainable development in Bangladesh. *OIDA International Journal of Sustainable Development, 8*(1), 77-83. https://papers.ssrn.com/sol3/papers.cfm?abstract_id=1675563

Keller, B., & Mbwewe, D. C. (1991). Policy and planning for the empowerment of Zambia's women farmers. *Canadian Journal of Development Studies, 1*(12), 75–88. doi:10.1080/02255189.1991.9669421

Alvares, D. F., & Soares, J. C. (2021). Innovation in tourism and startups in Brazil, Spain and Portugal. *Smart Tourism, 2*(2).

Alwakid, W., Aparicio, S., & Urbano, D. (2020). Cultural antecedents of green entrepreneurship in Saudi Arabia: An institutional approach. *Sustainability (Basel), 12*(9), 3673. doi:10.3390/su12093673

Antolin-Lopez, R., Martinez-del-Rio, J., & Cespedes-Lorente, J. J. (2019). Environmental entrepreneurship as a multi-component and dynamic construct: Duality of goals, environmental agency, and environmental value creation. *Business Ethics (Oxford, England), 28*(4), 407–422. doi:10.1111/beer.12229

Antoniuk Y. & Leirvik T. (2021). Climate Transition Risk and the Impact on Green Bonds. *Journal of Risk and Financial Management.* . doi:10.3390/jrfm14120597

Appiah, K., Du, J., Yeboah, M., & Appiah, R. (2019). Causal relationship between industrialization, energy intensity, economic growth and carbon dioxide emissions: Recent evidence from Uganda. *International Journal of Energy Economics and Policy, 9*(2), 237. doi:10.32479/ijeep.7420

Appiah, M., Gyamfi, B. A., Adebayo, T. S., & Bekun, F. V. (2023). Do financial development, foreign direct investment, and economic growth enhance industrial development? Fresh evidence from Sub-Sahara African countries. *Portuguese Economic Journal, 22*(2), 203–227. doi:10.1007/s10258-022-00207-0

Arnold, E., Barker, K., & Slipersæter, S. (2010). *Research Institutes in the ERA*. Europea. https://ec.europa.eu/research/era/index_en.htm

Arora, R., & Raj, M. (2020). A Comparative Study on the performance of Green and Traditional Bonds. *International Journal of Business and Management Invention., 9*(7), 40–46. doi:10.35629/8028-0907034046

Arthur, B., & Addai, B. (2022). The dynamic interactions of economic growth, foreign direct investment, and exchange rates in Ghana. *Cogent Economics & Finance, 10*(1), 2148361. doi:10.1080/23322039.2022.2148361

Asaolu, I., Alaofe, H., Gunn, J. K., Adu, A., Monroy, A., Ehiri, J., Hayden, M. H., & Ernst, K. (2018). Measuring women's empowerment in sub-Saharan Africa: Exploratory and confirmatory factor analyses of the demographic and health surveys. *Frontiers in Psychology, 9*(994), 1–10. doi:10.3389/fpsyg.2018.00994 PMID:29971030

Assembly, G. (2030). *A/RES/71/313: Work of the Statistical Commission pertaining to the 2030 Agenda for Sustainable Development*.

Auzzir, Z., Haigh, R., & Amaratunga, D. (2018). Impacts of disaster on SMEs in Malaysia. *Procedia Engineering, 212*, 1131–1138. doi:10.1016/j.proeng.2018.01.146

Azam, M. S. E., & Abdullah, M. A. (2024). SMEs, Employment Generation, and Islamic Finance. [IJIEF]. *International Journal of Islamic Economics and Finance, 7*(1), 433–454.

Babović, M. (2023). *Progress report on the implementation od sustainable development goals by in the Republic of Serbia*. Statistical Office of the Republic of Serbia.

Babu, G. S., & Sridevi, K. (2019). A study on issues and challenges of startups in India. *International Journal of Financial Management and Economics, 2*(1), 44–48. doi:10.33545/26179210.2019.v2.i1a.16

Baek, I. M., & Okawa, T. (2001). Foreign exchange rates and Japanese foreign direct investment in Asia. *Journal of Economics and Business, 53*(1), 69–84. doi:10.1016/S0148-6195(00)00038-2

Baguma, R., Carvalho, J.Á., Cledou, G., Estevez, E., Finquelievich, S., Janowski, T., Lopes, N. and Millard, J. (2016). *Knowledge Societies Policy Handbook*.

Baillie, R. T., Bollerslev, T., & Mikkelsen, H. O. (1996). Fractionally integrated generalized autoregressive conditional heteroskedasticity. *Journal of Econometrics*, *74*(1), 3–30. doi:10.1016/S0304-4076(95)01749-6

Balasubramanyam, V. N., & Mahambre, V. (2001). *India's Economic Reforms and the Manufacturing Sector*. (Lancaster University Working Paper 2001/010).

Banerjee, S., Alok, S., & George, B. (2020). Determinants of women empowerment as measured by domestic decision-making: perspective from a developing economy. *International Symposia in Economic Theory and Econometrics*. In *Advanced Issues in the Economics of Emerging Markets* (Vol. 27, pp. 1–12). Emerald Group Publishing Limited. doi:10.1108/S1571-038620200000027001

Banger, N., Pallavi, K., & Shetty, S. J. (2022). A Review Paper on Cloud Computing Architecture, Types, Advantages and Disadvantages. International Journal of Advanced Research in science [IJARSCT]. *Tongxin Jishu*, *2*(2), 14–22. doi:10.48175/IJARSCT-3144

Bank Negara Malaysia. (2006). *Bank Negara Malaysia Annual Report 2006*. Bank Negara Malaysia.

Barrell, R., & Pain, N. (1996). An Econometric Analysis of U.S. Foreign Direct Investment. *The Review of Economics and Statistics*, *78*(2), 200. doi:10.2307/2109921

Bayeh, E. (2016), The role of empowering women and achieving gender equality to the sustainable development of Ethiopia, *Pacific Science Review B: Humanities and Social Sciences,* 37-42. doi:10.1016/j.psrb.2016.09.013

Bertasini, M. (2020). *Startups value proposition in the tourism and art sector: an empirical analysis of digital and innovative trends.*

Bhati, Dr. Bharat. (2021). An Empirical Study on Environmental Seriousness and Green Product Purchasing. *Cosmos An International Journal of Management*, *10*(2), 22–29. doi:10.46360/cosmos.mgt.420211005

Biswas, D., Saha, S. K., Sarkar, A. P., Mondal, T., Haldar, D., & Sarkar, G. N. (2020). Participation in household decision-making among married women in rural and urban areas of Bankura, West Bengal: A comparative study. *International Journal of Health & Allied Sciences*, *9*(2), 170–174. doi:10.4103/ijhas.IJHAS_108_19

Blonigen, B. A. (1997). Firm-Specific Assets and the Link between Exchange Rates and Foreign Direct Investment. *The American Economic Review*, *87*(3), 447–465.

Bloom, D., & Canning, D. (2003). The Health and Poverty of Nations: From theory to practice. *Journal of Human Development*, *4*(1), 47–71. doi:10.1080/1464988032000051487

Boateng, R. N., Tawiah, V., & Tackie, G. (2022). Corporate governance and voluntary disclosures in annual reports: A post-International Financial Reporting Standard adoption evidence from an emerging capital market. *International Journal of Accounting & Information Management*, *30*(2), 252–276. doi:10.1108/IJAIM-10-2021-0220

Borensztein, E., De Gregorio, J., & Lee, J.-W. (1998). How does foreign direct investment affect economic growth? *Journal of International Economics*, *45*(1), 115–135. doi:10.1016/S0022-1996(97)00033-0

Boström, M., Andersson, E., Berg, M., Gustafsson, K., Gustavsson, E., Hysing, E., Lidskog, R., Löfmarck, E., Ojala, M., Olsson, J., Singleton, B., Svenberg, S., Uggla, Y., & Öhman, J. (2018). Conditions for transformative learning for sustainable development: A theoretical review and approach. *Sustainability (Basel)*, *10*(12), 4479. doi:10.3390/su10124479

Broadstock, D. C., Chan, K., Cheng, L. T., & Wang, X. (2021). The role of ESG performance during times of financial crisis: Evidence from COVID-19 in China. *Finance Research Letters*, *38*, 101716. doi:10.1016/j.frl.2020.101716 PMID:32837385

Brown, K., & Corbera, E. (2003). Exploring equity and sustainable development in the new carbon economy. *Climate Policy*, *3*, S41–S56. doi:10.1016/j.clipol.2003.10.004

Brundtland, G. H. (1987). *Our Common Future World Commission On Environment And Developement.*

Bruton, G. D., Zahra, S. A., Van de Ven, A. H., & Hitt, M. A. (2022). Indigenous theory uses, abuses, and future. *Journal of Management Studies*, *59*(4), 1057–1073. doi:10.1111/joms.12755

Bryan, B. A., Gao, L., Ye, Y., Sun, X., Connor, J. D., Crossman, N. D., Stafford-Smith, M., Wu, J., He, C., Yu, D., Liu, Z., Li, A., Huang, Q., Ren, H., Deng, X., Zheng, H., Niu, J., Han, G., & Hou, X. (2018). China's response to a national land-system sustainability emergency. *Nature*, *559*(7713), 193–204. doi:10.1038/s41586-018-0280-2 PMID:29995865

Bulsara, H. P., Gandhi, S., & Chandwani, J. (2015). Social Entrepreneurship in India: An Exploratory Study. *International Journal of Innovation*, *3*(1), 7–16. doi:10.5585/iji.v3i1.20

Burck, J., Höhne, N., Hagemann, M., Gonzales-Zuñiga, S., Leipold, G., Marten, F., Schindler, H., Barnard, S., & Nakhooda, S. (2016). *Brown to green: Assessing the g20 transition to a low-carbon economy*. Climate Transparency.

Byrne, B. M. (2010). *Structural Equation Modeling with Amos Basic Concepts, Applications, and Programming* (2nd ed.). New York Taylor and Francis Group.

Cahapin, E. L., Malabag, B. A., Samson, B. D., & Santiago, C. S. Jr. (2022). Stakeholders' Awareness and Acceptance of The Institution's Vision, Mission and Goals and Information Technology Program Objectives in A State University in The Philippines. *Globus Journal of Progressive Education*, *12*(1), 51–60. doi:10.46360/globus.edu.220221006

Cai, W., & Zhou, X. (2014). On the drivers of eco-innovation: Empirical evidence from China. *Journal of Cleaner Production*, *79*, 239–248. doi:10.1016/j.jclepro.2014.05.035

Cai, Y., & Lattu, A. (2022). Triple Helix or Quadruple Helix: Which Model of Innovation to Choose for Empirical Studies? *Minerva*, *60*(2), 257–280. doi:10.1007/s11024-021-09453-6

Carayannis, E. G., & Campbell, D. F. (2014). Developed democracies versus emerging autocracies: Arts, democracy, and innovation in Quadruple Helix innovation systems. *Journal of Innovation and Entrepreneurship*, *3*(1), 12. doi:10.1186/s13731-014-0012-2

Carayannis, E. G., & Campbell, D. F. J. (2009). "Mode 3" and "Quadruple Helix": Toward a 21st century fractal innovation ecosystem. *International Journal of Technology Management*, *46*(3/4), 201. doi:10.1504/IJTM.2009.023374

Carayannis, E. G., Grigoroudis, E., Stamati, D., & Valvi, T. (2021). Social Business Model Innovation: A Quadruple/Quintuple Helix-Based Social Innovation Ecosystem. *IEEE Transactions on Engineering Management*, *68*(1), 235–248. doi:10.1109/TEM.2019.2914408

Carroll, A. B. (1979). A Three-Dimensional Conceptual Model of Corporate Performance. *Academy of Management Review*, *4*(4), 497–505. doi:10.2307/257850

Carroll, A. B. (1999). Corporate Social Responsibility: Evolution of a Definitional Construct. *Business & Society*, *38*(3), 268–295. doi:10.1177/000765039903800303

Carroll, A. B. (2016). Carroll's pyramid of CSR: Taking another look. *International Journal of Corporate Social Responsibility*, *1*(1), 3. doi:10.1186/s40991-016-0004-6

Casey, C. (2024). *Governing the Firm in the Social Interest: Corporate Governance Reimagined*. Taylor & Francis.

Caves, R. E. (1996). *Multinational Enterprise and Economic Analysis* (2nd ed.). Cambridge University Press.

Cekrezi, A (2015), Factors Affecting Performance of Commercial Banks in Albania, *The European Proceedings of Social & Behavioral Sciences EpSBS*, eISSN: 2357-1330, 2015. doi:10.15405/epsbs.2015.05.3

Center for Climate and Energy Solutions. (2022, December 1). *Global Emissions*. C2ES. https://www.c2es.org/content/international-emissions/

Chaaben, N., Elleuch, Z., Hamdi, B., & Kahouli, B. (2022). Green economy performance and sustainable development achievement: Empirical evidence from Saudi Arabia. *Environment, Development and Sustainability, 26*(1), 1–16. doi:10.1007/s10668-022-02722-8 PMID:36320556

Chang, E., Chin, H., & Lee, J. W. (2022). Pre-crisis commitment human resource management and employees' attitudes in a global pandemic: The role of trust in the government. *Human Resource Management, 61*(3), 373–387. doi:10.1002/hrm.22097

Chatterjee, N. (2022). Households' Willingness to Pay for Improved Water Supply System in the Dryland areas of West Bengal – an estimation using Double-Bounded Dichotomous-Choice Model. *Economic Affairs, 67*(5), 787–795. doi:10.46852/0424-2513.5.2022.12

Chatterjee, T., Bhattacharjee, K., & Das, R. C. (2024). Long-run and Short-run Dynamic Linkages Among Capacity Utilization, Inflation and Per Capita Income: Theoretical and Empirical Enquiries for Panel of Countries. *Global Business Review, 09721509231219318*, 09721509231219318. Advance online publication. doi:10.1177/09721509231219318

Chaves, R., & Monzón, J. L. (2012). Beyond the crisis: The social economy, prop of a new model of sustainable economic development. *Service Business, 6*(1), 5–26. doi:10.1007/s11628-011-0125-7

Chen, L., & Ulmer, J. (2021). Volatility and Risk – FIGARCH Modelling of Cryptocurrencies, https://lup.lub.lu.se/luur/download?func=downloadFile&recordOId=9050072&fileOId=9050077

Cheng, B., Ioannou, I., & Serafeim, G. (2007). *Corporate social responsibility and access to finance.* (Harvard Business School Working Paper, No. 09-047). https://doi.org/ doi:10.2139/ssrn.1253170

Cheng, S., & Ali, S. (2023). A tiered pathway toward sustainability: The role of public administrators in advancing social equity in US local governments. *Public Administration Review, 83*(4), 878–894. doi:10.1111/puar.13617

Chenhall, R. H., & Moers, F. (2015). The role of innovation in the evolution of management accounting and its integration into management control. *Accounting, Organizations and Society, 47*, 1–13. doi:10.1016/j.aos.2015.10.002

Chen, J. H., & Huang, Y. F. (2013). The study of the relationship between carbon dioxide (CO2) emission and economic growth. *Journal of International and Global Economic Studies, 6*(2), 45–61.

Chen, J., & Xie, L. (2019). Industrial policy, structural transformation and economic growth: Evidence from China. *Frontiers of Business Research in China, 13*(1), 1–19. doi:10.1186/s11782-019-0065-y

Cheong, C., & Choi, J. (2020). Green Bonds: A Survey. *Journal of Derivatives and Quantitative Studies., 28*(4), 175–189. doi:10.1108/JDQS-09-2020-0024

Chew, R., & Chew, S. B. (2008). A study of SMEs in Singapore. *Journal of Enterprising Communities: People and Places in the Global Economy.*

Choi, I. (2001). Unit root tests for panel data. *Journal of International Money and Finance, 20*(2), 249–272. doi:10.1016/S0261-5606(00)00048-6

Choudhary, A., & Singh, V. (2020). In N. Capaldi, S. O. Idowu, & R. Schmidpeter (Eds.), *Exploring the Impact of Corporate Social Responsibility on Poverty Reduction BT - Responsible Business in a Changing World: New Management Approaches for Sustainable Development (B. Díaz Díaz* (pp. 329–338). Springer International Publishing., doi:10.1007/978-3-030-36970-5_18

Chourabi, H., Nam, T., Walker, S., Gil-Garcia, J. R., Mellouli, S., Nahon, K., . . . Scholl, H. J. (2012, January). Understanding smart cities: An integrative framework. In *2012 45th Hawaii international conference on system sciences* (pp. 2289-2297). IEEE.

Chowdhury, E. K., Dhar, B. K., Gazi, M., & Issa, A. (2022). Impact of Remittance on Economic Progress: Evidence from Low-Income Asian Frontier Countries. *Journal of the Knowledge Economy*, 1–26.

Cini, M., & Borragán, N. P. S. (2022). *European Union politics*. Oxford University Press. doi:10.1093/hepl/9780198862239.001.0001

Clapp, C., Alfsen, K., Torvanger, A., & Lund, H. (2015). Commentary: Influence of Climate Science on Financial Decisions. *Nature Climate Change*, *5*(2), 83–85. doi:10.1038/nclimate2495

Clemente, Paul Timothy A. (2023). Operations Strategy of Air Bed and Breakfast (AIRBNB): Basis for An Enhanced Business Model. *Globus An International Journal of Management & IT, 14*(2), 06-25. doi:10.46360/globus.mgt.120231002

Cochran, S. J., Mansur, I., & Odusami, B. (2012). Volatility persistence in metal returns: A FIGARCH approach. *Journal of Economics and Business*, *64*(4), 287–305. doi:10.1016/j.jeconbus.2012.03.001

Cortellini, G., & Panetta, I. (2021). Green Bond: A Systematic Literature Review for Future Research Agendas. *Journal of Risk and Financial Management*, *14*(589), 1–29. doi:10.3390/jrfm14120589

Corvello, V., Verteramo, S., Nocella, I., & Ammirato, S. (2023). Thrive during a crisis: The role of digital technologies in fostering antifragility in small and medium-sized enterprises. *Journal of Ambient Intelligence and Humanized Computing*, *14*(11), 14681–14693. doi:10.1007/s12652-022-03816-x PMID:35340698

Crescini, C. L., & Avila, E. C. (2023). Perceived Effects of Covid-19 Crisis on Budget Consumption of Filipino Families. *Cosmos An International Journal of Management*, *12*(2), 105–115.

Cushman, D. (1985). Real Exchange Rate Risk, Expectations, and the Level of Direct Investment. *The Review of Economics and Statistics*, *67*(2), 297–308. doi:10.2307/1924729

D'Amato, D., & Korhonen, J. (2021). Integrating the green economy, circular economy and bioeconomy in a strategic sustainability framework. *Ecological Economics*, *188*, 107143. doi:10.1016/j.ecolecon.2021.107143

Dabeedooal, Y. J., Dindoyal, V., Allam, Z., & Jones, D. S. (2019). Smart tourism as a pillar for sustainable urban development: An alternate smart city strategy from Mauritius. *Smart Cities*, *2*(2), 153–162. doi:10.3390/smartcities2020011

Dadras, O., & Hazratzai, M. (2023). Survey based women empowerment index for Afghanistan (SWEI A): An explanatory and confirmatory factor analyses. *Social Indicators Research*, *170*(3), 1059–1074. doi:10.1007/s11205-023-03241-3

DamodaranK. (2021). Women in decision making roles in India: An analytical study. *Human Rights International Research Journal*, 9(2): 101-109. doi:10.6084/m9.figshare.20324652

Daryakin, A. A., Sklyarov, A. A., & Khasanov, K. A. (2019). *Nº 04 - Ano 2019* (Special Edition, Vol. 8). The role of Key Performance Indicators (KPI) in Banking Activities, Periódico do Núcleo de Estudos e Pesquisas sobre Gênero e Direito Centro de Ciências Jurídicas - Universidade Federal da Paraíba. doi:10.22478/ufpb.2179-7137.2019v8n4.48458

Das, D. (2013). Tourism Industry in North-East Indian States: Prospects and Problems. *Global Research Methodology Journal, 2*(7), 1–6.

Dash, D. P., Sethi, N., & Barik, P. C. (2023). Dynamics of Foreign Aid and Human Development in South and South-East Asia: Analyzing the Effectiveness of Macro-Institutional Factors. *International Economic Journal, 37*(4), 646–674. doi:10.1080/10168737.2023.2261011

Das, S. (2017). Economic growth and women empowerment through education: A study on santal at Birbhum, West Bengal. *International Journal of Engineering Development and Research, 3*(5), 392–398. https://www.ijedr.org/papers/IJEDR1703057.pdf

David, D., Gopalan, S., & Ramachandran, S. (2020). *The Startup Environment and Funding Activity in India.* (Working Paper). Asian Development Bank Institute, Tokyo, June.

Davis, L. M., Schensul, S. L., Schensul, J., Verma, R., Nastasi, B. K., & Singh, R. (2014). Women's empowerment and its differential impact on health in low-income communities in Mumbai, India. *Global Public Health: An International Journal for Research, Policy and Practice, 9*(5), 481–494. doi:10.1080/17441692.2014.904919 PMID:24766149

De Mello, L. R. Jr. (1997). Foreign Direct Investment in Developing Countries and Growth: A Selective Survey. *The Journal of Development Studies, 34*(1), 1–34. doi:10.1080/00220389708422501

de Melo Neto, J. J., & Fontgalland, I. L. (2023). The BRICS in the sustainable agenda: Performance analysis of ESG indices in the financial markets in Brazil, China, India and South Africa. *International Journal of Business, Economics and Management, 10*(1), 1-11. https://ideas.repec.org/a/pkp/ijobem/v10y2023i1p1-11id3325.html

Dees, S. (1998). Foreign direct investment in China: Determinants and effects. *Economics of Planning, 31*(2/3), 175–194. doi:10.1023/A:1003576930461

Del Baldo, M. (2010). Corporate social responsibility and corporate governance in Italian SMEs: Towards a territorial model based on small champions of CSR? *International Journal of Sustainable Society, 2*(3), 215–247. doi:10.1504/IJSSOC.2010.034762

Department of Public Enterprises. (2010). Guidelines on Corporate Social Responsibility for CPSES. In *Corporate Social Responsibility for Central Public Sector Enterprises.* http://pib.nic.in/newsite/erelease.aspx?relid=68604

Deschryver, P., & Mariz, F. (2020). What Future for the Green Bond Market? How Can Policymakers, Companies, and Investors Unlock the Potential of the Green Bond Market? *Journal of Risk and Financial Management, 13*(61), 1–26. https://www.climatebonds.net/market/data/. doi:10.3390/jrfm13030061

Dhone, N., & Perumandla, S. (2024). Integrating Corporate Governance and Sustainability Practices in Indian SMEs Amid Industry 4.0: A Systematic Review. *IUP Journal of Corporate Governance, 23*(1).

Dimes, R., & Molinari, M. (2023). *Non-financial reporting and corporate governance: a conceptual framework.* Sustainability Accounting, Management and Policy Journal.

Dong, F., Wang, Y., Su, B., Hua, Y., & Zhang, Y. (2019). The process of peak CO_2 emissions in developed economies: A perspective of industrialization and urbanization. *Resources, Conservation and Recycling, 141*, 61–75. doi:10.1016/j.resconrec.2018.10.010

Douglas, J. L. (2008), The Role of a Banking System in Nation-Building, *Maine Law Review, 60.* https://digitalcommons.mainelaw.maine.edu/mlr/vol60/iss2/14

Du Pisani, J. A. (2006). Sustainable development – historical roots of the concept. *Environmental Sciences (Lisse), 3*(2), 83–96. doi:10.1080/15693430600688831

Du, X. L., & Chen, S. J. (2015), The application of factor analysis method in performance evaluation of listed banking business, *Proceedings of the 2015 International Conference on Education, Management, Information and Medicine, Advances in Economics, Business and Management Research.* Atlantis. https://www.atlantis-press.com/proceedings/emim-15/21527 doi:10.2991/emim-15.2015.156

Duarah, I., & Mili, B. (2013). Tourism Potentiality in North East India. *International Journal ofScience and Research (IJSR), 2*(10), 1-3.

Đuričin, S., Beraha, I., Jovanović, O., Mosurović Ružičić, M., Lazarević-Moravčević, M., & Paunović, M. (2022). The Efficiency of National Innovation Policy Programs: The Case of Serbia. *Sustainability (Basel), 14*(14), 8483. doi:10.3390/su14148483

Dutta, A. (2016). Start-up Initiative. *IOSR Journal of Business and Management, 15010*(2), 93–97. doi:10.9790/487X-15010020293-97

Dwivedi, D. M. C. (2022). A Study on Advanced Innovation Managing Risk and Rewards. *Cosmos Journal of Engineering & Technology, 12*(1), 45–47.

Dwivedi, M. C. (2022). Assessing the Socioeconomic Implications of Climate Change. *Cosmos An International Journal of Art & Higher Education, 11*(2), 20–23.

Dwivedi, M. C. (2022). Assessing The Socioeconomic Implications of Climate Change. *Cosmos An International Journal of Art & Higher Education, 11*(2), 20–23. doi:10.46360/cosmos.ahe.520222004

Dwivedi, Y. K., Hughes, L., Kar, A. K., Baabdullah, A. M., Grover, P., Abbas, R., Andreini, D., Abumoghli, I., Barlette, Y., Bunker, D., Chandra Kruse, L., Constantiou, I., Davison, R. M., De', R., Dubey, R., Fenby-Taylor, H., Gupta, B., He, W., Kodama, M., & Wade, M. (2022). Climate Change and COP26: Are digital technologies and information management part of the problem or the solution? An editorial reflection and call to action. *International Journal of Information Management, 63*, 102456. doi:10.1016/j.ijinfomgt.2021.102456

Dynamic CSR Report. (n.d.). CSR. https://www.csr.gov.in/content/csr/global/master/home/ExploreCsrData/dynamic-csr-report-search.html

Edelman. (2020). Washington, DC: Depicting trans spatialities. In *Transvitalities* (pp. 30–56). Routledge. doi:10.4324/9781351128025-3

Edward, J. J., & Ngasamiaku, W. M. (2021). An Empirical Investigation of the Role of Manufacturing and Economic Growth: The Case Study of Tanzania. *ORSEA Journal, 11*(1).

Ejsmont, K., Gladysz, B., & Kluczek, A. (2020). Impact of industry 4.0 on sustainability-bibliometric literature review. *Sustainability (Basel), 12*(14), 5650. doi:10.3390/su12145650

Elfaki, K. E., Khan, Z., Kirikkaleli, D., & Khan, N. (2022). On the nexus between industrialization and carbon emissions: Evidence from ASEAN+ 3 economies. *Environmental Science and Pollution Research International, 29*(21), 1–10. doi:10.1007/s11356-022-18560-0 PMID:35013968

Elken, M., & Wollscheid, S. (2016). The relationship between research and education: typologies and indicators. In Research and Education.

Ellili, N. O. D. (2023). Impact of corporate governance on environmental, social, and governance disclosure: Any difference between financial and non-financial companies? *Corporate Social Responsibility and Environmental Management, 30*(2), 858–873. doi:10.1002/csr.2393

Eltweri, A., Faccia, A., & Foster, S. (2022). International Standards on Auditing (ISAs) Adoption: An Institutional Perspective. *Administrative Sciences*, *12*(3), 119. doi:10.3390/admsci12030119

Employment to population ratio, 15+, total (%) (modeled ILO estimate) - India. (n.d.). World Bank. https://data.worldbank.org/indicator/SL.EMP.TOTL.SP.ZS?locations=IN

Erumban, A. A., & De Vries, G. J. (2021). *Industrialization in developing countries: is it related to poverty reduction?* (UNU-WIDER Working Paper No. 2021/172). doi:10.35188/UNU-WIDER/2021/112-9

Esa, E., Mohamad, N. R., Wan Zakaria, W. Z., & Ilias, N. (2022). Are corporate governance and reputation two sides of the same Coin? Empirical Evidence from Malaysia. *The Journal of Asian Finance, Economics, and Business*, *9*(1), 219–228.

Escobar, A. (1995). Encountering Development. In Encountering Development. doi:10.1515/9781400839926

ESG. (2021). *How to Calculate an ESG Score for a Bank*. ESG. https://www.esgthereport.com/how-to-calculate-an-esg-score-for-a-bank/

EtzkowitzH.LeydesdorffL. (1995). The Triple Helix — University-Industry-Government Relations: A Laboratory for Knowledge Based Economic Development. *EASST Review*, *14*(1), 14–19. https://ssrn.com/abstract=2480085

European Commission. (2021). *The EU's 2021-2027 long-term Budget and NextGenerationEU. Facts and figures*. (Issue September). Europea. https://op.europa.eu/en/publication-detail/-/publication/d3e77637-a963-11eb-9585-01aa75ed71a1/language-en

European Union. (2006). Community Framework for State Aid for Research and Development and. *Official Journal of the European Union*, 1–26. https://eur-lex.europa.eu/legal-content/EN/TXT/PDF/?uri=CELEX:52006XC1230(01)

Eurostat. (2022). *R&D Expenditure*. Eurostat. https://ec.europa.eu/eurostat/statistics-explained/index.php?title=R%26D_expenditure&oldid=551418#:~:text=In 2020%2C EU Research and,year when it recorded 2.23%25.&text=In 2020%2C the EU spent,compared with 1.97%25 in 2010.

Facevicova, K., & Kynclova, P. (2020). How Industrial Development Matters To The Well-Being Of The Population, Some Statistical Evidence. United Nations Industrial Development Organization. Vienna: United Nations Industrial Development Organization.

Fibryanti, Y. V., & Nurcholidah, L. (2020), Analysis of Factors that affect the Financial Performance of the Banks, *Proceedings of the 3rd Green Development International Conference (GDIC, 2020) Advances in Engineering Research*, Atlantis press. DOI:10.2991/aer.k.210825.087

Filho, W. L., Amaro, N., Avila, L. V., Brandli, L., Damke, L. I., Vasconcelos, C. R. P., Hernandez-Diaz, P. M., Frankenberger, F., Fritzen, B., Velazquez, L., & Salvia, A. (2021). Mapping sustainability initiatives in higher education institutions in Latin America. *Journal of Cleaner Production*, *315*, 128093. doi:10.1016/j.jclepro.2021.128093

Filieri, R., D'Amico, E., Destefanis, A., Paolucci, E., & Raguseo, E. (2021). Artificial intelligence (AI) for tourism: An European-based study on successful AI tourism start-ups. *International Journal of Contemporary Hospitality Management*, *33*(11), 4099–4125. doi:10.1108/IJCHM-02-2021-0220

Findlay, R. (1978). Relative Backwardness, Direct Foreign Investment, and the Transfer of Technology: A Simple Dynamic Model. *The Quarterly Journal of Economics*, *92*(1), 1–16. doi:10.2307/1885996

Fox, T. (2004). Corporate Social Responsibility and Development: In quest of an agenda. *Development*, *47*(3), 29–36. doi:10.1057/palgrave.development.1100064

Friedman, M. (n.d.). A Friedman doctrine-- The Social Responsibility of Business Is to Increase Its Profits. *The New York Times*. https://www.nytimes.com/1970/09/13/archives/a-friedman-doctrine-the-social-responsibility-of-business-is-to.html

Froot, K. A., & Stein, J. C. (1991). Exchange Rates and Foreign Direct Investment: An Imperfect Capital Markets Approach. *The Quarterly Journal of Economics*, *106*(4), 1191–1217. doi:10.2307/2937961

Fuss, S., Szolgayova, J., Obersteiner, M., & Gusti, M. (2008). Investment under market and climate policy uncertainty. *Applied Energy*, *85*(8), 708–721. doi:10.1016/j.apenergy.2008.01.005

Ganda, F. (2019). The impact of industrial practice on carbon emissions in the BRICS: A panel quantile regression analysis. *Progress in Industrial Ecology. Progress in Industrial Ecology*, *13*(1), 84–107. doi:10.1504/PIE.2019.098813

Gautam, R. S., Bhimavarapu, V. M., Rastogi, S., Kappal, J. M., Patole, H., & Pushp, A. (2023). Corporate Social Responsibility Funding and Its Impact on India’s Sustainable Development: Using the Poverty Score as a Moderator. In Journal of Risk and Financial Management (Vol. 16, Issue 2). doi:10.3390/jrfm16020090

GavriilidisK. (2021). Measuring Climate Policy Uncertainty. SSRN. https://ssrn.com/abstract=3847388 doi:10.2139/ssrn.3847388

Ghalanos, A. (2020). *Introduction to the rugarch package*. (Version 1.4-3). Cran R Project. https://cran.r-project.org/web/packages/rugarch/vignettes/Introduction_to _the_rugarch_package.pdf

Ghouri, A. M. (2023). *Big Data and Predictive Analytics and Malaysian Micro*. Small and Medium Businesses.

Ghouse, S. M., & Chaudhary, M. (2024). Artificial Intelligence (AI) for Tourism Start-Ups. In Innovative Technologies for Increasing Service Productivity (pp. 161-178). IGI Global. doi:10.4018/979-8-3693-2019-8.ch010

Glass, A. J., & Saggi, K. (1999). Foreign Direct Investment and the Nature of R&D. *The Canadian Journal of Economics. Revue Canadienne d'Economique*, *32*(1), 92. doi:10.2307/136397

Godin, B. (2003). The emergence of S&T indicators: Why did governments supplement statistics with indicators? *Research Policy*, *32*(4), 679–691. doi:10.1016/S0048-7333(02)00032-X

Golightly, L., Chang, V., Xu, Q. A., Gao, X., & Liu, B. S. (2022). Adoption of cloud computing as innovation in the organization. *International Journal of Engineering Business Management*, *14*, 18479790221093992. doi:10.1177/18479790221093992

Gonçalves, H., Magalhães, V. S., Ferreira, L. M., & Arantes, A. (2024). Overcoming Barriers to Sustainable Supply Chain Management in Small and Medium-Sized Enterprises: A Multi-Criteria Decision-Making Approach. *Sustainability (Basel)*, *16*(2), 506. doi:10.3390/su16020506

Gounder, R., & Xing, Z. (2012). Impact of education and health on poverty reduction: Monetary and non-monetary evidence from Fiji. *Economic Modelling*, *29*(3), 787–794. doi:10.1016/j.econmod.2012.01.018

Goyal, S., Agrawal, A., & Sergi, B. S. (2020). Social entrepreneurship for scalable solutions addressing sustainable development goals (SDGs) at BoP in India. *Qualitative Research in Organizations and Management*, *16*(3/4), 509–529. doi:10.1108/QROM-07-2020-1992

Grandori, A. (2022). Constitutionalizing the corporation. In *The corporation: Rethinking the iconic form of business organization*. Emerald Publishing Limited. doi:10.1108/S0733-558X20220000078004

Gregori, P., & Holzmann, P. (2020). Digital sustainable entrepreneurship: A business model perspective on embedding digital technologies for social and environmental value creation. *Journal of Cleaner Production*, *272*, 122817. doi:10.1016/j.jclepro.2020.122817

Gretzel, U., Zhong, L., & Koo, C. (2016). Application of smart tourism to cities. *International Journal of Tourism Cities*, *2*(2). Advance online publication. doi:10.1108/IJTC-04-2016-0007

Griffin, K., & McKinley, T. (1994). Human Development and Sustainable Development BT - Implementing a Human Development Strategy (K. Griffin & T. McKinley (Eds.); pp. 96–102). Palgrave Macmillan UK. doi:10.1007/978-1-349-23543-8_6

Griggs, D., Stafford Smith, M., Rockström, J., Öhman, M. C., Gaffney, O., Glaser, G., Kanie, N., Noble, I., Steffen, W., & Shyamsundar, P. (2014). An integrated framework for sustainable development goals. *Ecology and Society*, *19*(4), art49. doi:10.5751/ES-07082-190449

Grinsted, A., Moore, J. C., & Jevrejeva, S. (2004). Application of the cross wavelet transform and wavelet coherence to geophysical time series. *Nonlinear Processes in Geophysics*, *11*(5/6), 561–566. doi:10.5194/npg-11-561-2004

Gudwani, S., & Kaur, N. (2023). A Study, Challenges and Issues of Indian Startups on Economic Growth. *European Chemical Bulletin*, *12*(S3), 6590–6595.

Güldenberg, S., & Leitner, K.-H. (2008). *Strategy Processes in Research and Development Organisations: Why Knowledge Management is still more isolated than integrated.*

Gungor, H., & Simon, A. U. (2017). Energy consumption, finance and growth: The role of urbanization and industrialization in South Africa. *International Journal of Energy Economics and Policy*, *7*(3), 268–276.

Guo, H., Huang, L., & Liang, D. (2022). Further promotion of sustainable development goals using science, technology, and innovation. *Innovation (Cambridge (Mass.))*, *3*(6), 100325. doi:10.1016/j.xinn.2022.100325 PMID:36193207

Guo, J. Q., & Trivedi, P. K. (2002). Firm-Specific Assets and the Link between Exchange Rates and Japanese Foreign Direct Investment in the United States: A Re-examination. *The Japanese Economic Review*, *53*(3), 337–349. doi:10.1111/1468-5876.00232

Guo, Y., Liu, H., & Chai, Y. (2014). The embedding convergence of smart cities and tourism internet of things in China: An advance perspective. [AHTR]. *Advances in Hospitality and Tourism Research*, *2*(1), 54–69.

Gupta, A. C., & Chatterjee, N. (2021). Economic Values for the Environment with special reference to the Contingent Valuation Method, in Environmental Management: Issues and Concerns in Developing Countries, Springer and Capital Publishing Company. doi:10.1007/978-3-030-62529-0_14

Gupta, S. (2021). A Review on Social Entrepreneurship and Challenges in India. [IJIREM]. *International Journal of Innovative Research in Engineering & Management*, *8*(6), 298–301.

Gupta, T., & Khan, S. (2023). Education and International Collaboration in The Digital Age. *Globus Journal of Progressive Education*, *13*(1), 79–87.

Gusakov, A. A., Haque, A. U., & Jogia, A. V. (2020). Mechanisms to support open innovation in smart tourism destinations: Managerial perspective and implications. *Polish Journal of Management Studies*, *21*(2), 142–161. doi:10.17512/pjms.2020.21.2.11

H. W. Arndt. (1987). *ECONOMIC DEVELOPMENT THE HISTORY OF AN IDEA.* The University of Chicago Press Chicago and London. doi:10.4324/9781315774206-29

Haider, S., Adil, M., & Ganaie, A. (2019). Does industrialisation and urbanisation affect energy consumption: A relative study of India and Iran? *Economic Bulletin*, *39*(1), 176–185.

Hair, J. F., Black, W. C., Babin, B. J., & Anderson, R. E. (2010). *Multivariate Data Analysis* (7th ed.). Pearson., https://books.google.co.in/books/about/Multivariate_Data_Analysis.html?id=SLRPLgAACAAJ&redir_esc=y

Hajmohammad, S., Klassen, R. D., & Vachon, S. (2024). Managing supplier sustainability risk: An experimental study. *Supply Chain Management*, 29(1), 50–67. doi:10.1108/SCM-02-2023-0106

Hamad, S. B., & Karoui, A. (2011). The SMEs governance mechanisms practices and financial performance: Case of Tunisian industrial SMEs. *International Journal of Business and Management*, 6(7), 216–225.

Hanaysha, J. R., Al-Shaikh, M. E., Joghee, S., & Alzoubi, H. M. (2022). Impact of innovation capabilities on business sustainability in small and medium enterprises. *FIIB Business Review*, 11(1), 67–78. doi:10.1177/23197145211042232

Haq, M. U. (1995). Reflections On Human Development. In Reflections On Human Development. doi:10.1093/oso/9780195101911.001.0001

Hariram, N. P., Mekha, K. B., Suganthan, V., & Sudhakar, K. (2023). An Integrated Socio-Economic-Environmental Model to Address Sustainable Development and Sustainability. *Sustainability (Basel)*, 15(13), 10682. doi:10.3390/su151310682

Harris, J.M. (2000). Basic principles of sustainable development. *Dimensions of Sustainable Development*, 21-41.

Harrison, C., & Donnelly, I. A. (2011, September). *A theory of smart cities*. In *Proceedings of the 55th Annual Meeting of the ISSS-2011*, Hull, UK.

Harris, R. S., & Ravenscraft, D. (1991). The Role of Acquisitions in Foreign Direct Investment: Evidence from the U.S. Stock Market. *The Journal of Finance*, 46(3), 825–844. doi:10.1111/j.1540-6261.1991.tb03767.x

Hayzoun, H., Garnier, C., Durrieu, G., Lenoble, V., Bancon-Montigny, C., Ouammou, A., & Mounier, S. (2014). Impact of rapid urbanisation and industrialisation on river sediment metal contamination. *Environmental Monitoring and Assessment*, 186(5), 2851–2865. doi:10.1007/s10661-013-3585-5 PMID:24389842

Herath, D. (2009). The Discourse of Development: Has it reached maturity? *Third World Quarterly*, 30(8), 1449–1464. doi:10.1080/01436590903279216

Hewa, S. I., Chen, J., & Mala, R. (2023). Corporate responses to climate change risks: Evidence from Australia. *Australasian Journal of Environmental Management*, 30(2), 1–27. doi:10.1080/14486563.2023.2220297

Hisham, S. A. H. S. (2023). *Impact of technology adoption as a key growth contributor for women micro businesses in Malaysia*. University of Wales Trinity Saint David.

Hitka, M., Lorincová, S., Ližbetinová, L., Bartáková, G. P., & Merková, M. (2017). Cluster analysis used as the strategic advantage of human resource management in small and medium-sized enterprises in the wood-processing industry. *BioResources*, 12(4), 7884–7897. doi:10.15376/biores.12.4.7884-7897

Ho, C. Y., & Siu, K. W. (2007). A dynamic equilibrium of electricity consumption and GDP in Hong Kong: An empirical investigation. *Energy Policy*, 35(4), 2507–2513. doi:10.1016/j.enpol.2006.09.018

Holzmann, P., Breitenecker, R. J., Schwarz, E. J., & Gregori, P. (2020). Business model design for novel technologies in nascent industries: An investigation of 3D printing service providers. *Technological Forecasting and Social Change*, 159, 120193. doi:10.1016/j.techfore.2020.120193

Hong, Y., Zhang, R., & Zhang, F. (2024). Time-varying causality impact of economic policy uncertainty on stock market returns: Global evidence from developed and emerging countries. *International Review of Financial Analysis*, 91, 102991. doi:10.1016/j.irfa.2023.102991

Hristov, I., Chirico, A., & Ranalli, F. (2022). Corporate strategies oriented towards sustainable governance: Advantages, managerial practices, and main challenges. *The Journal of Management and Governance*, 26(1), 75–97. doi:10.1007/s10997-021-09581-x

Hu, M. W. (2010). SMEs and economic growth: Entrepreneurship or employment. *ICIC Express Letters*, 4(6), 2275–2280.

Huong, T. T. X., Nguyen, M. L. T., & Lien, N. T. K. (2020). An empirical study of the real effective exchange rate and foreign direct investment in Vietnam. *Investment Management & Financial Innovations*, 17(4), 1–13. doi:10.21511/imfi.17(4).2020.01

Ibrahim, N. M. N., & Mahmood, R. (2016). Mediating role of competitive advantage on the relationship between entrepreneurial orientation and the performance of small and medium enterprises. *International Business Management*, 10(12), 2444–2452.

Idowu, A., Ohikhuare, O. M., & Chowdhury, M. A. (2023). Does industrialization trigger carbon emissions through energy consumption? Evidence from OPEC countries and high industrialised countries. *Quantitative Finance and Economics*, 7(1), 165–186. doi:10.3934/QFE.2023009

Imeokparia, P. O., & Ediagbonya, K. (2014). Small and Medium Scale Enterprises (SMEs): A catalyst in promoting economic development in Nigeria. *Journal of Education and Practice*, 5(33), 92–98.

Im, K. S., Pesaran, M. H., & Shin, Y. (2003). Testing for unit roots in heterogeneous panels. *Journal of Econometrics*, 115(1), 53–74. doi:10.1016/S0304-4076(03)00092-7

Indian Ministry Of Corporate Affairs, & Werner, W. J. (2009). Corporate Social Responsiblility Voluntary Guidelines. *Journal of Health Population and Nutrition, 27*(4), 545–562. http://www.ncbi.nlm.nih.gov/pubmed/20304693%5Cnhttp://www.mca.gov.in/Ministry/latestnews/CSR_Voluntary_Guidelines_24dec2009.pdf

Innig, C. (April 9, 2021). *In Banking, sustainability is the new digital, now what?* Banking Blog. https://bankingblog.accenture.com/banking-sustainability-new-digital-now-what

International Finance Corporation. (2019), *Emerging Market Green Bonds Report*. IFC. https://www.ifc.org/content/dam/ifc/doc/mgrt/amundi-ifc-research-paper-2018.pdf

International Finance Corporation. (2022), *Green and Social Bond Impact Report*. IFC. https://www.ifc.org/content/dam/ifc/doc/2023/IFC-GreenSocialBondReport-Final.pdf

Ishak, N. F., & Thiruchelvam, V. (2024). Sustainable innovations in Malaysia's public procurement: Strategic policy initiatives and coherences. *International Journal of Innovation Science*, 16(2), 338–372. doi:10.1108/IJIS-08-2022-0144

Islam, M. R. (2010), Women's empowerment for sustainable development in Bangladesh. *OIDA International Journal of Sustainable Development, 8*(1), 77-83. https://papers.ssrn.com/sol3/papers.cfm?abstract_id=1675563

Islamic Financial Services Board (2006). Guiding principles on corporate governance for institutions offering only Islamic financial services (excluding Islamic insurance (takaful) institutions and Islamic mutual funds).

Islam, M. S., Akash, M., Farhan, S., Jahid, M. J. I., & Ovi, M. O. H. (2023). Understanding the Factors that Influence Financial Literacy in Small Businesses: Evidence from Bangladesh. *International Journal of Research and Innovation in Social Science*, 7(12), 492–505. doi:10.47772/IJRISS.2023.7012041

Jaeger, P. T., Lin, J., & Grimes, J. M. (2008). Cloud computing and information policy: Computing in a policy cloud? *Journal of Information Technology & Politics*, 5(3), 269–283. doi:10.1080/19331680802425479

Jain, R. K., Triandis, H. C., & Weick, C. W. (2010). Managing Research, Development, and Innovation: Managing the Unmanageable. In Managing Research, Development, and Innovation: Managing the Unmanageable. doi:10.1002/9780470917275

Jaish, A. A., Murdipi, R., Razak, D. A., & Alwi, N. M. (2023). The Impact of Digitalization Towards the Sustainability of Malaysian SMEs: The Dynamic Capabilities Perspective. In *From Industry 4.0 to Industry 5.0: Mapping the Transitions* (pp. 3–12). Springer Nature Switzerland. doi:10.1007/978-3-031-28314-7_1

Jan, A. A., Lai, F. W., Asif, M., Akhtar, S., & Ullah, S. (2023). Embedding sustainability into bank strategy: Implications for sustainable development goals reporting. *International Journal of Sustainable Development and World Ecology*, *30*(3), 229–243. doi:10.1080/13504509.2022.2134230

Jaouad, E., & Lahsen, O. (2018), Factors Affecting Banks Performance: Empirical Evidence from Morocco, European Scientific Journal, 14. doi:10.19044/esj.2018.v14n34p255

Jarakunti, T. (2023). Social Entrepreneurship – Prospects and Challenges. *Iconic Research and Engineering Journals*, *6*(12), 663–668.

Jasrotia, A., & Gangotia, A. (2018). Smart cities to smart tourism destinations: A review paper. *Journal of tourism intelligence and smartness, 1*(1), 47-56.

Jayanthi, D. (2019). A Study About Entrepreneurship in India and Its Promotion Under 'Startup India' Scheme. *Iconic Research and Engineering Journals*, *2*(11), 118–126.

Jennifer, & Radianto, W. & Kohardinata, C. (2022). Determinant Effect of CASA and NPM on Market Ratio of Banks Listed In IDX. *Business and Finance Journal, 7*(2). . DOI: https://www.researchgate.net/publication/368776396_DETERMINANT_EFFECT_OT_CASA_AND_NPM_ON_MARKET_RATIO_OF_BANKS_LISTED_IN_IDX doi:10.33086/bfj.v7i2.3490

Jermsittiparsert, K. (2021). Does urbanization, industrialization, and income unequal distribution lead to environmental degradation? Fresh evidence from ASEAN. *International Journal of Economics and Finance Studies*, *13*(2), 253–272. doi:10.34109/ijefs.20212012

Ji, H., Zhou, S., Wan, J., & Lan, C. (2024). Can green innovation promote the financial performance of SMEs? Empirical evidence from China. *Corporate Social Responsibility and Environmental Management*, *31*(2), 1288–1302. doi:10.1002/csr.2633

Jing, J., Wang, J., & Hu, Z. (2023). Has corporate involvement in government-initiated corporate social responsibility activities increased corporate value?—Evidence from China's Targeted Poverty Alleviation. *Humanities & Social Sciences Communications*, *10*(1), 355. doi:10.1057/s41599-023-01869-7

Johansen, S. (1988). Statistical Analysis of Cointegration Vectors. *Journal of Economic Dynamics & Control*, *12*(2–3), 231–254. doi:10.1016/0165-1889(88)90041-3

Johansen, S., & Juselius, K. (1990). Maximum Likelihood Estimation and Inference on Cointegration– with Applications to the Demand for Money. *Oxford Bulletin of Economics and Statistics*, *52*(2), 169–210. doi:10.1111/j.1468-0084.1990.mp52002003.x

Joshi, S., Sharma, M., Bartwal, S., Joshi, T., & Prasad, M. (2024). Critical challenges of integrating OPEX strategies with I4. 0 technologies in manufacturing SMEs: A few pieces of evidence from developing economies. *The TQM Journal*, *36*(1), 108–138. doi:10.1108/TQM-08-2022-0245

Joss, S., Cook, M., & Dayot, Y. (2017). Smart cities: Towards a new citizenship regime? A discourse analysis of the British smart city standard. *Journal of Urban Technology*, *24*(4), 29–49. doi:10.1080/10630732.2017.1336027

Jouda, H., & Abu Dan, M. (2022). The Role of Scientific Research on Sustainable Development Into Organizations. SSRN *Electronic Journal*. doi:10.2139/ssrn.4233050

Kahouli, B., Miled, K., & Aloui, Z. (2022). Do energy consumption, urbanization, and industrialization play a role in environmental degradation in the case of Saudi Arabia? *Energy Strategy Reviews*, *40*, 100814. doi:10.1016/j.esr.2022.100814

Kalymbetova, A., Zhetibayev, Z., Kambar, R., Ranov, Z., & Izatullayeva, B. (2021). The effect of oil prices on industrial production in oil-importing countries: Panel cointegration test. *International Journal of Energy Economics and Policy*, *11*(1), 186–192. doi:10.32479/ijeep.10439

Kamalaveni, R., & Buvaneswaran, V. (2019). A Study on Problems and Prospects of Social Entrepreneurs in Tamilnadu. *CIKITUSI Journal for Multidisciplinary Research*, *6*(4), 392–400.

Kao, C. (1999). Spurious regression and residual-based tests for cointegration in panel data. *Journal of Econometrics*, *90*(1), 1–44. doi:10.1016/S0304-4076(98)00023-2

Kapur, S. K. (2022, December 19). *Dr Samir Kapur in Voices*. TOI, India. https://timesofindia.indiatimes.com/blogs/voices/innovations-in-tourism-industry-to-attract-travellers/

Kauffman, J. (2009). Advancing sustainability science: Report on the International Conference on Sustainability Science (ICSS) 2009. *Sustainability Science*, *4*(2), 233–242. doi:10.1007/s11625-009-0088-y

Kaur, G., & Dhiman, B. (2024). Co-integration and Causal Relationship between Energy Commodities and Energy Stock Index: Empirical Evidence from India. In *BIO Web of Conferences* (*Vol. 86*, p. 01053). EDP Sciences. 10.1051/bioconf/20248601053

Kaur, K. (2021). Social Entrepreneurship: Major Challenges Faced by Social Entrepreneurs in India. [IJCRT]. *International Journal of Creative Research Thoughts*, *9*(4), 1738–1741.

Kaur, S., Kumar, P., & Ansari, M. A. (2024). An analysis of Indian FDI inflows through an augmented gravity model: Exploring new insights. *International Economics and Economic Policy*, ●●●, 1–21. doi:10.1007/s10368-024-00594-z

Keho, Y. (2016). What drives energy consumption in developing countries? The experience of selected African countries. *Energy Policy*, *91*, 233–246. doi:10.1016/j.enpol.2016.01.010

Keller, B., & Mbwewe, D. C. (1991). Policy and planning for the empowerment of Zambia's women farmers. *Canadian Journal of Development Studies*, *1*(12), 75–88. doi:10.1080/02255189.1991.9669421

Khan, J. (2015). The Role of Research and Development in Economic Growth:a Review. *Journal of Economics Bibliography*, *2*(3), 128–133. doi:10.1453/jeb.v2i3.480

Khan, M. S., Woo, M., Nam, K., & Chathoth, P. K. (2017). Smart city and smart tourism: A case of Dubai. *Sustainability (Basel)*, *9*(12), 2279. doi:10.3390/su9122279

Khan, S., Akbar, A., Nasim, I., Hedvičáková, M., & Bashir, F. (2022). Green finance development and environmental sustainability: A panel data analysis. *Frontiers in Environmental Science*, *10*, 2134. doi:10.3389/fenvs.2022.1039705

Khan, S., & Freeda Maria, S. M. (2022). What innovations would enable the tourism and hospitality industry in India to re-build? *Worldwide Hospitality and Tourism Themes*, *14*(6), 579–585. doi:10.1108/WHATT-05-2022-0053

Khedhiri, M. (2022). Empowering The Saudi's Higher Education System: Real Strategies Towards A World-Class Status. *Globus Journal of Progressive Education*, *12*(2), 82–87. doi:10.46360/globus.edu.220222013

Kheeche, R. S. (2020). Impact of information technology on Indian social values. *International Journal of Advanced Research in Commerce. Management and Social Science*, *03*(04), 167–172.

Mert, M., Bölük, G., & Çağlar, A. E. (2019). Interrelationships among foreign direct investments, renewable energy, and CO 2 emissions for different European country groups: A panel ARDL approach. *Environmental Science and Pollution Research International*, *26*(21), 21495–21510. doi:10.1007/s11356-019-05415-4 PMID:31127517

Mervar, A. (1999). PREGLED MODELA I METODA ISTRAŽIVANJA GOSPODARSKOG RASTA. *Privredna Kretanja i Ekonomska Politika*.

Mervar, A. (2003). Esej o novijim dorinosima teoriji ekonomskog rasta. *Ekonomski Pregled*.

Mgbemene, C. A., Nnaji, C. C., & Nwozor, C. (2016). Industrialization and its backlash: Focus on climate change and its consequences. *Journal of Environmental Science and Technology*, *9*(4), 301–316. doi:10.3923/jest.2016.301.316

Miedema, S. S., Haardorfer, R., Girard, A. W., & Yount, K. M. (2018). Women's empowerment in East Africa: Development of a cross-country comparable measure. *World Development*, *110*(C), 453–464. doi:10.1016/j.worlddev.2018.05.031

Mijares, I. I. I. III, & Benjamin, F. (2023). Development and Validation of a Supplementary learning Material in Earth Science. *Cosmos An International Journal of Art & Higher Education*, *12*(1), 56–76. doi:10.46360/cosmos.ahe.520231005

Millemaci, E., & Ofria, F. (2014). Kaldor-Verdoorn's law and increasing returns to scale: A comparison across developed countries. *Journal of Economic Studies (Glasgow, Scotland)*, *41*(1), 140–162. doi:10.1108/JES-02-2012-0026

Mishra, P. K., & Tripathi, P. (2018), Women and sustainable development goals, 29-38. https://www.researchgate.net/publication/327814277_Women_and_Sustainable_Development_Goals

Mishra, L. (2021). Corporate social responsibility and sustainable development goals: A study of Indian companies. *Journal of Public Affairs*, *21*(1), e2147. doi:10.1002/pa.2147

Misra, R., Srivastava, S., Mahajan, R., & Thakur, R. (2021). Decision making as a contributor for women empowerment. *Journal of Comparative Asian Development*, *18*(1), 79–99. doi:10.4018/JCAD.2021010104

Mitra, N., & Schmidpeter, R. (2017). The why, what and how of the CSR mandate: The India story. *Corporate Social Responsibility in India: Cases and Developments after the Legal Mandate*, 1–8.

Mitra, S., Kumar, H., Gupta, M. P., & Bhattacharya, J. (2023). Entrepreneurship in smart cities: Elements of start-up ecosystem. *Journal of Science and Technology Policy Management*, *14*(3), 592–611. doi:10.1108/JSTPM-06-2021-0078

Mittal, B., & Garg, S. (2018). A Conceptual Study of Startup India-A Rejuvenation. *Journal of Commerce and Trade*, *13*(1), 1–14. doi:10.26703/JCT.v13i1-1

Mohnot, R., Banerjee, A., Ballaj, H., & Sarker, T. (2024). Re-examining asymmetric dynamics in the relationship between macroeconomic variables and stock market indices: Empirical evidence from Malaysia. *The Journal of Risk Finance*, *25*(1), 19–34. doi:10.1108/JRF-09-2023-0216

Mora, H., Morales-Morales, M. R., Pujol-López, F. A., & Mollá-Sirvent, R. (2021). Social cryptocurrencies as model for enhancing sustainable development. *Kybernetes*, *50*(10), 2883–2916. doi:10.1108/K-05-2020-0259

Mosikari, T. (2024). Heterogenous Effect of Industrialisation on Environmental Degradation in Southern African Customs Union (SACU) Countries: Quantile Analysis. *Economies*, *12*(3), 71. doi:10.3390/economies12030071

Muhammad, M. Z., & Char, A. K., bin Yasoa, M. R., & Hassan, Z. (2010). Small and medium enterprises (SMEs) competing in the global business environment: A case of Malaysia. *International Business Research*, *3*(1), 66.

Munir, K., & Ameer, A. (2020). Nonlinear effect of FDI, economic growth, and industrialization on environmental quality: Evidence from Pakistan. *Management of Environmental Quality*, *31*(1), 223–234. doi:10.1108/MEQ-10-2018-0186

Muñoz, P., & Cohen, B. (2018). Sustainable entrepreneurship research: Taking stock and looking ahead. *Business Strategy and the Environment*, *27*(3), 300–322. doi:10.1002/bse.2000

Murdiati, E., Jawazi, J., Zakaria, N. B., & Musa, K. (2023). Does University–Industry Engagement Assist Women in Generating Business Income in Emerging Economies? Evidence from Malaysia. *Economies*, *11*(9), 239. doi:10.3390/economies11090239

Nagaraj, R. (2011). Industrial Performance, 1991-2008: A Review. In D. M. Nachane (Ed.), *India Development Report, Oxford University Press, 69-80.*

Nambisan, S. (2017). Digital Entrepreneurship: Toward a Media and Communication Perspective of Entrepreneurship. *Entrepreneurship Theory and Practice*, *41*(6), 1029–1055. doi:10.1111/etap.12254

Nam, K., Dutt, C. S., Chathoth, P., & Khan, M. S. (2021). Blockchain technology for smart city and smart tourism: Latest trends and challenges. *Asia Pacific Journal of Tourism Research*, *26*(4), 454–468. doi:10.1080/10941665.2019.1585376

Nam, T., & Pardo, T. A. (2011, June). Conceptualizing smart city with dimensions of technology, people, and institutions. In *Proceedings of the 12th annual international digital government research conference: digital government innovation in challenging times* (pp. 282-291). ACM. 10.1145/2037556.2037602

Narayan, M., Mohanty, B., & Kumar, M. (2019). Growth pattern and trends in startup funding in India. *International Journal of Innovative Technology and Exploring Engineering*, *8*(12), 3721–3724. doi:10.35940/ijitee.L2654.1081219

Nasir, M. A., Canh, N. P., & Le, T. N. L. (2021). Environmental degradation & role of financialisation, economic development, industrialisation and trade liberalisation. *Journal of Environmental Management*, *277*, 111471. doi:10.1016/j.jenvman.2020.111471 PMID:33049616

Nasrallah, N., & El Khoury, R. (2022). Is corporate governance a good predictor of SMEs financial performance? Evidence from developing countries (the case of Lebanon). *Journal of Sustainable Finance & Investment*, *12*(1), 13–43. doi:10.1080/20430795.2021.1874213

Nations, U. (n.d.). *Human Development Index.* Human Development Reports. https://hdr.undp.org/data-center/human-development-index#/indicies/HDI

Naz, F. (2006). Arturo Escobar and the development discourse: An overview. *Asian Affairs*, *28*(3), 64–84.

Ndagu, W., & Obuobi, R. (2010). *Strengthening SMEs: A Guide to Business Management and Governance for Small and Medium Enterprises in East Africa.*

Ndiaya, C., & Lv, K. (2018). Role of industrialization on economic growth: The experience of Senegal (1960-2017). *American Journal of Industrial and Business Management*, *8*(10), 2072–2085. doi:10.4236/ajibm.2018.810137

NelsonR. R. (1993). National Innovation Systems: A Comparative. In *Analysis University of Illinois at Urbana-Champaign's Academy for Entrepreneurial Leadership Historical Research Reference in Entrepreneurship.* https://ssrn.com/abstract=1496195

Neves, P. (2018). *Literature Review on Sustainable Development - The spirit and critics of SD and SDGs.* How to Implement Partnerships Based on Sustainable Development (SD)to Achieve the Sustainable Development Goals (SDGs). https://doi.org/ OECD/Eurostat. (2022). *Researchers by sector 2021.* https://ec.europa.eu/eurostat/databrowser/view/rd_p_persocc/default/table?lang=en doi:10.13148/PN.2018.30.01.006

Newell, P., & Frynas, J. G. (2007). Beyond csr? Business, poverty and social justice: An introduction. *Third World Quarterly*, *28*(4), 669–681. doi:10.1080/01436590701336507

Nguyen, Q. H. (2021). Impact of investment in tourism infrastructure development on attracting international visitors: A nonlinear panel ARDL approach using Vietnam's data. *Economies, 9*(3), 131. doi:10.3390/economies9030131

Nishant, R., Kennedy, M., & Corbett, J. (2020). Artificial Intelligence for Sustainability: Challenges, Opportunities and A Research Agenda. *International Journal of Information Management, 53*, 102104. doi:10.1016/j.ijinfomgt.2020.102104

Nor-Aishah, H., Ahmad, N. H., & Thurasamy, R. (2020). Entrepreneurial leadership and sustainable performance of manufacturing SMEs in Malaysia: The contingent role of entrepreneurial bricolage. *Sustainability (Basel), 12*(8), 3100. doi:10.3390/su12083100

Northup, T., Santana, A. D., Choi, H., & Puspita, R. (2022). Personality traits, personal motivations, and online news and social media commenting. *Journal of Media and Communication Studies, 14*(3), 68–78. doi:10.5897/JMCS2022.0775

Odeleye, A. T., & Olunkwa, N. C. (2019). Industrialization: Panacea for economic growth. *Academic Journal of Economic Studies, 5*(2), 45-51. https://ir.unilag.edu.ng/handle/123456789/12302

OECD. (2011). Fostering Innovation to Address Social Challenges. In *Innovation Strategy* (p. 99). https://www.oecd.org/sti/inno/47861327.pdf

OECD. (2015). The Measurement of Scientific, Technological and Innovation Activities. In *Frascati Manual 2015*. Guidelines for Collecting and Reporting Data on Research and Experimental Development.

Ogbechie, C., & Arije, A. (2023). Corporate Governance in Africa: Key Challenges and Running Effective Boards. In *Sustainable and Responsible Business in Africa: Studies in Ethical Leadership* (pp. 265–290). Springer Nature Switzerland.

Ogwara, N. O., Petrova, K., & Yang, M. L. (2022). Towards the development of a cloud computing intrusion detection framework using an ensemble hybrid feature selection approach. *Journal of Computer Networks and Communications, 2022*, 1–16. doi:10.1155/2022/5988567

Olaoye, I. J., Ayinde, O. E., Ajewole, O. O., & Adebisi, L. O. (2021). The role of research and development (R&D) expenditure and governance on economic growth in selected African countries. *African Journal of Science, Technology, Innovation and Development, 13*(6), 663–670. doi:10.1080/20421338.2020.1799300

Olayungbo, D. O. (2021). Global oil price and food prices in food importing and oil exporting developing countries: A panel ARDL analysis. *Heliyon, 7*(3), e06357. Advance online publication. doi:10.1016/j.heliyon.2021.e06357 PMID:33748459

Olofsdotter, K. (1998). Foreign direct investment, country capabilities and economic growth. *Weltwirtschaftliches Archiv, 134*(3), 534–547. doi:10.1007/BF02707929

Opoku, E. E. O., & Boachie, M. K. (2020). The environmental impact of industrialization and foreign direct investment. *Energy Policy, 137*, 111178. doi:10.1016/j.enpol.2019.111178

Organization for Economic Co-operation and Development. (2004). *OECD Principles of Corporate Governance*. OECD Publications Service.

Our World in Data team. (2023). *Achieve gender equality and empower all women and girls*. OurWorldInData.org. https://ourworldindata.org/sdgs/gender-equality

Ozdemir, H. (2018). *The road to women's empowerment in a man's crop: A field study of Ugandan women's empowerment process in the coffee farming industry*. https://www.diva-portal.org/smash/get/diva2:1284575/FULLTEXT01.pdf

Pakkan, S., Sudhakar, C., Tripathi, S., & Rao, M. (2022). A correlation study of sustainable development goal (SDG) interactions. *Quality & Quantity*. doi:10.1007/s11135-022-01443-4 PMID:35729959

Panagariya, A., (2004), India in the 1980s and 1990s: A Triumph of Reforms. *International Monetary Fund. 4* (43). . doi:10.5089/9781451846355.001

Panait, M., Ionescu, R., Radulescu, I. G., & Rjoub, H. (2022). The Corporate Social Responsibility on Capital Market: Myth or Reality? In Research Anthology on Developing Socially Responsible Businesses (pp. 1721-1754). IGI Global.

Pandey, A., Tiwari, D., & Singh, R. (2023). Environmental Social and Governance Reporting in India: An Overview. *EPRA International Journal of Multidisciplinary Research (IJMR), 9*(8), 47-51. https://www.eprajournals.net/index. php/IJMR/article/view/2554

Pandey, P., Choubey, K. A., & Rai, G. (2021). The involvement of women as the domestic decision maker: A study of Patna Metropolitan City, Bihar, India. *Sociedade & Natureza, 33*, 1–9. doi:10.14393/SN-v33-2021-62053

Pandey, P., & Shukla, R. (2021). The Process of Social Entrepreneurship: Opportunities and Challenges. *Emerge Managing Innovation and Entrepreneurship in New Normal, 1*, 97–103.

Pankaj, L., & Seetharaman, P. (2021). The balancing act of social enterprise: An IT emergence perspective. *International Journal of Information Management, 57*, 102302. doi:10.1016/j.ijinfomgt.2020.102302

Pan, S. L., Carter, L., Tim, Y., & Sandeep, M. S. (2022). Digital Sustainability, Climate Change, and Information Systems Solutions: Opportunities for Future Research. *International Journal of Information Management, 63*, 102444. doi:10.1016/j.ijinfomgt.2021.102444

Pansa, L. (2023). Social Enterprises in India: The Issues, Challenges and Its Performance Measurement. *International Journal of Current Research, 15*(01), 23587–23595.

Papagiannidis, S., & Marikyan, D. (2022). Environmental Sustainability: A Technology Acceptance Perspective. *International Journal of Information Management, 63*, 102445. doi:10.1016/j.ijinfomgt.2021.102445

Parveen, S., Khan, A. Q., & Farooq, S. (2019). The causal nexus of urbanization, industrialization, economic growth and environmental degradation: Evidence from Pakistan. *Review of Economics and Development Studies, 5*(4), 721–730. doi:10.26710/reads.v5i4.883

Pata, U. K., & Zengin, H. (2020). Testing Kaldor's growth laws for Turkey: New evidence from symmetric and asymmetric causality methods. *Çankırı Karatekin Üniversitesi İktisadi ve İdari Bilimler Fakültesi Dergisi, 10*(2), 713-729. doi:10.18074/ckuiibfd.625455

Pata, U. K. (2018). The effect of urbanization and industrialization on carbon emissions in Turkey: Evidence from ARDL bounds testing procedure. *Environmental Science and Pollution Research International, 25*(8), 7740–7747. doi:10.1007/s11356-017-1088-6 PMID:29288303

Paunović, M., Mosurović Ružičić, M., & Lazarević Moravčević, M. (2022). Business process innovations in family firms: evidence from Serbia. *Journal of Family Business Management*. doi:10.1108/JFBM-03-2022-0044

Pavlatos, O. (2021). Drivers of management control systems in tourism start-ups firms. *International Journal of Hospitality Management, 92*, 102746. doi:10.1016/j.ijhm.2020.102746

Pawni, B. and Sailaja, V. (2022). Social Entrepreneurship in India: Opportunities and Challenges. *International Journal of Advanced Research in management (IJARM), 13*(1), 237-245.

Pazaitis, A., Kostakis, V., & Bauwens, M. (2017). Digital economy and the rise of open cooperativism: The case of the Enspiral Network. *Transfer: European Review of Labour and Research, 23*(2), 177–192. doi:10.1177/1024258916683865

Pennington, A., Orton, L., Nayak, S., Ring, A., Petticrew, M., Sowden, A., White, M., & Whitehead, M. (2018). The health impacts of women's low control in their living environment: A theory-based systematic review of observational studies in societies with profound gender discrimination. *Health & Place, 51*, 1–10. doi:10.1016/j.healthplace.2018.02.001 PMID:29482064

Perron, P. (1988). Trends and random walks in macroeconomic time series: Further evidence from a new approach. *Journal of Economic Dynamics & Control, 12*(2-3), 297–332. doi:10.1016/0165-1889(88)90043-7

Pesaran, M. H., Shin, Y., & Smith, R. P. (1999). Pooled mean group estimation of dynamic heterogeneous panels. *Journal of the American Statistical Association, 94*(446), 621–634. doi:10.1080/01621459.1999.10474156

Petreski, M. (2009). Analysis of exchange-rate regime effect on growth: Theoretical channels and empirical evidence with panel data. *Economics Discussion Paper,* (2009-49). doi:10.2139/ssrn.1726752

Pierce, P., Ricciardi, F., & Zardini, A. (2017). Smart cities as organizational fields: A framework for mapping sustainability-enabling configurations. *Sustainability (Basel), 9*(9), 1506. doi:10.3390/su9091506

Pinki. (2021). Environmental Sustainability and Economic Growth during Covid-19 Pandemic. *Cosmos An International Journal of Management, 11*(1), 120-124.

Pooja, H. R. (2019). A descriptive study of opportunities and challenges of Startup India Mission. *International Journal of Advance Research and Innovative Ideas in Education, 2*(3), 2395–4396.

Poverty headcount ratio at $2.15 a day (2017 PPP) (% of population) - India | Data. (n.d.). World Bank. https://data.worldbank.org/indicator/SI.POV.DDAY?locations=IN

Prabhavati, K., & Dinesh, G. P. (2018), Banking: D definition and evolution, *International Journal of scientific and engineering research, 9*(8). https://www.ijser.org/researchpaper/Banking-Definition-and-Evolution.pdf

Pratley, P., & Sandberg, J. F. (2018). Refining the conceptualization and measurement of women's empowerment in Sub-Saharan Africa using data from the 2013 Nigerian demographic and health survey. *Social Indicators Research, 140*(2), 777–793. doi:10.1007/s11205-017-1811-1

Presenza, A., Abbate, T., Meleddu, M., & Sheehan, L. (2020). Start-up entrepreneurs' personality traits. An exploratory analysis of the Italian tourism industry. *Current Issues in Tourism, 23*(17), 2146–2164. doi:10.1080/13683500.2019.1 677572

Qaiser, S. (2020). Relationship Between Industrialization and Economic Growth: An Empirical Study of Pakistan. *International Journal of Management. Accounting & Economics, 7*(12). doi:10.5281/zenodo.4482746

Qin, Lv., Wang, Y., Zhang, D., Yang, M., & Zheng, Y. (2020), Performance evaluation of commercial banks based on factor analysis, *E3S Web Conf. 2020 International Conference on Energy Big Data and Low-carbon Development Management (EBLDM 2020)*. IEEE. 10.1051/e3sconf/202021402017

Racine, J. L., Goldberg, I., Goddard, J. G., Kuriakose, S., & Kapil, N. (2009). *Restructuring of Research and Development Institutes in Europe and Central Asia.*

Raghavendran, C. V., Satish, G. N., Varma, P. S., & Moses, G. J. (2016). A study on cloud computing services. [IJERT]. *International Journal of Engineering Research & Technology (Ahmedabad), 4*(34), 1–6.

Raheem, I. D., & Ogebe, J. O. (2017). CO2 emissions, urbanization and industrialization: Evidence from a direct and indirect heterogeneous panel analysis. *Management of Environmental Quality, 28*(6), 851–867. doi:10.1108/MEQ-09-2015-0177

Rahman, M. M., Alam, K., & Velayutham, E. (2021). Is industrial pollution detrimental to public health? Evidence from the world's most industrialised countries. *BMC Public Health*, 21(1), 1175. doi:10.1186/s12889-021-11217-6 PMID:34144705

Rahman, N. A., Yaacob, Z., & Radzi, R. M. (2016). The challenges among Malaysian SME: A theoretical perspective. *WORLD (Oakland, Calif.)*, 6(3), 124–132.

Rajani, K. (2023). A Study on Opportunities and Challenges of Startups in India. [IJM]. *International Journal of Management*, 14(4), 251–256.

Rajaraman, V. (2014). Cloud computing. *Resonance*, 19(3), 242–258. doi:10.1007/s12045-014-0030-1

Ramli, A. M., Asby, P. N. K., Noor, H. M., & Afrizal, T. (2022). Challenges Encountered by SMEs in Tourism Industry: A review from 2017 to 2021. *Journal of ASIAN Behavioural Studies*, 7(21), 1–13. doi:10.21834/jabs.v7i21.405

Rao, S. R., & Kumar, L. (2016). Role of Angel Investor in Indian Startup Ecosystem. *FIIB Business Review*, 5(1), 3–14. doi:10.1177/2455265820160101

Raphael, G. (2024). Causality between Financial Development and Foreign Direct Investment: Evidence from Tanzania. *International Journal of Business, Law, and Education*, 5(1), 158–176. doi:10.56442/ijble.v5i1.242

Rashid, A., Akmal, M., & Shah, S. M. A. R. (2024). Corporate governance and risk management in Islamic and convectional financial institutions: Explaining the role of institutional quality. *Journal of Islamic Accounting and Business Research*, 15(3), 466–498. doi:10.1108/JIABR-12-2021-0317

Ratha, K. C. (2019). Growing industrialisation and its cumulative impacts: Insights from the Mahanadi River basin. *Social Change*, 49(3), 519–530. doi:10.1177/0049085719863904

Rawal, T. (2018). A Study of Social Entrepreneurship in India. [IRJET]. *International Research Journal of Engineering and Technology*, 5(1), 829–837.

Razak, D. A., Abdullah, M. A., & Ersoy, A. (2018). Small, medium enterprises (SMEs) in Turkey and Malaysia a comparative discussion on issues and challenges. *International Journal of Business, Economics, and Law*, 10(49), 2–591.

Rehman, A., Ma, H., & Ozturk, I. (2021). Do industrialization, energy importations, and economic progress influence carbon emission in Pakistan. *Environmental Science and Pollution Research International*, 28(33), 45840–45852. doi:10.1007/s11356-021-13916-4 PMID:33881694

Reserve Bank of India. (2023), *Sovereign Green Bonds – Full Auction Results*. Reserve Bank of India. https://www.rbi.org.in/scripts/BS_PressReleaseDisplay.aspx?prid=55190

Roche, J. (2005). *Corporate governance in Asia*. Routledge. doi:10.4324/9780203461723

Rodriguez-Sanchez, I., Williams, A. M., & Brotons, M. (2019). The innovation journey of new-to-tourism entrepreneurs. *Current Issues in Tourism*, 22(8), 877–904. doi:10.1080/13683500.2017.1334763

Rodrik, D. (2008). The Real Exchange Rate and Economic Growth. *Brookings Papers on Economic Activity*, 2008(2), 365–412. doi:10.1353/eca.0.0020

Roseland, M. (2000). Sustainable community development: Integrating environmental, economic, and social objectives. *Progress in Planning*, 54(2), 73–132. doi:10.1016/S0305-9006(00)00003-9

Rost, B. (2010). Basel committee on banking supervision. In *Handbook of transnational economic governance regimes* (pp. 319–328). Brill Nijhoff. doi:10.1163/ej.9789004163300.i-1081.238

Royal, S., Chaudhary, N., Dalal, R. C., & Kaushik, N. (2023). A Nexus Between Sustainability, Openness, Development, and Urbanisation: Panel Data Evidence from Quad Nations. [Ikonomicheski Izsledvania]. *Economic Studies Journal*, *32*(3), 178–196.

Roy, C., Chatterjee, S., & Gupta, S. D. (2018). Women empowerment index: Construction of a tool to measure rural women empowerment level in India. *Anveshak -. International Journal of Management*, *7*(1), 199–212. doi:10.15410/aijm/2018/v7i1/119887

Ružičić Mosurović, M., & Obradović, V. (2020). *Strateško upravljanje projektima u naučnoistraživačkim organizacijama.* Udruženje za upravljanje projektima Srbije, IPMA Serbia.

Ružičić Mosurović, M., Obradović, V., & Iganjatović, M. (2021). Strategic Manaiginig Innovation in SROs in Serbia: Should it be resistible? *Responsible and Resistible Project Management*, 211–216. https://ipma.rs/wp-content/uploads/2022/10/Zbornik-2021.pdf

Ružičić, M. M., Miletić, M., & Dobrota, M. (2021). Does a national innovation system encourage sustainability? Lessons from the construction industry in Serbia. *Sustainability (Basel)*, *13*(7), 3591. Advance online publication. doi:10.3390/su13073591

Sadorsky, P. (2013). Do urbanization and industrialization affect energy intensity in developing countries? *Energy Economics*, *37*, 52–59. doi:10.1016/j.eneco.2013.01.009

Sadorsky, P. (2014). The effect of urbanization and industrialization on energy use in emerging economies: Implications for sustainable development. *American Journal of Economics and Sociology*, *73*(2), 392–409. doi:10.1111/ajes.12072

Saebi, T., Foss, N. J., & Linder, S. (2019). Social entrepreneurship research: Past achievements and future promises. *Journal of Management*, *45*(1), 70–95. doi:10.1177/0149206318793196

Sahoo, M., & Sethi, N. (2020). Impact of industrialization, urbanization, and financial development on energy consumption: Empirical evidence from India. *Journal of Public Affairs*, *20*(3), e2089. doi:10.1002/pa.2089

Sallam, M. (2021). The role of the manufacturing sector in promoting economic growth in the Saudi economy: A cointegration and VECM approach. *The Journal of Asian Finance. Economics and Business*, *8*(7), 21–30. doi:10.13106/jafeb.2021.vol8.no7.0021

Samsunnehar & Sarkar, S. (2021). Decision making power of homemakers in a rural muslim community of West Bengal: An Empirical Study. *Space and Culture, India, 9*(3), 45–60. doi:10.20896/saci.v9i3.1198

Sangwan, D. S. (2022). Impact of Russia Ukraine war on Indian Economy. Globus An International Journal of Medical Science. *Engineering and Technology*, *11*(1), 36–39.

Sanyal, K. (2014). *Rethinking Capitalist Development Primitive Accumulation, Governmentality and Post-Colonial Capitalism-Routledge India.* Routledge India. doi:10.4324/9781315767321

Saqib, N., Usman, M., Radulescu, M., Sinisi, C. I., Secara, C. G., & Tolea, C. (2022). Revisiting EKC hypothesis in context of renewable energy, human development and moderating role of technological innovations in E-7 countries? *Frontiers in Environmental Science*, *10*, 2509. doi:10.3389/fenvs.2022.1077658

Sarah, R. M. (2017). The benefits of good corporate governance to small and medium enterprises (SMEs) in South Africa: A view on top 20 and bottom 20 JSE listed companies. *Problems and Perspectives in Management*, (15, Iss. 4), 271–27. doi:10.21511/ppm.15(4-1).2017.11

Savio, R., D'Andrassi, E., & Ventimiglia, F. (2023). A Systematic Literature Review on ESG during the COVID-19 Pandemic. *Sustainability (Basel)*, *15*(3), 2020. doi:10.3390/su15032020

Schaltegger, S., Lüdeke-Freund, F., & Hansen, E. G. (2016). Business Models for Sustainability: A Co-Evolutionary Analysis of Sustainable Entrepreneurship, Innovation, and Transformation. *Organization & Environment*, *29*(3), 264–289. doi:10.1177/1086026616633272

Schlierer, H. J., Werner, A., Signori, S., Garriga, E., von Weltzien Hoivik, H., Van Rossem, A., & Fassin, Y. (2012). How do European SME owner-managers make sense of 'stakeholder management?: Insights from a cross-national study. *Journal of Business Ethics*, *109*(1), 39–51. doi:10.1007/s10551-012-1378-3

Schölmerich, M. J. (2013). On the impact of corporate social responsibility on poverty in Cambodia in the light of Sen's capability approach. *Asian Journal of Business Ethics*, *2*(1), 1–33. doi:10.1007/s13520-012-0016-6

Sekeran, U., & Bougie, R. (2010). *Research method for business: skin building Approach* (5th ed.). John Wiley and Sons Ltd.

Sell, M., & Minot, N. (2018). What factors explain women's empowerment? Decision-making among small-scale farmers in Uganda. *Women's Studies International Forum*, *71*, 46–55. doi:10.1016/j.wsif.2018.09.005

Sen, A. (1982). *Poverty and famines: an essay on entitlement and deprivation*. Oxford university press.

Sen, A. (2000). *Develeopment as freedom*. Anchor Books.

Sengupta, J. (2014). *Theory of Innovation*. Springer International Publishing. doi:10.1007/978-3-319-02183-6

Seth, R., Gupta, S., & Gupta, H. (2021). ESG investing: a critical overview. *Hans Shodh Sudha*, *2*(2), 69-80. https://hansshodhsudha.com/volume2-issue2/October_December%202021_%20article%207.pdf

Settembre-Blundo, D., González-Sánchez, R., Medina-Salgado, S., & García-Muiña, F. E. (2021). Flexibility and resilience in corporate decision making: A new sustainability-based risk management system in uncertain times. *Global Journal of Flexible Systems Managment*, *22*(S2, Suppl 2), 107–132. doi:10.1007/s40171-021-00277-7

Shaari, M. S., Abdul Karim, Z., & Zainol Abidin, N. (2020). The effects of energy consumption and national output on CO2 emissions: New evidence from OIC countries using a panel ARDL analysis. *Sustainability (Basel)*, *12*(8), 3312. doi:10.3390/su12083312

Shahbaz, M., & Lean, H. H. (2012). Does financial development increase energy consumption? The role of industrialization and urbanization in Tunisia. *Energy Policy*, *40*, 473–479. doi:10.1016/j.enpol.2011.10.050

Shah, W. U. H., Hao, G., Yan, H., Yasmeen, R., Padda, I. U. H., & Ullah, A. (2022). The impact of trade, financial development and government integrity on energy efficiency: An analysis from G7-Countries. *Energy*, *255*, 124507. doi:10.1016/j.energy.2022.124507

Sharma, R. K. (2014). Industrial development of India in pre and post reform period. *IOSR Journal of Humanities and Social Science*, *19*(10), 01-07.

Sharma, A., & Sharma, R. P. (2023). A Research Study on Eco-Friendly Green Products: Understanding Consumer Perceptions and Preferences. *Globus An International Journal of Management & IT*, *14*(2), 81–83. doi:10.46360/globus.mgt.120231011

Sharma, M., & Choubey, A. (2022). Green banking initiatives: A qualitative study on Indian banking sector. *Environment, Development and Sustainability*, *24*(1), 293–319. doi:10.1007/s10668-021-01426-9 PMID:33967597

Sharma, N. N. (2000). Ecotourism in North East India–A marketing Alternative in the next millennium. *Management and Labour Studies*, *25*(3), 177–190. doi:10.1177/0258042X0002500303

Wang, Z., Rasool, Y., Zhang, B., Ahmed, Z., & Wang, B. (2020). Dynamic linkage among industrialisation, urbanisation, and CO2 emissions in APEC realms: Evidence based on DSUR estimation. *Structural Change and Economic Dynamics*, *52*, 382–389. doi:10.1016/j.strueco.2019.12.001

Wang, Z., Shi, C., Li, Q., & Wang, G. (2011). Impact of heavy industrialization on the carbon emissions: An empirical study of China. *Energy Procedia*, *5*, 2610–2616. doi:10.1016/j.egypro.2011.03.324

Warth, L., & Koparanova, M. (2012). *Empowering Women for Sustainable Development*. United Nations Economic Commission for Europe. https://unece.org/DAM/Gender/publications_and_papers/UNECE_Discussion_Paper_2012.1.pdf

Weller, K., & Holaschke, M. (2022). Whose stream is this anyway? Exploring layers of viewer-integration in online participatory videos. *Journal of Media and Communication Studies, 14*(1), 17-32. IJCRT22A6128.pdf

Wells, H., & Thirlwall, A. P. (2003). Testing Kaldor's growth laws across the countries of Africa. *African Development Review*, *15*(2-3), 89–105. doi:10.1111/j.1467-8268.2003.00066.x

Williams, C. (2011). Research methods. [JBER]. *Journal of Business & Economics Research*, *5*(3). doi:10.19030/jber.v5i3.2532 PMID:21543382

Williams, J., Debski, I., & White, R. T. (2008). *Business Expenditure on Research and Development in New Zealand - future potential and future industries*. Ministry of Research, Science, and Technology.

Wood, J. (2020). Why this moment could be decisive for tackling climate change: Report, https://www.weforum.org/agenda/2020/07/how%20covid-19-could-spark-climate-change-recovery-sustainability/

World Bank. (2019), *Green Bond Impact Report*. World Bank. https://documents1.worldbank.org/curated/en/961221573041494528/pdf/Financial-Year-2019.pdf

World Bank. (2022), *Sustainable Development Bonds & Green Bonds Impact Report*. World Bank. https://thedocs.worldbank.org/en/doc/33420eed17c2a23660b46dc208b01815-0340022023/original/World-Bank-IBRD-Impact-Report-FY22.pdf

Wuttke, M., & Vilks, A. (2014). Poverty alleviation through CSR in the Indian construction industry. *Journal of Management Development*, *33*(2), 119–130. doi:10.1108/JMD-11-2013-0150

Xue, S., Genmao, Z., Boxin, H., Jiahui, H., & Salman, S. A. (2024). The Perception of SMEs towards the Corporate Governance in Malaysia. *The Journal of Research Administration*, *6*(1).

Yahyaoui, I., & Bouchoucha, N. (2021). The long-run relationship between ODA, growth and governance: An application of FMOLS and DOLS approaches. *African Development Review*, *33*(1), 38–54. doi:10.1111/1467-8268.12489

Yakovleva, N. (2017). *Corporate social responsibility in the mining industries*. Routledge. doi:10.4324/9781315259215

Yamaguchi, N. U., Bernardino, E. G., Ferreira, M. E. C., de Lima, B. P., Pascotini, M. R., & Yamaguchi, M. U. (2023). Sustainable development goals: A bibliometric analysis of literature reviews. *Environmental Science and Pollution Research International*, *30*(3), 5502–5515. doi:10.1007/s11356-022-24379-6 PMID:36418837

Yapraklý, S. (2006). An Econometric Analysis on the Economic Determinants of Foreign Direct Investments in Turkey. *Dergisi*, *21*(2), 23–48.

Yousef, H. A., ElSabry, E. A., & Adris, A. E. (2024). Impact of technology management in improving sustainability performance for Egyptian petroleum refineries and petrochemical companies. *International Journal of Energy Sector Management*, *18*(3), 517–538. doi:10.1108/IJESM-02-2023-0002

Zafar, A., & Mustafa, S. (2017). SMEs and its role in economic and socio-economic development of Pakistan. *International Journal of Academic Research in Accounting, Finance and Management Sciences*, *6*(4).

Zafar, A., Ullah, S., Majeed, M. T., & Yasmeen, R. (2020). Environmental pollution in Asian economies: Does the industrialisation matter? *OPEC Energy Review*, *44*(3), 227–248. doi:10.1111/opec.12181

Zafeiriou, E., Azam, M., & Garefalakis, A. (2022). Exploring environmental–economic performance linkages in EU agriculture: Evidence from a panel cointegration framework. *Management of Environmental Quality*, *34*(2), 469–491. doi:10.1108/MEQ-06-2022-0174

Zeng, B., Tan, Y., Xu, H., Quan, J., Wang, L., & Zhou, X. (2018). Forecasting the Electricity Consumption of Commercial Sector in Hong Kong Using a Novel Grey Dynamic Prediction Model. *Journal of Grey System*, *30*(1), 159.

Zeng, J. (2018). Fostering path of ecological sustainable entrepreneurship within big data network system. *The International Entrepreneurship and Management Journal*, *14*(1), 79–95. doi:10.1007/s11365-017-0466-3

Zhanbayev, R. A., Irfan, M., Shutaleva, A. V., Maksimov, D. G., Abdykadyrkyzy, R., & Filiz, Ş. (2023). Demoethical model of sustainable development of society: A roadmap towards digital transformation. *Sustainability (Basel)*, *15*(16), 12478. doi:10.3390/su151612478

Zhang, L., Zhang, X., An, J., Zhang, W., & Yao, J. (2022). Examining the Role of Stakeholder Oriented Corporate Governance in Achieving Sustainable Development: Evidence from the SME CSR in the Context of China. *Sustainability (Basel)*, *14*(13), 8181. doi:10.3390/su14138181

Zhang, Z., Zhu, H., Zhou, Z., & Zou, K. (2022). How does innovation matter for sustainable performance? Evidence from small and medium-sized enterprises. *Journal of Business Research*, *153*, 251–265. doi:10.1016/j.jbusres.2022.08.034

Zheng, Y., Rashid, M. H. U., Siddik, A. B., Wei, W., & Hossain, S. Z. (2022). Corporate social responsibility disclosure and firm's productivity: Evidence from the banking industry in Bangladesh. *Sustainability (Basel)*, *14*(10), 6237. doi:10.3390/su14106237

Zhou, D., Siddik, A. B., Guo, L., & Li, H. (2023). Dynamic relationship among climate policy uncertainty, oil price, and renewable energy consumption—Findings from TVP-SV-VAR approach. *Renewable Energy*, *204*, 722–732. https://www.mca.gov.in/Ministry/latestnews/National_Voluntary_Guidelines_2011_12jul2011.pdf. doi:10.1016/j.renene.2023.01.018

Zhu, W., Zhang, L., & Li, N. (2014). Challenges, function changing of government and enterprises in Chinese smart tourism. *Information and communication technologies in tourism*, *10*, 553-564.

Zorgati, I., Albouchi, F., & Garfatta, R. (2024). Financial contagion during the COVID-19 pandemic: The case of African countries. *International Journal of Accounting. Auditing and Performance Evaluation*, *20*(1/2), 23–42. doi:10.1504/IJAAPE.2024.135531

About the Contributors

Biswajit Paul is presently working at the PG and Research Department of Commerce of University of Gour Banga, Malda, West Bengal, India as an Assistant Professor. He did his undergraduate, post-graduate studies and Ph.D. (research studies) from the University of Calcutta. He has teaching experience of more than fifteen years in different colleges and universities. He worked as Guest Faculty at the Department of Commerce of Vivekananda College, Thakurpukur, Kolkata; Panihati Mahavidyalaya, Sodepur, North 24 Parganas, West Bengal; and Acharya Jagadish Chandra Bose College, Kolkata. After that he worked as Contractual Whole Time Teacher at the Department of Commerce of Vivekananda College, Thakurpukur, Kolkata. He also worked as Coordinator and Contractual Whole Time Teacher at the Department of Commerce (Post-Graduation under Calcutta University) of Naba Ballygunge Mahavidyalaya, Kolkata. He also worked as a Visiting Faculty in Sikkim Manipal University (DE), Vidyasagar University (DE) and IGNOU. Dr. Paul has ten years of research experience in the field of Developmental Economics, Macroeconomic Issues, Finance and Rural/Urban Development and allied areas. His academic and research contributions include the publications of more than eighty research articles and chapters in renowned National and International journals, books, and conference proceedings. He achieved three best paper awards in International seminars. Apart from this, he presented many research papers in different National and International conferences, seminars, and symposiums. He also authored seven text books published by reputed publishers and two International edited books. He acted as the reviewer of many reputed National and International journals and edited books. Dr. Paul is associated with different learned academic associations and societies as member or life member.

Sandeep Poddar, Deputy Vice Chancellor (Research & Innovation), Member of Board of Studies, Lincoln University College, Malaysia, has been graduated from University of Calcutta in 1993 with Honours in Zoology, he has obtained Post Graduate Diploma in Dietetics from All India Institute of Hygiene and Public Health 1995, Master of Science in Zoology with specialization in Biochemical Genetics from Dayalbagh Educational Institute 1998 with distinction. He has completed PhD in Zoology from Vivekananda Institute of Medical Sciences on Cytotoxicity in 2004. After completing PhD he pursued Post Doctoral Research in different projects on Hemoglobinopathies and Oral Cancer mutation. Dr Sandeep also completed his MBA from Lincoln University College, Malaysia. He has published several research papers, filed patent and organized international conferences, and also edited books in Malaysia, Australia and India. He is active member of different organizations, Indian Science Congress Association, Indian Science News Association, World Academy of Sciences, Mental Health Innovation Network, UK, Malaysian Society for Molecular Biology and Biotechnology, Fellow member of World

Researchers Associations. Dr Sandeep is founder Assistant Secretary of Dr Tarak Nath Podder Memorial Foundation, Kolkata, India

***

Bhaskar Bagchi works as a Professor in the Department of Commerce, University of Gour Banga, Malda, West Bengal, India. He has teaching and research experience of more than 21 years and is an active reviewer of many reputed international journals. He has guided research scholars in M.Phil and Ph.D. He has published books on finance and has several publications in the leading finance journals of the world. He has also chaired technical sessions at national and international conferences. His areas of interest include capital markets and financial econometrics. He is also a member of different learned academic bodies.

Sandip Basak is presently engaged as an Assistant Professor in the department of commerce, Dwijendralal College, West Bengal, India and he is pursuing his Ph.D. from University of Calcutta, India. His Research Interests are ESG Reporting, Sustainable Investing, Social Development and Women Empowerment. He has done his M.Phil degree from University of Calcutta, India. He is an Associate Member of Institute of Cost Accountants of India and Life Member of IAA and IAARF.

Samprit Chakraborti, Dean(academics) at ICFAI Business School, Kolkata, has a vast teaching experience of 22 years. He has authored many research papers in National and International journals of repute

Barendra Nath Chakraborty is a Ph.D. scholar in the Department of Commerce at Cooch Behar Panchanan Barma University, West Bengal, India. He is a recipient of the prestigious silver medal in MA Economics. His current endeavours delve into the nuanced application of econometric and time series analysis tools across the domains of finance, macroeconomics, and environmental economics. He has actively engaged in esteemed national and international conferences, further enriching his academic discourse, and contributing significantly to the scholarly landscape.

Nilendu Chatterjee, PhD is an Assistant Professor in the Department of Economics, Bankim Sardar College, West Bengal, India. He has research interest in Resource economics, General Equilibrium, and Development Economics. He has published number research articles in several international journals of economics including Journal of the Knowledge Economy, International Journal of Sustainable Economies Management, Economic Affairs, Foreign Trade Review. He has also contributed several chapters in edited volumes published from Springer, Emerald, Routledge, IGI Global, etc.

Reuben Das is a dedicated faculty member with 12 years of experience in Umeschandra College's Commerce Department. An academic with a passion for financial management, he holds dual Masters degrees in both Commerce and Business Administration (Finance). Possessing expertise in Marketing and Financial Planning, he is committed to nurturing future business leaders.

Raktim Ghosh is presently serving as a State Aided College Teacher – I in the Department of Commerce at the Maharaja Srischandra College, Kolkata, West Bengal, India. He completed his graduation

Anirban Mandal is currently working as a Faculty Member in ICFAI Business School, Kolkata. He has worked as an Associate Professor and Head of the Department in the School of Management and Commerce at Brainware University. He has done his Ph.D. from KIIT University, Bhubaneswar, India. He has more than 16 years of teaching experiences in different renowned colleges and institutions of West Bengal and also a Visiting Faculty in Pelita Harapan University, Jakarta, Indonesia. He has authored many research papers in National and International journals of repute. He acted as Resource person in different National and International Seminars. Orcid: 0000-0002-5130-5424

Biswajit Paul is presently serving as an Assistant Professor in the PG and Research Department of Commerce at the University of Gour Banga, Malda, West Bengal, India. Dr. Paul completed his Under-graduate, Postgraduate, and Research Studies (Ph.D.) at the University of Calcutta. He has more than 15 years of teaching experience. His academic and research contributions include the publication of more than fifty research papers in renowned journals, books, and conference proceedings. Apart from this, he has presented many research papers at different National and International Conferences, Seminars, and Symposiums. He has also authored seven text books published by reputed publishers.

Payel Roy has a PhD degree in Finance and more than 12 years of teaching experience in a renowned college in North Kolkata, India under University of Calcutta, the author is relocated to the United States in March 2023 in search of Post doctoral opportunities. Her interest areas are finance, women empowerment, socio-economic diversity and the like. Currently the author is working independently on sustainability issues.

Syed Ahmed Salman is a Senior Lecturer at Lincoln University college. He completed his PhD. in Islamic Banking and Finance from Institute of Islamic Banking and finance, International Islamic University Malaysia and a researcher in Islamic finance, especially in Takaful. Dr. Salman is actively involved in professional organizations. He is a Shari'ah Complaint Officer at Eco-Ethics Business Consultancy in Canada and he has been providing his service to Global Illuminators as a scientific review committee. He has also been providing his services to quite a few journals as a reviewer. Research Interests: Islamic banking, Takaful (Islamic insurance), Shari'ah Governance and Waqf

Ashish Kumar Sana is presently working as a Professor in the Department of Commerce, University of Calcutta. He was the former Head, Department of Commerce and Former Director, University of Calcutta - Calcutta Stock Exchange Centre of Excellence in Financial Markets (CUCSE-CEFM). He was the editor of the Research Journal, Business Studies (UGC --- CARE Listed Journal Group I) published by the Department of Commerce, University. He was the Associate Editor of the Research Journal, Indian Accounting Review published by the Indian Accounting Association Research Foundation, Kolkata. Prof. Sana has more than 22 years of experience in teaching undergraduate and postgraduate courses in Commerce and Management in different colleges and Universities. In addition to his academic experience, he has over 5 years of administrative experience in the fields of Accounting and Auditing. He has authored more than ten books in the field of Financial Markets, Financial Management, Auditing Business Communication and other related fields. His research interests are Accounting Theory, Capital Markets, Microfinance, Small Business, Women Empowerment and Social Development. Under his supervision, ten scholars have been awarded Ph.D. degree while 14 students have been awarded M.Phil. degree from the University of Calcutta. He has published more than 60 articles in different journals and edited books in national and international repute. He has presented several research papers national and international level seminars and conferences India and abroad. He has acted as the chairperson in different seminars and conferences and delivered keynote addresses in many international and national conferences and seminars. He has completed three UGC research projects on Capital Market, Small Business and Women Empowerment. He has been received best papers from different conferences from India and abroad. Presently, he is actively associated as a member and expert in different Research Journals, Committees and Boards of different Universities and other Academic institutions. He is also the Executive Member of the Indian Accounting Association and Joint Secretary, IAA Kolkata Branch.

Yamla Sathiyaseelan holds the position of Lecturer and Deputy Dean at the Faculty of Business, Lincoln University College. Furthermore, she has the position of Internal Auditor at Lincoln University College. She possesses a total of ten years of combined academic and corporate experience. She possesses extensive knowledge and expertise in the fields of Accounting and Auditing. She is keenly interested in Accounting, Financial Accounting, Auditing, Corporate Governance, and Business Management.

Index

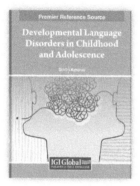

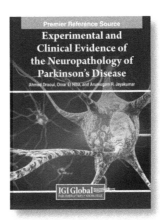
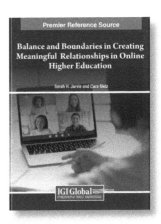

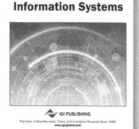